D0011390

DARWIN'S LEAP OF FAITH

JOHN ANKERBERG & JOHN WELDON

HARVEST HOUSE PUBLISHERS
Eugene, Oregon 97402

Part I

Evolution
and the
Modern World

*To the Staff of
Harvest House Publishers*

Contents

PART III
EVOLUTION AND THE SCIENTIFIC EVIDENCE

Note to the Reader

The authors are not scientists nor do they have science backgrounds, so why should a scientist or layman buy a book by non-scientists on a scientific issue? Because the content is valuable nonetheless. One prepublication reviewer (Ph.D. Biology) said that if any evolutionist read the entire book, including the citations, he didn't see how that person could continue to believe in evolution. Another reviewer (M.A. Zoology) referred to it as "an outstanding and detailed analysis of the myth of macroevolution. . . ."

True, we do not have science backgrounds and this will probably be obvious to any scientist who reads our book. Further, in some subjects of this book we are stronger than in others. But we have tried to set out the issues forthrightly to show why we think it is not logically possible to accept an evolutionary origin of life. We have also indicated why we believe the evidence points more strongly to creation.

Some readers will wonder why we have frequently cited scientists, both evolutionists and creationists. The reason is because as scientists, they *are* authorities in their respective fields. For example, in our chapter on the fossil record, it is one thing for us as non-scientists to claim that a key evidence for evolution is nonexistent, i.e., that there are no demonstrated fossil transitions. But it is more powerful to cite evolutionists exclusively who agree that the fossil evidence is lacking. It's one thing for authors with doctorates outside the sciences to claim such and such in a particular area of science. It is entirely another for scientists to make the same claims. Were we only speaking alone, many people would respond, "Why should I accept these claims?" Even with footnote documentation, the impact is hardly the same as reading words that come from a scientist's own mouth. It is still true today that when science (or a scientist) speaks, people listen. So we would also encourage the reader to listen to the important statements that we cite.

Granted, it can sometimes be work to read quotations. But since all are there by design and since the reader will forfeit a good deal of important information if he or she were to neglect them, we would strongly encourage the effort. We also understand why some will object to the use of many secondary references which was unavoidable. However, 1) when used, only reliable secondary sources were cited; 2) these almost always contained the primary reference which is listed first for the reader's convenience; 3) most secondary references are *not* creationists' citations of evolutionists; and 4) the quality of an argument/content, not its secondary nature, was our primary concern. Of course, it is always possible that a secondary reference has inadvertently misrepresented the original text. We would appreciate being informed of any instance where this occurs. Further, our citation of evolutionists does not, in any manner, imply their criticisms of evolution are endorsements of creation.

Finally, our criticism of evolutionary theory and methodological naturalism, which is quite rigorous in places, should not be construed as disrespect for those who hold such views. From our perspective as theists, our criticism stems from a concern over the often painful consequences of materialism. However, although we are critical of evolutionists, we recognize not all are diehard materialists or atheists. To the contrary, some are theistic or agnostic. Others are wavering in their commitment to evolution or in the process of becoming creationists. Our concern is more with an errant scientific philosophy and an abuse of science that it never deserved.

Science is a truly marvellous discipline that has brought much to be thankful for, and dedicated scientists are to be commended for their sacrifice. Unfortunately, as is frequently the lot common to man, scientists and their discipline may also succumb to an erosion of either philosophy or ethics.

Hopefully, it will be a love for science, the search for truth, and ethical considerations that will guide and safeguard the science of the twenty-first century.

False facts are highly injurious to the progress of science, for they often endure long. . . .

—CHARLES DARWIN
THE DESCENT OF MAN

The contemplation of things as they are, without substitution or imposture, without error or confusion, is in itself a nobler thing than a whole harvest of invention.

—FRANCIS BACON

L. Tiger, an anthropologist at Rutgers, contends that Darwinian science inevitably will, and should, have legal, political, and moral consequences. . . .

—SCIENTIFIC AMERICAN, OCTOBER 1995, p. 181

Preface

Darwin's theory of evolution is arguably the single most profound theory emphasized by science in the twentieth century. In terms of its impact and implications, nothing else even comes close.

But despite its weight in the world of ideas, and despite its dominance, paradoxes abound for the evolutionary establishment.

Most people consider evolution to be an indisputable fact. But then how do we account for statements by reputable scientists such as the following? Molecular biologist and medical doctor Michael Denton concludes, "Ultimately the Darwinian theory of evolution is no more nor less than the great cosmogenic myth of the twentieth century."[1] Other scientists actually now refer to evolution as "a fairy tale." For example, Dr. Louis Bounoure, Director of the Zoological Museum and Director of Research at the National Center of Scientific Research in France declares, "Evolution is a fairy tale for grownups."[2]

If evolution were an undeniable fact, how do we account for the thousands of scientists worldwide, creationists and noncreationists alike, who say the theory of evolution is false scientifically; indeed, that it has more conclusive evidence against it than any evidence ever offered for it? Many of these scientists have their Ph.D.s in the "hard" sciences (biology, paleontology, genetics, biochemistry, etc.) from leading American universities such as Harvard, Princeton, and U.C. Berkeley.

If evolution were a fact, proven beyond doubt, or even a convincing theory, we could not *possibly* expect to see thousands of reputable scientists rejecting it outright. At best, we would discover only a few fringe "scientists" who would deny it—just like a few fringe "scientists" might be found in the Flat Earth Society (if such a society exists).

The fact that a lesser number of scientists reject evolution is not the issue here, as some evolutionists maintain. The issue is that thousands of credible scientists would not deny the theory of evolution if it were a proven fact. Something else, then, must account for belief in evolution, something other than the scientific data.

Perhaps things aren't as they seem to most of the world.

Evolutionists say the scientific evidence for evolution is overwhelming. But critics of the theory allege that this evidence is seriously misunderstood. And if the scientific evidence is really undeniable, why have evolutionists lost hundreds of *scientific* debates to creationists? Again, perhaps there is more than meets the eye in the creation-evolution controversy.

On the one hand, evolutionists everywhere say that the theory of evolution represents the epitome of good science and that a theory of creation cannot possibly be scientific. As the American Anthropological Association declared in an official statement, "evolution is . . . a cornerstone of twentieth century science in general."[3] The American Society of Parasitologists declared, "Creationism is not a science and cannot become a science."[4]

Even Pope John Paul II issued a formal statement in 1996, widely reported in the press, affirming that some evolution is compatible with Catholic beliefs. He is the fourth pope to affirm this.

On the other hand, many scientists with multiple doctorates in science, including Dr. Dmitri Kouznetsov and the late Dr. A. E. Wilder-Smith, have rejected evolution as *bad* science and say creation can be and is a legitimate scientific theory. And leading theologians other than the pope say evolution is bad science and worse theology.

Is it conceivable that most scientists are uninformed on the true nature of science? And perhaps even the pope was wrong— and the religious implications of evolution are more complex than assumed.

We find additional paradoxes as science moves rapidly into the twenty-first century. Scientific materialism, naturalism, and atheism remain a dominant and powerful Western worldview, both philosophically and practically. Yet the authors of texts like *Cosmos, Bios, Theos*, written by 60 leading scientists including 24 Nobel Prize winners, repeatedly inform us that only *God* can explain the complexity and order of life as we know it. How can this be if materialism and naturalism are as sacrosanct as proponents allege? As Arthur L. Schawlow, winner of the Nobel Prize for Physics, observes, when confronted with the marvels of life and the universe, "The only possible answers are religious . . . I find a need for God in the universe and in my own life."[5]

An even more surprising statement came from perhaps the most famous existentialist atheist of the twentieth century, Jean Paul Sarte, who publicly stated his "faith" in God just prior to his death. Although a committed atheist since the age of 11, he declared: "As for me, I don't see myself as so much dust that has appeared in the world but as a being that was expected, prefigured, called forth. In short, as a being that could, it seems, come *only* from a creator; and this idea of a creating hand that created me refers me back to God. Naturally this is not a clear, exact idea that I set in motion every time I think of myself. It contradicts many of my other ideas; but it is there, floating vaguely. And when I think of myself I *often* think rather in this way, for want of *being able* to think otherwise."[6]

How do we explain all of this? If matter alone can explain the origin of life and all its glory, why do some Nobel prize winners invoke the belief in God to explain it? Again, if evolution is a fact, why do thousands of scientists reject it? Thousands of qualified scientists simply do not reject facts of science.

Perhaps things aren't quite as they seem to committed naturalists? And perhaps most scientists and most Americans are wrong to believe in evolution so uncritically.

"So what?" some might say. So everything. Whether or not evolution is true makes all the difference in the world. Whether or not we believe it has profound implications. The theory of evolution has significantly impacted almost everyone's life. As the great novelist Aldous Huxley correctly declared, "Evolution has resulted in the world as we know it today."[7] That is no small declaration. For those who think about it, such a statement is indeed profound. No one can overestimate the importance of evolution if it is true or its consequences if it is false.

The issue of evolution is crucial today because, whether right or wrong, it tells us who we are. And no one can ignore their own portrait.

We hope open-minded evolutionists will find much that is challenging to their beliefs in this book and that they will further consider the ethical implications of continuing to advocate an undemonstrated explanation of origins as a proven scientific fact. Evolution is simply a *belief* that people may accept or reject—no more, no less. But beliefs should be accepted on the basis of the evidence, without allowing philosophical premises (e.g., naturalism) to skew the interpretation of the evidence.

However, another purpose in writing this book is to help those in the Christian community who currently assume that the theory of evolution is true and, who consciously or unconsciously, have accepted the logical consequences. Given the major philosophical, theological, biblical, and moral implications of evolution, Christian interest in this subject is more than justified. If evolution isn't even a good scientific theory as critics charge, then these Christians should feel intellectually satisfied in letting the Scripture speak for itself about creation and related issues. There is no need to revise the historic orthodox theology of biblical anthropology, harmartiology, bibliology, or soteriology—i.e., the nature of man/the Fall, sin, inerrancy, and salvation. In essence, there is no need to misinterpret the Bible in light of the "truth" of evolution.

To put it another way, there is no need for any Christian to feel intimidated by science just for accepting what the Bible plainly declares. In the end, the weight of the evidence tells us the Bible will always prove true.[8] No Christian should think there will be legitimate evidence, scientific or otherwise, to deny what God has clearly spoken.

Evolutionists are, unfortunately, often rather condescending to Christians for allegedly taking an irrational "leap of faith" in believing in God, miracles, and the supernatural. Not only are their charges false (as we indicated in *Ready with an Answer*[9]), we will seek to show evolutionists themselves take an incredible "leap of faith" that far exceeds in credulity anything Christians have ever believed.

1

The Big Gamble

Why the Creation/Evolution
Issue Is So Important

Trust the evolutionary process. It's all going to work out all right.

— Timothy Leary,
The Politics of Ecstasy

A Bad Idea?

Someone once cleverly remarked that Darwin had the luck to please everyone who had an axe to grind. In this book we are not going to please everyone, but we are going to examine Darwin's theory critically, and show its outgrowth for both science and society. Our central thesis will be to show that the theory of evolution* is scientifically in error and that, therefore, its overarching consequences are also in error.

Historically and at present, many have argued that general acceptance of the theory of evolution has had greater consequences than realized for religion, morality, and mankind's sense

---

*The term "evolution" is used to refer to the general theory that all life on earth has evolved from non-living matter and progressed to more complex forms with time; hence, it refers to macroevolution and not microevolution (minor changes within species illustrated in crossbreeding, such as varieties of dogs or varieties of corn).

of purpose in life, and has even influenced, to some extent, recent totalitarian governments and the very respect for authority that holds a society together.

Of course, the truth or falsity of a theory cannot be judged on the basis of its legacy alone, but neither can it ultimately be separated from it. If bad ideas produce a bad harvest, and if evolution is a bad idea, this needs to be pointed out even if some people are offended. Far-reaching ideas that impact our day-to-day lives need to be carefully evaluated, especially if we are frequently unaware of their impact. With evolution, this kind of evaluation is rarely attempted, partly because the theory is so widely accepted that it is deemed unquestionable. But this only makes such critique all the more necessary.

A scientific evaluation is, of course, vital and it forms the heart of this book. To determine if evolution is true or false is clearly necessary. However, as much as this can accomplish, it can never tell the whole story. Thus, to briefly explore its impact on history and on people's lives is also vital because it completes the subject. To expose the social harm evolutionary ideas have wrought, intentional or not, is to be alerted to future ill advised theories.

Some ideas are so bad that it may be argued they should be rejected on the basis of their implications alone. As we will see, evolution seems to be one of those ideas.

Encountering the Meaning of Life

There is little doubt that the legacy of Darwin's theory has, in whole or part, dealt with life and death issues. Evolution significantly impacts our views of both life and death in the logical development of its philosophical outlook.

All of us know by experience that, generally, life is good, but very fragile. The Princess Diana tragedy that touched the world illustrates how life can be here one moment and gone the next instant. Or, consider another tragedy, the fate of the Boeing 727 jumbo jet, flight JAL #123, and its 520 passengers. It took this aircraft a full nine minutes to crash.

On that jumbo jet all 520 passengers were killed—people who fully expected to be alive the next day, but never saw the wonder of another dawn.

For many of us, it often takes exposure to a disaster of this nature to make us ponder the meaning of life. And it is here more than anywhere that the creation/evolution issue is personalized. In the end, the issue of origins involves much more than a scientific theory or theological doctrine. It tells us who we are and it impacts how we live. Indeed, our collective view of origins can dramatically affect how efficiently and ethically we function as a society.

In this first chapter, we feel it important to examine some of the implications and impacts of evolutionary theory both for us as individuals and in terms of recent history. We think this information will be both surprising and useful to our readers in light of the content of the remainder of this book. So, to begin, what does evolution really mean to each of us personally?

Evolutionary Kin?

Although most people may not have considered the implications of evolution to them individually, they are quite pronounced and quite personal. In the evolutionary or materialistic worldview, unfortunately, man has no special or unique relevance other than that which he may arbitrarily choose to give himself. As the late leading evolutionist George Gaylord Simpson observed:

> In the world of Darwin, man has no special status other than his definition as a distinct species of animal. He is in the fullest sense a part of nature and not apart from it. He is *akin,* not figuratively, but literally, *to every living thing, be it an amoeba, a tapeworm, a seaweed, an oak tree, or a monkey*—even though the degrees of relationship are different and we may feel less empathy for forty-second cousins like the tapeworm than for, comparatively speaking, brothers like the monkeys. . . ."[1]

Simpson's reference to mankind being literally related to tapeworms is apropos. Darwin himself believed we were descended from something like tapeworms. In their book *Evolving,* Ayala and Valentine agree, "To be sure, both butterflies and humans have descended from a remote common ancestor, most likely a small wormlike marine animal resembling a flat worm."[2]

If humans are only advanced animals that nature has bestowed her favors on by chance, then where do we draw the line as to which animals have which rights and which rights (or animals) are most important to preserve? According to evolution, man is quantitatively better than the animals (has a bigger brain) but not qualitatively better (created in God's image). It is therefore ethically wrong to violate the rights of other animals, who are our literal brothers, evolutionarily speaking.[3] (At least according to popular views of evolution.)

As the national director of PETA (People for the Ethical Treatment of Animals), Ingrid L. Newkirt, stated, "A rat is a pig is a dog is a boy!"[4] By this line of reasoning, apparently, all "higher" forms of life are to be considered equal. More startling, a representative of The Church of Euthanasia believes animal rights are actually superior to human rights. In all seriousness, she told a national TV audience, "If we are going to kill off species, let's kill humanity first because humans are only a minor species with a minor role to play in the overall diversity of Nature."[5] Other animal rights groups maintain that "eating meat is murder" or "man is the tyrant species" and that killing cows and chickens is equal to "the Holocaust perpetrated by the Nazis."[6]

If evolution is true, we can hardly avoid the conclusion. We are all just animals and the animal rights groups seem to have a valid argument. We have no right at all to violate the rights of other animals. All of sentient nature is equally valuable and, as far as rights go, "A rat . . . is a boy." Marvin M. Lubenow, an expert on human fossils, comments as follows and then summarizes the argument:

> While it is difficult to prove that evolution is largely responsible for this equating of human and animal rights, it is more than coincidence that all of the animal-rights advocates who have expressed themselves publicly on the subject are evolutionists. According to evolution, it is merely the "luck of the draw" that man has evolved a big brain. . . . Had certain mutations not happened in our ancestors and instead happened in the ancestors of the chimpanzees, we might be where they are and they might be where we are. . . . Hence, I have no ethical right to use my superiority, achieved by chance, to violate the rights of other animals who through no fault of their own did not evolve the same abilities.[7]

The animal rights groups have taken us here to one of the logical if idealistic consequences of the philosophy of evolution.* But as we will see, there are others. The scientific literature of recent years has justified everything from adultery and homosexuality to irresponsible genetic engineering and barbarous fetal research on the basis of our animal status, in accordance with evolutionary principles.

Chance and Dignity

If man is only an animal, an accident of nature, a collection of chance mutations, the question logically arises, where does he then derive ultimate meaning, dignity, or absolute values?

According to naturalistic evolution, a trinity of basic factors—matter, time, and chance—has created the entire universe and all that lives within it. Nobel prize winning biologist Jacque Monod echoes the sentiments of many when he comments in his *Chance and Necessity*, "[Man] is alone in the universe's unfeeling immensity, out of which he emerged by chance . . ."[8] and, ". . . chance *alone* is at the source of every innovation, of all creation in the biosphere. Pure chance, absolutely free but blind, [is] at the very root of the stupendous edifice of evolution. . . ."[9]

As noted evolutionist J. W. Burrow writes in his introduction to *The Origin of Species:*

> Nature, according to Darwin, was the product of blind chance and a blind struggle, and man a lonely, intelligent mutation, scrambling with the brutes for his sustenance. To some the sense of loss was irrevocable; it was as if an umbilical cord had been cut, and men found themselves part of "a cold passionless universe." Unlike nature as conceived by the Greeks, the Enlightenment, and the rationalist Christian tradition Darwinian nature held no clues for human conduct, no answers to human moral dilemmas.[10]

---

*In another sense, it can be argued the evolution popularizers are wrong. Based on theories of natural selection and survival of the fittest, genuine evolutionary scientists could easily maintain that "might makes right," in spite of the implications for the human animal, as seen, for example, in the abuse of social Darwinism.

This depressing view of man as a "lonely intelligent muta-tion" and of the chance origin of all life is sharply contrasted with the Judeo-Christian tradition which views the universe not as the purposeless product of blind forces but as the inten-tional product of an infinite-personal God who created man in his own image, giving him inherent dignity and value far above that of the animals.[11]

Unfortunately, the picture of mankind given by modern evolutionary science is one of cosmic isolation. God not only doesn't exist for us; He never existed. He never will. Religion is just an opiate for those troubled by this fact. Man lives alone within a truly massive but terribly impersonal universe—a uni-verse which endlessly piques our awe and curiosity but which, strangely, cannot provide us with a final justification for the things we seem to value most deeply—faith in God, purpose in life, love, caring for others.

As professor William Provine of Cornell University argues, "The implications of modern science, however, are clearly in-consistent with most religious traditions. . . . No inherent moral or ethical laws exist, nor are there absolute guiding principles for human society. The universe cares nothing for us and we have no ultimate meaning in life."[12] Thus, as Monod concludes, for good or ill, ". . .our system of values is free for us to choose."[13] And, people everywhere today are indeed choosing their values, often with little regard for the welfare of others and often with great consequences.

Regardless, not surprisingly, in a universe so large and un-certain, millions of men ponder the meaning of their existence. When all is said and done, was there any real purpose in life? As Leslie Paul once observed, "If no one knows what time, though it will be soon enough by astronomical clocks, the lonely planet will cool, all life will die, all mind will cease, and it will all be as if it had never happened. That, to be honest, is the goal to which evolution is traveling, that is the benevolent end of the furious living and furious dying. . . . All life is no more than a match struck in the dark and blown out again. The final result . . . is to deprive it completely of meaning."[14]

J.D. Bernal, a professor of x-ray crystallography gave the following evolutionary definition of life: "Life is a partial, continuous, progressive, multiform and continually interactive, self-realization of the potentialities of atomic electron states."[15]

If we really are mere brothers to the flatworm and mere potentialities of electron states, the implications are hardly insignificant. They go to the heart of how we see ourselves, how we live, and how we treat our fellow man.

Logically considered, the materialistic view is not highly flattering to us. After death, in the cosmic perspective, men and women are, in the ultimate sense, little more than ephemeral 70 year conglomerates of atoms coalescing for one brief second in eternity.

Contrasting Worldviews

In the West there are two basic worldviews which have dominated modern thinking. The first is the naturalistic world-view we have just discussed, which may also be termed "secular humanism" or "scientific materialism." As noted, this view assumes man is the end product of the chance workings of an impersonal cosmos. The "noble" human animal must face his meaningless existence courageously and live and die with dignity. But individually and cosmically, when it is over, it is really over. Little, if anything, ever finally matters.

The second view is represented by the Judeo-Christian worldview. It teaches that men and women are the product of divine creation, beings who are endowed with dignity and eternal value because they are created in the image of an infinite-personal God who loves them sacrificially.

Whatever position we adopt, few would argue that the consequences are incidental. As we will seek to show, our answer to the question of origins makes a great deal of difference. For example, consider just a few contrasts between the materialistic and Judeo-Christian worldviews in the chart on the next page.

Perhaps it is the magnitude of difference between these worldviews, as well as their respective implications, which has led thinking people to increasingly concede the importance of origins in public discussion. Our view of origins affects and even determines our attitudes toward the most important matters of public policy, including criminology, sex education, and religious freedom, to name a few. Not surprisingly, polls

	Materialistic View	**Christian View**
Ultimate Reality	Ultimate reality is impersonal matter. No God exists.	Ultimate reality is an infinite, personal, loving God.
Universe	The universe was created by chance events without ultimate purpose.	The universe was lovingly created by God for a specific purpose.
Man	Man is the product of impersonal time plus chance plus matter. As a result, no man has eternal value or dignity nor any meaning other than that which is subjectively derived	Man was created by God in His image and is loved by Him. Because of this, all men are endowed with eternal value and dignity. Their value is not derived ultimately from themselves, but from a source transcending themselves, God Himself.
Morality	Morality is defined by every individual according to his own views and interests. Morality is ultimately relative because every person is the final authority for his own views.	Morality is defined by God and immutable because it is based on God's unchanging character.
Afterlife	The afterlife brings eternal annihilation (personal extinction) for everyone.	The afterlife involves either eternal life with God (personal immortality) or eternal separation from Him (personal judgment).

consistently reveal that most Americans wish to see the theory of divine creation taught in addition to the theory of evolution:

> A massive majority (86% to 88%) of the national public supports teaching the theory of creation in public schools rather than just evolution (AP-NBC News Poll), including nearly equal superma-jorities of Protestants and Catholics . . . more than two-thirds of lawyers nationally agree (66%–26%) and find dual instruction constitutional (63%–26%) (American Bar Association Com-mission Poll); majorities (80% at Ohio State, 56% at Oberlin) of university students at secular institutions agree . . . two-thirds (67%–25%) of public school boards members concur (American School Board Journal poll); and a substantial minority (42.3%–53.7%) of even public school biology teachers favor the theory of creation over the theory of evolution (Austin Analytical Consulting poll).[16]

The Big Gamble

This openness to a creationist view of origins perhaps re-flects an intuitive sense that life really does have meaning. Christians would argue that materialists and many other evolu-tionists are taking a big gamble on their future. They are betting their convictions about ultimate reality on the assumption that their worldview is correct. Ultimate reality is material (matter), not spiritual (God). And if there is no God who created us, there is no God who judges us.

We do not believe this gamble is wise for reasons that will become increasingly evident. Put bluntly, the odds that evolu-tion is true are much less than one chance in a thousand billion. By illustrating this extremely small number, one chance in a trillion, we can show the inadvisability of basing one's view of reality on such odds.

Imagine a mountain one cubic mile in size composed of one trillion Excedrin capsules. Every capsule but one is laced with deadly strychnine. The odds are one trillion to one that anyone could, by chance, pick out the only safe capsule.

No one in his or her right mind would step blindfolded into this mountain, arbitrarily select a capsule, and swallow it, no matter how bad the headache. No one would do it even if there

were only *two* capsules and the odds were 50/50. Yet evolutionists are gambling against far worse odds than one chance in a
trillion (chapters 11 and 17). As the previous chart reveals, the
truth is that more than our physical life is at stake in the current
debate. We are dealing with ultimate issues of origins (naturalistic evolution vs. divine creation) and final destiny (extinction
vs. heaven or hell).

If the creationists are right, and the biblical view of origins
true, this controversy is of greater concern than materialists now
think. When the final breath is drawn, evolutionists may have
more pressing matters to discuss than lack of fossil transitions.

Risking one's money at Las Vegas is one thing. Gambling
one's soul on evolution is another matter entirely.

Losing God and Social Manipulation

As we documented elsewhere, no one familiar with recent
Western history can deny that the theory of evolution bears
tremendous responsibility for undermining faith in a personal
creator God, faith in the Bible, and furthering Christianity as a
whole. In fact, according to noted evolutionary critic and U.C.
Berkeley law professor Phillip Johnson, evolution is "the key
philosophical concept that has allowed the atheists and agnos-
tics to dominate the whole intellectual world and government
world," leading to "the complete marginalization of theism" in
these realms.[17] The implications of this historically recent turn
to secularism have been vast. Philosopher Will Durant once
noted: "By offering evolution in place of God as a cause of history, Darwin removed the theological basis of the moral code of
Christendom. And the moral code that has no fear of God is
very shaky. That's the condition we are in. . . . I don't think man
is capable yet of managing social order and individual decency
without fear of some supernatural being overlooking him and
able to punish him."[18] That Durant's assessment was correct
can be seen all around us.

Every day in the world, the nihilistic implications of evolution are being worked out in the lives of men, women, and children—in the relativism, amoralism, hedonism, and practical
atheism that flow from a view of origins that tells us that we are
chance mutations, evolved animals with absolutely no final

meaning or relevance in life. Indeed, most of the ills of modern society stem from the lack of morals and purposelessness derived from a materialistic, evolutionary philosophy. "No God exists, this life is all there is" has generated far more social pathology than most people ever suspect.[19]

Prevalent Despair

We earlier stated that evolution is based upon the basic premise that time plus the impersonal (matter) plus chance formed all living things. That's our birthright and our epitaph. In essence, man becomes a tragic accident revolving at dizzying speeds hurling through the dark corridors of space. The gut-wrenching despair of modern man seen everywhere around us (see the chart on the next page for illustrations) is directly traceable to the implications of naturalistic evolution and anti-theism.[20] To the extent evolution has removed God from the consciousness of modern man, it bears responsibility for the lostness and terror of modern man apart from God.

Again, philosophical worldviews molded by materialistic premises are reflected in the day to day living of millions of individuals. This was recognized by Sedgwick, a Cambridge geologist and colleague of Darwin. Sedgwick derided Darwin's *Origin of Species* as "a dish of rank materialism cleverly cooked and served up merely to make us independent of a Creator."[21] Sedgwick felt, quite correctly, that Darwin had shown every criminal how to justify his ways. But he also believed that if Darwin's teachings were widely accepted humanity "would suffer a damage that might brutalize it and sink the human race into a lower grade of degradation than any into which it has fallen since its written records tell us of its history."[22]

In the minds of many critics of evolution, Sedgwick's fears came true. Darwin's ideas were broadly accepted and since then mankind has suffered a brutality that has sunk it into one of the lowest grades of degradation it has ever endured.

The last 75 years have witnessed some of the greatest horrors of all human history—principally the result of Nazi and communist atrocities. Alexander Soltzenitzen claims that "from 1917 to 1959 socialism cost the Soviet Union 110 million lives."[23] In communist China the leaders may have put to death

THE DESPAIR OF MODERN MAN

The philosopher Ionesco points out, "Cut off from his religious, metaphysical, and transcendental roots, man is lost; all his actions become senseless, absurd, useless." Theodore Dreiser writes, "As I see him, the unutterably infinitesimal individual weaves among the mysteries a floss-like and wholly meaningless course—if course it be. In short, I catch no meaning from all I have seen, and pass quite as I came, confused and dismayed." Albert Camus observed, "Up 'til now man derived his coherence from his Creator. But from the moment that he consecrates his rupture with him, he finds himself delivered over to the fleeting moment and to wasted sensibility." U.C.L.A. Professor of Philosophy Donald Kalish argues, "There are no ethical truths . . . you are mistaken to think that anyone ever had the answers. There are no answers. Be brave and face up to it." Nietzsche opined, "Everything lacks meaning. . . . What does nihilism mean? That the highest values devalue themselves." He referred to ". . . The advantage of our times, nothing is true, everything is permitted." Hegel wrote, "World history is not the ground of happiness. The periods of happiness are empty pages." Novelist Henry Miller complained, "I see that behind the nobility of [man's] gestures there lurks the specter of the ridiculousness of it all. . . . He is not only sublime, but absurd. Once I thought that to be human was the highest aim man could have, but I see now that it was meant to destroy me. Today I am proud to say that I am inhuman . . . a man who belongs to this race must stand up on the high place with gibberish in his mouth and rip out his entrails." LSD Guru Timothy Leary declared, ". . . all purposes, including your own, are solemn self-deceptions." Andy Warhol objected, "I wish I were a machine." Psychoanalyst Eric Fromm laments, "Alienation as we find it in modern society is almost total; it pervades the relationship of man to his work, to the things he consumes, to the state, to his fellow man, and to himself."[20]

some 30 million others.[24] Millions more have been slaughtered in Cambodia and other Southeast Asian countries. And some two billion men and women have had their individual freedoms denied and been politically enslaved to Marxist ideology. Nor have these ideologies been expunged. In Germany today neo-Nazism has become a powerful social force and neofascism is rising in Italy—incredibly, under the leadership of Mussolini's own granddaughter. Despite the collapse of Communism in Europe and Russia, Marxist theory still rules over a billion people in China and other countries, and there is no guarantee that Russia and Eastern Europe will continue their move toward democracy.

What does any of this have to do with evolution? In the following material we will seek to show not only that evolutionary ideas have consequences but that evolutionary theory has been a basis for both modern despair and destructive political regimes.

In a universe that is ultimately meaningless, what happens to individual and societal ethics? Why shouldn't the more powerful or more intelligent among us manipulate the less intelligent and powerful for whatever purposes they deem "good" and "worthy?"

If, according to some, modern man "is nothing but a complex biochemical mechanism powered by a combustion system which energizes a computer with prodigious storage facilities for retaining encoded information," why shouldn't he be manipulated by those with power and the courage to do so?[25]

Our century is replete with examples.

We do not offer the following examples to argue that the theory of evolution is directly responsible for the terrible events cited. Obviously, many factors were at work, including human evil and, in all likelihood, demonic evil as well.

What we do claim is that evolutionary theory provided logical impetus and encouragement for such events, and this is of concern.

Of course, any idea, theory, or doctrine can be misused. It can be misinterpreted or misapplied by unscrupulous people for whatever reason. The problem with evolution is that what we discuss below does not involve misinterpretations or misapplications but logical derivations and applications of the theory.

Evolutionary Ethics?

If we examine the two most obvious horrors of the twentieth century, Nazism and Marxism, it seems logical that the implications of evolutionary theory applied socially were partly responsible. Did a pragmatic approach to evolutionary ethics among elitist powers help produce Hitler's racist eugenics where the fit live and the unfit die, or the Communist destruction of those considered expendable for the welfare of the state? Christian values could never have resulted in such acts, but evolutionary values could produce such results. How do we know?

Sir Arthur Keith, a physical anthropologist and one of the greatest evolutionists of recent times, was strongly opposed to Christianity and devoted more time to studying evolutionary ethics than perhaps any of his contemporaries. His *Evolution and Ethics* illustrates that the ethics taught by Christianity and the ethics of evolution are not reconcilable. For example, "Christ's teaching is . . . in direct opposition to the law of evolution" and, "Christian ethics are out of harmony with human nature and secretly antagonistic to Nature's scheme of evolution and ethics."[26] He confesses, ". . . the conclusion I have come to is this: the law of Christ is incompatible with the law of evolution. . . . Nay, the two laws are at war with each other. . . ."[27]

Keith recognized that evolutionary theory supports the argument that the final purpose of our existence is to promote evolution—and, therefore, whatever accomplishes this goal is to be considered good and moral. That which hinders evolution may be considered its opposite.

Keith also understood that if we follow evolutionary ethics to their strict, logical conclusion, we must "abandon the hope of ever attaining a universal system of ethics" because "the ways of national evolution, both in the past and in the present, are cruel, brutal, ruthless and without mercy."[28]

When Christianity advocates mercy, love, and selflessness, it may be considered the antagonist of evolutionary ethics. For example, according to Keith, "the Sermon on the Mount is a condemnation of the evolutionary ladder" and Christianity has supposedly failed because it is anti-evolutionary.[29]

World Wars

Thus, when we examine the social and political influence of Darwinian theory in the latter half of the nineteenth and twentieth century, Keith was correct—the moral consequences are frightening. Professor of History at Columbia University Jacques Barzun observes that "No one who has not waded through some sizeable part of the literature of the period 1870–1914 has any conception of the extent to which it is one long call for blood. . . ."[30] And this call for blood was conducted and justified in the "scientific" evolutionary jargon of the day.

Bernhardi, a German general at the turn of the century, extolling militarism in his *Germany and the Next War* (1911) claimed that from an evolutionary viewpoint, it is biologically right to crush the weaker peoples of the earth. "Might is at once the supreme right" and "War is a *biological* necessity of the first importance."[31] Dr. Henry Morris documents that "Darwin, Nietzsche, and Haeckel . . . laid the foundations for the intense German militarism that eventually led to the Great War of 1914-18. There were others who participated in the development, of course, including many of the German generals and political leaders, all very much under the spell of the German variety of social Darwinism. General Friedrich von Bernhardi said: 'War gives a biologically just decision, since its decisions rest on the very nature of things. . . . It [war] is not only a biological law, but a moral obligation, and, as such, an indispensable factor in civilization.' "[32]

Keith himself, writing prior to 1947, observed the chilling impact of Darwinian theory upon the world's chances for peace:

> It was often said in 1914 that Darwin's doctrine of evolution had bred war in Europe, particularly in Germany. An expression of this belief is still to be met with. In 1935, a committee of psychologists, representing 30 nations, issued a manifesto in which it was stated that "war is the necessary outcome of Darwin's theory. . . ."
> The law of evolution, as formulated by Darwin, provides an

explanation of wars between nations, the only reasonable explanation known to me.[33]

And he supplies the following illustration:

To see evolutionary measures and tribal morality being applied
vigorously to the affairs of a great modern nation, we must turn
again to Germany of 1942. We see Hitler devoutly convinced that
evolution produces the only real basis for a national policy . . .
The means he adopted to secure the destiny of his race and
people were organized slaughter, which has drenched Europe in
blood. . . . Such conduct is highly immoral as measured by every
scale of ethics, yet Germany justifies it; it is consonant with tribal
or evolutionary morality. Germany has reverted to the tribal past,
and is demonstrating to the world, in their naked veracity, the
methods of evolution. . . .

Thus,

The German Fuhrer, as I have consistently maintained, is an
evolutionist; he has consciously sought to make the practice of
Germany conform to the theory of evolution. . . .[34]

Hitler saw in evolutionary theory the scientific justification
for his personal views as much as social Darwinists of the
nineteenth century did for their terrible abuses. "There is no
question that evolutionism was basic in all Nazi thought, from
beginning to end. Yet, it is a remarkable phenomenon how few
are aware of this fact today."[35]

In *The Natural Sciences Know Nothing of Evolution*, the late
distinguished scientist A. E. Wilder-Smith cited leading existen-
tial psychologist Eric Fromm:

The "religion" of social Darwinism belongs to the most dangerous elements within the thoughts of the last century. It aids the
propagation of ruthless, national and racial egoism by establishing it as a moral norm. If Hitler believed in anything at all, then it
was in the laws of evolution, which *justified and sanctified his
actions and especially his cruelties.*[36]

Not unexpectedly, "In the biological theory of Darwin,
Hitler found his most powerful weapon against traditional
values"[37] and "[Hitler] stressed and singled out the idea of
biological evolution as the most forceful weapon against tradi-

tional religion and he repeatedly condemned Christianity for its opposition to the teaching of evolution."[38]

Hitler, who obviously hated Christianity, said, "I regard Christianity as the most fatal, seductive lie that ever existed."[39] Reflecting evolutionary values, he wrote the following in *Mein Kampf*, "He who would live must fight; he who does not wish to fight in this world where permanent struggle is the law of life, has not the right to exist"; "I do not see why man should not be just as cruel as nature"; "Nature likes bastards only a little"; and finally, "all that is not [of pure] race in this world is trash." [40]

In destroying the Jews, blacks, and Gypsies, Hitler professed he was only helping natural selection and improving human biology.[41] Indeed, as an article in *Time* magazine (Oct. 28, 1996) pointed out, "According to Darwinism, the evil in nature lies at its very roots, instilled by its creator, natural selection. After all, natural selection is chronic competition untrammeled by moral rules."

Dr. Robert Clark observes, "Evolutionary ideas—quite undisguised—lie at the basis of all that is worst in *Mein Kampf* and in [Hitler's] public speeches. . . ."[42] According to Hitler's reasoning, since all natural history was simply a struggle for survival of the fittest, any action was justified in order to facilitate the victory of the "higher" and "purer" species. For Hitler, brutality toward other nations actually became acts of virtue in his quest to "purify" the race.

Dr. Robert Ley, head of the Nazi Labor Front wrote about the war of 1940 as follows: "War is not in contrast to peace, but simply another form of expression of the uninterrupted battle of nations and men. It is an expression of the highest and best in manhood."[43]

Because Hitler understood the implications of evolution, evolutionary precepts were pounded into the German people and swayed them.[44] The schools were profoundly influenced as biology was purposely infused with an evolutionary bias. Who should be surprised that the German Youth Movement sided with the German states' view of not supporting the struggles of the weak? "Inferior" individuals were to be sacrificed for the health of both the state and the "purity" of the human stock itself.

Yet, incredibly, one can read through scores of books on Hitler and the Third Reich and find little or no mention of the impact evolutionary theory had on Hitler—simply because writers are either afraid of being classed as antievolutionary or prefer not to admit the influence of evolution.[45]

In Italy, the fascist Mussolini also ridiculed the idea of ongoing peace as a barrier to the process of evolutionary advancement:

> Mussolini's attitude was completely dominated by evolution. In public utterances, he repeatedly used the Darwinian catchwords while he mocked at perpetual peace, lest it should hinder the evolutionary process. For him, the reluctance of England to engage in war only proved the evolutionary decadence of the British Empire.[46]

In *Twentieth Century in Crisis: Foundations of Totalitarianism*, Larry Azar evaluates the rise of totalitarianism in the twentieth century. Azar supplies over 300 references to support critical statements such as the following: "The impact of evolution on human thought cannot be exaggerated"; "Darwinian evolution . . . shattered the very foundations of morality itself"; "This doctrine of racial supremacy Hitler took at face value. . . . He accepted evolution much as we today accept Einsteinian relativity"; and "Sixty-three million people would be slaughtered in order to obey the evolutionary doctrine that perishing is a law of nature."[47]

But Darwinism's horrific consequences were evident not only within the two major world wars of the twentieth century. Even in the late nineteenth century we find its inhuman influences. For example, the complete extermination of the native peoples of Tasmania resulted from the influence of early Darwinism. Jerry Bergman, Ph.D., writes in the abstract of his article, "Nineteenth Century Darwinism and the Tasmanian Genocide":

> It was widely believed in the nineteenth century that the Tasmanians were a living link between modern humans and their primitive ancestors. Given the presuppositions of naturalistic evolution, the Tasmanian people were often seen as less than human and, consequently, many people felt that it was not wrong

or immoral to treat them like animals. This attitude eventually influenced behavior which resulted in the total extermination of the native Tasmanians. Today it is concluded that they were a distinct racial group similar to the Australian aborigines that possessed a unique culture and were fully human. This event is only one of many examples of the numerous tragedies that evolutionary naturalism has produced in modern times.[48]

Marx and Darwin

Finally, Darwinism was effectively used to propagate Communist ideology as well. Karl Marx "felt his own work to be the exact parallel of Darwin's" and he was so grateful that he wanted to dedicate a portion of *Das Kapital* to Darwin, who declined the honor.[49]

Marx wrote to Engels concerning the *The Origin of Species*, that this was the book which "contains the basis in natural history for our views."[50] In 1861 he also wrote, "Darwin's book is very important and serves me as a basis in natural selection for the class struggle in history. . . ."[51] Thus, as Burrow observes, "Even Marx and Engels adopted Darwinism as the biological counterpart to the class war. . . ."[52]

Indeed:

> . . . Marx and Engels based their communistic philosophy squarely on the foundation of evolutionism. . . . Marx and Engels were doctrinaire evolutionists, and so have all Communists been ever since. Since atheism is a basic tenet of Marxism in general, and Soviet Communism in particular, it is obvious that evolution must be the number one tenet of communism. Lenin and Trotsky and Stalin were all atheistic evolutionists, and so are today's Communist leaders. In fact, they have to be in order ever to get to be Communist leaders . . . . The continuing commitment of modern communism to atheistic evolutionism is evident in communistic publications all over the world.[53]

Significantly, at the time of Marx's death in 1883, his ideas had made little or no impact. Marxist philosophy seems to have gained little ground historically until evolutionary theory had been sufficiently accepted, providing a scientific basis for denying the existence of God and supplying a drastically revised view of man's nature and the historical process. Thus, in some ways, Darwinism appears to have been a key agent for bringing about ideological changes for fostering the growth and application of communist theory.[54]

Dr. A. E. Wilder-Smith remarks: "The political and anti-religious propaganda put out since Marx's time writhes with the most primitive Darwinism" observing that communism "brutalizes those it is forced upon."[55]

Marx's philosophy, like Hitler's, reflected the brutality of Darwinian nature. He referred to "the disarming of the bourgeoisie . . . revolutionary terror . . . and the creation of a revolutionary army . . . liberty is dismissed as a purely bourgeois ideal. . . ." Further, the revolutionary government would "have neither time nor opportunity for compassion or remorse. Its business is to terrorize its opponents into acquiescence. It must disarm antagonism by execution, imprisonment, forced labor, control of the press. . . ."[56]

Clearly, some of the most inhuman actions ever seen have been perpetuated in the name of national socialist or Marxist "social advancement," based on evolutionary philosophies:

> The world today, for the most part, despises Hitler—Stalin, also. Both rejected the ethics of loving neighbors as set forth in the Bible, and both slaughtered millions. Stalin selfconsciously chose Darwin. Hitler tried to ram survival of the fittest down the world's throat. Entomologist Vernon L. Kellogg, mentioned by Gould, summarized the position held, "That human group which is in the most advanced evolutionary state . . . should win in the struggle for existence. . . ."[57]

Consider the following terrorist communiqué as reported on the CBS Evening News February 21 and 22, 1985, "Life has no special sacred character"; "Hate is your law and revenge is your first privilege."

Where did the terrorists who stated these things get such ideas? From Jesus? Would it be surprising to discover they devised them logically, as evolutionary materialists, in combination with their Marxist philosophy? According to evolutionary principles there can be no special sacred character to life since it simply arose by chance, exists a brief time and is forever ended.

It has no ultimate meaning, no special value. And certainly, in a reading of the writings of Karl Marx and other communist leaders one can understand the concept that hate and revenge are laws or privileges. This is exactly what Marxist idealogy has spawned in the last 100 years, leading to the deaths of some 150 million people.

Given the impact of Hitler, Marx, and their associates and the demonstrable connection of their anti-human philosophies to evolutionary atheism, the comments of historical philosopher John Koster should be considered relevant:

> Many names have been cited beside that of Hitler to explain the Holocaust. Oddly enough, Charles Darwin's is almost never among them. [Yet] . . . Darwin's and Huxley's picture of man's place in the universe prepared the way for the Holocaust. . . . Hitler and Stalin between them murdered more innocent victims than had died in all the religious wars in mankind's history. They murdered these victims not with the misguided intentions of saving their souls or punishing their sins, but because they were competitors for food and obstacles to "evolutionary progress." Many humanitarians, Christian, Jewish, or agnostic, have understood the relationship between Nietzsche's ideas and Hitler's mass murder teams and crematoria. Few have traced the linkage back one step further to Darwin, the "scientist" who directly inspired Nietzsche's superman theory and the Nazi corollary that some people were subhuman. The evidence was all there—the term neo-Darwinism was openly used to describe Nazi racial theories. The expression "natural selection," as applied to human beings, turns up at the Wannsee Conference in the prime document of the Holocaust. . . .
>
> We can see the events of Hitler's Germany and of Stalin's Russia as a meaningless collection of atrocities which took place because Germans and Russians are terrible people, not like us at all. Or we can realize that imposing the life-is-pathology theories of Huxley and Darwin, of clinical depression masquerading as science, played a critical role in the age of atrocities. And we can take warning. People have to learn to stop thinking of other people as machines and learn to think of them as men and women possessed of souls. . . .
>
> History doesn't need another one hundred million deaths to prove that scientific atheism is a form of mental illness.[58]

It should surprise no one that amoral theories reflecting nature's "Darwinian methods," methods which have a utilitarian ethic, can play such a part in human affairs. As you read our next chapter on the overall influence of evolution in the modern world, perhaps you can now see why many people today are increasingly concerned.

Ideas do have consequences.

2

The World As We Know It

The Influence of Evolution in the Modern Era

. . . there are no living sciences, human attitudes, or institutional powers that remain unaffected by the ideas . . . released by Darwin's work.

—Philosopher J. Collins, in Miller and Levine's *Biology* (Prentice Hall, 1995), p. 313.

In the history of mankind, few theories have had the impact that evolution has. To illustrate, let us briefly survey what leading scientists, biographers, and thinkers in diverse fields have stated about the influence of evolution. Only then can we begin to understand the tremendous impact of evolution and its importance for our own lives today—and possibly the lives of our own children tomorrow.

As you begin to think about this subject more critically, ponder the following statements. Biologist and ecologist Sir Julian Huxley wrote that, "Evolution . . . is the most powerful and most comprehensive idea that has ever arisen on earth."[1] A quarter century ago, the famous evolutionary zoologist Ernest Mayr of Harvard University observed that evolution was coming to be regarded as "perhaps the most fundamental of all intellectual revolutions in the history of mankind."[2] Indeed, it was. Few can logically deny that "Almost the entire intellectual world has accepted it today."[3] The definitive modern biography of Charles Darwin by James Moore, *Darwin: The Life of a Tormented Evolutionist* points out that, "More than any modern thinker—even Freud or Marx—[Darwin] . . . has transformed the way we see ourselves on the planet."[4]

Darwin's Origin of Species

In terms of modern influence, Darwin's text was unlike that of almost any other book. Wendell R. Bird is a prominent American attorney and Yale Law School graduate who argued the major creationist case on the issue of creation/evolution before the U.S. Supreme Court. In his 1,100 page criticism of evolutionary theory, *The Origin of Species Revisited: The Theories of Evolution and of Abrupt Appearance*, he observes of *On the Origin of Species*, "That single volume has had a massive influence not only on the sciences, which increasingly are built on evolutionary assumptions, but on the humanities, theology, and government."[5]

Physicist H. S. Lipson further observed of *On the Origin of Species*, "It is perhaps the most influential book that has ever been published. . . . "[6]

In his *Mankind Evolving*, eminent biologist Theodosius Dobzhansky observes that the publication of Darwin's book in 1859 "marked a turning point in the intellectual history of mankind" and "ushered in a new understanding of man and his place in the universe."[7] He observes that even a hundred years after Darwin "the idea of evolution is becoming an integral part of man's image of himself. The idea has percolated to much wider circles than biologists or even scientists; understood or misunderstood, it is a part of mass culture."[8]

Influence Outside of Science

Consider some examples. Writing in *Scientific American* for September 1978, page 47, Harvard scientist Ernest Mayr observed that, "Man's worldview today is dominated by [evolution] . . ." and he stated in *Science* magazine for June 2, 1972, page 981 that it "not only eliminated man's anthropocentrism, but affected every metaphysical and ethical concept, if consistently applied."[9] Leading ecologist Rene Dubois observed in *American Scientist* for March, 1965, page 6, that: "Evolutionary concepts are applied also to social institutions and to the arts. Indeed, most political parties, as well as schools of theology, sociology, history, or arts, teach these concepts and make them the basis of their doctrines."[10]

Robert B. Downs, a former president of the American Library Association, also writes concerning the influence of Darwin's text:

> Of these celebrated names [of the nineteenth century], and in fact among all the millions born in the nineteenth century, none, with the possible exception of Karl Marx, did as much as Darwin to change the main trends of thought, and to produce a new outlook in human affairs. . . . Viewed in retrospect, Darwin's impress on nearly all major fields of learning was, and continues to be, profound. The doctrine of organic evolution has been accepted by biologists, geologists, chemists, and physicists, by anthropologists, psychologists, educators, philosophers, and sociologists, and even by historians, political scientists, and philologists. Charles Ellwood declared: "When one reflects upon the immense influence which Darwin's work has had on practically all lines of human thought, and especially on the biological, psychological, and social sciences, one is forced to conclude that . . . Darwin must be given the seat of highest honor as the most fructifying thinker which the nineteenth century produced, not only in England, but in the whole world. And the social significance of Darwin's teachings is even yet only beginning to be apprehended."
> Anthony West concurred, in writing of the *Origin of Species*: "The effect was truly tremendous. Almost by the mere statement of a new principle of approach, dynamic, not static, he revolutionized every department of study, from astronomy to history, from paleontology to psychology, from embryology to religion."[11]

Thus, evolutionary critic and molecular biologist Michael Denton further illustrates the dramatic influence of this dominant theory in disciplines outside the natural sciences, pointing out that even the terrible social and political upheavals of the twentieth century "would have been impossible" apart from the philosophical sanction provided by Darwinism:

The twentieth century would be incomprehensible without the Darwinian revolution. The social and political currents which have swept the world in the past eighty years would have been impossible without its intellectual sanction. . . . The influence of evolutionary theory on fields far removed from biology is one of the most spectacular examples in history of how a highly speculative idea for which there is no really hard scientific evidence can come to fashion the thinking of a whole society and dominate the outlook of an age.

Indeed:

Today it is perhaps the Darwinian view of nature more than any other that is responsible for the agnostic and skeptical outlook of the twentieth century. . . . [It is] a theory that literally changed the world. . . ."[12]

Dr. Bernard Stonehouse has held university posts at Oxford, Canterbury, and Yale and is currently editor of the *Polar Record* at the Scott Polar Research Institute in Cambridge. He observes that the theory of evolution "ran like wildfire through every other branch of philosophy. It penetrated even religion and morality to become, as clerical opponents feared it would, an aspect of common sense. . . .[Yet] If Darwinism turns out to be nonsense, the basis for much of our everyday thinking is suspect, and we may all have to look for something better."[13]

But if evolution has permeated practically the entire fabric of our culture and provides the basis for modern man's worldview and thus his subsequent actions, wouldn't it appear to be one of the most important issues there is? Who can argue that this creation-evolution issue is unimportant? Indeed, how an individual views his origin, his beginning, greatly conditions his worldview, the decisions he makes, his actions, and even his general lifestyle. As the philosopher Francis Schaeffer once noted, people live more consistently with their own presuppositions than even they themselves may realize.[14]

An Emerging Religion?

In light of this, it must be emphasized that the theory of evolution today is *far* more than a mere scientific theory. It is a grand, unifying materialistic philosophy that actually has most of the elements of a religion, as we will see in Chapter 17.

Sir Julian Huxley wrote that "Our present knowledge indeed forces us to the view that the whole of reality is evolution—a single process of self transformation."[15] This is why Dobzhansky could observe: "Evolution comprises all the stages of the development of the universe: the cosmic, biological, and human or cultural developments. Attempts to restrict the concept of evolution to biology are gratuitous. Life is a product of the evolution of inorganic nature, and man is a product of the evolution of life."[16]

If all reality involves and is evolution, and if evolution is our maker, then it is evolution that we must trust and evolution we must bow before. Perhaps evolution *should* become the guiding principle of humanity.[17] Sir Julian Huxley became UNESCO's first Director-General. In its formative years, UNESCO's basic philosophy also served to guide the United Nations. In that connection Huxley observed in *The Humanist* for March-April, 1979, pages 35 and 36, "It is essential for UNESCO [United Nations Educational, Scientific, and Cultural Organization] to adopt an evolutionary approach. . . . The general philosophy of UNESCO should, it seems, be a scientific world humanism, global in extent and evolutionary in background. . . . Thus the struggle for existence that underlies natural selection is increasingly replaced by conscious selection, the struggle between ideas and consciousness."[18] Former powerful United Nations Assistant Secretary-General Robert Muller, a promoter of New Age beliefs around the world, agreed when he observed: "I believe the most fundamental thing we can do today is to believe in evolution."[19]

As an indication of the extent to which some people almost worship evolution, consider the statement by the influential Roman Catholic priest and mystic, Pierre Teilhard de Chardin: "[Evolution] is a general postulate to which *all theories, all hypotheses, all systems* must henceforward bow and which they must satisfy in order to be thinkable and true. Evolution is a light which illuminates *all facts*, a trajectory which *all* lines of thought *must* follow."[20]

In conclusion, evolution today influences or dominates our primary and secondary schools, academic study in the universities, the media, psychology, sociology, history, literature, education, ethics, law and constitutional law, religion, and seemingly, nearly all segments of society in most nations throughout the world.

This is why most people who think of evolution as strictly a scientific discipline are wrong. No solely scientific theory has the incredible *nonscientific* impact (social, religious, political) that evolutionary theory has—not even the theory of gravity or the atomic theory. As noted, evolutionary influence and appropriation make it seem more like a religion, as many commentators have argued. This is one reason some can make the unexpected claim that evolution "is being vigorously and more and more successfully promoted as the coming world religion, world culture and world government."[21]

In order to understand the influence of this seemingly god-like theory over the minds of people worldwide, consider a selected list of dominant or influential philosophies and religions which assume or incorporate evolution: naturalism, existentialism, materialism, Marxism, atheism, humanism, occultism, Hinduism, Buddhism, Taoism, liberal Judaism and Christianity (including process theology), much or most of Islam and Roman Catholicism, and most cults, new religions, and branches of the New Age movement.

Because these philosophies and ideologies collectively touch the vast majority of the earth's population, one could argue that, at least in one sense, the *underlying*, unspoken, religion of the world *is* a philosophy of evolution.

But again what if the theory of evolution is wrong? Wouldn't it then be true that *everything* evolution has touched would be affected in a prejudicial or even harmful way? Given the influence of evolutionary thinking, the implications are hardly small.

As we saw, one only need examine the twentieth century and take note of the terrible impact of evolutionary materialism to see how true this is. Ideologies like Nazism, Marxism, and atheism have collectively destroyed tens of millions of lives.

The modern relativism, selfism, nihilism, despair, and lawlessness so prevalent today are destroying tens of millions more. All this has been sanctioned and supported by evolution's materialistic creed and "survival of the fittest" code, as we and others have documented elsewhere. Thus, "Evolutionary theory does indeed dominate modern thought in virtually every field— every discipline of study, every level of education, and every area of practice. This fact in itself indicates the tremendous responsibility that evolutionism must assume for present world conditions."[22] Again, Aldous Huxley, one of the twentieth century's foremost novelists, was correct when he noted, "Evolution has resulted in the world as we know it today."[23]

Part II

Evolution
and the
Politics
of Science

3

Seeing Things Differently
Science, Evolution, and the Interpretive Process

Evolutionists consistently maintain that evolution is a true scientific theory devoid of speculation, dogma, or faith. As the following official statement from the Association of Pennsylvania State College and University Biologists declares, "The Theory of Evolution meets the criteria of science and the criteria of a scientific theory and is not based on faith, mere speculation or dogma. . . . To state, as Creationists do, that the Theory of Evolution is 'only' a theory illustrates ignorance of science and the scientific method."[1]

Science Misunderstood

Many popular misunderstandings concerning the nature of science exist today. Philosopher of science Dr. J.P. Moreland discusses some of these misconceptions and observes that even "scientists today, in contrast to their counterparts in earlier generations, are often ill-equipped to define science, since such a project is philosophical in nature."[2] The surprising truth is that most scientists apparently *are* ignorant about the real nature of science, as W. R. Bird and others have documented in detail.[3] Bird and Moreland further cite several standard definitions of science given in such texts as *College Physics, Biological Science,* and Webster's *New Collegiate Dictionary*, as well as Judge William R. Overton's definition of science in the decision against creationism in the famous creation science trial in Little Rock, Arkansas, December 1981. They observe that none of these definitions of science is adequate.[4]

It is not our purpose at this point to discuss the problems involved in the definition of science.[5] We do need to know that the interaction of science and philosophy is a complex one and that there is no universally accepted, entirely clear-cut definition of what science is.* We are on safer ground if we define science in a general way, noting its methodology, i.e., the scientific method. For our purposes, the *Oxford American Dictionary* (1982) definition of science is adequate: "A branch of study which is considered either with a connected body of *demonstrated truths* or with *observed facts* systematically classified and more or less colligated and brought under *general laws*, and which includes *trustworthy methods* for the discovery of *new truth* within its own domain" (emphasis added).

---

*Science educator William F. McComas (Ph.D. in Science Education), writing in *Skeptic* magazine (vol. 5, no. 2) discusses 15 of the most common " 'Myths of Science' that are common in science textbooks, in classroom discourses, and in the mind of adult Americans": 1) hypotheses become theories which in turn become laws; 2) scientific laws are absolute; 3) a hypothesis is an educated guess; 4) a general and universal scientific method exists; 5) evidence accumulated carefully will result in sure knowledge; 6) science and its methods provide absolute proof; 7) science is procedural more than creative; 8) science and its methods can answer all questions; 9) scientists are particularly objective; 10) experiments are the principle root of scientific knowledge; 11) conclusions in science are reviewed for accuracy; 12) acceptance of new scientific knowledge is straightforward; 13) models represent reality; 14) science and technology are the same and 15) science is a solitary pursuit. We would recommend interested readers secure this article.

In simple terms the scientific method involves but is not limited by the following:

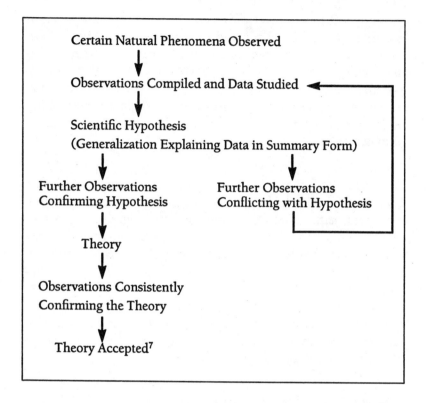

Ideally scientific work involves an orderly method of defining a particular problem, gathering the relevant data, formulating a hypothesis, interpreting one's results, reaching a logical conclusion and peer review. Science and the scientific method deal with *hypotheses, theories* and *laws,* general definitions of which are given below.[6]

1. *Hypothesis: The American Heritage Dictionary of Science* defines *hypothesis* and provides an illustration in the following manner: "a proposition assumed as a basis for reasoning and often subjected to testing for its validity: *a speculation in regard to the probable cause of a phenomenon is called a hypothesis. A*

hypothesis gains in reliability each time a prophecy is based upon it and found to be correct (Parks and Steinbach, *Systematic College Chemistry*, p. 304)."

A hypothesis is never proved nor verified in a final sense, it is only supported or disproved depending on how the experiment comes out. The reason for this is that a false hypothesis may predict a result that has a different cause from that hypothesized. In other words, a hypothesis "designates a merely tentative explanation of the data, advanced or adopted provisionally, often as the basis of a theory or as a guide to further observation or experiment."[7]

2. *Theory:* A theory is more than a single hypothesis, it's a collection of them. For example, the theory of evolution consists of multiple hypotheses about mutation, population dynamics, natural selection, genetic drift, origin of life experiments, and so on. *The American Heritage Dictionary of Science* defines theory as "an explanation or model based on observation, experimentation, and reasoning, especially one that has been tested and confirmed as a general principle helping to explain and predict natural phenomena."[8] As terms in science, theory and hypothesis mean a "generalization reached by inference from observed particulars and proposed as an explanation of their cause, relations, or the like."[9]

3. *Law:* The term scientific law refers to "a statement of what always occurs under certain conditions."[10] In essence, a law is simply a declaration of something that has always been observed to be true under the given conditions. A scientific law does not provide the kind of explanation that is found in a hypothesis or theory. For example, the law of gravity states that all airborne objects left to themselves will fall to the earth. A theory of gravitation would seek to explain why that is the case. Thus, scientific theories do not become laws; they *explain* laws.

When it comes to evolution, how do we properly classify the concept? Is it a scientific law, theory, or hypothesis? It is certainly not a scientific law or fact; neither does it adequately fit the above definition of theory, and while in certain ways evolution may legitimately be considered a tentative theory or hypothesis, even this has its problems. If by hypothesis we mean a "speculation in regard to the cause of a phenomenon" or "a merely tentative explanation of the data," evolution would fit as a weak hypothesis.[11] But if by hypothesis we mean "a generalization reached by inference from observed particulars and proposed as a *well-supported* explanation of their cause, relation, or the like" the term is not applicable. As far as we can see, the most accurate classification for evolution would be a materialistic postulate, a statement about origins based on scientific naturalism that is accepted as true without proof.

In essence, the theory of evolution should never have been accepted as a legitimate scientific theory. True science uses logical inference from empirical observations to arrive at truth.[12] What the proper definition of science and description of the scientific method will indicate is that, while scientists who study nature may utilize the scientific method, evolutionary theory *itself* is not ultimately good science because evolution has few, if any, "demonstrated truths" or "observed facts." It does not arrive at truth inductively, i.e., the supporting of a general truth (evolution) by observing particular cases that exist.[13] A strictly limited change within species can be demonstrated, such as crossbreeding among some plants and animals, but this has nothing to do with evolution as commonly understood, nor, when examined critically, can the mechanisms involved explain how evolution might occur.

Let's further explain why we do not think the term theory is appropriately applied to evolution. As noted, in science, the term has a more profound meaning than in common usage. In science, the phrase, "It's *just* a theory" is inappropriate. A good scientific theory explains a great deal of scientific knowledge, including "both laws and the facts dependent on scientific laws."*[14]

---

*Evolutionists argue that with the phrase "the theory of evolution" the term theory refers primarily to the long debated *mechanism* of evolution, not its factuality. Thus, "to call evolution a theory implies no more doubt about its factuality than referring to atomic theory or the theory of gravitation. . . ."[15] The problem is that evolution is assumed to be true apriori—even when almost every aspect of evolution is debatable, not just its mechanism.

"'*Theory*'—to a scientist—is a concept firmly grounded in and based upon facts, contrary to popular opinion that it is a hazy notion or undocumented hypothesis. Theories do not become facts; they explain facts. A theory must be verifiable. If evidence is found that contradicts the stated theory, the theory must be modified or discarded."[16]

Evolution is not verifiable; it explains few facts, and it contradicts several scientific laws. Further, there is a great deal of undeniable evidence against it. So, scientifically, it must be modified or discarded. It is inappropriate to apply the term *scientific theory* to evolution. Applied to evolution, the term actually fits the popular idea much better, e.g., " a hazy notion or undocumented hypothesis."

After citing evolutionists who confess that evolution is not scientifically provable, Dr. Randy L. Wysong observes, ". . . evolution is not a formulation of the true scientific method. [These scientists] realize [that, in effect] evolution means the initial formation of unknown organisms from unknown chemicals produced in an atmosphere or ocean of unknown composition under unknown conditions, which organisms have then climbed an unknown evolutionary ladder by an unknown process leaving unknown evidence."[17]

Not Good Science

An extensive discussion of the philosophical nature and definition of science proves why modern evolutionary theory does not only not fit a proper definition of science, but is frequently distorting to science. In fact the *radical* definition of science promoted by the evolutionary establishment "has been contrived recently for the obvious purpose of excluding the theory of abrupt appearance [e.g., scientific creation] by definition."[18] For example:

> The McLean opinion, which was a 1982 decision of a federal trial court judge, gave the following definition of science:
> More precisely, the essential characteristics of science are:
>
> 1. It is guided by natural law;
> 2. It has to be explanatory by reference to natural law;

3. It is testable against the empirical world;
4. Its conclusions are tentative, i.e., are not necessarily the final word; and
5. It is falsifiable.

That definition is absolutely incorrect as a demarcation of science from nonscience. . . . The *MacLean* definition does not resemble, or come close to resembling, any definition of science existing in the philosophy of science literature, and has not been endorsed subsequently by any philosopher of science, except by certain courtroom witnesses from the *MacLean* trial. . . . In fact, the *MacLean* definition of science was contrived by the American Civil Liberties Union (ACLU) for the tactile purpose of excluding "creation-science" by definition from being scientific.[19]

As Bird noted earlier,

One philosopher of science has responded that "the criteria which Judge Overton offered [in *MacLean*] as 'essential conditions' of science are nothing of the sort," and that the *MacLean* opinion made "anachronistic efforts to revive a variety of discredited criteria" and gave "a false stereotype of what science is." Another philosopher of science described the *MacLean* criteria as "demonstrably false," as discussed further below.[20]

One reason this definition is inadequate is its assumption of scientific naturalism in points one and two. Scientific naturalism is the belief that everything in the universe can be explained through a closed system of material causes without recourse to a creator. This is simply not good science as, for example, Dr. J. P. Moreland points out so well in *The Creation Hypotheses* (1996). If science must be ruled by a philosophy of naturalism, it can no longer be properly considered scientific.

In other words, Judge William Overton's decision ruling that equal classroom treatment for creation science and evolution science was unconstitutional was itself based on a faulty definition of science, and therefore invalid. This decision involved not only bad legal reasoning but bad science as well. It has even been criticized by a number of evolutionists. For example, evolutionist Dr. Larry Lauden, Professor of Philosophy of Science at the University of Pittsburgh wrote that, "The victory in the Arkansas case was hollow, for it was achieved only at the expense of perpetuating and canonizing a false stereotype of what science is and how it works. If it goes un-challenged by the scientific community, it will raise grave doubts about that community's intellectual integrity."[21]

Despite the absence of both good legal reasoning and the principles of science in this case (and many others), not only did the great majority of evolutionists in the scientific commu-nity never challenge the decision but they have constantly used Judge Overton's erroneous decision in defense of evolution whenever the subject of creation is raised.[22] Yet to depend on a false definition of science would seem to show the weakness of their own case for evolution. As Dr. Gish and others point out, not only have evolutionists falsely attacked scientists who are creationists, they have also been, regrettably, "especially vicious and slanderous" in their methods.[23] "It is unfair, unethical, and demeaning to science as a profession for evolutionists to inces-santly charge creation scientists with quoting out of context, misquoting, distorting science, and telling outright falsehoods. These tactics are simply an admission of weakness on the part of evolutionists and of their inability to refute scientific chal-lenges to their sagging theory. If the facts are on their side, they should simply state the facts, and the facts would speak for themselves."[24]

Regardless of the bias against creationism in the *MacLean* court, to the extent that the findings of science *hinge* upon demonstrated truths and observed facts, evolutionary theory has little to do with the findings of science. Evolution is more properly considered a naturalistic philosophy or worldview that seeks to explain the origin of life materialistically. The late A. E. Wilder-Smith, who held three earned doctorates in science, ob-served, "As Kerkut has shown [in *The Implications of Evolution*], neo-darwinian thought teaches seven main postulates. Not one of these seven theses can be proved or even tested experimen-tally. If they are not supported by experimental evidence, the whole theory can scarcely be considered to be a *scientific* one. If the seven main postulates of Neodarwinism are experimentally untestable, then Neodarwinism must be considered to be a phi-losophy rather than a science, for science is concerned solely with experimentally testable evidence."[25] Dr. Wilder-Smith pursued this theme in *The National Sciences Know Nothing of Evolution* and other works.

Dr. Gish further argues that evolution does not meet the criteria of empirical science:

> Strictly defined, *empirical science* is our attempt to observe, understand, and explain events, processes, and properties that are *repeatably observable*. On the basis of such theories, predictions can be made concerning related natural phenomena or future natural events. Thus, experiments can be conceived and performed to test the theory and which may possibly show that the theory is wrong, if it is wrong. This property of potential falsifiability is an important element of a true scientific theory. Empirical science and scientific theories thus are restricted to attempts to explain the *operation* of the universe and of the living things it contains. They are about the real world out there, the here and now.[26]

Obviously, theories concerning origins such as the origin of the universe, the origin of our galaxy or solar system, the origin of planet earth or of life on planet earth are, strictly, outside the domain of empirical science. Origins cannot be observed nor can they be repeated. Only subsidiary hypotheses that are potentially capable of being falsified can be considered. So in this sense it is not possible to falsify either evolution or creation per se. But it is possible that the preponderance of the evidence would falsify enough subsidiary hypotheses to make one the more logical option.

And yet the dilemma here is more profound. Evolutionary theory is sufficiently outside the domain of science, and over the years it has become so adept at elasticity, that it can stretch itself to explain virtually all contrary data, no matter how definitive.

This explains one reason why Dr. Paul Ehrlich and Dr. L. C. Birch, evolutionary biologists at Stanford University and the University of Sydney respectively, wrote the following in the prestigious journal, *Nature*: "Our theory of evolution has become . . . one which cannot be refuted by any possible observations. Every conceivable observation can be fitted into it. It is thus 'outside of empirical science' but not necessarily false."[27] Actually, as we will see later, for all practical purposes evolution *is* falsifiable.

If evolution is such a mercurial theory that "it no longer makes any difference what the data may be,"[28] because ways will be found to fit all data to it, of what relevance is the theory? The theory is untestable, "nonfalsifiable," and can accommodate even the most complete refutations of its basic postulates. It can encompass almost anything. In the end, isn't evolution closer to a dogma, something to be accepted as true without question? And isn't dogma a property of religion, not science?[29]

Dr. Willem J. Ouweneel, Research Associate in Developmental Genetics, Ultrech, Netherlands, with the Faculty of Mathematics and Natural Sciences, points out in his article "The Scientific Character of the Evolution Doctrine," what is now obvious to more and more scientists: "It is becoming increasingly apparent that evolutionism is not even a good scientific theory."[30] He argues that evolution should not be considered a *scientific* fact, theory, hypothesis, or postulate. For example, evolutionary theory is not, strictly, a *scientific* postulate because to be so: (a) it must be in accordance with the principal laws of mathematics and natural science; (b) it must not be more complicated than necessary for the explanation of observed phenomena; (c) it must give rise to conclusions which can be controlled by further experimental observations and testing; (d) it must conform to the general data of science; (e) alternate hypotheses must be shown to be wrong or less acceptable; and (f) the reliability of a scientific conception is inversely proportional to the number of unproven postulates on which it is founded. Evolution fails all six criteria for categorization as a scientific postulate. This is why Dr. Ouweneel properly concludes that evolution is actually a *materialistic* postulate rather than a credible scientific theory.[31] As philosopher and non-creationist Dr. David Berlinski pointed out in the September 1996 issue of *Commentary:* ". . . As our knowledge increases, the crude Darwinian scheme seems progressively remote from the evidence. . . . Still, the real infirmities of Darwin's theory are conceptual and not empirical. Darwin's theory of evolution remains little more than a collection of anecdotal remarks."

But one would never know this from reading the scientific literature, literature which constantly assures the world that evolution is a scientific fact. The principal reason evolution "must" be a scientific fact is because of the naturalistic bias that pervades the scientific world—a bias which, in the end, is unnecessary and in many ways even harmful to the cause of science.[32]

Assumptions and Interpretation

At this point, it is necessary to discuss the *interpretation* of scientific data.

One frequently reads in evolutionary literature such declarations as "evolution is a fact" and "the weight of the evidence for it is beyond persuasive." On the other hand, one reads just as commonly in antievolutionary literature that "evolution is a myth" and "the amount of faith it takes to believe in evolution is beyond belief."

How is that we can get such extremely divergent views from the *same* set of data when *all* these statements come from scientists? The reason is simple: it has to do with how one interprets the data. Evolutionary theory does not depend on the credibility of the data used but rather upon the subjective interpretation given the data within metaphysical assumptions held by scientists. "Data do not speak for themselves: they must be interpreted. They often say what the individual wants them to say."[33] Thus, if one is a scientific naturalist, then one can only conclude the data *must* fit the evolutionary scenario. Indeed, all sorts of technical scientific experimentation, argumentation, and philosophizing are pressed to support the idea of evolution, and to be sure, the weight of tens of thousands of technical scientific papers in support of evolution certainly seems impressive. When scientists read this literature, especially outside their own field, it convinces them evolution is true.

The difficulty is that the interpretation is highly strained and that most scientists rarely consider the evidence *against* evolution or the evidence *for* creation. In other words, they never fairly look at the other side because based on "the authority of science" they assume that evolution must be true. And again, the data *can* be made to fit into an evolutionary framework. It's just that the data, when examined critically, doesn't fit.

An illustration can be seen in the legal courtroom. The defendant is either innocent or guilty of the crime specified.

Both the defense and prosecution have the same set of data with which to work—the facts that have been painstakingly gathered by police and other investigators. The prosecutor will do his best to use the same facts to prove guilt that the defense attorney will use to prove innocence.

This illustrates how the same evidence can be interpreted in two different ways even though the data actually best fit only one decision. And usually, it takes some time to sort out where the weight of the evidence lies, especially if one attorney is particularly clever and/or manipulative of the law. Interested laymen trying to sort out the creation/evolution controversy find themselves in a similar situation. One reason it takes time to render a verdict is because of the philosophical assumptions most materialistic scientists bring to their study of science, the application of which is tantamount to a manipulation of the data.

Creationists see things quite differently because they do not start from the perspective of scientific naturalism but of theistic science or creation science. When creationists look at evolution through the eyes of mathematical probabilities; the fossil record; information theory and the vast information content in living things; the laws of thermodynamics, biogenesis and noncontradiction; comparative studies in physiology/anatomy/taxonomy/embryology/morphology/genetics and biochemistry; and sciences such as anthropology, geology, and biology, they find it hard to believe that anyone who fairly examines this issue could state that evolution is a fact—or even a credible theory. This is why creationists argue that any open-minded individual, scientist or layman, who will objectively evaluate all the evidence, will discover that such evidence comes down heavily on the side of creation.

Thus, when Edward O. Dodson, an evolutionary biologist, says, "Despite the controversy over cladism, there is still a vast array of evidence for evolution, drawn from such diverse fields as biogeography, comparative anatomy, comparative embryology, comparative physiology, comparative biochemistry, paleontology, genetics, and cytology,"[34] one must recognize that we are dealing with interpretation based on preexisting philosophical premises (e.g., scientific naturalism). The creationist evaluates in the exact same areas to either disprove evolution or explain the data better from a creationist viewpoint. As an example, the facts of anatomy are disputed by almost no one; however, even among evolutionists the interpretation of those facts is both difficult and tentative. This is illustrated in the area of comparative anatomy/homology by such texts as G. DeBeer's *Homology: An Unsolved Problem* and Marvalee H. Wake, ed., *Hyman's Comparative Vertebrate Anatomy*. These texts illustrate why creationists argue that the scientific facts in these areas better support creation.

Consider another illustration from biogeography, the study of the geographic distribution of plants and animals. Nationally respected zoologist Gareth J. Nelson wrote the following in a preface to W. R. Bird's, *The Origin of Species Revisited*. While accepting that "the book has virtue as criticism of evolutionary theory" he argues Bird should also have dealt with biogeography which he says is inexplicably missing from Bird's argument. "The facts of geographic distribution are not in short supply. They have been considered the most convincing evidence of evolution."[35]

This is hardly the case. For example, Kurt P. Wise, who received his Ph.D. in paleontology from Harvard University, observes that one must distinguish microbiogeography from macrobiogeography. Microbiogeography involves the fact that very similar species are often found near to one another *as if* they evolved from one another. Dr. Wise points out this can only be evidence for microevolution, the evolution of populations, not for macroevolution or the origin of major groups. Concerning macrobiogeography, he observes "There are very few examples of macrobiographical evidences for macroevolution, and none of them is very strong. The best-known claim is the concentration of marsupials in Australia. But there are several reasons that marsupials in Australia are actually a poor example. . . ."[36]

Biogeography aside, we are amazed that the vast array of evidence against evolution presented by Bird does not seem to faze Dr. Nelson. But this is just the point. As Nelson says of Bird's book, "Its argument will not convince my evolutionist colleagues. . . ."[37]

Committed scientific naturalists of today will *not* be convinced by creationist arguments, no matter how persuasive, because their philosophical assumptions *prevent* it.

Noted Berkeley law professor Phillip E. Johnson has written a most important book, *Reason in the Balance: The Case Against Naturalism in Science, Law and Education*. This book discusses the philosophical assumptions underlying modern belief in evolution and explains why evolutionists have such a problem with creationism. What is "reasonable" is not determined by a search for truth but by preconceived notions as to what constitutes reasonable. The accepted definition of science today involves the idea that matter is the final absolute and the only cause for all existence. As a result, any supernatural or nonphysical explanation for reality is entirely unacceptable and considered unreasonable in the field of science. In essence, what Darwin hoped to achieve with *On the Origin of Species*, the eviction of God from the realm of scientific investigation, has actually been achieved. Religious explanations are not credible because religious explanations are preconceived as not credible. Religious explanations are not scientific because religious explanations cannot be scientific.[38]

Yet consider the following statement by noted creationist Dr. Jerry Bergman, author of *The Criterion* which, as we detail later, documents scores of cases of inexcusable biases against creationists:

> This reviewer has read most of the three dozen or so books often termed anti-creationist, written to lambast and "refute" the conclusions of those who argue in favor of a designed worldview. Most are written by individuals who have a limited first-hand understanding of the intelligent design view. Many simply repeat incorrect statements until conclusions which lack foundation are accepted because they are so often repeated. Those who have completed extensive research in the creationist movement such as Numbers and Toumey have effectively refuted, or at least critiqued, some of the many false conclusions that are mainstay among evolutionary naturalists."[39]

The book reviewed by Jerry Bergman is by Christopher P. Toumey, *God's Own Scientists: Creationists in a Secular World* published by Rutgers University Press, 1994. Toumey shows that the common interpretation of creationism and creationists by those who are committed to naturalistic evolution, is frequently highly inaccurate. In fact, he concludes that, "scientific creationism has changed the nation's assumptions about the credibility of evolutionary thought and has given conservative Christians reason to believe that science is the Bible's best friend. . . . Modern creationism cannot be reduced to either scientific illiteracy or a slavish devotion to . . . Scripture. In fact it is a rich, complicated, and varied system of knowledge, values and beliefs. . . . ICR's [Institute for Creation Research] followers take science more seriously than most scientists do."[40]

So we see that the creation/evolution controversy is really an issue of the *interpretation* of scientific data. The creationist has just as valid a right to his scientific interpretation of the data as does the evolutionist. And only the fact that creation involves a legitimate scientific view can explain why a minority of scientists, on a regular basis, reject evolution and come to accept creation. In fact, we are convinced that, were the case for creation presented adequately, almost any jury in the United States would logically conclude that not only is creation scientific and at least an equally credible option to evolution, but that creation actually offers a far better choice scientifically. If the creationist camp were allowed to present its case with its best legal, philosophical, and scientific proponents including leading non-creationist anti-evolutionist scientists, we think there should be little doubt as to the outcome of a jury's decision.

The Theological Dimension

Finally, in one sense, there is also a theological dimension to the interpretation of scientific data. Christians, at least, should be aware of the information given in Romans chapter one as it relates to the creation/evolution controversy. The Scripture clearly declares God's displeasure at men who suppress the truth about God, even *after* God has made this truth plain to them: "The wrath of God is being revealed from heaven against all the godlessness and wickedness of men who suppress the truth by their wickedness, since what may be known about God is *plain* to them, because God *has made it plain* to them. For since the creation of the world God's invisible qualities—his eternal power and divine nature—have been *clearly seen*, being *understood* from what has been made, so that men are *without excuse*. For although they *knew God*, they neither glorified him as God nor gave thanks to him, but their thinking became futile and their foolish hearts were darkened" (Romans 1:18-21, emphasis added).

If God has been their teacher, there is hardly a possibility of failure. Only the deliberate suppression of evidence can account for the resulting unbelief. Considering the biblical testimony of the unregenerate state of the human mind and heart, the normal approach for secular scientists to take is to reject evidence clearly seen—or even to be hostile toward the evidence for creation. According to Romans 1, the evidence for divine creation is not dim and hidden, but "*clearly* seen, being *understood* through what has been made." This is why God says unbelievers are without excuse, because they willfully "suppress the truth" concerning the existence of God and His nature. Again, all people—including scientists—will tend to reject the witness of God in nature or deliberately corrupt it because of the condition of their heart, *not* because of the condition of nature. As the Apostle Peter says similarly concerning another divine reality, divine judgment, "They deliberately forget" this (2 Peter 3:5).

In essence, one could expect that materialistic scientists would intentionally devise conceptual frameworks that would interpret nature without God or put God at a distance, which was exactly what Darwin intentionally did. (See the important work by Neal C. Gillespie, *Charles Darwin and the Problem of Creation.*) All their facts would be interpreted through this biased and flawed naturalistic conceptual framework.[42]

So what may be just as important as the scientific evidence itself is the theological bias that can reside in men's hearts and prevent them from fairly examining the evidence. As Dr. Jerry Bergman wrote in a review of the materialistically oriented *Dictionary of Science and Creationism* (Promethius Books), "While reviewing this book, it soon became apparent that it conformed to a hypothesis of mine about those who write books against creationism: many have personal vendettas against Christianity."[43] Anyone who understands how such individuals have used the concept of evolution against God, biblical authority, and the Christian faith, and in support of all kinds of philosophical, moral, social, and political ills, understands the implication only too well.

All this brings us to the related theological issue of spiritual deception. It is difficult to deny the statement of zoologist Dr. Bolton Davidheiser (Ph.D., Johns Hopkins University), who wrote in the introduction to his *Evolution and the Christian Faith*, "It is of the utmost importance for Christians to realize that a very real struggle is going on and that the theory of evolution is a very important factor in the accelerating trend toward apostasy."[44] Because of its materialistic premises, evolution must be considered an important philosophical and scientific instrument to hinder acceptance of the Gospel and to reject the Christian faith, as we documented elsewhere. If even Darwin himself referred to his theory as "the devil's gospel," then perhaps our comments here are not out of place. In a letter to Huxley dated August 8, 1860, he referred to Huxley as "my good and kind agent for the propagation of the Gospel—i.e., the devil's gospel."[45]

Speaking of the devil, the Scripture informs us that Satan has "blinded the minds of unbelievers . . ." (2 Corinthians 4:4). How does he do this? One way is through anti-Christian philosophies and religions. Indeed, as we have studied the world's major religions, scores of cults, and numerous philosophies, we have been struck by a fact common to them all: in their own unique way they each insulate their advocates against the Gospel. Perhaps this is one reason why the Bible calls Satan "the god of this age" (2 Corinthians 4:4). Perhaps it is also why theologians of such repute as Dr. Merrill Unger, writing in *Demons in the World Today*, can comment that evolution: "opposes the Word of God so flagrantly that it should be labeled 'a doctrine of demons.' " (See 1 Timothy 4:1.)[46] Nor are we surprised that occultism and endless revelations from the spirit world endorse evolution enthusiastically.

Actually, it can be argued that this classification as a "doctrine of demons" is not only valid for the theory in terms of its negative moral, theological, and nihilistic implications, which are consequential enough; it is also true for the doctrine scientifically speaking. In other words, the *scientific* doctrine of evolution could also be so labeled. Why? Consider the major implication of such science naturalistically. As Sir Julian Huxley once noted, the idea of God as Creator is entirely "removed . . . from the sphere of rational discussion."[47] That's no small victory.

In our next two chapters we show how naturalistic biases hurt the cause of science. First, in Chapter 4, we will illustrate how the assumption of materialism requires scientists to conclude evolution must be a fact. In other words, if matter alone is the ultimate reality and no God exists, then natural processes alone must account for evolution. The only possible way we could have come into being is through naturalistic evolution. Any other view is ruled out by definition. Put simply, we exist, therefore evolution must be an undeniable scientific fact.

In Chapter 5, we will show how naturalistic science damages the cause of science by its powerfully biased approach to creation science.

4

It Must Be True (Science Says So)

The Scientific Establishment and Evolution

*Dogmatic assertions are inconsistent with objective considera-
tion of any subject. Science is always tentative and does not pretend to offer ultimate truth.*

—West Virginia Academy of Science[1]

Evolution is a fact, fact, FACT!

—Michael Ruse[2]

Evolution continues to be set forth as an established scientific
fact by the scientific community. Again, the only reason evolution "must" be a scientific fact is the naturalistic, anti-
supernatural bias that pervades the scientific world. This bias
was evident in the life of the four pillars of nineteenth century
evolution—Darwin, Spencer, Huxley, and Wallace—and among
scientists today who *assure* us that evolution is a scientific fact.[3]
Lewontin of Harvard, writing in *BioScience*, illustrates the trend
by calling for evolutionists to clearly declare that "evolution is a
fact not a theory," while simultaneously chiding "creationist
know-nothings."[4]

Dogmatic Assertions

Consider in detail how leading scientists are damaging the integrity of their own profession by making dogmatic assertions that far exceed the domains of legitimate scientific conclusion. Is it not misrepresentation for the scientific world to declare that evolution is demonstrated fact when it is no such thing? Consider the following illustrations from the official declarations of noted scientific organizations and then from noted scientists. As we will discuss, our belaboring the point is necessary to our argument, hence we encourage the reader to read the statements below. This will supply a perspective perhaps not otherwise attainable.

American Society of Parasitologists
"Evolution . . . is believed by nearly all professional life scientists. . . . Virtually all scientists accept the evolution of current species from fewer, simpler, ancestral ones as undisputed fact."[5]

Geological Society of America
". . . we geologists find incontrovertible evidence in the rocks that life has existed here on earth for several billions of years and that it has evolved through time."[6]

North Carolina Academy of Science
". . . evolution [is] an established law of nature. . . . "[7]

Society for Amateur Scientists
". . . that life has adapted and changed through time is as well established as the fact that the earth goes round the sun."[8]

Society of Vertebrate Paleontology
"[Evolution has] come to be regarded as a confirmed fact, as certain as the drift of continents through time or the lawful operation of gravity. . . . [Scientists] do not argue about whether evolution took place: that is a fact."[9]

Committee for Scientific Investigation of Claims of the Paranormal
"Evolution . . . is as well established in science as are the principle of gravity and the fact that the earth orbits the sun. . . . Virtually no active scientist challenges the fact that evolution has occurred."[10]

American Association for the Advancement of Science
". . . the evidences in favor of the evolution of man are sufficient to convince every scientist of note in the world."[11]

University of California Academic Senate
". . . virtually all biological scientists are agreed on the broad features of the theory of evolution of life forms, the evidence for which is completely overwhelming."[12]

American Geological Institute
"Scientific evidence indicates beyond any doubt that life has existed on Earth for billions of years. This life has evolved through time producing vast numbers of species of plants and animals. . . ."[13]

American Institute of Biological Sciences
"The theory of evolution is the only scientifically defensible explanation for the origin of life and development of species. . . . As a community, biologists agree that evolution occurred and that the forces driving the evolutionary process are still active today. This consensus is based on more than a century of scientific data gathering and analysis."[14]

Science Museum of Minnesota
"All scientific disciplines are united in demonstrating the evolution of life on this planet. . . . It is widely accepted within the scientific community that evolution itself is fact."[15]

Similar official pronouncements have been made by the following organizations: Academy of Science of the Royal Society of Canada, Alabama Academy of Science, American Association of Physical Anthropologists, American Astronomical Society, American Chemical Society, American Geological Institute, American Geophysical Union, American Physical Society, American Psychological Association, American Society for Biological Chemists, California Academy of Sciences, Iowa Academy of Science, Kentucky Academy of Science, Louisiana Academy of Sciences, National Academy of Sciences, New York Academy of Sciences, Society for the Study of Evolution, Southern Anthropological Society, and the West Virginia Academy of Science, as well as numerous educational, religious, and civil liberties organizations.[16]

Again, we are belaboring the point for a purpose. All of these highly respected and reputable scientific organizations are declaring that evolution is an undisputed fact—based on incontrovertible evidence no less. Yet nothing could be further from the truth. Doesn't this give the reader some idea of the power of a false premise to thoroughly distort entire branches of science?

We are now going to give a similar list of noted evolutionary scientists who declare the same thing. We are going to such lengths to document the many claims for evolution because people don't realize the collective weigh such declarations have in convincing people of the truth of evolution.

Most people today, including most scientists, believe evolution is a fact largely because evolutionary scientists authoritatively declare it so. "Science says so" is still a powerful persuader. Regrettably, most scientists have apparently never taken the time to investigate the matter for themselves. And, given the following declarations, perhaps it's no wonder.

It is simply not possible to make our point effectively without providing citations such as these: if evolution is universally declared a fact, and yet this is demonstrably false, then it's hard to avoid the conclusion that modern science is responsible for *misleading* the American public on an extremely crucial subject. So below we offer the comments of many noted evolutionary scientists. Perhaps the reader will wish to think through the implications. (Emphases are added.)

More Dogmatic Assertions

Pierre-Paul Grassé, the renowned French zoologist and past president of the French Academy of Sciences, states in his *Evolution of Living Organisms*: "Zoologists and botanists are nearly unanimous in considering evolution *as a fact* and not a hypothesis. I agree with this position and base it primarily on documents provided by paleontology, i.e., the [fossil] history of the living world."[17]

Theodosius Dobzhansky, who, according to another leading evolutionist, Stephen J. Gould of Harvard, is "the greatest evolutionist of our century,"[18] asserts in his award-winning text, *Mankind Evolving*, "the *proofs of evolution* are now a matter of elementary biology. . . . In Lamark's and Darwin's times evolution was a hypothesis; in our day it is *proven*."[19]

The late world famous scientist George Gaylord Simpson, distinguished professor of vertebrate paleontology at the

Museum of Comparative Zoology at Harvard emphasized in *The Meaning of Evolution*, "*Ample proof* has been repeatedly presented and is available to anyone who really wants to know the truth. . . . In the present study the *factual truth* of organic evolution is taken as *established*. . . ."[20]

Simpson also cited Darwin's *Origin of Species* (1859) as "the work that first substantially established this truth."[21] Even the National Academy of Sciences agrees: "it was Darwin, above all others, who first marshaled the convincing critical evidence for biological evolution."[22] Yet anyone who has critically read Darwin's *Origin of Species* knows how extremely weak his arguments were. As we will illustrate in Chapter 8, Darwin himself was unable to logically resolve serious doubts as to the validity of his own theory.

Nevertheless, noted evolutionist G. Ledyard Stebbins writes, "The origins of races and species by evolution is a *demonstrated fact* supported by experimental evidence *as strong as* the evidence for the existence of atoms, electrons, protons, and other particles of matter."[23] Everett C. Olson, Professor of Geophysical Sciences at the University of Chicago and Chairman of the Interdivisional Committee on Paleozoology, states in his *The Evolution of Life*: "In spite of all the accumulated *evidence* some people still do not 'believe' in evolution. For the most part those who reject the basic concept of evolution *know little about it*."[24]

Ashley Montagu of Princeton University has stated that, "The attack on evolution, the *most thoroughly authenticated fact in the whole history of science*, is an attack on science itself."[25]

The late Carl Sagan was a distinguished Cornell University astronomer and Pulitzer Prize winning author. He is perhaps best known as the host and co-writer of the *Cosmos* television series seen in 60 countries by approximately 3 percent of all people on earth. The hard cover edition of *Cosmos* was on the *New York Times* best-seller list for 70 weeks and may be the best-selling science book in the English language in the twentieth century. In this book, Sagan simply states, "Evolution is *a fact*, not a theory."[26] The eminent anthropologist Konrad Lorenz observed in *Intellectual Digest*, "It is *not* a theory, but an *irrefutable historical fact*, that the living world—since its origin—has evolved from 'below' to 'above.' "[27]

Rene Dubos, one of the country's leading ecologists, stated in *American Scientist*, "Most enlightened persons now accept as a *fact* that everything in the cosmos—from heavenly bodies to human beings—has developed and continues to develop through evolutionary processes."[28] Noted geneticist Richard Goldschmidt of the University of California also stated in *American Scientist*, "Evolution of the animal and plant world is considered by all those entitled to judgment *to be a fact* for which *no further proof* is needed."[29]

Another prominent evolutionist, Sir Julian Huxley, claimed in his famous keynote address at the Darwin Centennial held in 1959 at the University of Chicago, "The first point to make about Darwin's theory is that it is *no longer* a theory, *but a fact*. No serious scientist would deny the fact that evolution has occurred, just as he would not deny the fact that the earth goes around the sun."[30]

But all this is nothing new. Confident assertions of this nature have been put forth for decades. Consider some examples. In *Scientific Monthly* for October 1930 (p. 290) William Patton of Dartmouth University stated, "Evolution itself has long since passed out of the field of scientific controversy. There is *no other subject* on which scientific opinion is so completely unanimous. It is the one great truth we *most surely* know."[31] Calvin S. Hall of Western Reserve University noted in the *Sigma Xi Quarterly* of March 1938 (p. 19) that if someone were not an evolutionist, their "views deserve little serious consideration."[32] In 1939, H. H. Newman of the University of Chicago claimed in his *Evolution: Genetics and Eugenics* (p. 51), "There is no rival hypothesis except the outworn and completely refuted idea of special creation, now retained only by the ignorant, the dogmatic, and the prejudiced."[33] In 1942 Michael F. Guyer observed in his *Speaking of Man* (p. 302) that every biologist who truly understands the evidence must conclude that all life has evolved.[34] In 1942 Paul Weatherwax of Indiana University argued in *Plant Biology* (p. 370), "The doctrine [of evolution] is no longer questioned by any biologist."[35] Again, in 1942, Gilbert M. Smith of Stanford University wrote in *A Textbook of General Botany* (4th edition, p. 630), "No one who, since the publication of *Origin of Species* in 1859, has impartially investigated this evidence has questioned the validity or the usefulness of the idea of continuous evolution."[36]

Edwin Grant Conklin of Princeton University emphasized in *Man, Real and Ideal* (1943, p. 28), "The *fact* of evolution is no longer questioned by men of science."[37] In 1947 William Howells of the University of Wisconsin declared in *Mankind So Far* (p. 5), "The 'theory of evolution' is an overworked term, in the popular usage, and unfortunate besides, since it implies that, after all, there may be something dubious about it. Evolution *is a fact*, like digestion."[38] In 1956, Alexander Gordon of the University of Colorado stated in *General Biology* (p. 808), "The *proofs* of evolution are not merely adequate; they are *overwhelming*. The *fact* of organic evolution is a part of the thinking of every individual who may properly call himself a biologist."[39] Finally, Marston Bates of Harvard University said in his *The Nature of Natural History* (1950, p. 222) that as far as the evidence for evolution is concerned, "there is no more question of this among contemporary scientists than there is of the relative movements of the planets within the solar system. . . ."[40]

Even the famous historian, H. G. Wells, observed in 1946 in his *Mind at the End of Its Tether* (p. 30), ". . . no rational mind can question the *invincible nature* of the evolutionary case."[41] And in *The Human Organism and the World of Life* (1938, p. 293) it was asserted, "No unprejudiced student can possibly reject what the authors of *The Science of Life* have termed 'the incontrovertible fact of evolution,' and no responsible scientist does reject it."[42]

A State of Mind, a Mental Prison

Evolution is so widely accepted and its worldview is so dominant in the modern world that every generation accepts it almost without question, interpreting all facts of the natural world in light of its alleged truth.

As we have seen in the above citations, anyone who doubts the theory of evolution may be viewed as ignorant, incompetent, or irresponsible.

However, creationists and other non-evolutionary scientists argue that evolution cannot logically be considered a fact *apart* from any real evidence: "All the hard data in the life sciences show that evolution is not occurring today, all the real data in the earth sciences show it did not occur in the past, and all the genuine data in the physical sciences show it is not possible at all. Nevertheless, evolution is almost universally accepted as a fact in all the natural sciences."[43]

Consider the comments of the late Canadian scholar, Arthur C. Custance (Ph.D. anthropology), author of the seminal ten-volume *The Doorway Papers*. He was a member of the Canadian Physiological Society, a fellow of the Royal Anthropological Institute, and a member of the New York Academy of Sciences. In "Evolution: An Irrational Faith" he observes, ". . . virtually all the fundamentals of the orthodox evolutionary faith have shown themselves to be either of extremely doubtful validity or simply contrary to fact. . . . So basic are these erroneous [evolutionary] assumptions that the whole theory is now largely maintained *in spite of* rather than *because of* the evidence. . . . As a consequence, for the great majority of students and for that large ill-defined group, 'the public,' it has ceased to be a subject of debate. Because it is both incapable of proof and yet may not be questioned, it is virtually untouched by data which challenge it in any way. It has become in the strictest sense *irrational*. . . . Information or concepts which challenge the theory are almost never given a fair hearing. . . ."[44]

In fact, in the opinion of this erudite scholar, "Evolutionary philosophy has indeed become *a state of mind*, one might almost say a kind of mental prison rather than a scientific attitude. . . . To equate one particular interpretation of the data with *the data itself* is evidence of mental confusion. . . . The theory of evolution . . . is detrimental to ordinary intelligence and warps judgment."[45]

He concludes, "In short, the premises of evolutionary theory are about as invalid as they could possibly be. . . . If evolutionary theory was strictly scientific, it should have been abandoned long ago. But because it is more philosophy than science, it is not susceptible to the self-correcting mechanisms that govern all other branches of scientific enquiry."[46]

This last statement is very true. As we will see in Part III, if evolution *were* strictly scientific, it would of necessity have been discarded over one hundred years ago. The fact that it remains is proof it is not strictly scientific.[47]

5

Truth in Advertising

Damaging the Cause
of Science

Perhaps we should reflect for a moment on what we have just read in our last chapter. If evolution is not a fact, and yet the scientific world declares evolution is a fact, then the unkind conclusion is that the scientific world is either deceived or somehow doesn't know the meaning of the term "fact." The *Macmillan Dictionary for Students* (1984) defines fact as "something known to be true or real; that which has actually occurred." For reasons that we will demonstrate later, it is impossible that evolution can be "*known* to be true." Further, the evidence declares that evolution has not occurred and could never occur.

Unintentional Damage

Scientists who declare that evolution is a fact should recognize the damage they do to the credibility of science—and not just evolutionary science but all of science. As more and more

75

people gradually learn the truth that, deliberately or innocently, science has mislead them on an extremely crucial issue, their trust in the authority of science will be over. The implications are hardly small.

The public trusts the scientific world to know the difference between fact and speculation, between the proper interpretation of observable data that can be proven valid and unwarranted conclusions derived from faulty premises. When scientists everywhere assert that a highly suspect, indeed incredible, theory is "an established fact of science," why should anyone trust scientists to tell them the truth in other areas? If the scientific world won't tell the truth in so critical an area as our own origins, with vast implications for each of us, why should it tell the truth in matters of lesser import? In fact, the public's trust in science has already eroded significantly because of consequences stemming from its adherence to naturalism,[1] and because of sloppy science generally, as the recent book *Junk Science* illustrates.

One of those logical consequences is a nihilistic outlook on life, as we documented in Chapter 1. Even an article in the prestigious journal *Science* for August 15, 1997, correctly warned, "much of the anti-science mood in the country today stems from the perception that by venerating meaninglessness, science has become inhuman."[2] But most scientists are unaware of how the theory of evolution *itself* damages the progress of science.

Consider again the comments of the Canadian scholar Arthur C. Custance, discussing a text by noted evolutionist G. G. Simpson, *This View of Life*: "Throughout the book this begging of the issue runs like an unending refrain. Evolution is a fact, not a theory; evolution is one of the few *basic* facts; it is an unassailable fact; a fact supported by all other facts; a fact which only dishonest biologists would argue against. . . . According to Simpson, those who refuse to accept it are either idiotic, dishonest, or both."[3]

Custance's comment here is significant because it applies to so many modern science textbooks. Custance also says, "Observing the literature carefully over a period of some 40 years, it is my impression that the sense of urgency and special pleading in assuring the public that Darwin was right, has increased steadily with the passage of time."[4]

Actually, as more and more damaging evidence accumulates against the idea of evolution, it is presented more forcefully as fact. This cannot be science (or reason) operating, this is *emotion* and "politically correct" science, pure and simple. And if scientists do science on the basis of *emotion* and "political correctness," we are all in trouble.

Of course, lay people aren't the only ones realizing that the scientific establishment has been less than truthful. Many scientists who investigate the matter openly are also discovering that the theory of evolution has little or no evidence in its behalf. As Dr. Isaac Manly (MD, Harvard Medical School) comments, "What I have learned in the past ten years of review of recent scientific knowledge of cellular morphology and physiology, the code of life (DNA), and the lack of supporting evidence for evolution in the light of recent scientific evidence is a shocking rebuttal to the theory of evolution. . . . There is no evidence of any kind for this theory."[5] Dr. Manly also commented that, as he read Darwin's *Origin of Species*, he was "struck by the lack of any real evidence for Darwin's theories."[6]

We continue to have the same conclusion as we read modern evolutionary literature. Manly is correct concerning Darwin's successor's attempts to prove evolution: "they were quite willing to speculate and theorize to degrees of absurdity to prove the unprovable."[7]

Indeed, the conclusions of noted U.C. Berkeley law professor Phillip E. Johnson can be multiplied hundreds of times from scientists on the basis of scientific evidence alone. Johnson stated evolution "is not only unproven but actually contrary to the overwhelming weight of the evidence. . . . [W]hat is presented to the public as scientific knowledge about evolutionary mechanisms is mostly philosophical speculation and is not even consistent with the evidence once the naturalistic spectacles are removed. If that leaves us without a known mechanism of biological creation, so be it: it is better to admit ignorance than to have confidence in an explanation that is not true."[8]

Even evolutionist Grassé, among the most distinguished of French zoologists, remarks that "the explanatory doctrines of biological evolution do not stand up to an in-depth criticism," while evolutionist Bethel sees "Darwin's theory . . . on the verge of collapse."[9]

If scientists want the public to trust them, and to pay taxes to fund their research, then perhaps they should start telling us the truth. Until that time, by declaring evolution a fact, they will only damage their own cause.

The same article in *Science* magazine for August 15, 1997 correctly warned (citing geneticist Francisco Ayala), "The financial structure of American research depends on the goodwill of a body politic that values religion. We are not wise to have the body politic seeing science as antagonistic to spiritual commitment."[10]

Voices for Evolution

As one example of how modern naturalistic science can damage the name of science, consider the book *Voices for Evolution*, published by the National Center for Science Education (NCSE) in Berkeley. This text contains the official statements of some 70 scientific, religious, educational, and civil liberty organizations who virtually demand the teaching of evolution, almost always as fact, in public schools, and who demand we reject or strongly oppose the teaching of creation science as a legitimate second theory for an explanation of origins. This text is so full of distortions one hardly knows where to start. The NCSE states its goal plainly enough in the foreword, "The short-term immediate goal of NCSE . . . is to keep 'scientific' creationism from being taught as legitimate science in public schools."[11]

What is so disconcerting is that this text offers an accurate representation of the views of the scientific establishment, mainline religion, and numerous educational organizations in America. Yet it shows an ignorance as to the true nature of science, the true nature of creation science and the undeniable facts of science as they relate to the creation/evolution controversy. Worse yet, it clearly shows a naturalistic bias which serves to distort science. We earlier cited experts relative to the "evolution is a fact" bias. Consider other examples:

Distortion One: Creation Is
Not a Valid Scientific Theory

Abundant documentation exists proving that creation can be a valid *scientific* theory. But apparently some people don't want the public to know this. If the evolutionary establishment is properly informed on the nature of science, then they are misleading the public by the following pronouncements. If they are not properly informed as to the nature of science, then they should not make pronouncements as to what is or isn't scientific.

Isaac Asimov in the introduction to Voices for Evolution
"There is no trace of anything scientific in creationism . . . "[12]

Academy of Science of the Royal Society of Canada
". . . 'scientific creationism' has nothing to do with science or the scientific method."[13]

American Association for the Advancement of Science
". . . the theory of creation is neither scientifically grounded nor capable of performing the roles required of scientific theories. . . . 'Creationist Science' has no scientific validity. . . ."[14]

American Society of Parasitologists
"Creationism is not a science and cannot become a science."[15]

Iowa Academy of Science
"Creationism is not science and the Academy deplores and opposes any attempt to disguise it as science."[16]

University of California Academic Senate
". . . a description of special creation as a scientific theory is a gross misunderstanding of the nature of scientific inquiry."[17]

Georgia Citizens' Educational Coalition
"We oppose the teaching of 'creationism' as science in Georgia's public schools. Creationism is based on . . . religious belief . . . not on scientific theory."[18]

American Civil Liberties Union
"ACLU also opposes the inculcation of religious doctrines even if they are presented as alternatives to scientific theories. 'Creation science' in all guises, for example 'abrupt appearance theory' or 'intelligent design theory,' is just such religious doctrine."[19]

New York State Education Department
". . . 'scientific creationism' is not accepted as science by the majority of experts working in those fields of science related to origins."[20]

American Humanist Association
"Creationism is not scientific: it is a purely religious view held by some religious sects and persons. . . ."[21]

The above are only a few examples of the scientific, educational, and civil liberties organizations making such statements. Indeed, virtually all of the organizations cited are opposed to the teaching of creation as a scientific alternative to evolution in public school classrooms. However, if scientific creation is legitimate, as it is, then these organizations are more concerned with scientific *indoctrination* than scientific education. And recent history has shown how perilous this can be. In this particular case, here is why they are wrong.

Many noted scientists and experts on the nature of the relationship between science and religion have attested to the scientific case for creation. For example, the volumes by Bird, Moreland (ed.), and Geisler and Anderson are only some of those demonstrating that creation can be scientific.[22]

Bird also points out that, "Seven of the fifteen judges of the U.S. Court of Appeals for the Fifth Circuit agreed that the theory of creation is 'scientific evidence' that 'has no direct religious reference whatever,' and two of the nine justices of the U. S. Supreme Court agreed. They correctly point out that concepts of creation always have been a basic part of science, and are still a vital part of cosmology. . . ."[23]

In *What Is Creation Science?* Morris and Parker also demonstrate that creation can be scientific.[24] Morris has a Ph.D. from the University of Minnesota with a major in hydraulics and hydrology and minors in geology and mathematics. He is a full member of Sigma Xi and Phi Beta Kappa and a Fellow of the American Association for the Advancement of Science. Morris has published dozens of research papers in refereed scientific journals, and has spent 28 years on the faculties of five major universities and partaken in scores of debates with evolutionists. Gary Parker earned his Ph.D. in biology with a cognate in geology (paleontology) and has several academic awards including election to the National Universities Scholastic Honorary Society, Phi Beta Kappa, and a Science Faculty Fellowship from the National Science Foundation. His research in amphibian endocrinology earned his election to the American Society of Zoologists.

Dean H. Kenyon, Ph.D., professor of biology and coordinator of the general biology program at San Francisco State University wrote the foreword to the above text by Morris and Parker. Dr. Kenyon is one of America's leading non-evolutionary scientists and has a Ph.D. in biophysics from Stanford University.[25] A former evolutionist and co-author of *Biochemical Predestination*, a standard work on the evolutionary origin of life, Kenyon now believes that the current situation where most consider creation science simply a religion in disguise "is regrettable and exhibits a degree of close-mindedness quite alien to the spirit of true scientific inquiry."[26] Kenyon is only one prominent scientist who has "extensively reviewed the scientific case for creation" and finds it legitimate.[27]

In Volume 1 of his *The Origin of Species Revisited*, W. R. Bird presents scientific evidence for what he terms the theory of abrupt appearance, similar to the theory of creation. He offers seven lines of evidence in support of abrupt appearance: "These lines of evidence are affirmative in the sense that, if true, they support the theory of abrupt appearance. They are not negative in the sense of merely identifying weaknesses of evolution. Nor do they depend on any assumption that the theories of abrupt appearance and evolution are the only scientific alternatives, except for the probability argument in part."[28]

These seven lines of evidence include: 1) the empirical evidence of systematic abrupt appearance; 2) the empirical evidence of systematic gaps; 3) the argument from comparative morphology involving empirical evidence of systematic similarity and stasis of organisms; 4) the information content argument relating to natural laws of information science; 5) the probability argument dealing with the laws of statistics; 6) the genetics argument dealing with the natural law of limited change; and 7) the comparative discontinuity argument dealing with empirical evidence from comparative anatomy, comparative biochemistry, and classification.

In essence, "The theory of abrupt appearance is scientific. It consists of the empirical evidence and scientific interpretation that is the content of this chapter. The theory of abrupt appearance also satisfies the various definitions of science in a manner comparable to evolution, as discussed in chapters 9 and 10. Its many testable and falsifiable claims are summarized in sections 10.3(a) and 10.4(a). The theory of creation similarly can be scientific, as a number of its opponents concede."[29]

W. R. Bird demonstrates that the theory of abrupt appearance is not only scientifically evidential, in Volume 2 he shows it is scientifically testable and refutable. In the area of biology, he shows that the affirmative evidence for abrupt appearance in paleontology, comparative morphology, information content, probability, genetics, and comparative discontinuity not only have testable claims but they affirm the theory of abrupt appearance. In the area of biochemistry, he shows that the argument from information content, probability, isomers, biogenesis and thermodynamics are not only testable, but also affirm abrupt appearance. And in terms of cosmology, he shows that thermodynamics, information content, the anthropic principle, heterogeneity, star and galaxy formation, and radio halos are testable and provide evidence for abrupt appearance.[30]

Dr. Wilder-Smith also presents a scientific creation alternative to Neo-Darwinism in his *A Basis for a New Biology* and *The Scientific Alternative to Neo-Darwinian Evolutionary Theory: Information Sources and Structures*.[31]

The scientific case for creation is also ably marshalled by several leading scientists in J. P. Moreland's (ed.), *The Creation Hypothesis* (InterVarsity, 1994). Some of the contributors include: William A. Dembski who holds a Ph.D. in mathematics from the University of Chicago and a Ph.D. in philosophy from the University of Illinois, Chicago, and has conducted doctoral and postdoctoral research at Cornell (math), MIT (math), the University of Chicago (math and physics), and Princeton (computer science) and has been a National Science Foundation doctoral and postdoctoral fellow. Stephen C. Meyer has degrees in physics and geology and a Ph.D. from Cambridge in the history and philosophy of science. Charles Thaxton has a Ph.D. in chemistry from Iowa State University and was a postdoctoral

fellow at Harvard University as well as a postdoctoral appoint-
ment in the molecular biology laboratory at Brandeis University. Kurt P. Wise has degrees in geophysical science from the
University of Chicago and a M.A. and Ph.D. in paleontology
from Harvard University.

Collectively, the authors in this volume alone have published hundreds of scientific articles in refereed scientific
journals. They are only nine examples of thousands which
make the evolutionists' claims amusing: "No reputable scientist
believes in creation."

Finally, if creationism is really only a religion, why do
evolutionists consistently lose their *scientific* debates to creationists? Such debates have been held since 1970. In 1979, *The
Wall Street Journal* for June 15 reported, "The creationists tend
to win" the debates. Six months later a report in *Bioscience* for
January 30, 1980 agreed: "Why do creationists seem to be the
consistent winners in public debates with evolutionists?"[32] In
an ICR letter of August 1979, Henry Morris could report: "By
now, practically every leading evolutionary scientist in this
country has declined one or more invitations to a scientific
debate on creation/evolution."[33] One wonders why if evolution
is a proven scientific fact and creation only a religion?

By 1993, creationists were still leading, even according to
the evolutionists. Evolutionists had 20 years to improve their
debating record and yet did not. Today, these debates are "almost
always won by creationists, according to evolutionists. . . ."[34]
and Dr. Morris says of Duane Gish who has had over 300 formal
debates, "at least in our judgment and that of most in the audiences, he always wins."[35] In conclusion, in all these debates that
"have been conducted throughout the U.S. and in other countries during the past 20 years, creationists have carefully avoided
all references to religious concepts and literature and have based
their arguments strictly on scientific evidence, such as the fossil
record, the laws of thermodynamics, the complexity of living
organisms and probability relationships, etc. The fact that evolutionists themselves admit that creationists have won most of the
debates does seem to be saying something important."[36]

Perhaps all this helps explain why, despite erroneous and
biased legal decisions, polls indicate most people favor the idea

of schools teaching the theory of creation in addition to the theory of evolution. This includes more than 85 percent of the national public, two thirds of lawyers nationally (who also find it constitutional), most university presidents at secular universities, and two-thirds of public school board members. One poll indicated 42 percent of public school biology teachers now favor the theory of creation over the theory of evolution.[37] Yet very few schools actually allow their teachers the option of a two model approach. *Something* would certainly seem to need addressing here.

Distortion Two: Poisoning the Well

Remember, among these organizations are some of the most prestigious and respected in America. But note how the reader is prejudiced against creation beforehand by the terms and language used. Among logical fallacies, this is known as "poisoning the well"—the attempt to refute an argument beforehand by discrediting the source of the evidence for the argument: "Everyone knows creationists are pseudoscientific religionists, so why trust their arguments?"

The obvious bias against creationism can be seen in the following examples:

Society for Amateur Scientists
"SAS [Society for Amateur Scientists] will never participate in creationist research."[38]

American Civil Liberties Union
"To reject creationism as science is to defend the most basic principles of academic integrity and religious liberty."[39]

California Academy of Sciences
"The appropriate place in the science curriculum for the notion that organisms have been designed is the same as that for the notion that the earth is located at the center of the universe."[40]

Utah Science Teachers Association
"[Teachers in the state of Utah should] help students understand that accepting the theory of evolution by natural selection need not compromise their religious beliefs. . . . [and] help students

understand that creationism, as taught by prominent creationist organizations of the day, is pseudoscience and not science."[41]

These are only a few of the declarations that could be cited. What's worse, scientists who are creationists are actually regarded as *incapable* of understanding *any* of the sciences because the scientific disciplines can, supposedly, be understood *only* in terms of the theory of evolution. We find it incredible that respected scientific organizations would make these kinds of statements. Consider some examples (emphases added):

American Anthropological Association
". . . evolutionary theory is *the indispensable foundation* for the *understanding* of physical anthropology and biology. . . ."[42]

American Psychological Association
"Principles of evolution are *an essential part* of the knowledge base of psychology. Any attempt to limit or exclude the teaching of evolution from the science curriculum would deprive psychology students of *a significant part* of their education."[43]

Society of Vertebrate Paleontology
"[Besides paleontology and biology] evolution is equally basic to geology, because the patterns of rock formations, geomorphology, and fossil distributions in the world *make no sense* without the underlying process of change through time."[44]

National Association of Biology Teachers
"Teaching biology in an effective and scientifically honest manner *requires* classroom discussions and laboratory experiences of evolution. . . . Effective teaching of cellular and molecular biology *requires* inclusion of evolution."[45]

Freedom From Religion Foundation
"Biology *makes no sense* without recognizing the fact [of evolution]."[46]

In other words, none of the thousands of creationist or nonevolutionary scientists who reject evolution are considered capable of understanding scientific disciplines such as biology, anthropology, paleontology, geology, or molecular biology! But there's more. Creationists and other nonevolutionary scientists aren't considered able to understand *any* of the sciences. Indeed, creationists, etc., can't even *teach* biology apart from evolution:

Georgia Citizens' Educational Coalition
"It is *no longer possible to teach biology* without the study of the scientific theory of evolution, which has been universally accepted into mankind's general body of knowledge, and stands today as the organizing principle of biology and the general theory of life."[47]

Humanist Association of Canada
"A student *cannot possibly understand* any of the life sciences without understanding the process of evolution that is the foundation of these sciences."[48]

Biological Sciences Curriculum Study
"It is *no longer possible* to give a complete or even a coherent account of living things without the story of evolution."[49]

Society for Amateur Scientists
"Genetics, astronomy, geology, paleontology, biology, physiology, anatomy, and physics all speak with one voice. . . . The evidence [for evolution] is abundant and irrefutable."[50]

In light of such statements, no wonder so many people think creation is pseudoscience and creationists scientific know-nothings. Sources quoted in this book and others liken creationism to such false ideas as a flat earth, astrology, the anti-germ theory, and even divination by goat entrails![51] No wonder the terms used in rejecting creation science are so adamant: "deplores and opposes," "strongly opposed," "strongly deplores," "condemns," "vigorously opposes," etc.

In the introduction to *Voices for Evolution*, the late scientist Isaac Asimov calls creation, "nothing but a disgraceful imposture" pointing out that "creationists do not hesitate to distort scientific findings, to misquote scientists, and to play upon the emotions and prejudices of their unsophisticated followers." Creation is regarded as "unscientific gibberish" because it believes the literal words of the Bible are true.[52] The Council for Democratic and Secular Humanism tells us that "biblical creationism is an ongoing and *serious threat* to science education, responsible research, critical thought, and free inquiry."[53]

In light of this, it is hardly surprising that we find the following descriptions of creationists, creationism, and teaching creation in science classrooms. Some of the leading scientific, religious, and educational organizations in the country employ the following terms:

> Creationist pseudoscience; bad science; the forces of unreason; counterfeiters; misleading to students; artificial; denigration of legitimate science; misnamed religious propaganda; myth; ignorance; bigotry; a threat to the very integrity of science.[54]

When modern science speaks in such a manner, it should not be surprised that tens of millions of Americans who are creationists would learn not to trust modern science. If science says that the scientific evidence for belief in a divine Creator is a horrible thing to allow in children's science classrooms, scientists shouldn't be surprised at the outcome.

Thankfully however, one can find rare glimpses of the truth. Consider again the West Virginia Academy of Science declaration that, "Dogmatic assertions are inconsistent with objective considerations of any subject. Science is always tentative and does not pretend to offer ultimate truth."[55] The Association of Pennsylvania State College and University Biologists says that biology teachers in Pennsylvania should teach the theory of evolution "not as absolute truth . . ." but as the most widely accepted scientific theory.[56] The Iowa Department of Public Instruction emphasizes that evolution should be taught as a well-supported scientific theory, "not a fact. . . ."[57]

If science should not be dogmatic and evolution should not be presented as a fact, then all the "voices for evolution" must be wrong in dogmatically declaring it a fact.

Distortion Three: Errors as to the Scientific Status of Creation and Evolution

In light of our previous discussion, we will simply list these without comment. Such declarations reveal the unfortunate depth of misinformation on this subject.

When Russell L. French, one of America's leading educators, read W. R. Bird's 1,100-page critique, *The Origin of Species*

Revisited, which covers almost everything important in the creation-evolution controversy (including scientific, educational, and legal aspects), he commented as follows: "This book is frightening to me because it clearly demonstrated to me how much I did *not* know until I had read it. If that was my condition, what about others, perhaps a majority, in our society?"[58]

Regrettably, most people in our society are ignorant on this subject, including the prestigious organizations listed below:

American Society of Parasitologists
"The 123-year history of creationism clearly shows it to . . . be overwhelmingly rejected by the majority of Christian denominations and by scientists of all faiths."[59]

The National Committee for Public Education and Religious Liberties
"Teaching creationism is impermissible as a matter of law, either in lieu of scientific evolution or as a 'companion theory.' "[60]

Louisiana Academy of Sciences
". . . organic evolution is amenable to repeated observation and testing. . . ."[61]

National Academy of Sciences
"[Teaching creation science] would be contrary to the nation's need for a scientifically literate citizenry and for a large, well-informed pool of scientific and technical personnel. . . . Special creation is neither a successful theory nor a testable hypothesis for the origin of the universe, the earth, or of life thereon. Creationism reverses the scientific process. . . ."[62]

National Academy of Sciences
"Its documentation is almost entirely limited to the special publications of its advocates. And its central hypothesis is not subject to change in light of new data or demonstration of error. Moreover, when the evidence for creationism has been subjected to the tests of the scientific method, it has been found invalid."[63]

New Orleans Geological Society
"Creation-science data almost invariably are of questionable quality, obsolete, or taken out of context from the scientific literature. Even well-known creation scientists such as Duane Gish of the Institute for Creation Research have readily admitted that

creation science is not at all scientific. . . . Creationism, as a scientific concept, was dismissed over a century ago and subsequent research has only confirmed that conclusion. Scientific creationism threatens to do great damage to the credibility of legitimate scientific research. . . ."[64]

New York Academy of Sciences
"Scientific creationism is a religious concept masquerading as a scientific one."[65]

American Humanist Association
"There are no alternative theories to the principle of evolution . . . that any competent biologist of today takes seriously."[66]

Society for the Study of Evolution
"The study of evolution is an empirically based science which employs the scientific process of hypothesis testing."[67]

Society for Amateur Scientists
"None of the arguments which scientific creationists make against evolution withstands scrutiny and most were first refuted nearly a century ago. And the creationists have never been able to martial quality evidence that strongly supports their ideas."[68]

West Virginia Academy of Science
"Their claim that scientific creationism is independent of biblical creationism, which they admit is religious, is demonstrably false."[69]

Committee for Scientific Investigation of Claims of the Paranormal
". . . Virtually no active scientist challenges the fact that evolution has occurred. . . . There is no scientific evidence supporting the instantaneous creation of the earth and all the creatures on it. . . ."[70]

Freedom from Religion Foundation
"The only 'evidence' creationists present is the story in Genesis, or other religious texts, that must be accepted by faith, not by rational principles of verification."[71]

Institute for First Amendment Studies
"By faith [creation scientists] begin with belief in creationism—then they search for evidence to back that belief. True scientists study the evidence, drawing their conclusions from that evidence."[72]

Upon reflection, such statements are incredible. The false-hood of *all* the above statements is either documented in this book or in other scientific and philosophical literature.[73] But we would be remiss not to point out two additional statements from this book. First, according to the National Association of Biology Teachers, "science is a constantly self-correcting endeavor to understand nature and natural phenomena" and second, from the Iowa Academy of Science on Pseudoscience, "in contrast to pseudoscientists, scientists seek out, expose, and correct any logical fallacies or other errors which could weaken their theories or interpretations. To assure complete scrutiny, open criticism is not only tolerated but often rewarded, particularly when it results in significant revisions of established views."[74]

If this were true, first, science *would* be teaching a proper definition of science. Second, it would *not* be teaching evolution as a fact. Third, creation would *not* be falsely ridiculed and rejected out of hand on the basis of solely naturalistic presuppositions or other bias. Fourth, creation scientists would not be subject to the extreme prejudice they are currently subject to. Fifth, creation scientists would be rewarded for their research, which has not only advanced science by correcting the deficiencies and errors in evolutionary theory, but has presented quality evidence for a more believable theory of origins.

Even though the definition of science is a philosophical one, *scientists* should know the definition of science—what it is, what it isn't, and what it involves or doesn't involve. This is part of their responsibility as scientists. If American university life isn't educating them properly on this subject, then so much worse for the state of modern American education.

We can clearly see how and why science suffers today—its own biases and prejudices force it to deal unfairly with the scientific data and to distort the truth. To portray evolution as science fact (and therefore sacrosanct) while portraying creation as merely faith (and therefore suspect) is a reversal of reality. As we will see later, it is evolution that rests on faith, and creation that employs good science. When the American Institute of Biological Sciences says that "creationism is based almost solely on religious dogma stemming from faith rather than demonstrable facts" it is not looking at the issues fairly.[75]

And when the American Civil Liberties Union apparently deliberately distorts the nature of true religious faith, which is based on logic and sound evidence as we demonstrated in *Ready with an Answer*, it can hardly expect sympathy from those who know better. Consider this statement for example: "Creationism necessarily rests on the unobservable; it can exist only in the ambiance of faith. Faith—[i.e.,]belief that does not rest on logic or on evidence—has no role in scientific inquiry."[76]

Again, we will later see exactly where an irrational faith lies and where the scientific evidences leads.

Unfortunately, the majority of Americans have no idea of the unjustifiable abuse that creationism is subject to by the evolutionist establishment. It would be unfair of us not to point out that even though this establishment claims to function according to the principles of objectivity and fairness, this is simply not the case. Our next chapter will document this in detail.

6

Professional Objectivity and the Politics of Prejudice

Science vs. Creation

Mainstream scientists would welcome *the development of a coherent creation model.* . . .

—Victor Bernard, *Free Inquiry,* Summer 1991,
p. 34, emphasis added.

Perhaps most people today assume that science is free of personal bias, indoctrination, and fraud. But as our last chapter indicated this is not necessarily the case. Although it is true that a science like mathematics, with its tight logical structure, would almost preclude fraud, and that highly mathematical sciences would have a built-in protection against fraud, the truth is that there are very few scientific disciplines immune to charges of bias, indoctrination, or fraud.[1]

This subject is of no small importance in the creation/evolution debate because, if fraud is already somewhat widespread within science, and if scientists are doing research and interpreting data that must be placed into a false theory, then bias and fraud are actually made that much easier. After all, if one is *forced* to fit data into a false theory, it makes the "tweaking" of the evidence all the more probable.

Evolutionary Fraud

If we understand how an evolutionary bias so thoroughly dominates modern science in all the disciplines, the following comments from a book documenting scientific fraud in detail are relevant indeed:

> Fraud in science is of course the abnegation of a researcher's fundamental purpose, the search for truth. It is thus an act of considerable moment. . . . Those who falsify scientific data probably start and succeed with the much lesser crime of improving upon existing results. Minor and seemingly trivial instances of data manipulation—such as making results appear just a little crisper or more definitive than they really are, or selecting just the "best" data for publication and ignoring those that don't fit the case—are probably far from unusual in science. But there is only a difference in degree between "cooking" the data and inventing a whole experiment out of thin air.
>
> A continuous spectrum can be drawn from the major and minor acts of fabrication to self-deception, a phenomenon of considerable importance in all branches of science. . . . In the spectrum that runs from hard sciences to soft sciences, from physics to sociology, the center is probably occupied by biology, a discipline in which fraud is by no means rare.[2]

First, let us note that many evolutionists are not beyond stooping to fraud in order to defend evolution. In Volume 2 of his *The Origin of Species Revisited*, Bird supplies examples of the lack of professional integrity and scientific fraud that are "so widespread":

> Many examples of scientific dishonesty with data and observation also exist. These include many instances of evolutionists' suppression or discounting of unfavorable data, according to Lipson: "In fact, evolution became in a sense a scientific religion; almost all scientists have accepted it and many are prepared to 'bend' their observations to fit in with it."
>
> Eisley and Romar mention casual discarding of anomalous fossils; Weidenreich describes how "paleontological facts are disregarded and replaced with purely speculative constructions" on the evolution of man; and Keith recounts arbitrary rejection of human remains mixed with alleged pre-human remains.

Another category of concern is ideological suppression of dis-
favored views (Section 9.7(b)) and particularly of the theory of
creation (Sections 9.7(d) and 18.2).

Some evolutionists have been guilty of serious misquotations.
. . . Scientists have used and do use outdated or repudiated information in order to support a preferred result, or disregard meaningful information because it conflicts with the preferred result.
. . . Scientists sometimes do alter scientific theory or change scientific terminology to meet legal or political advantage, whether
pursuant to the Marxist beliefs of many modern biologists or the
Victorian economic view of many early Darwinians.[3]

Consider an illustration from the modern Big Bang theory
of the origin of the universe (which we discuss in Chapter 10).
According to The *Los Angeles Times*, January 21, 1979, Nobel
laureate Hannes Alfven described the Big Bang theory in less
than glowing terms: "incredible," "insane," and "fanatical." "If
judged without bias and compared to what is known about the
universe, 'the Big Bang theory' will collapse," Alfven said in an
interview with The *Times*.

Alfven has received such criticism, and his ideas have been
subjected to such biased attack, that he commented, "If once a
school is established, this school fights with all means, even
dirty means, for its life, and criticism of this school is not allowed." Alfven points out that the Big Bang theory has been, in
the words of The *Times* "continually twisted and shoved about
to make it fit contradictory observations, rather than simply
discarded."

For example, efforts to show that the periodic elements
were formed in the first half hour after the Big Bang have failed
to account for any of them except helium. If this aspect of the
theory constituted 91 predictions "then certainly not more than
one of these predictions is correct," and "the other 90 predictions are wrong."

The prominent Swedish biologist, Søren Løvetrup, in his
Darwinism: The Refutation of a Myth wrote concerning Neo-
Darwinism, "To all intents and purposes, the theory has been
falsified so why has it not been abandoned? I think that the
answer to this question is that current evolutionists follow

Darwin's example. They refuse to accept falsifying evidence."[4] Is refusal to accept evidence good science?

Let us not forget that scientists are people and people are often not objective and neutral. Scientists, of course, should work harder at being objective because of the limits and goals of the scientific disciplines, but this doesn't mean personal preferences or ideologies never get in the way of their research. The scientific community does have its share of ambition, suppression of truth, fraud, prejudice, plagiarism, and manipulation of data. This is further illustrated by Tel Aviv Medical School's Professor of Urology Alexander Kohn in his *False Prophets: Fraud and Error in Science and Medicine* (1986), by Broad and Wade's *Betrayers of the Truth: Fraud and Deceit in the Halls of Science* (1982), by the appropriately named text, *Junk Science* (1997), and other books and articles.

Bias Against Creation

The August 15, 1997 issue of *Science* cited Francis Collins, director of the National Human Genome Research Institute at the National Institutes of Health: "When scientists like me admit they are believers, the reaction from colleagues is, 'How did this guy ever get tenure?' " David Scott, a former U.C. Berkeley physicist, was also correct when he remarked, "In postmodern academic culture, the majority of scientists think that to be taken seriously they must scoff at faith." This is so even though the truly great scientists of the past almost never did this.

W. R. Bird offers many examples of the "widespread bias" among the evolutionary establishment. Evolutionists themselves have conceded the unjustified bias against creation by the scientific world:

> Strong opposition to the theory of creation is not surprising in view of the widespread scientific bias in favor of evolution, which Patterson describes as "an intellectual fashion, a substitute for religion, an entrenched dogma," which Hardin refers to as "quite remarkable ferocity" toward doubters and which Grene sees as "a religion of science that Darwinism chiefly held, and holds men's minds . . . an orthodoxy preached by its adherents with religious fervor." Prangle refers to "the bluster and unscientific indignation into which rationalism collapses when Neo-Darwinians

try to suppress alternative theories," and Provine acknowledges for example that "most biological scientists are intolerant of creationism."

Bird's next statement is what is so ironic.

The determined and adamant opposition of most scientists to scientific alternatives is what is surprising.[5]

Many contemporary examples show that most scientists have biases against creation science. We have cited a sufficient number to remove any doubt. When one of the greatest thinkers and scholars of modern times, Mortimer J. Adler of the University of Chicago, referred to evolution as a "popular myth," the well known materialist and critic Martin Gardner actually included him in his study of quacks and frauds in *Fads and Fallacies in the Name of Science.*[6] Philosopher and historian Dr. Rousas Rushdoony was entirely correct when he observed of evolution, "To question the myth or to request proof is to be pilloried as a modern heretic and fool."[7]

The case of Immanuel Velikovsky's *Worlds in Collision* (1950) is too well known to discuss other than to mention that a scientist's legitimate ideas were suppressed from publication because of pressure from a scientific establishment that did not like his ideas.

Evolutionists often belittle creationists as "non-scientists" and ask "If creationist theories are really scientific, why are they never published in reputable scientific journals?" As the McLean trial pointed out, "There is . . . not one recognized scientific journal which has published an article espousing the creation science theory. . . ."[8] Well, the reason is because scientific journals *refuse* to publish such articles because they don't like creationism.

The evolutionist Strike, professor of philosophy of education at New York College of Agricultural and Life Sciences of Cornell University is entirely correct when he writes "[t]he referee system has rejected creationism" and "[creationism] is not seen as an acceptable scientific option by the referee system of science. . . ."[9]

It is an unfortunate arrogance that criticizes creation scientists for not publishing in the scientific journals when those scientific journals refuse to accept legitimate scientific papers merely because they do not like their implications.

Dr. Arno Penzias, who won the Nobel Prize for Physics, writes:

> Today's dogma holds that matter is eternal. The dogma comes from the intuitive belief of people (including the majority of physicists) who don't want to accept the observational evidence that the universe was created—despite the fact that the creation of the universe is supported by all the observable data astronomy has produced so far. As a result, the people who reject the data can arguably be described as having a "religious" belief that matter must be eternal. . . . Since scientists prefer to operate in the belief that the universe must be meaningless—that reality consists of nothing more than the sum of the world's tangible constituents—they cannot confront the idea of creation easily, or take it lightly.[10]

One of the greatest modern evolutionists, G. G. Simpson, comments that most paleontologists "find it logical, if not scientifically required, to assume that the sudden appearance of a new systematic group is *not* evidence for creation. . . ."[11]

Tom Bethell, a writer for the Hoover Institute of California and *National Review*, observes that even though "there is almost no evidence to support it," nevertheless, "evolution is perhaps the most jealously guarded dogma of the American public philosophy. Any sign of serious resistance to it has encountered fierce hostility in the past, and it will not be abandoned without a tremendous fight. . . . Darwinism will be defended to the bitter end."[12]

In our last chapter, we documented a scientific bias against the concept of creation science itself. In this chapter we will document the evolutionist bias against creationists themselves. We will reveal the extent to which creationists have been forced to suffer as a result of the bigotry of modern science.

Wilder-Smith and Kenyon

Consider the cases of two leading scientists. As noted, Dr. A. E. Wilder-Smith earned three doctorates in the field of science; his noteworthy academic career spanned over 40 years and included the publication of over 100 scientific papers and over 40 books published in 17 languages. Before discussing his own case, he illustrates with two others where eminent scientists have been silenced because they dared question evolutionary belief:

> Over and above this, the situation is such today that any scientist expressing doubts about evolutionary theory is rapidly silenced. Sir Fred Hoyle, the famous astronomer, was well on his way to being nominated for the Nobel Prize. However, after the appearance of his books expressing mathematically based doubts as to Darwinism, he was rapidly eliminated. His books were negatively reviewed and no more was heard about his Nobel Prize. The case of the halo dating methods developed by Robert V. Gentry tell a similar story. Gentry gave good evidence that the earth's age, when measured by the radiation halo method using polonium, might not be so great as had been thought when measured by more conventional methods. A postulate of this type would have robbed Darwinism of its main weapon, namely long time periods. Gentry lost his research grants and job at one sweep.
>
> It is by such methods, often bordering on psychoterror, that the latter day phlogiston theory (Neodarwinism) still manages to imprint itself in pretty well all scientific publications today. I myself gave the Huxley Memorial Lecture at the Oxford Union, Oxford University, on February 14, 1986. My theses were well received even by my opponents in the debate following the lecture. But I have been to date unable to persuade any reputable scientific journal to publish the manuscript. The comment is uniformly that the text does not fit their scheme of publications.
>
> I recently (December 1986) received an enquiry from the Radcliffe Science Library, Oxford, asking if I had ever really held the Huxley Memorial Lecture on February 14, 1986. No records of my having held the lecture as part of the Oxford Union debate could be found in any library nor was the substance of this debate ever officially recorded. No national newspapers, radio or TV station breathed a word about it. So total is the current censorship on any *effective* criticism of neo-darwinian science and on any genuine alternative.[13]

Now consider the case of Professor Dean Kenyon. Kenyon is one of America's leading non-evolutionist scientists. He received his Ph.D. in biophysics from Stanford University and teaches biology and evolution at San Francisco State University. He is co-author of one of the standard texts on the subject, *Biochemical*

Predestination, and has done original research for many years on the origin of life and published many technical articles.

Kenyon's problem originated when he added three lectures on the subject of biological origins in his introductory biology course at San Francisco State University. In these he presented data which gave credibility to the theory of intelligent design. Dr. John Hafernik, Chair of the Biology Department, viewed this as teaching creation and told Kenyon not to teach this in his biology class. He also said that *only non-theistic evolution* could be taught. Because of his sin of questioning the orthodox dogma, Kenyon was removed from teaching the introductory biology course and reassigned to teaching primarily labs—work often given to graduate students.

This is hardly a unique situation. So, the first thing to note is what the evolutionary establishment does even to its own members who simply question evolution. Kenyon had not only his Ph.D. in biophysics from Stanford University, he did postdoctoral work at the University of Southern California, at Berkeley, Oxford University in England, and NASA. Again, he was the co-author of the seminal theoretical work on biochemical evolution, *Biochemical Predestination*, a book that according to Meyer offered "what was arguably the most plausible evolutionary account of how a living cell might have organized itself from chemicals in the 'primordial soup.'"

Kenyon was a committed evolutionist throughout most of his academic career. Eventually, based on his own research, he began to question the evolutionary viewpoint. This research required him to logically conclude that it was impossible for life to evolve naturalistically. He did what any good scientist would do; he looked for other alternatives.

Kenyon was not attempting to insert religion or creation in his classroom, but simply presenting to students the logical implications of the results of his research.

Kenyon's case was such a blatant example of academic bigotry that even the San Francisco State University's Academic Freedom Committee ruled in Kenyon's favor. It argued the university is not permitted to require professors to teach a particular orthodoxy but should encourage dialogue and even controversy. But did Kenyon's evolutionary colleagues respect the views of the committee? Not at all. Kenyon was still not permitted to teach his course. "In spite of the extensive well-documented 16-page report strongly in favor of Dr. Kenyon signed by five fellow professors at his university, the biology chair refused to assign Kenyon the basic biology course. . . ."

Even the *Wall Street Journal* and the American Association of University Professors openly came out in support of Kenyon. But not his biology colleagues. "They voted twenty-seven to five with two abstentions to force him to censor all critiques of naturalism and favorable evidence of theism. Mims was absolutely correct when he described this case as an illustration of pathological science: 'Dr. Kenyon's case raises the troubling secondary issue of institutionalized pathological science practiced by scientists whose faith in what they have failed to prove is as dogmatic as that of the staunchist religious fundamentalist. Professor Kenyon's research has convinced him to reject Darwin's unproved speculation that life arose spontaneously. Although his views are at least as philosophically tenable as those of the Darwinists, to the Darwinists Dr. Kenyon is a threat. . . . Any so-called scientific institution or publication that reassigns a distinguished professor or fires a columnist solely because of a scientific view that leaves room for God is neither scientific nor American.' "[14]

Thousands of Cases

Dr. Jerry Bergman and others have documented that there are *thousands* of cases of discrimination against creation scientists—of competent science teachers being fired merely because they taught a "two model approach" to origins; of highly qualified science professors being denied tenure because of their refusal to declare their faith in evolution; of students' doctoral dissertations in science rejected simply because they supported creation; of students being expelled from class for challenging the idea that evolution is a fact, and so on.[15]

Prominent lawyer Wendell R. Bird, author of *The Origin of Species Revisited*, observes that "most of higher education is dogmatic and irrationally committed to affirm evolution and to suppress creation science, not on the basis of the scientific evidence but in disregard of that evidence."[16] He correctly refers to the "intolerance," "hysteria," and "unfairness" of the evolutionist establishment and to the "intolerable denials of tenure, denials of promotion, denials of contract renewals, denials of earned degrees, denials of admission into graduate programs, and other discrimination against that minority that disagrees with the prevailing dogmaticism and dares affirm creation science. . . . From my research for published articles in the *Yale Law Journal* and *Harvard Journal of Law and Public Policy*, and from my legal work in First Amendment litigation, it is my professional judgment that the cases of discrimination reported [by Bergman] . . . are a very tiny fraction of the general pattern and practice of discrimination against creationists and creation science at both the college and university level and the secondary and elementary school level."[17]

Lawyer John Edismoe also declares the cases cited by Bergman are only "the tip of the iceberg."[18]

Even the Institute for Creation Research (ICR) in Santee, California was subject to a wholly irrational vendetta under the leadership of superintendent of public instruction Bill Hoenig and the California Department of Education. Hoenig attempted to eliminate the Master of Science degree programs from the ICR graduate school wholly without justification. In 1989 the California Department of Education "imposed on all public schools a Science Framework that states evolution to be as sure a scientific fact as gravity or electricity, and therefore to be taken as the basic premise in all courses of instruction—all subjects at all levels. Creation is to be eschewed as strictly a religious belief of an insignificant fundamentalist fringe. This framework requires all textbooks and courses to conform to this premise."[19] The attack was so blatant and prejudiced that even the California Republican Assembly issued a resolution calling for an investigation of such actions by several state and federal agencies. The resolution resolved that it "opposes any action taken by the State Department of Education which would deny a private institution its rights to practice academic and religious freedom" noting that "Superintendent Hoenig has for several years publicly endorsed and promoted exclusive evolution teaching and has openly opposed the teaching of creation in California's public school science classes, and has now publicly stated his intention to deny I.C.R. their academic and religious freedom to include their interpretation of scientific data in their graduate level science classes by rescinding their license to operate."[20]

Perhaps it goes without saying, but had not Wilder-Smith, Kenyon, and the ICR taken appropriate measures to achieve justice, nothing would have been done to correct the obvious injustice.

In doing research for his book *The Criterion*, Dr. Bergman interviewed over 100 creationists who had at least a master's degree in science, the majority with a Ph.D. degree—among them Nobel prize winners and those with multiple doctorates in science. "Nevertheless, all, without exception, reported that they had experienced some discrimination...some cases were tragic in the extent, blatancy, and consequences of the discrimination."[21] For example, "over 12 percent of those interviewed stated that they had received death threats, highly emotional non-verbal feedback, or irrational verbalizations against them." Further, "Many persons who were denied degrees or lost jobs were forced to move to another community and start over. ...Many creationists publish under pseudonyms; others are extremely careful to hide their beliefs while earning their degree and come out of the closet only after they have the degree in hand or have earned tenure."[22]

Professor Michael Behe, in *Darwin's Black Box*, a masterful refutation of naturalistic evolution at the biochemical level, illustrates the bias against creationism with examples:

> Richard Dawkins has written that anyone who denies evolution is either "ignorant, stupid or insane (or wicked—but I'd rather not consider that.)" It isn't a big step from calling someone wicked to taking forceful measures to put an end to their wickedness. John Maddox, the editor of *Nature*, has written in his journal that "it may not be long before the practice[!] of religion must be regarded as anti-science." In his recent book *Darwin's Dangerous Idea*, philosopher Daniel Dennett compares religious believers— 90 percent of the population—to wild animals who may have to be caged, and he says that parents should be prevented (presumably by coercion) from misinforming their children about the truth of evolution, which is so evident to him.[23]

One department supervisor stated, "You creationists are Stone Age Neanderthals, and if I had my way I would fire every one of you."[24] One creationist with a Ph.D. in biology from Harvard University had actively been seeking a teaching position for 12 years. One employer told him: "Frankly, I don't like holy people, fundamentalists, especially Baptists, Church of Christ types, Pentecostals or other seventeenth century retrogressives. If we find out we hired one, especially if they start talking to the other research scientists about their beliefs, I terminate them within the month. Usually they leave without much of a protest. And I've never had one bring suit even though firing on religious grounds is illegal, and I know that it is."[25]

Bergman also reports that this "religious censorship and intolerance" in higher education, according to several research studies that he recently completed "is extremely common." And, further, that, "In our colleges and universities alone, each year there are on the average of between two and four hundred cases of religious firings or clear, blatant incidence of job discrimination incidents because of religion. Almost none of these, unfortunately, are taken to the courts."[26]

Many evolutionists, of course, can also be defined as secular humanists or "free thinkers." The publications of such groups often publicly recognize Christians, particularly creationists, as "enemies." Bergman cites John Indo writing in the Winter 1981 issue of *Free Inquiry* who stated: "Logical thinking is antithetical to [religious fundamentalists]. . . . This is what is so hideous about them. Their limited little minds function only in support of parochialist stupidity. . . . Frankly speaking . . . we must stop them at all costs. Otherwise, disaster will be the result."[27] Writing in "Freedom from Religion" *American Atheist* for February 1984, Charles Edelman stated that Christians are either mentally retarded or insane and should be prevented from having children.

> I am arguing for more than a separation of state and church; I am arguing for a separation of fantasy and reality as a necessary precondition for producing mentally healthy and responsible citizens. No nation, in this day and age, can afford mass insanity, not with the kind of weapons man is capable of producing.

There are laws in most states which prevent the insane and the feeble minded from having or raising children. Since no one but a moron or a lunatic can believe . . . the Christian religion . . . is the indisputable truth, one wonders why believers are excluded from such prudent legal restrictions. I question the right of the insane to perpetuate insanity however numerous they may be . . . I am for keeping religion out of the schools; I am for keeping religion out of the churches and the homes; in fact, I am for abolishing religion all together.[28]

The American Civil Liberties Union is frequently at the forefront of this bigotry that opposes creation science.[29] Even the prestigious National Academy of Sciences has publicly attacked creationism, a violation of its earlier principles. On April 27, 1976, the Academy adopted an official resolution "affirming freedom of inquiry and expression," noting that "the search for knowledge and the understanding of the physical universe and of the living things that inhabit it should be conducted under conditions of intellectual freedom, without religious, political, or ideological restriction."[30] Yet in their 1984 booklet "Science and Creationism: A View from the National Academy of Sciences" they state they "cannot remain silent" and that "the tenets of 'creation science' are not supported by scientific evidence, [and] that creationism has no place in a science curriculum at any level."[31]

Given the fact that thousands of scientists now reject evolution and accept creation, and given the fact that the National Academy of Sciences in its 1984 brochure cited no evidence for evolution, one can't help but think this prestigious academy a bit awkward when it condemns scientists for the religious *implications* of their views or scientific work.

Another important example is the discrimination against research physicist Robert V. Gentry, the world's leading authority on polonium halos. The significance of Gentry's research is that these radio halos strongly imply, if not demand, an extremely young earth. This is, of course, contrary to the accepted view that the earth is billions of years old and therefore, presumably, old enough for evolution to have occurred. It could not, of course, have occurred in a few tens of thousands of years. We should note that despite the attempts of some of the world's best scientists to refute Gentry's conclusions, his research apparently remains unrefuted.[32]

Yet there is little doubt Gentry was grossly discriminated against *only* because the results of his experiments supported the creationist position. Consider that Gentry has published in the most prestigious of scientific magazines for over 15 years— *Science*, *Nature*, annual reviews of *Nuclear Science*, *Geotimes*, etc.[33] For 15 years he was a visiting scientist in the chemistry division of the Oak Ridge National Laboratory. He is a member of the American Association for the Advancement of Science, The American Physical Society, The American Geophysical Union, Sigma Ki, and the New York Academy of Sciences, and is listed in "Who's Who in America." But these credentials were apparently not good enough for the ACLU and the National Science Foundation, which rejected further funding of his work.[34] The NSF discriminated against Dr. Gentry in spite of the fact that its own Affirmation states, "Freedom of inquiry and dissemination of ideas require that those so engaged be free to search where their inquiry leads without fear of retribution and consequence of the unpopularity of their conclusions."[35]

Additional Examples

Consider other illustrations of religious bigotry from the evolutionary establishment:[36]

• Dr. Bergman states that several of his colleagues told him that if they discovered one of their students was a conservative Christian, they would fail him or her. One professor said, "I don't think this kind of people should get degrees and I'm going to do what I can to stop them." Bergman observes that "some professors are openly advocating failing creationists" and he cites examples.

• A professor of biology at a large state university was denied tenure admittedly because of his creationist views although he had more publications in scientific journals than any other member of his department (well over 100), many of them in the most prestigious journals in his field. When the university that granted his Ph.D. in biology learned he was an active creationist, they assembled a committee to rescind his degree six years *after* it was issued!

• A Michigan science teacher was fired shortly after he donated several boxes of books on creationism to the school library. A "South Dakota Outstanding Teacher of the Year" recipient was also fired because he was teaching creation in class.

• Dr. David A. Warriner received his B.S. in chemistry from Tulane University, his Ph.D. from Cornell University and was close to a second Ph.D. He was invited to join the Natural Science Department at Michigan State University *as* a creationist. After four years his department head suggested tenure but the dean claimed Warriner had "damaged the image of science" for the university and he was dismissed. He has been unable to find a teaching position at any other university.

• A creationist working on his Ph.D. in zoology at a major university, with almost straight A's, expressed serious reservations about evolution to his dissertation committee. He was required to take four more courses in evolutionary biology before they would permit him to graduate. After the courses were completed, his dissertation committee asked whether he now "believed in evolution." When he replied he was "more firmly convinced of the validity of creationism than ever before," the dissertation committee broke their agreement and refused to grant his degree.

• A researcher at a Cancer Research Center who had earned an excellent reputation for his six years of work was forced to resign once his creationist views became known.

• N. Chandra Wickramasinghe of the University College in Cardiff, Wales and co-worker with Fred Hoyle, one of the world's best known living astronomers, allegedly received death threats merely for speaking out in favor of a two-model teaching position.

• Byron Nelson was denied his Master of Science in Genetics at Rutgers University because of his creationism despite an almost straight-A GPA.[37]

• Paul Oles, an astronomer and program director with the prestigious Buhl Planetarium in Pittsburgh, experienced censorship of his creationist ideas when his *Popular Science* column was cancelled after he decided to go public with his views on creationism.[38]

- In his text, *Remember Thy Creator*, G. Richard Culp gives several other illustrations of discrimination. A candidate for the Ph.D. degree in zoology from the University of Michigan, one of the nation's most respected schools in the sciences, was asked during his Ph.D. examination whether he believed in evolution and he replied in the negative. The student was refused his degree.

- Dr. Erville Clark was denied his Ph.D. in biology at Stanford University merely because he was a creationist.[39]

- George Mulfinger, a well-known creationist and professor of physics in Greenville, South Carolina, was refused his Ph.D. because he was a creationist. This was despite graduating summa cum laude with straight A's in all his graduate work.[40]

- Internationally known creationist Dr. John N. Moore, a professor of natural science at Michigan State University (currently professor emeritus) was denied the right to present a paper at the October 1983 National Association of Biology Teachers Convention in Philadelphia because of the paper's *alleged* creationist content.[41]

The compiler of most of the above illustrations, Dr. Jerry Bergman, was denied tenure at Bowling Green State University in Ohio and fired because of his creationist beliefs and for writing the booklet "Teaching About the Creation/Evolution Controversy." He was fired in spite of the fact that his own colleagues' evaluation of his work was almost without exception extremely complimentary and students praised his teaching. He had published over 100 articles and monographs, many of which were published in the best journals—in fact, he published more than the rest of his department combined.[42] "Over a dozen major due process and procedural violations in the administration's handling of his tenure decision and subsequent appeals have been documented. . . ."[43]

Apparently, even librarians engage in censorship against creation. Jim Melnick's study in the *Newsletter on Intellectual Freedom*, May 1982, observed that:

Significant creationist literature has been self-censored from nearly every major secular university library in America. An OCLU computer search conducted in March 1982 indicated that of the over 3,000 institutions on the OCLU list, only 33 subscribe to the Creation Research Society Quarterly, without question the preeminent journal in the field of scientific creationism and read throughout the world. . . . The entire "progressive" state of New York has one lone subscription, at King's College, a Christian school. The Ivy League schools are strangely silent, though in the name of academic freedom and in order to provide necessary source material, I have seen very anti-Semitic periodicals, pro-apartheid magazines, and many other "nasty" items on many of those shelves. Where are the creationist periodicals?[44]

The Creation Research Society itself has been forced to strictly guard its membership list of 700 scientists because of concerns over discrimination.[45]

Obviously, the evolutionist Michael Ruse is correct when he states, "I must point out that orthodox scientists loathe scientific creationism and do all in their power to oppose it."[46] One wonders if the evolutionary establishment is actually proud that there is "a widespread bias against discontinuist and particularly creationist scientists and educators by many educational institutions and technical publications. . . ."[47]

Evolutionary Indoctrination

The truth is that the teaching of evolution involves a widespread indoctrination in our school systems and society. "Most modern classrooms simply indoctrinate students in evolutionary theory and censor alternative scientific theories."[48]

To see the importance of this, consider what indoctrination is:

Indoctrination occurs when a teacher "attempts to inculcate into the minds of his pupils his own beliefs and attitudes, and also ideas which are no means certain without the suggestion of possible alternatives." . . . That produces "mindless acceptance of conventional attitudes and beliefs". . . and "the child is cut off from all but a narrow band of possibilities."

Indoctrination in schools and universities is particularly effective (and thus dangerous) because of the influence of the teacher, the peer group, and the text. "The teacher ... is an 'authority figure' with 'tremendous influence because of the knowledge he has acquired and because of the power vested in him.' "[49]

The hypocrisy in all this seems evident enough. The evolutionist establishment demands freedom of expression for itself but refuses to allow its opposition this freedom. As Dr. Thomas Dwight of Harvard observed, "The tyranny in the matter of evolution is overwhelming to a degree of which the outsider has no idea."[50] In our colleges and universities today, the Christian faith can be ridiculed, Marxism can be espoused, the Constitution criticized, marriage degraded, morality demeaned, occultism promoted, and homosexuality practiced—but the theory of evolution is somehow sacrosanct. Chicago University's Professor Paul Shoray observed, "There is no cause so completely immune from criticism today as evolution."[51]

Even the head of the biology department at an ivy league university tore out an article in *Systematic Zoology* because it was critical of natural selection. When confronted he said, "Well of course I don't believe in censorship in any form, but I just couldn't bear the idea of my students reading that article."[52]

The solution to this problem is for creationists to begin to start using legal measures in order to preserve their academic freedoms. The discrimination we have been discussing is absolutely illegal and, if for no other reason than responsibility to our society and the law, Christians should not hesitate to press lawsuits to preserve the granting of their degrees, their scientific research, or their jobs.

Some evolutionists might respond to this like children, who, having invented the rules of the game in their favor, complain upon losing. But to demand that everyone else *think* like evolutionists (play by our rules or don't play at all) is the height of arrogance. Given the evolutionist response to creationism, one would think that creationists were witches, lepers, and criminals all rolled into one.

What are evolutionists really afraid of? Are they afraid of a legitimate scientific theory having religious implications? Can anything else explain the fact that those who hold to creation are unfairly ridiculed, condemned *a priori*, labeled deceivers, frauds, and fools merely because of their beliefs?

This is one more example of how the secular scientific community in general has only damaged its own credibility. If evolutionists don't like creation, the rational alternative is an intelligent agnosticism—not dogmatism.

7

The Retreat from Good Science

Evolution and the Great Escape, Part 1

Our next two chapters will discuss *why* most scientists accept evolution. In this section, we will underscore the theme of a great escape—in this chapter an escape from good science and in the next chapter an escape from God. When scientists accept evolution because 1) they wrongly think there are no other scientific alternatives, 2) they misinterpret the data, 3) everyone else believes it, or 4) they prefer its philosophical implications, they are not performing good science. Obviously, scientists are not consciously seeking to engage in bad science, but they do so by default when they neglect to think through the issues more clearly and thoroughly.

Much of the problem here involves in the philosophy of science and modern science's unjustified domination by scientific naturalism. Since we have discussed these elsewhere, we will not do so in detail here (see note 5). Our main purpose in these two chapters is to show that modern science's acceptance of evolution is directly related to its doing science poorly.

The history of science reveals many instances where the majority of scientists were convinced of a particular theory and yet were wrong. Further, when it comes to the discussion of the creation/evolution issue, many scientists today are simply closed minded. Why? Because modern science is committed to the ideologies of scientism and scientific naturalism and any time a philosophical commitment to a particular ideology exists, there is a reluctance to consider alternate viewpoints.

Scientism assumes that science constitutes the apex of truth and that anything that disagrees with science or is incapable of scientific investigation is false, not rational, or irrelevant.

Naturalism assumes the whole history of the cosmos must submit to the principles of natural science. Everything in the universe can be explained through a closed system of material causes and effects without recourse to a Creator.[1]

In this scheme of things, God is irrelevant and science itself becomes captive to atheism. Basil Willey states that "Science must be provisionally atheistic, or cease to be itself."[2] Seemingly even most scientists who are Christians have, regrettably, accepted the legitimacy of scientific naturalism. Raymond Grizzle writes, "God cannot be a part of a scientific description . . . any description that implies a creator will probably be looked at as improper. . . ."[3]

Nancey Murphy, evolutionist and philosopher at Fuller Theological Seminary, makes the incredible statement that "Christians and atheists alike must pursue scientific questions in our era without invoking a Creator" and "For better or worse, we have inherited a view of science as methodologically atheistic."[4] According to *Science* (August 15, 1997) the once evangelical Fuller Seminary itself will soon "publish a book acknowledging a natural [evolutionary] origin for the human family tree."

The sad part is that scientism and scientific naturalism have long been discredited; university libraries are replete with books showing their flaws and weaknesses. Scientism and scientific naturalism are simply false and can logically be shown false.[5] This means that scientists are engaging in science and interpreting data *with false premises.* Unfortunately, they are blinded by their own assumptions. We find this especially ironic for scientists who are Christians

Regardless, consider the comments of Dr. A. E. Wilder-Smith, the deliverer of the Huxley Memorial Lecture at the Oxford Union, Oxford University, February 14, 1986: "May not a future generation well ask how any scientist, in full possession of his intellectual faculties and with adequate knowledge of information theory could ever execute the feat of cognitive acrobatics necessary to sincerely believe that a (supremely complex) machine system of information, storage and retrieval, servicing millions of cells, diagnosing defects and then repairing them in a teleonomic Von Newman machine manner, arose in randomness—the antipole of information?"[6] In other words, "How could any scientist in possession of the facts we now have logically continue to exercise faith in naturalistic evolution?" As molecular biologist Michael Denton observes of the created order of living things, "To common sense it does indeed appear absurd to propose that chance could have thrown together devices of such complexity and ingenuity that they appear to represent the very epitome of perfection."[7]

There are many reasons why scientists would accept a discredited theory such as evolution. Among them we mention four, each of which involves inadequate or poor science.

1. A false belief can be accepted when scientists mistakenly assume there are no legitimate scientific theories to replace it.

Dr. Wilder-Smith observes that when the modern scientific establishment adheres to evolutionary belief, it is "certainly not because experimental evidence encourages the establishment to do so."[8] He explains that a commitment to materialism is the problem. Thus, "There exists at present no other *purely scientific* alternative which postulates a purely scientific *materialistic* basis for biogenesis and biology. . . . Scientists whose upbringing and education are Darwinian and therefore naturalistic, have for this reason no real alternative to Darwinism. Here we have perhaps one of the main reasons for the victory of Darwinism even today, even though the accumulating evidence of science is steadily against the theory."[9]

But what if there is a legitimate scientific option to evolution which is not materialistic? As we saw, Yale Law School graduate Wendell R. Bird fully documents that the theory of "abrupt appearance" is entirely scientific—and also that such a theory was capable of being advanced scientifically by scientists of an earlier era. Further, he shows that creation itself is not *necessarily* religious; it too can be fully scientific.[10] The discussion in J. P. Moreland, ed., *The Creation Hypothesis* (IVP, 1994) reveals that theistic science is anything but an oxymoron and merits real consideration among scientists. In fact, unless we arbitrarily, or by default, allow scientific naturalism to provide the rules of the game convenient to its own worldview, the concept of theistic science *must* be considered a valid competing hypothesis to the current naturalistic paradigm. The question of whether or not scientific naturalism can be challenged is long past, and the issue of a scientific theory of creation is already settled.

2. *A false theory can be accepted because scientific facts can be misinterpreted or unnaturally forced to fit a dominant theory.*

The facts of the natural world are in the possession of every scientist, whether creationist or evolutionist. The issue in debate is the interpretation of those facts, whether it concerns biogeography, the fossil record, origin-of-life experiments, or homologous (similar) structures. Evolution may initially seem to make sense in light of the evidence for something like genetic variation and adaptation or other alleged evidence. The error is to extrapolate from relatively minor phenomena to truly gargantuan conclusions. The fact that living things were created with a very vital if limited genetic variability, or have adaptive powers in relation to their environment is hardly proof that matter, chance, and time alone could eventually give rise to man. Small differences related to geographic spread and history (biogeography) may indeed occur between groups of plants or animals, as Darwin noted on his journey to the Galapagos Islands. But this has nothing to do with proof of evolution, or evolution per se.

Developing new strains of corn or wheat or breeds of cattle are simply intraspecies events and hardly evidence that narrows the tremendous gap evolution must cross from one type of species to another. Even "new" species formed experimentally, such as the cross between a radish and cabbage (*Raphanobrassica*), on the basis of genetic principles cannot be considered evicence for evolution.

The only evidence we have is in the area of what is termed microevolution, which is basically powerless when it comes to offering real evidence for macroevolution. Variation and macroevolution are two very different things. Yet scientific facts may not only *seem* to fit a false theory, but the facts themselves may become irrelevant when the presentation of a particular worldview becomes paramount:

> Yet no matter how convincing such disproofs [of evolution] might appear, no matter how contradictory and unreal much of the Darwinian framework might now seem to anyone not committed to its defense, as philosophers of science like Thomas Kuhn and Paul Feyerabend have pointed out, it is impossible to falsify theories *by reference to the facts* or indeed by any sort of rational or empirical argument. The history of science amply testifies to what Kuhn has termed "the priority of the paradigm" and provides many fascinating examples of the *extraordinary lengths* to which members of the scientific community will go to defend a theory just as long as it holds sufficient intrinsic appeal.[11]

In other words, once scientists are trained to interpret data in a particular manner, they rarely question the relevance of their interpretations. The perceptual grid of scientific naturalism forces data to be interpreted in very specific evolutionary ways that are simply not correct. Worse, scientific data *must* be made to fit the prevailing dominant theory. (Thomas Kuhn pointed this out in *The Structure of Scientific Revolutions*.)

For example, the geocentric theory of the sun orbiting the earth dominated science for several hundred years. Although a heliocentric alternative was considered as early as the Greek astronomers, the geocentric theory was, by the late middle ages, "a self-evident truth, the one and only sacred and unalterable picture of cosmological reality."[12] But, as with all false theories, there were innumerable facts which got in the way. The response of scientists was to invent "explanations" to account for the irregularities. More and more explanations were required to deal with more and more problems presented by undeniable facts, and by the early sixteenth century the entire Ptolemaic system had become "a monstrosity" of fantastically involved explanations and counter-explanations.[13] Nevertheless, "so ingrained was the idea that the earth was the center of the universe that hardly *anyone*, even those astronomers who were well aware of the growing unreality of the whole system, *ever bothered to consider an alternative theory.*"[14]

The eighteenth century concept of phlogiston is also instructive. The theory of phlogiston "assumed that all combustible bodies, including metals, contained a common material, phlogiston, which escaped on combustion but could be readily transferred from one body to another."[15] Scientific experiments with zinc and phosphorus appeared to prove the phlogiston theory.[16] The concept was fully accepted for a hundred years and debated for another hundred years before it was finally disproven. But in fact, "The theory was a total misrepresentation of reality. Phlogiston did not even exist, and yet its existence was firmly believed and the theory adhered to rigidly for nearly 100 years throughout the eighteenth century."[17]

As was true for the geocentric theory, awkward facts were cunningly assimilated, explained away, or ignored. It was the false theory *itself* which determined how science dealt with facts. The facts had to bow to the truth of phlogiston. Thus, as time progressed and discoveries were made which made it increasingly difficult to believe in phlogiston, the theory was not rejected but "was modified by the insertion of more and more unwarranted and *ad hoc* assumptions about the nature of phlogiston."[18]

In his *Origins of Modern Science*, Professor H. Butterfield observes how the phlogiston theory actually led to scientists being intellectually incapacitated to deal with the evidence: ". . . the last two decades of the eighteenth century give one of the most spectacular proofs in history of the fact that able men who had the truth under their very noses, and possessed all the ingredients for the solution of the problem—the very men who had actually made the strategic discoveries—were incapacitated by the phlogiston theory from realizing the implications of their own work."[19]

In a similar fashion Denton comments ". . . it is not hard to find inversions of common sense in modern evolutionary thought which are strikingly reminiscent of the mental gymnastics of the phlogiston chemists or the medieval astronomers. . . . The Darwinist, instead of questioning the orthodox framework as common sense would seem to dictate, attempts of justifying his position by *ad hoc* proposals . . . which to the skeptic are self-apparent rationalizations to neutralize what is, on the face of it, hostile evidence."[20]

Thus, the great many intractable scientific problems with modern evolutionary belief do *not* constitute a disproof of Darwinian claims but merely require adjustment to the belief in order that the belief be preserved at all costs.

3. A false belief can be accepted because scientists assume the belief to be true only because of broad general support among scientists.

In the case of evolution, no one questions the basic idea because everyone seems to accept the basic idea: "The fact that every journal, academic debate, and popular discussion assumes the truth of Darwinian theory tends to reinforce its credibility enormously. This is bound to be so because, as sociologists of knowledge are at pains to point out, it is by conversation in the broadest sense of the word that our views and conceptions of reality are maintained and therefore the plausibility of any theory or world view is largely dependent upon the social support it receives rather than its empirical content or rational consistency. Thus all the pervasive affirmation of the validity of Darwinian theory has had the inevitable effect of raising its status to an impregnable axiom which could not even conceivably be wrong."[21]

Hence the constant refrain that evolution is an "undisputed scientific fact." As atheist Richard Dawkins, author of *The Blind Watchmaker* and *The Selfish Gene*, asserts: "The theory is about as much in doubt as [that] the earth goes around the sun."[22] Once the scientific community elevates a theory, in this case evolution, to a self-evident truth, defending it becomes irrelevant and there is "no longer any point in having to establish its validity by reference to empirical facts."[23] Further, all disagreement with the current view becomes irrational by definition. As

P. Feyerabend argues in his article "Problems of Empiricism" in *Beyond the Edge of Certainty*: "The myth is therefore of no objective relevance, it continues to exist solely as the result of the effort of the community of believers and of their leaders, be these now priests or Nobel Prize winners. Its 'success' is entirely manmade."[24]

4. A false belief can be accepted by scientists because they prefer its philosophical implications.

Many materialistic scientists are also atheists and therefore more than happy to accept the atheistic implications of naturalistic evolution. Here, as we indicate below and in our next chapter, the very purpose of evolution is to explain things without recourse to God. Scientists are only men, and if the unregenerate bent of the human heart underscores the attempt to escape God, then naturalistic evolution is certainly an appealing idea. If there is no God, there are no necessary moral standards and one may happily discover justification for any conceivable belief or lifestyle.

Many modern scientists have pointed out with seeming satisfaction that, given evolution, there is no need even to consider God. This tends to make one suspect that some of these scientists may have ulterior motives for wanting evolution to be true.[25] For example, in his *Heredity, Race and Society*, Theodosius Dobzhansky observes, "Most people, however, greeted the scientific proof of this view [i.e., evolution] as a great *liberation from spiritual bondage*, and saw in it the promise of a better future."[26] As noted novelist Aldous Huxley, grandson of "Darwin's bulldog," Thomas Henry Huxley, once confessed in his *Ends and Means*: "I had motives for not wanting the world to have a meaning; consequently I assumed that it had none, and was able without any difficulty to find satisfying reasons for this assumption. Most ignorance is invincible ignorance. We don't know because we don't want to know." And "The philosopher who finds no meaning in the world is not concerned exclusively with a problem in pure metaphysics; he is also concerned to prove that there is no valid reason why he personally should not do as he wants to do, or why his friends should not seize political power and govern in the way they find most advantageous to themselves. . . . For myself, as, no doubt, for most of my contemporaries, the philosophy of meaninglessness was essentially an instrument of liberation."[27] Huxley proceeds to identify this liberation as being political, economic, and sexual and, no doubt, like many other modern materialists, he found evolutionary belief quite satisfying.

8

The Retreat from God

Evolution and the Great Escape, Part 2

In an earlier chapter, we mentioned that there was a theological dimension to the interpretation of scientific data—scientists, as fallen people, would have a tendency to skew the data of the natural world in such a way as to avoid or escape ideas of design, God, and teleology. In fact, this is what they do. Huxley's quote in the last chapter is to the point.

If people can "avoid" God, they have little reason to worry over things like responsibility to God and divine judgment and, as a result, they can pretty much live as they please—at least they think so. Of course, many scientists believe in God, but often a God of their own devising, a convenient God who makes no demands on them. What they try to avoid is the *biblical* God who holds them accountable. This is why Darwin's *Origin* was far less a rejection of theism generally than a specific rejection of the God of Genesis. The closer one gets to the biblical God, the greater the discomfort and the greater the personal investment in the materialistic interpretation of the data. For some this is a conscious act; for others less so but true nonetheless.

Scientific naturalism solves all kinds of problems like this. The evidence for design, creation, and the God of the Bible can simply be dismissed as "irrelevant" or "nonexistent."

In this section, we wish to document in more detail the final point of our last chapter, briefly touched upon, that scientists can accept a false theory because they prefer its philosophical or theological implications.

Many people aren't aware that when Darwin first published the *Origin of Species*, it was largely rejected by the scientific world of his day, which almost universally held to a belief in divine creation. Not only did his *Origin* receive endless critical reviews,[1] but "The scientific world also was almost wholly against the *Origin*. In later years, T. H. Huxley, speaking of the year 1860, described the situation by saying, 'The supporters of Mr. Darwin's views were numerically, extremely insignificant. There is not the slightest doubt that if a general council of the church scientific had been held at that time, we should have been condemned by an overwhelming majority.'"[2]

Darwin's Doubts

Darwin himself expressed serious doubts about the idea of evolution. He attempted to rationalize these doubts, but their force and power remained with him and also remain to this day. In the sixth chapter of *Origin*, "Difficulties on Theory," Darwin remarked, "Long before having arrived at this part of my work, a crowd of difficulties will have occurred to the reader. Some of them are so grave that to this day I can never reflect on them without being staggered. . . ."[3]

In his chapter on instinct he conceded such "simple" instincts as bees making a beehive could be "sufficient to overthrow my whole theory."[4] For example, "nothing at first can appear more difficult to believe than that the more complex organisms and instincts should have been perfected, not by means superior to, though analogous with, human reason, but by the accumulation of innumerable slight variations. . . ."[5]

And to think that the eye could evolve "by natural selection, seems, I freely confess, absurd in the highest possible degree."[6]

In his chapter on the imperfections in the geological record he complained that the complete lack of fossil intermediates in the geological record was perhaps "the most obvious and gravest objection which can be urged against my theory."[7] He further confessed that other difficulties he discussed here were "all undoubtedly of the gravest nature. . . ."[8]

He later stated that the various difficulties of his theory had weighed heavily on him for many years,[9] and that he was "well aware that scarcely a single point is discussed in this volume on which facts cannot be adduced, often apparently leading to conclusions directly opposite to those at which I have arrived."[10] Indeed, Darwin was "deeply conscious of his ignorance."[11] In his personal letters he wrote of having "awful misgivings" of having "deluded myself" and of having "devoted myself to a phantasy."[12]

What explains Darwin's doubts? Darwin's own reason informed him that the evidence for intelligent design was overwhelming, as we documented elsewhere.[13] Although he was "determined to escape from design and a personal God at all costs,"[14] he never really could. Thus, he confessed to the "impossibility of conceiving this immense and wonderful universe, including man with his capacity of looking far backwards and far into futurity, was a result of blind chance or necessity."[15]

But then, because Darwin's mind was really descended from lower life forms, how could its reasoning processes ultimately be trusted? Darwin confessed, "But then arises the doubt, can the mind of man, which has, as I fully believe, been developed from a mind as low as that possessed by the lowest animals, be trusted when it draws such grand conclusions? . . . Would anyone trust in the convictions of a monkey's mind, if there are any convictions in such a mind?"[16]

In essence, Darwin's inability to either accept divine creation or to escape it caused his own reasoning processes to become strained. As Dr. Clark and Dr. Bales observe, "Reason led Darwin to God, so Darwin killed reason. He trusted his mind when reasoning about evolution, but not about God. . . . As

Arnold Lunn put it: 'A clear thinker would never have been guilty of such inconsistent reasoning. If Darwin was not prepared to trust his mind when it drew the "grand conclusion" that God existed, why was he prepared to trust when it drew the depressing conclusion that a mind of such bestial origin could not be trusted to draw any conclusion at all?' "[17] Thus, "To the end of his life, the old warfare continued in Darwin's mind. Try as he would, he could not escape from God. Gradually his emotional life atrophied under the strain of the battle. Religious feeling disappeared and with it much else besides. . . . The world became cold and dead. As we have already seen, even his reasoning powers became distorted when he dwelled upon subjects even remotely concerned with his conflict. Finally the time came for Charles Darwin to die with the conflict still unresolved."[18]

In the end, Darwin had apparently received a taste of his own medicine.[19] He had deprived the universe of God and all meaning, and it had cost him dearly.[20] Darwin could not live with God but neither could Darwin escape God. The battle endured throughout his life and it not only made him physically ill, it also cost him, to some degree, his mental health. Most biographers of Darwin acknowledge his rejection of Christian faith. In fact, Darwin said, "I can hardly see how anyone could wish Christianity to be true." What they don't usually do is reveal the consequences. James Moore's definitive biography, *Charles Darwin: The Life of a Tormented Evolutionist*, is a notable exception, as well as the volumes by Clark and Bales and Sunderland. Dr. Robert E. D. Clark (Ph.D., Cambridge) shows how tortured Darwin's life was because of his rejection of God. Again, as noted earlier, Darwin even referred to his theory as "the devil's gospel."[21] What concerned Darwin was not the initial critical response to his *Origin of Species*. Even after the battle was "won" and his reputation assured, his psychological suffering and physical symptoms continued. In other words, Darwin was dealing with a much deeper and fundamental feeling—guilt. As far as the Christian faith was concerned, he had not only banished the biblical God from his own life, but, it seemed, from the entire universe as well. He had killed God for everyone.

Darwin's real problem lay with the *suppression* of his own religious needs: "His life was one long attempt to escape from Paley [i.e., his *Natural Theology*], to escape from the church, to escape from God. It is this that explains so much that would otherwise be incongruous in his life and character."[22]

Darwin's Agenda

Perhaps to soothe his fears, Darwin adopted a philosophy convenient to his own rejection of God, logical positivism. Logical positivism held that only science, mathematics, and logic were meaningful for ascertaining facts and that religion, ethics, and metaphysics were meaningless. Having adopted this philosophy, Darwin was hardly unbiased in his scientific methodology. Robert Kofahl, Ph.D., argues that Darwin's particular philosophy of science was intended to invoke naturalism and to remove the concept of divine intervention from the category of scientific thinking and endeavor—a feat that, if successful, would have profound consequences: "It is this author's opinion that Charles Darwin had a hidden agenda for science. There is much evidence for this in his writings. Neal Gillespie (1979) of Georgia State University in his important book, *Charles Darwin and the Problem of Creation*, established the fact that Darwin espoused logical positivism as his philosophy of science. His hidden agenda, then, was to remove from the thinking of all scientists any concepts of special creation, divine intervention, or divine teleology in the natural world. That this agenda has been achieved with almost total global success in the spheres of science, education, and scholarly disciplines is obvious to any informed observer."[23]

Professor Marvin L. Lubenow's comments on this bias of Darwin are important enough to cite in some detail:

> Not only was Darwin's contribution primarily philosophical, it was a philosophy bent on a specific mission: to show that creation is unscientific. The most extensive research into Darwin's religious attitudes and motivations has been done by historian Neal C. Gillespie (Georgia State University). He begins his book with this comment: "On reading the *Origin of Species*, I, like many others,

became curious about why Darwin spent so much time attacking the idea of divine creation."

Gillespie goes on to demonstrate that Darwin's purpose was not just to establish the concept of evolution. Darwin was wise enough not to stop there. Darwin went for the jugular vein. Darwin's master accomplishment was to convince the scientific world that it was unscientific to believe in supernatural causation. His purpose was to "ungod" the universe. Darwin was a positivist. This is the philosophy that the only true knowledge is scientific knowledge; no other type of knowledge is legitimate. Obviously, to accept that premise means to reject any form of divine revelation. Darwin accomplished one of the greatest feats of salesmanship in the history of the world. He convinced scientists that it was unscientific to deal with God or creation in any way. *To be scientific, they must study the world as if God did not exist.* . . .

In all of this, it is important to realize that Darwin was not an atheist. He did not exterminate God. He just evicted God from the universe which God had created. All that God was allowed to do was to create the "natural laws" at the beginning. From then on, nature was on its own. With God out of the picture, evolution fell into place rather easily, since evolution seemed to be the only viable alternative to Special Creation. . . .

We are now getting down to basics. The real issue in the creation/evolution debate is not the *existence* of God. The real issue is the *nature* of God. To think of evolution as basically atheistic is to misunderstand the uniqueness of evolution. Evolution was not designed as a general attack against theism. It was designed as a specific attack against the God of the Bible, and the God of the Bible is clearly revealed through the doctrine of creation. Obviously, if a person is an atheist, it would be normal for him to also be an evolutionist. But evolution is as comfortable with theism as it is with atheism. An evolutionist is perfectly free to choose any god he wishes, as long as it is not the God of the Bible. The gods allowed by evolution are private, subjective, and artificial. They bother no one and make no absolute ethical demands. However, the God of the Bible is the Creator, Sustainer, Savior, and Judge. All are responsible to him. He has an agenda that conflicts with that of sinful humans. For man to be created in the image of God is very awesome. For God to be created in the image of man is very comfortable.

Evolution was originally designed as a specific attack against the God of the Bible, and it remains so to this day. While Christian

Theistic Evolutionists seem blind to this fact, the secular world sees it very clearly.[24]

Evolutionists' Agenda

Secular scientists today face the same quandary as Darwin and they respond in a similar fashion. They cannot imagine the universe occurring by blind chance. Yet, as materialists, they find the idea of divine creation uncomfortable at best. Like Darwin, they have an agenda for the scientific data. For these scientists, evolution is accepted as a philosophical necessity more than a scientific conviction.

Theologians have recognized this all along. Dr. Clark Pinnock is correct when he observes, "The reason evolution is believed and taught as a fact is not due to the evidence for it, but rather due to the *need* for it."[25] Dr. Greg Bahnsen concurs, "Evolution is not a testable scientific hypothesis at all, but rather a philosophical paradigm preferred by some men to discredit the Biblical doctrine of creation."[26]

Dr. George Wald, the Nobel Prize winning biologist at Harvard, agrees:

> The reasonable view was to believe in spontaneous generation; the only alternative, to believe in a single, primary act of supernatural creation. There is no third position. For this reason many scientists a century ago chose to regard the belief in spontaneous generation as a philosophical necessity. . . . Most modern biologists, having viewed with satisfaction the downfall of the spontaneous generation hypothesis, yet unwilling to accept the alternative belief in special creation, are left with nothing.[27]

But how wise is it to be "left with nothing"? The eminent space scientist Dr. Wernher von Braun is, quite correctly, convinced that science and belief in a Creator go hand in hand:

> I find it as difficult to undertand a scientist who does not acknowledge the presence of a superior rationality behind the existence of the universe as it is to comprehend a theologian who would deny the advances of science. And there is certainly no scientific reason why God cannot retain the same relevance in our modern world that He held before we began probing His creation with telescope, cyclotron, and space vehicles. Our

survival here and hereafter depends on adherence to ethical and spiritual values.[28]

Evolution became accepted because it was philosophically comfortable to a generation of materialists who were, in effect, practical atheists who would not accept a theory of divine creation. As we saw, more than one materialist has confessed that removing the idea of God as Creator opened up an entirely new realm of philosophical and personal living. The irony is that most scientists accepted evolution, even *though* they were not convinced as to its legitimacy[29] and even *though* it left them in a worse state scientifically and philosophically than the acceptance of creation.

In *Why Scientists Accept Evolution*, Dr. Clark and Dr. Bales further document this and point out that "men often accept evolution because the only alternative is creation by God."[30] Indeed, the four pillars of nineteenth-century Darwinism— Charles Darwin, Herbert Spencer, Thomas Henry Huxley, and Alfred Russell Wallace—all accepted evolution (despite their doubts) because they had *first* rejected Divine creation and simply had no other option. Because they were biased against the supernatural and preferred not to believe in the Creator God of Genesis, evolution was accepted by default:

> The reason these men accepted evolution is not brought out clearly in their scientific works but in their letters, biographies and autobiographies which many scientists have never examined. ... The eminent evolutionists of the nineteenth century accepted evolution because of their anti-supernatural bias, and not because of the weight of the scientific evidence. . . . [31]

Most importantly, it "was not a study of nature itself that led men to search for some hypothesis of natural evolution, but rather the desire to escape the supernatural."[32]

Thus, even today many frank scientists have confessed that the reasons behind their belief in evolution are primarily philosophical, *not* scientific.

Scientist Louis T. More observed, "When, however, we examine these causes for our belief [in evolution] we find that *accepting our desire to eliminate special creation* and, generally, what we call the miraculous, most of them can be considered only as secondary reasons to confirm a theory already advanced."[33]

Professor Delage, a Professor of Comparative Zoology at the University of Paris, explains that "Darwin's everlasting title to glory will be that he explained the seemingly marvelous adaptation of living things by the mere action of natural factors" rather than by recourse to God.[34]

Another scientist, Du Bois-Raymond, noted what he felt was one of the most important aspects of Darwin's theory. Thus, "The possibility, ever so distant, of banishing from nature its seeming [divine] purpose, and putting a blind necessity everywhere in the place of final causes, appears, therefore, as one of the greatest advances in the world of thought. . . ."[35]

Finally, G. Fana confesses, "Let us admit, without further preamble: the success attained by the theory of evolution is not due primarily to its self evident character, for even the most generally admitted facts cannot always be reconciled with it, but rather to the sympathy of the scientific world for the 'dogma' of scientific materialism."[36]

Paradoxically, the theory of special creation is rejected primarily because it is seen as "incredible" in light of a far more incredible materialism. The great biologist D. N. S. Watson once observed that evolution was accepted not because it had been observed to occur or was supported by logically coherent arguments but because it fit certain facts and "because no alternative explanation is credible."[37] As scientist H. S. Shelton stated, "I regard the hypothesis of special creation as too foolish for serious consideration."[38] C. H. Darlington of Oxford University noted, "We owe to *The Origin of Species* the overthrow of the myth of Creation, especially the dramatic character of the overthrow."[39] And Julian Huxley remarked "Darwinism removed the whole idea of God as the Creator of organisms from the sphere of rational discussion. . . ."[40]

But, the dogma of materialism has consequences—it causes scientists to neglect their scientific and ethical responsibilities to let the facts of science lead them. Because most scientists are unwilling to accept where these facts lead—to divine creation—"they frame whatever hypotheses are necessary to sustain a hypothesis of evolution."[41] One is reminded of physicist

Ernest Mach's quip, often quoted by Einstein, which asserts: "When the observed facts come into conflict with a cherished theory, then it is so much worse for the facts." If evolutionary biologists are in the habit of ignoring the most relevant criticisms of their theory, where is the fair play in the assessment of scientific data?

One can wade through hundreds of evolutionary textbooks and notice that although almost all are certain as to the *fact* of evolution, all are equally uncertain when it comes to the *details* of a mechanism like evolution.[42] The problem is compounded because even though most specialists may be well aware of the problems in their own domain they *assume* the evidence for evolution is well established in other fields. Yet, it never is. This conclusion becomes all the more evident when one examines the doubts that different scientists have expressed in their own specialties concerning evolution.[43]

But the problem is compounded because the deception is artificially reinforced in each succeeding generation—without anyone even noticing. The delusion is so magnificent it perpetuates itself invisibly. Evolution is so widely assumed to be true that even questioning it is considered illogical. Because "the fact of evolution is accepted by every biologist"[44] and because the doctrine is so universally accepted, "it is received by each oncoming generation for the simple reason that each generation finds that evolution is a part of the scientific world outlook in which it is reared."[45]

Personal Preference

The above indicates that evolution's acceptance today is due more to personal preference than to scientific evidence.[46] Two decades after the publication of the *Origin of Species*, Darwinism had become scientifically respectable largely because scientists *wanted* it to be respectable. And this is somewhat ironic.

The irony is two fold. First, as we show in this volume, evolution has no evidence to support it, and in light of what it requires us to believe, is more properly considered a bizarre philosophical idea than a scientific fact.

Second, the modern theory of evolution has only replaced one religious faith (supernatural creation) for another religious faith (materialistic evolution). Few can logically deny that *both* theories require faith in the miraculous. But as we will see, evolutionists have embarrassingly discarded one miracle of divine creation for thousands or millions of miracles of evolution. Indeed, not only must they accept the miracles that, as materialists, they find so disagreeable, they must accept them endlessly. Based on what we know about the impossibility of life evolving naturalistically, biochemistry, mutations, and the information content in living things, each of the thousands of steps of evolution for the many thousands of life forms on this planet must have required a miracle.

For example, leading scientist N. Chandra Wickramasinghe writes that, "Contrary to the popular notion that only creationism relies on the supernatural, evolutionism must as well, since the probabilities of random formation of life are so tiny as to require a 'miracle' for spontaneous generation 'tantamount to a theological argument.' "[47]

This is why the Nobel prize winner and atheist Sir Francis Crick acknowledges in his *Life Itself*, "An honest man, armed with all the knowledge available to us now, could only state that in some sense, the origin of life appears at the moment to be almost a miracle, so many are the conditions which would have had to have been satisfied to get it going."[48]

As anthropologist Loren Eiseley observes in his *The Immense Journey*, "After chiding the theologian for his reliance on myth and miracle, science found itself in the unenviable position of having to create a mythology of its own: namely, the assumption that what, after long effort, could not be proved to take place today had, in truth, taken place in the primeval past."[49]

Thus, evolution demands faith in impotent natural processes rather than faith in what must logically be acknowledged as a far more credible option—creation by an infinite Designer. Only the logic of supernatural design explains why thousands of competent scientists remain either strict creationists or theists who accept that the universe can only be accounted for on the basis of a divine power. Nor is this surprising—until the acceptance of Darwin's theory of evolution shortly after 1859, almost all scientists accepted that life was a miracle requiring belief in God to rationally explain it. They agreed with one of the greatest scientists of all time, Sir Isaac Newton, who declared in his *Mathematical Principles of Natural Philosophy*, "This most beautiful system of the sun, planets, and comets could only proceed from the counsel and domain of an intelligent and powerful Being."[50]

In the end, what more fair-minded scientists readily confess today—the practical necessity for belief in a Creator—many materialistic scientists are increasingly finding themselves troubled over. Because the hard data of science continues to mount a stronger and stronger case for creation, they are, embarrassingly, finding themselves in the theologian's chair by default. And they can't be happy about this. As Dr. Robert Jastrow observed in his *God and the Astronomers*, "For the scientist who has lived by his faith in the power of reason, the story ends like a bad dream. He has scaled the mountains of ignorance; he is about to conquer the highest peak; as he pulls himself over the final rock, he is greeted by a band of theologians who have been sitting there for centuries."[51] This explains why committed evolutionists will only continue to skew the data to even more absurd lengths in order to maintain their faith in materialism.

They have no other choice.

This concludes our introduction to the subject of evolution. We now proceed to an evaluation of the alleged evidences for evolution.

Part III

Evolution
and the
Scientific
Evidence

9

Evolution, Logic, and Increasing Doubts

An Introduction to
the Evidence

I have often thought how little I should like to have to prove organic evolution in a court of law.

—Errol White, *presidential address, "A Little on Lungfishes,"*
Proceedings of the Linnean *Society of London,* 177:8 (1966)

Evolutionists tell us that the evidence for evolution can be found in numerable scientific disciplines. Consider two examples: A National Academy of Sciences official statement declares, "Evidence for relation by common descent [evolution] has been provided by paleontology, comparative anatomy, biogeography, embryology, biochemistry, molecular genetics, and other biological disciplines."[1]

The Council for Democratic and Secular Humanism, in another official statement further alleges, "Physico-chemical development paved the way for the origin of life about four billion years ago. Subsequent organic evolution is now documented by empirical evidence from geology, paleontology, biogeography, anthropology, and genetics as well as comparative studies in taxonomy, biochemistry, embryology, anatomy, and physiology."[2]

No one denies that evolutionists see evidence for evolution everywhere. No one disagrees that a vast amount of data has been assembled offering alleged evidence for evolution. As we noted earlier, the problem is not the data, the facts themselves, but how one interprets the data and the critical spirit one brings to one's scientific reading. As Isaac Manly, M.D. comments, when one looks critically at the evidence for evolution, its logic breaks down: "There is even a certain amount of 'logic' to the evidence cited unless one looks at the evidence critically and with basic understanding of biological processes."[3]

Famous actor Richard Dreyfuss made the following comment on "The Galapagos Islands" on the WNET/Nature program for February 26, 1997. With emotion, he described a spectacular display of sea lions surfing the waves on the very islands whose name is so frequently associated with Charles Darwin. As he watched in amazement he commented, "I'm trying to understand the *science* of evolution. But right now, all I can see is a miracle."

Although his initial hunch was more valid, as the program progressed, and Dreyfuss discussed more and more of the "evidence" for evolution, the case for evolution was made to seem plausible by the explanation of vast time periods and micromutations leading to vital changes so that new species could be produced. By the end of the TV program, Dreyfuss was informing viewers as to how eminently reasonable belief in evolution was.

When evolutionists like biologist Edward O. Dodson, co-author of *Evolution: Process and Product*, say there is "a vast array of evidence for evolution," one must be aware of the necessary interpretive lenses placed on the data to arrive at the conclusion.[4] When a creationist such as Dr. Kurt Wise declares that, "Macroevolution is a powerful theory of explanation for a wide variety of physical data"[5] one must understand this as a credible statement only if evolution is *possible*. Something that never happened can't explain anything. Frankly, as we will show, we think the *impossibility* of evolution makes all such alleged evidences and explanatory powers irrelevant. As Dr. Heribert-Nilsson points out in our chapter on fossils, it is rather pointless to discuss "the digestion or the brain functions of a ghost."

An Embarrassing Silence

In his book, *Darwin on Trial*, U.C. Berkeley law professor Phillip E. Johnson relates a remarkable lecture given by evolutionist Colin Patterson at the American Museum of Natural History in 1981. Patterson is the senior paleontologist at the British Natural History Museum and the author of that museum's general text on evolution. He asked his audience one simple but key question which reflected his own doubts about much of what has been thought to be secure knowledge about the process of evolution. Here is what he asked his audience of expert evolutionists:

> "Can you tell me anything you know about evolution, any one thing . . . that is true?" I tried that question on the geology staff at the Field Museum of Natural History and *the only answer I got was silence.* I tried it on the members of the Evolutionary Morphology seminar in the University of Chicago, a very prestigious body of evolutionists, and all I got there *was silence for a long time* but eventually one person said, "I do know one thing—it ought not to be taught in high school."[6]*

Johnson believes that, viewed strictly from the point of view of logic and the accepted canons of scientific research, the Darwinian theory is severely lacking in confirmatory evidence. He shows how scientists have put the cart before the horse, prematurely accepting Darwin's theory as fact and then scrambling to find evidence for it. In the process, Darwinism itself has become a pseudo-science held by its devotees in spite of, rather than because of, the evidence.[8]

This same lack of evidence has led philosophers such as Karl Popper to state: "I have come to the conclusion that Darwinism is not a testable scientific theory, but a *metaphysical research*

---

*Johnson does not cite this incident to imply that Patterson's highly skeptical views are widely held in the scientific community. Patterson was being provocative on purpose and came "under heavy fire" from Darwinists after a bootleg transcript of the lecture was circulated. This caused him to disavow the entire business. Johnson's point is that whether or not Patterson intended his comments for public distribution, he did make a crucial point—scientists know very little about how complex living beings on our planet came into existence.[7]

programme—a possible framework for testable scientific theories. . . . I do not think that Darwinism can explain the origin of life. I think it quite possible that life is so extremely improbable that nothing can 'explain' why it originated. . . ."[9]

Increasingly, evolutionary scientists are dissatisfied today: they think evolution is true, but are more and more confronted by the necessity for faith.[10]

The Evidence for Evolution

The common popular evidences cited in favor of evolution are logical, philosophical, and scientific. One of the alleged logical arguments is this: hundreds of thousands of scientists worldwide simply cannot *all* be so wrong as to have accepted a genuinely false theory—not in the twentieth and twenty-first centuries, the world's most productive era of modern science.

But technological advancement and evolutionary theory are not the same thing. Further, the argument from the majority is itself a logical fallacy. The number of proponents accepting a given theory doesn't prove anything. The proof is in the weight of the evidence. As we saw earlier, the majority can be wrong.

Another common argument for evolution is that it's the only *possible* explanation for our existence. Since we exist, and evolution is the only way we could have gotten here, evolution must be true. But this is another logical fallacy, known as faulty dilemma—limiting options when other legitimate explanations exist.

Most people are persuaded by the alleged scientific evidence—origin of life experiments that allegedly indicate that precursors to life could randomly form and evolve; mutations and natural selection as the apparent mechanism of evolution (mutations do occur; natural selection is alleged to demonstrate evolution); the fossil record with its history of past life in such a fashion that it supposedly shows evolutionary ascent; comparative anatomy/biochemistry/genetics physiology which purport to reveal evolutionary similarity and common descent; biogeography, the geographical distribution of plants and animals which allegedly demonstrate evolutionary relationships; the study of hominid fossils, (the remains of man-like primates from which humans supposedly evolved) and so on.

Although space prohibits examining all the alleged evidences for evolution, we will examine in detail or summary most of the above key evidences. If these key evidences are valid, then evolution may be considered demonstrated. If they are found wanting, then any additional evidence for evolution, major or minor, should also be considered suspect.

Evolutionists say that the proof of evolution *can* be found in the fossil record, natural selection, comparative anatomy, fossil man, and biogeography. But we are convinced that not only is there no proof in any of these areas—there is not even good evidence. This is why we are unable to trust evolutionary scientists when they say there is proof of evolution in other areas as well. The truth is that, when examined critically, all these alleged evidences break down. In fact, we can go further and declare that virtually all such evidence supports special creation, either directly or indirectly.[11]

However, in the remainder of this book, we will do more than examine the foundational weaknesses in the evidence for evolution. We will also discuss such key areas as information theory, design, abiogenesis, molecular evolution, probability factors, the second law of thermodynamics, cosmogony, the myth of chance, and various scientific laws to prove that not only did evolution not happen, it could *never* happen. The discussion of these areas, especially in light of the lack of evidence for evolution in other areas, dismisses any and all of the alleged additional evidence for evolution.

The point must be made that if evolution is biologically and mathematically *impossible*, then *no evidence exists for it anywhere because it never happened.* If it never happened, then the logical, experimental, and evidential dilemmas faced by evolutionists today are only to be expected. Further, theists of any persuasion cannot be accused of being dogmatic or narrow-minded when they simply allow the facts of science to speak for themselves.

Thus, we will not only prove there is no credible and/or demonstrable evidence for evolution in the areas evolutionists cite in favor of evolution, we will prove that it could never happen to begin with. By doing this, we will further document our conclusions in Chapters 7 and 8 that evolution is accepted for reasons other than legitimate scientific data.

Again, because of how they interpret nature, evolutionists do believe the scientific evidence is compelling. If this really isn't the case, why then do evolutionists believe as they do? We think this is explained by several factors: 1) they may not have looked at the data objectively (i.e., they assume the evidence is good without critical analysis); 2) they may have a personal bias in favor of naturalism (they choose to accept evolution on faith, look at the data selectively, and convince themselves the evidence is good); 3) they may have never been exposed to the weight of the evidence against evolution (like that found in the volumes by Bird, Denton, Behe, Milton, MacBeth, Moorehead and Kaplan, Gentry, Grassé, Shute, and others[12]) and/or given it a fair hearing; or 4) they just aren't thinking clearly. In fact, we have talked with many people committed to evolution whose basic problem is simply that they fail to think clearly.

Evolution and Logical Fallacies

When one reads evolutionary literature, one discovers evolutionary faith is replete with an acceptance of logical fallacies. The examples below are illustrative.

The logical fallacy known as "invincible ignorance" happens when a person adopts a particular viewpoint, rigidly maintaining it despite all evidence to the contrary. Regardless of mounting, even definitive, evidence, the person's faith in his particular point of view remains.

The fallacy of provincialism is when one sees things solely from the perspective of one's own particular group (in this case the evolutionary establishment). Other viewpoints, especially those with religious implications, are simply not accepted or tolerated. Thus, as we saw earlier in Chapters 5 and 6, dogmatism is a strong component of modern evolutionary belief. Proponents also engage in special pleading—they selectively accept data supporting their position while rejecting data that does not support it. In fact, they support their position with a confidence entirely out of proportion to the evidence.

In his book on logical fallacies, *Don't You Believe It*, A. J. Hoover summarizes the 30 common logical fallacies he discusses.[13] Significantly, almost all of them are applicable to how evolutionists deal with the data or how they respond to creationism. Consider a few illustrations:

Hasty Generalization—basing a general statement on too small a sample; building general rules from accidental or exceptional situations. (Microevolution is evidence of macroevolution; origin of life experiments in the laboratory can be extrapolated to the actual evolution of life in the primitive oceans, alleged transitionary forms [*Archaeopteryx, Semouria,* etc.] prove evolution.)

Begging the Question (petitio principii)—reasoning in a circle, using your conclusion as a premise, assuming the very thing to be proved as proof of itself. (Natural selection; paleoanthropology; geologic record.)

Misuse of Authority—attempting to prove a conclusion by appealing to a real or alleged authority in such a way that the conclusion does not necessarily follow. (All competent scientists declare evolution is a *fact!*)

Misuse of Analogy—trying to prove something by improper use of a parallel case. (Hominid fossils prove evolution.)

Chronological Snobbery (argumentum ad futuris)—attempting to refute an idea merely by dating it, usually dating it very old. (Creationism was refuted long ago.)

Argument to the Future—trying to prove something by appealing to evidence that might be turned up in the (unknown) future. (As science progresses, proof of evolution will eventually be forthcoming.)

Poisoning the Wells—attempting to refute an argument by discrediting in advance the source of the evidence for the argument. (Creationists are "know-nothings" opposed to modern science; they get their arguments mostly from the book of Genesis.)

Appeal to Force (agumentum ad baculum)—substituting force or the threat of force for reason and evidence. (Evolutionists' intimidation of creationist students and professors.)

Appeal to the People (argumentum ad populum)—trying to establish a position by appealing to popular sentiments instead of relevant evidence. (Everybody believes in evolution, therefore it must be true.)

The Fallacy of Extension—attacking an exaggerated or caricatured version of your opponent's position, i.e., to attack a "straw man." (Creationism is only the religious doctrine of a small but vocal minority.)

Hypothesis Contrary to Fact—arguing from "what might have been," from a past hypothetical condition. (The fossil record.)

The Ultimate Fallacy: Pigheadedness—refusing to accept a proposition even when it has been established by adequate evidence. (That evolution is false is established by the law of biogenesis, probability considerations, thermodynamics, etc.)

Thus, Professor Marvin Lubenow is quite correct when he writes, "As one studies evolutionist literature, one cannot help but notice in its practitioners both a lack of logic and an inability to weigh evidence properly. Legal experts have also noted this."[14] Indeed, when considering the alleged evidences for evolution, weighing the conclusions of legal experts—those trained to weigh evidence—is highly relevant.

Evolution and the Law

We earlier quoted Errol White as stating that he had often thought about how little he would like to have to attempt to prove organic evolution in a court of law. It's no wonder.

No evolutionary scientist anywhere could prove evolution in a legal forum, given competent cross-examination. It is significant that in recent years a number of well argued texts have been written by expert lawyers critiquing evolution based on the application of the laws of evidence. One is by Harvard trained Norman MacBeth. In *Darwin Retried*, he argued that not only was the evidence for evolution of insufficient quality to stand up in a modern court of law but that evolution itself had become a religious faith.[15]

Noted University of California law professor Phillip E. Johnson wrote *Darwin on Trial*, which is one of many significant critiques of evolution in recent years. He argues forcefully what is evident to everyone who has studied this issue objectively: 1) that evolution is ultimately a religious faith; 2) that if evolution were a true scientific hypothesis, an objective rigorous examination of the evidence would have caused it to be discarded a long time ago; 3) that it is not grounded on scientific facts but on the philosophy of naturalism; and 4) that it is an illusion that a great body of empirical evidence can be marshaled in support of the truth of evolution.[16]

A final example is by W. R. Bird, a Yale Law School graduate who argued the major case on the issue before the U.S. Supreme Court. W. R. Bird is a member of the most prestigious legal organization, The American Law Institute, and is listed in the most selective directory, *Who's Who in the World*. His definitive critique of evolution, *The Origin of Species Revisited*, is a masterful analysis of evidential reasoning showing that evolution is without significant evidence and that the theory of abrupt appearance (roughly parallel to creationism) is the better scientific theory.[17]

One wonders, if evolution is *a fact of science*, how do legal experts trained in evaluating evidence declare it is without evidence? Or, how do scientists like Dave Nutting deliver lectures at national conferences with titles like "Fifty scientific reasons why evolution is wrong"?*

Evolution and the Classroom

This kind of critical information almost never gets into the classroom, where it is most needed, and, in fact should be expected. This explains why, according to Klein, a Regent Emerita of the New York State Board of Regents, "the theory of evolution continues to be presented in textbooks, encyclopedias, and

---

*While creationists, some lawyers who have examined the issue in detail, and many non-evolutionary scientists would all agree that a case for evolution *would not* stand under cross-examination in a modern law court, we think it is also significant, as we established in *Ready with an Answer,* that the case for the historic resurrection of Jesus Christ *would* stand in a modern court of law. Those who would respond that we are "blind" for declaring that a "fact" of science would not stand in a court of law but that "religious" suppositions would, are simply not looking at these issues objectively or in sufficient detail to understand the logic of the arguments. If they did, they would understand why evolution would not be proven in a court of law but the resurrection would.

research papers as if it were a proven and verifiable scientific fact."[18]

And, according to one court opinion, "Presently, the concepts of evolutionary theory ... permeate the public school textbooks," at least in biology and for some texts in other fields. "Evolution receives an average of 14,055 words in each of eight major biology textbooks published between 1980 and 1982, and seven devote at least 11,000 words to evolution. By contrast, neither the theory of abrupt appearance nor the theory of creation receives more than a paragraph in any but one of the roughly 30 textbooks for public school biology, neither is mentioned in most, and neither is mentioned in the rest except in criticism."[19]

Unfortunately, educators generally have no idea that they *are* legally permitted to criticize evolution—regardless of what course they teach. Sooner or later, evolution turns up in most courses anyway. Innovative teachers who wish to educate students through the Socratic method, for example, would discover that a few auxiliary lectures on "Weighing the evidence for evolution" will become a fascinating exercise in which to help students think independently and critically.

In fact, legal experts such as W. R. Bird in Vol. 2 of *The Origin of Species Revisited* have shown that the Establishment Clause of the First Amendment does *not* prevent teachers from offering scientific alternatives to evolution and that creation itself can be a legitimate scientific alternative. Teachers who would like to offer an alternative, especially as pedagogical method, and yet do not, have only been intimidated. They are fully within their rights to do so.

If Darwinism is false and evolution dead, then Bird's concluding paragraph in Vol. 2 must be true:

> Perhaps modern science classrooms are only Plato's cave in *The Republic,* and their certain truths are only deceptive images on the wall. Perhaps modern scientists are only Aristophanes' scientists contemplating gnats' anuses in *The Clouds,* or Swift's scientists soberly focusing microscopes on breasts and modifying objects to fit distorted mathematical laws in *Gulliver's Travels.* The dominant science mixes the hemlock to kill its rivals oftentimes; it

disestablishes the priests only to don their mantels, as Rousseau warned.[20]

Rejection on Scientific Grounds

An article of evolutionist Ronald Bailey in *Reason* attempts to explain why so many non-creationist political conservatives are now abandoning belief in evolution. Supposedly, it's not because of the scientific evidence. Bailey's argument assumes that evolution is true—and that recent new discoveries discredit or disprove the creationist's probability and design arguments (they don't). Incredibly, he argues that the only reason conservatives reject evolution is to preserve the moral order resulting from religious values. He cites Irving Kristol who correctly wrote, "If there is one indisputable fact about the human condition it is that no community can survive if it is persuaded—or even if it suspects—that its members are leading meaningless lives in a meaningless universe."[21] Bailey actually suggests that conservatives secretly *know* that evolution is true, but they lie and deceive the public and criticize evolution publicly in order to help preserve the moral order!

This entirely ignores the fact that evolution is being rejected today largely on *scientific* grounds, not social or moral grounds, and that the attack on evolution comes more from establishment science than from religious creationism.

Again, it should be emphasized that the attack on evolution comes more from *within* the halls of naturalistic science than from creationists. Certainly this speaks volumes as to the weakness of its evidence. B. Leith, who catalogued some of the dissent in *The Descent of Darwin: A Handbook of Doubts about Darwinism* (1982) observes, "The theory of life that undermined nineteenth century religion has *virtually become a religion itself* and in turn is being threatened by fresh ideas. The attacks are certainly not limited to those of the creationist and religious fundamentalists who deny Darwinism for political and moral reasons. The main thrust of the *criticism comes from within science itself.*"[22] A few recent examples are science journalist and engineer Richard Milton's *Shattering the Myth of*

Darwinism (1997) and biophysicist Lee M. Spetner's *Not by Chance! Shattering the Modern Theory of Evolution* (1997).

Scientists Who Face the Evidence

Evolutionists may declare that "denying Darwin is intellectually impossible," as Herbert Gintis did in *Commentary* magazine (September 1996) or that "the scientific community has no doubts" about evolution as an article in *Scientific American* (October 1997) claimed. But consider a few examples of the dissent culled from our own research.

Professor Wolfgang Smith received his Ph.D. in Mathematics from Columbia University. He has held faculty positions at the Massachusetts Institute of Technology and UCLA. He writes, "I am opposed to Darwinism, or better said, to the transformist hypothesis as such, no matter what one takes to be the mechanism or cause (even perhaps teleological or theistic) of the postulated macroevolutionary leaps. I am convinced, moreover, that Darwinism, in whatever form, is not in fact a scientific theory, but a pseudo-metaphysical hypothesis decked out in scientific garb. In reality the theory derives its support not from empirical data or logical deductions of a scientific kind but from the circumstance that it happens to be the only doctrine of biological origins that can be conceived with the constricted *Weltanschauung* [worldview] to which a majority of scientists no doubt subscribe."[23]

Dr. R. Merle d'Aubigne, head of the Orthopedic Department at the University of Paris remarks, "The origin of life is still a mystery. As long as it has not been demonstrated by experimental realization, I cannot conceive of any physical or chemical condition [allowing evolution]. . . . I cannot be satisfied by the idea that fortuitous mutation . . . can explain the complex and rational organization of the brain, but also of lungs, heart, kidneys, and even joints and muscles. How is it possible to escape the idea of some intelligent and organizing force?"[24]

Sir John Eccles, winner of the Nobel Prize for Physiology/Medicine says of evolution in "A Divine Design," "One of its weak points is that it does not have any recognizable way in which conscious life could have emerged. . . ."[25]

Professor Harry Rubin, Professor of Molecular Biology and Research Virologist to the Virus Laboratory, University of California Berkeley and recipient of numerous prestigious awards, accepts non-Darwinian evolution but still remarks, "Life, even in bacteria, is too complex to have occurred by chance."[26]

Nobelist and evolutionist Dr. Robert A. Millikan comments, "The pathetic thing is that we have scientists who are trying to prove evolution, which no scientist can ever prove."[27]

Dr. Albert Fleishmann, zoologist at Erlangen University, writes, "The theory of evolution suffers from grave defects, which are more and more apparent as time advances. It can no longer square with practical scientific knowledge."[28]

Famous Canadian geologist William Dawson says "the record of the rocks is decidedly against evolutionists."[29]

The highly regarded noncreationist anti-Darwinian French scientist Grassé says, "The explanatory doctrines of biological evolution do not stand up to an objective, in-depth criticism. They prove to be either in conflict with reality or else incapable of solving the major problems involved."[30]

Ken Hsu, the evolutionist professor at the Geological Institute in Zurich, E.T.H., and former president of the International Association of Sedimentologists, writes, "We have had enough of the Darwinian fallacy. Its about time we cry: 'The Emperor has no clothes.'"[31]

Lemoine, a former president of the Geological Society of France and director of the Natural History Museum in Paris, as well as the editor of the *Encyclopedie Francaise*, declares that, "The theories of evolution, with which our studious youth have been deceived, constitute actually a dogma that all the world continues to teach: but each, in his speciality, the zoologist or the botanist, ascertains that none of the explanations furnished is adequate. . . . [I]t results from this summary, that the theory of evolution is *impossible*."[32]

Julio Garrido, Sc.d., a member of the Spanish Royal Academy of Science and a former president of the French Society of Crystallography and Mineralogy quotes French scholar and mathematician Georges Salet concerning the last 150 years of attempts to find evidence for evolution or even explanations of it, "During the last one hundred and fifty years of research that has been carried out along this line, there has been no discovery of anything [confirming evolution]."[33]

Garrido also quotes French evolutionist Jen Rostand who writes, "The theory of evolution gives no answer to the important problem of the origin of life and presents only fallacious solutions to the problem of the nature of evolutive transformations. . . . [Because of this situation] We are condemned to believe in evolution. . . . Perhaps we are now in a worse position than in 1859 because we have searched for one century and we have the impression that the different hypotheses are now exhausted."[34]

Dr. Garrido himself writes that evolution "is a simplistic idea, almost an infantile idea" and even that it is a philosophical disease: "The evolutionary theory is one of these 'diseases,' because it is the corruption of philosophical prejudices regarding a pure scientific question."[35]

An article by Howard Byington Holroyd, Ph.D., retired head of the Department of Physics, Augustana College, Rock Island, Illinois, points out that evolution is nonsense. His research and calculations show "far beyond any reasonable doubt, that this theory is nothing more than physical and mathematical nonsense."[36]

R. Clyde McCone, Ph.D., Professor of Anthropology, California State University, Long Beach, states, "as an anthropologist, I object to evolution on the anthropological grounds that I have presented. There are no data for evolution."[37]

Roger Haines, Jr., J. D., research attorney for the California Third District Court of Appeals, Sacramento, writes that, "The arguments for macroevolution fail at every significant level when confronted by the facts."[38]

Finally, evolutionist and zoologist with the Department of Physiology and Biochemistry, University of Southampton (England), G. A. Kerkut writes the following conclusions in his *Implications of Evolution*. He refers to the seven basic assumptions of evolution and assesses their validity:

> The first assumption was that non-living things gave rise to living material. This is still just an assumption. . . . There is, however, little evidence in favor of biogenesis and as yet we have no indication that it can be performed. . . . It is therefore a

matter of faith on the part of the biologist that biogenesis did occur. . . .

The second assumption was that biogenesis occurred only once. This again is a matter for belief rather than proof. . . .

The third assumption was that Viruses, Bacteria, Protozoa and the higher animals were all interrelated. . . . We have as yet no definite evidence about the way in which the Viruses, Bacteria or Protozoa are interrelated.

The fourth assumption was that the Protozoa gave rise to the Metazoa. . . . Here again nothing definite is known. . . .

The fifth assumption was that the various invertebrate phyla are interrelated. . . . The evidence, then, for the affinities of the majority of the invertebrates is tenuous and circumstantial; not the type of evidence that would allow one to form a verdict of definite relationships.

The sixth assumption [is] that the invertebrates gave rise to the vertebrates. . . . As Berrill states, "in a sense this account is science fiction."

We are on somewhat stronger ground with the seventh assumption that the fish, amphibia, reptiles, birds, and mammals are interrelated. There is the fossil evidence to help us here, though many of the key transitions are not well-documented and we have as yet to obtain a satisfactory objective method of dating the fossils. . . . The evidence that we have at present is insufficient to allow us to decide the answer to these problems.[39]

Kerkut goes on to state that, in essence, evolution has to be taken on pure faith: the evidence is circumstantial and much of it can be argued either way. He says of these initial assumptions for evolution, "The evidence is still lacking for most of them."[40]

Scientists may claim evolution is a demonstrated fact, and this may routinely be stated in student textbooks, but this is wrong. Creationists have pointed this out for decades. And not without good cause.

Creation Evidence

In fact, creationist Dr. Duane Gish has actually debated leading evolutionists some 300 times and almost always won.[41] Creationist Dr. Henry Morris has spoken to some 3,000 audiences and never heard an evolutionist respondent offer convincing evidence for evolution.[42] The hundreds of scientists with the Creation Research Society, the Institute for Creation Research, and other creationist organizations (there are well over 100) have read literally thousands of evolutionary books and articles. They conclude there is little or no genuine evidence for the validity of evolution. In essence, the reason most people continue to believe in evolution is because of personal bias or because they are misinformed about the evidence against it.[43]

Scientists may choose not to listen to creationists. However, we don't see how any scientist can logically deny the conclusions given by W. R. Bird in his critique of evolution and presentation of the scientific evidence for abrupt appearance, or creation. He shows that of six scientific approaches to macroevolution (besides the theory of abrupt appearance), classical Darwinism must be considered wrong on key issues; that neo-Darwinism and punctuated equilibria cancel each other out by denying the relevance of the other's mechanism; and that the other three approaches are anti-Darwinian, with one opposing it and a second being agnostic toward macroevolution.[44]

In essence, all theories of evolution, whether Darwinian, neo-Darwinian, punctuated equilibria, or non-Darwinian, should now be considered *dead* despite their continuing popularity in the scientific world. The obituary has already been written due to the latest scientific discoveries and the failure of 150 years of scientific advancement to confirm evolution. Obviously then, something like theistic evolution would also be dead.

We emphasize again that the evidence of neither paleontology, phylogeny, taxonomy or classification, comparative anatomy, comparative embryology, comparative biochemistry, population genetics, artificial selection, biogeographical distribution, cytology, nor any other area offers real evidence for evolution.[45]

Only Two Options?

Sometimes, it is claimed there are many different legitimate origin theories. But this is not ultimately true. Native American, Hindu, Muslim, Aztec, etc., have creation accounts that are either myths or have no scientific validity. Scientifically the only real alternatives are creation or evolution. Thus, we think that to effectively disprove evolution is to effectively prove creation. And we are not alone in limiting our choices this way.

In a recent anti-creationist book, the evolutionist Futuyma writes, "Creation and evolution, between them, exhaust the possible explanations for the origin of living things."[46] George Wald, a Nobel Prize winner says that between spontaneous generation and a single primary act of supernatural creation, "There is no third position. . . ."[47]

Bird cites other evolutionists as admitting the same: O'Grady ("It [neo-Darwinism] has long been perceived as the only legitimate theory of evolution, and thus the only alternative to creationism."); H. Newman ("There is no rival hypothesis except the outworn and completely refuted idea of special creation, now retained only by the ignorant, the dogmatic, and the prejudiced."); D. Watson ("The only alternative, special creation, is clearly incredible."); J. Teller ("The concept of development was accordingly untrue, and special creation remained the only valid interpretation."); R. Jastrow ("Perhaps the appearance of life on the earth is a miracle. Scientists are reluctant to accept that view, but their choices are limited; either life was created on the earth by the will of a being outside the grasp of scientific understanding, or it evolved on our planet spontaneously. . . ."); M. Simpson ("If life was not created supernaturally, and if it did not simply develop from pre-existent 'seeds' present from the creation of the universe [whenever that was], life must have come forth from nonliving matter."); Alexander ("Indeed, at this moment creation is the only alternative to evolution."); P. Davis and E. Solomon ("Such explanations tend to fall into one or the other of two broad categories: special creation or evolution. Various admixtures and modifications of these two concepts exist, but it seems impossible to imagine an explanation for origins that lies completely outside the two ideas."[48]

Thus, it is not surprising that some evolutionists will accept the fact, that, as Miller and Fowler state, "a case against creation is a case for evolution and *vice versa*."[49] And evolutionist Naylor agrees that "Evidence in favor of one is necessarily against the other."[50]

From the perspective of chosen worldview options, only evolution or creation have the capacity to logically attract men's minds. Pantheism and related theories lie outside the realm of science and are self-refuting or disproven by modern science; directed panspermia theories are evolution in disguise and only push the problem back further; theistic evolution is sceintifically and biblically impossible; and other theories have serious or fatal problems as well. So, if evolution is disproved, creation is our only option. The remaining chapters in our book will disprove evolution, leaving creation the best choice. Perhaps then it should surprise no one that even a number of evolutionists have publicly declared that creation is the better theory.

Creation the Better Theory?

Evolutionary scientists generally claim that "No competent scientist believes in creation." But even some evolutionary scientists agree that the theory of special creation better fits the actual scientific data. Many more examples could be cited; the ones given are only for purposes of illustration. Our point is to show that evolutionists cannot be correct when they claim no serious scientist accepts creation or that creation is a useless religious theory without a shred of scientific evidence for it. If this were true other *evolutionists* could never claim that creation is the better scientific theory.

Of course, virtually all of the thousands of scientists who are creationists believe that whatever scientific field one is referring to, the actual scientific facts fit creation far better than evolution[51]:

> The true sciences of astronomy, physics, chemistry, biology, and especially thermodynamics, all give strong witness to the primeval special creation of all things, whereas the sciences of geophysics, geology, paleontology, and others similarly give clear testimony to the great Deluge. The fossil record, in particular, commonly alleged to provide the strongest evidence of evolution and the geological ages, instead can be understood much better in the framework of the Flood. . . . There is no scientific evidence for evolution that is not at least as well explained by creation, and there are now thousands of modern scientists who have abandoned evolution and become creationists.[52]

Below we cite representative statements of evolutionary scientists who are frank enough to admit that special creation is the better theory in whole or part. Unfortunately, as noted earlier, most scientists wrongly assume evolution has been proven in other fields and that their field of specialty is the only one with difficulties. For example, the botanist E. J. H. Corner of Cambridge University believes that evidence for evolution exists in certain other fields, although he admits to difficulty in finding evidence for evolution in his own field:

> Much evidence can be adduced in favor of the theory of evolution—from biology, biogeography, and paleontology, but I still think that, to the unprejudiced, the fossil record of plants is in favor of special creation. . . . Can you imagine how an orchid, a duck weed, and a palm have come from the same ancestry, and have we any evidence for this assumption? The evolutionist must be prepared with an answer, but I think that most would break down before an inquisition."[53]

In fact, as we will indicate in our remaining chapters, every field is fraught with difficulties. Those who recognize this are more open to considering creation.

Writing in the *Physics Bulletin* (Volume 31, No. 4, May 1980, 138), H. S. Lipson at the University of Manchester Institute of Science and Technology and a Fellow of the Royal Society states: "I have always been slightly suspicious of the theory of evolution because of its ability to account for *any* property of living beings (the long neck of the giraffe, for example). I have therefore tried to see whether biological discoveries over the last 30 years or so fit in with Darwin's theory. I do not think that they do." He further states, "In the last 30 years we have learned a great deal about life processes (still a minute part of what there is to know!) and it seems to me to be only fair to see how the theory of evolution accommodates the new evidence. This is what we should demand of a purely physical theory. To my mind, the theory does not stand up at all. I shall take only one example—breathing." And he proceeds to show how one cannot account for breathing on evolutionary assumptions. After further discussion, he asks, "How has living matter originated?" and concludes: "I think, however, that we must go further than this and admit that the only acceptable explanation is *creation*. I know that this is anathema to physicists, as indeed it is to me, but we must not reject a theory that we do not like if the experimental evidence supports it."[54] It is refreshing indeed to read such words. Without a few such statements like this one might think that truly open-minded evolutionists were themselves an extinct species.

In his *Biology, Zoology, and Genetics: Evolution Model Versus Creation Model 2*, A. Thompson observes, "Rather than supporting evolution, the breaks in the known fossil record support the creation of major groups with the possibility of some limited variation within each group"[55]

Dr. Austin Clark, the curator of paleontology at the Smithsonian Institution observed in "Animal Evolution:" "Thus so far as concerns the major groups of animals, the creationists seem to have the better of the argument."[56]

In the area of comparative biochemistry, Bird observes, "This comparative unrelatedness argument is an affirmative evidence for the theory of abrupt appearance, as not just Denton and Sermonti but Zihlman and Lowenstein acknowledge in reference to the comparative biochemistry evidence, saying that 'this constitutes a kind of "special creation" hypothesis.' "[57]

These citations and others reveal that some evolutionary scientists are frank enough to admit the theory of creation is in whole or part superior to the theory of evolution. In fact, the scientific evidence is so conclusive against evolution and for creation one is finally amazed that the idea of evolution so thoroughly dominates modern science. As noted, the reasons are not scientific. Were they scientific, virtually all scientists would be creationists—as the vast majority were in preceding centuries. Even such eminent scientists as Sir Fred Hoyle and N. Chandra Wickramasinghe, his research partner, in discussing the "theory that life was assembled by an [higher] intelligence" state, "Indeed, such a theory is so *obvious* that one wonders why it is not widely accepted as being self evident. The reasons are psychological rather than scientific."[58]

The remainder of this book will be devoted to showing why the evidence for evolution is lacking—and why it will never be forthcoming. We will show the scientific basis for the increasing dissatisfaction with evolution even among many evolutionary scientists. This is why creationists make statements like the following by leading Canadian medical specialist Evan Shute, M.D., author of *Flaws in the Theory of Evolution*: "Evolution will be a lost cause as soon as people hear all the evidence and not just the noise made by its proponents."[59] And "the fall of Darwinism will be the big story of the early 21st century . . ." states noted U.C. at Berkeley law professor Phillip E. Johnson, author of *Darwin on Trial, Reason in the Balance,* and *Defeating Darwinism by Opening minds.*[60]

10

The Greatest Magic in the World

Everything We See from Nothing at All

In the long run, the materialistic assumptions of modern scientific naturalism can only prove a serious embarrassment to modern science. Science is in the unenviable position of the emperor with no clothes. No one has the daring to tell the poor man he is naked until a little child exclaims what is obvious to everyone. Modern science, in its naturalistic speculation, is naked today, with only a few "children"—non-evolutionary and creationist scientists—willing to shout out the obvious.

We can illustrate the embarrassment of modern science by considering its attempt to explain the origin of the material universe from either 1) literally nothing or 2) virtually nothing. Equally embarrassing is its attempt to explain life from nonlife.

In fact, two of the most unbelievable scenarios of the modern evolutionary story are that 1) *nothing* created the material universe and 2) lifeless matter created all living diversity in its endless life forms.

Both of these scenarios are so implausible that, rationally, they must be considered nonsense. In fact, both assumptions are flat out impossible.

In this chapter (and later in Chapter 17) we will deal with the issues surrounding the idea that the material universe, in a naturalistic sense, arose from nothing. The remainder of the chapters in this section will examine the credibility of the idea that dead matter could produce the tremendous complexity of the natural and human worlds around us.

The dilemma for the evolutionary scientist should be obvious. In the first scenario, the scientist has only *nothing* to work with—not space, time, or quantum matter—only *nothing*. From *nothing* the evolutionist must explain how our amazingly ordered and spectacular universe came to be. Here we discover the "Big Bang" event that began with something much smaller than an atom, according to many cosmologists, and expanded to a universe with an alleged 30 billion-light-year diameter. (No implausibilities here.) In the second story, there is at least something to work with—a lifeless universe. Here, science must explain an entire series of impossible events—how prebiological evolution occurred (that is, how unorganized matter organized itself into the chemical precursors of life permitting upward evolution); how early microbial life evolved further in the primeval oceans; how subsequent ocean life evolved from this; how "water breathing" fish evolved into land animals; how reptiles evolved into birds (and, as some evolutionists maintain, how birds evolved from dinosaurs); how cold blooded reptiles evolved into warm blooded mammals, and how people came from lower animals.

If all this sounds like a lot to explain, it is. As we will see, it is too much to explain.

The Power of Nothing

Let's begin by seeing how modern science explains the existence of our universe. Science tells us it came into being from nothing.

Professor of Physics and Astronomy at the University of Hawaii, Victor J. Stenger asserts, "the universe exploded out of nothingness."[1]

Physicist Arno Penzias, a Nobel Prize winner for co-discovering the background radiation allegedly remaining from the "Big Bang," asserts that the simplest theory to explain the scientific data is the view "astronomers normally espouse, a creation out of nothing, the appearance out of nothing of a universe." Thus, "the universe was created out of nothing, in an instant, and continues to expand."[2]

In addition, the older steady state theory (continuous creation) teaches that hydrogen atoms abruptly appear "out of nothing."[3]

Perhaps the reader can begin to sense the problem here. The problem is that *literally* nothing—no space, time, atoms, etc.—can ever *explain* anything, let alone create it. Remember, "space" as we know it is not literally nothing. It has all kinds of particles and "stuff" in it. Indeed, how can we see starlight if the starlight isn't transmitted through space on something? So, if modern science asks us to accept its explanation of the universe, what are the scientific equations to show that matter arises from literally nothing? Or that space and time arise from literally nothing? Aren't these ideas just as incredible as the creation myths of ancient civilizations?

John Mather, NASA's principal researcher of the cosmic background radiation's spectral curve with the COBE satellite points out, "We have equations that describe the transformation of one thing into another, but we have no equations whatever for creating space and time. And the concept doesn't even make any sense in English. So I don't think we have words or concepts to even think about creating something from nothing. And I certainly don't know of any work that seriously would explain it when we can't even state the concept."[4]

It is true that some have argued the inflationary Big Bang theory put forth by MIT's Alan Guth in 1979 attempts to explain how a universe arises from *literally* nothing. "In this view the universe would originate as a quantum fluxuation starting from absolutely nothing. . . ."[5] But Guth later explains, "First of all, I will say that at the purely technical level, inflation [expansion] itself does not explain how the universe arose from nothing. . . . Inflation itself takes a very small universe and produces from it a very big universe. But inflation by itself does not explain where that very small universe came from."[6]

A Proton by Any Other Name

When Guth speaks of a "very small universe" he isn't kidding. The universe envisioned by his theory was only about one *trillionth* the size of a proton, and a proton is only a small fraction of the size of an atom. And yet in less than a nanosecond (one billionth of a second), the story goes, the "universe" was the size of a baseball and in a trillionth of a second later about six feet in diameter. At this point it was "cooled" to around one hundred billion degrees and quarks and electrons, the building blocks of atoms, were formed. When the universe was one one-millionth of a second old, atoms formed, quarks bonded to form protons and neutrons, which then formed nuclei, producing helium, supposedly the first element.

So the inflationary Big Bang model does not begin with literally nothing; it begins with something, however infinitesimal.[7]

But could the universe ever originate from literally nothing? And perhaps more amazingly, do scientists seriously propose this? Incredibly, yes, they do.

In fact, some scientists argue that creation from literally nothing can be scientifically defended as a *rational* concept. Indeed, "there are many ongoing efforts to find a natural explanation for how the universe could have originated from absolutely nothing."[8] However, we think these scientists have no choice other than to defend the rationality of nonsense since their naturalistic theories require such credulity.

Paul Davies writes in *Sky and Telescope* for January 1993 that it is "possible to imagine the universe coming into being from nothing entirely spontaneously" and that there is "no need for an external creator." Well, certainly that can be imagined, but that is not the issue. The issue is what is credible and what is rational. Consider the infinite difference between *nothing* that creates the universe and an *infinite God* that creates the universe. To argue that the universe originates spontaneously from nothing and therefore we don't need God to explain it is just more myth and nonsense given the public in the name of "science."

Better Science?

The late, famed science fiction writer and science popularizer Isaac Asimov characteristically dismissed creationism as "nonsense," "a disgraceful imposture," "unscientific gibberish," etc.[9]

Yet listen to Asimov's own *scientific* "explanation" for the origin of universe: "Where did the substance of the universe come from?. . . If $0 = + 1 + (-1)$, then something which is 0 might just as well become 1 and -1. Perhaps in an infinite sea of nothingness, globs of positive and negative energy in equal-sized pairs are constantly forming, and after passing through evolutionary changes, combining once more and vanishing. We are in one of these globs in the period of time between nothing and nothing, and wondering about it."[10]

Perhaps it should be evident even to leading science fiction writers where the "scientific gibberish" lies. But for argument's sake, let's say these scientists are right and that creation from literally *nothing*, in a naturalistic sense, can be considered scientifically rational. Then how much *more* scientifically rational is creation by an infinite, omnipotent God?

Most scientists, however, can't seem to accept a creation from literally nothing. As science writer Fred Heeren concludes:

> In other words, any kind of natural creation from absolutely nothing (*ex nihilo*), remains as unthinkable in this scientific age as it has always been for the philosophers. Some cosmologists would like to imply that they have found a way to explain this thorniest of cosmological realities, but all must stop short of claiming any true explanation for ultimate origins. The closest they can come to an explanation is to say that, given what we know of quantum fluxuations, something might come from *practically* nothing. George Smoot, principal investigator of the cosmic background's ripples with the COBE satellite, says: ". . . it is possible to envision creation of the universe from almost nothing—not nothing, but practically nothing. Almost creation *ex nihilo*, but not quite."

When pressed to answer how creation could begin with *nothing*, Tryon himself (the originator of the fluxuation/creation proposal) said, "It may well be that we will never have a confident answer." The earlier hope that something could have come from nothing now appears to be going the way of the "spontaneous generation" theory of the mid-1800's, the idea that life (even flies) could spontaneously spring from nonliving materials in a closed jar.

As it enters the 21st century, science has yet to come up with a natural explanation for the universe's origin, and it would seem that the supernatural explanation given in Hebrews 11:3 is still the best one we have: "By faith we understand that the universe was formed at God's command, so that what is seen was not made out of what was visible."[11]

Astrophysicist Herman J. Eckelmann, after discussing the impossibility of life evolving naturalistically quotes C. K. Chesterton:

"It is absurd for the evolutionist to complain that it is unthinkable for an admittedly unthinkable God to make everything out of nothing, and then pretend that it is *more* thinkable that nothing should turn itself into anything." This is a wonderful new gospel. It wants to be believed against all odds—literally. If we were to be able to derive a number that would express the chances of writing history in advance with such accuracy as the Bible does (and as Robert C. Newman describes in this volume and elsewhere) and multiply it by Hoyle's [one chance in] $10^{40,000}$ [for the evolution of a single bacterium to occur], what would we have? Some would say a much larger than ever reason for recognizing the existence of the truly awesome God of the Bible. . . . The Bible is accredited to us by the fulfilled prophecies conveyed within it. . . . The alternative [to accepting this] seems to be to believe in an eternally running-down universe being resupplied by the continuous creation of matter out of nothing by nothing at a rate that cannot be detected by experiment. No one has *ever* observed new matter emerge out of nothing. . . . Is it possible that one can have too high an emotional stake in wanting to have a Godless universe—one that avoids standards of right living and a Judgment Day when all accounts will be balanced?[12]

The first law of thermodynamics confirms that something does not arise from literally nothing. (And something one trillionth the size of a proton is close enough to literally nothing.) It appears an unfortunate commentary on the state of modern science that the majority of the scientific world believes that from nothing, nothing produced something and something (i.e., dead matter) produced life in all its varied glory.

The evolutionist scoffs at the creationist for believing an infinite God created the universe from nothing—nothing other than His command. But then he proceeds to argue that *nothing* created the universe from *nothing*! While divine creation from nothing is certainly incomprehensible to finite minds, the current scientific view is, surely, much less credible. Yet this is exactly what modern science teaches.

Since naturalism has ruled God irrelevant in the origins issue (see Romans 1:28), one is tempted to wonder whether, in response, God has now impelled naturalistic science to teach nonsense. Are most of the brilliant and dedicated minds in the scientific world now reduced to teaching nonsense? And some think God has no sense of humor.

Regardless, evolutionists cannot ridicule and outlaw creationists for believing in a creation from nothing when they teach the same thing. As Tipler, a prominent cosmologist and atheist writes concerning the errors of the McLean court decision against creationism:

> The sections of the opinion on cosmology make amusing reading for cosmologists. The 1981 Arkansas equal time law defined "creation-science" as "science" that involved, among other things, "Sudden creation of the universe, energy, and life from nothing." (Overton, 1982, p. 30). The judge thought such an idea inherently unscientific: ". . . Indeed, creation of the world 'out of nothing' is the ultimate religious statement because God is the only actor. . . . The idea of [sudden creation from nothing, or] creatio ex nihilo, is an inherently religious concept." (Overton, 1982). . . .
>
> The problem with this is that, as I pointed out in section 2 no. 2 the standard Big Bang theory has the Universe coming into existence out of nothing, and cosmologists use the phrase "creation of the universe" to describe this phenomenon. Thus if we accept Judge Overton's idea that creation out of nothing is inherently religious, and his ruling that inherently religious ideas cannot be taught in public education institutions, it would be illegal to teach the Big Bang theory at state universities. . . . [13]

This is the dilemma indeed. If the court has ruled that teaching a creation from nothing is illegal, then teaching the Big Bang theory is also illegal.

As for the intellectual dilemma modern science faces in attempting to explain everything from nothing apart from God, we are reminded of the analytically meaningless attempt of existentialist philosopher Martin Heidegger to explain the primacy of existence (which, in light of our discussion he appropriately termed "the Nothing") over essence (the "Negation" and the "Not").

Heidegger's obscurantism seemed profound to many; in fact it was also nonsense:

> What is to be investigated is being only and—*nothing* else; being alone and further—*nothing*; solely being, and beyond this—*nothing*. What about this *Nothing? . . . Does the Nothing exist only because the Not, i.e., the Negation, exists? Or is it the other way around? Does Negation and the Not exist only because the Nothing exists? . . .* We assert: *the Nothing is prior to the Not and the Negation. . . .* Where do we seek the Nothing? How do we find the Nothing? . . . We know the Nothing. . . . *Anxiety reveals the Nothing. . . .* That for which and because of which we were anxious, was "really"—nothing. Indeed: the Nothing itself—as such—was present. . . . *What about this Nothing?—The Nothing itself nothings* [sic].[14]

As modern scientists' "explanations" and theorizing are increasingly obscurantist, we can't help but wonder if one day they will end up at the same place as Heidegger—teaching a nonsense that sounds profound. Or are they already there? Inflationary cosmologist Andrei Linde actually claims he may be able to create "an entire universe in a laboratory" if he can only determine how to trigger inflation![15]

One is reminded of what the Apostle Paul wrote almost 2,000 years ago, "For even though they knew God, they did not honor Him as God, or give thanks; but they became futile in their speculations, and their foolish heart was darkened. Professing to be wise, they became fools. . . . For they exchanged the truth of God for a lie and worshiped and served the creature rather than the Creator, who is blessed forever. . . . And just as they did not see fit to acknowledge God any longer, God gave them over . . ." (Romans 1:21,22,25,28 NASB).

Modern evolutionary cosmology has been left to its own devices. It has ended in nonsense because it has ignored God. In Chapter 17 we will discuss this issue of nothing creating everything from a different vantage point in such a way as to really bring home the title of this book. We will further see just how nonsensical nontheistic origin theorizing has become.

Perhaps modern scientists should reconsider the truth of the old Latin phrase, *ex nihilo nihil fit*—"from nothing, nothing comes."

11

Alphabet Soup and Winning the Lottery
Origin of Life Experiments

Spontaneous generation—"the supposed production of living organisms from non-living matter . . . also called abiogenesis. . . ."
—The American Heritage Dictionary of Science
(1986), p. 618

Biogenesis—"the theory that living things can be produced only by other living things, and cannot develop spontaneously from nonliving materials."

—Ibid., p. 68

Do origin of life experiments prove evolution and is the spontaneous generation of life from dead matter a remote possibility, as evolutionists claim? Students in college classes today may be taught that experiments in the laboratory have "created life" from non-life and that this is proof of evolution. Such assertions usually come from nonscience teachers. Had this ever occurred, the news would be so momentous, the whole world would know it in a few hours. The truth is that life will never be created from non-life in the laboratory because such a feat is impossible, as we will seek to show.

What these teachers have misinterpreted are origin of life experiments designed to show how evolution might occur. But they show nothing of the kind; indeed, an examination of the scientific literature in the field shows how controversial this area is. First, we have no idea what the early environment of the earth was like and we will never be able to determine it, let alone reproduce it. Scientifically, this ends all discussion.

Second, whatever the composition of the alleged earliest oceans, primitive life could not have evolved. It would have been destroyed since all organic material would degrade spontaneously with time in accordance with the second law of thermodynamics.

Third, for life to evolve, oxygen had to be absent. But if it were absent, the ozone layer would also be absent and the ultraviolet radiation from the sun would have destroyed any life supposedly originating in the oceans.

Fourth, laboratory experiments have only been able to generate simple chemical building blocks, not the vastly more complex information carrying sequences necessary to life.

Fifth, the design inherent in these experiments is hardly based upon spontaneous processes. In other words, there is intelligent use of materials with the intention of obtaining desired results. But this is not consistent with the chance conditions that must have been present when life would have first evolved. The use of extremely complex instruments, laboratories, and billions of man hours only shows there is no chance of life evolving on its own spontaneously from dead matter. If intelligence is necessary to generate the results of these experiments, it must also be necessary to generate something far greater—life itself.

The Miller Experiment

In order to examine the claim that origin of life experiments have "proved" that life could evolve from non-life, we need to go back to the original experiments of Stanley Miller, published in *Science* magazine in 1953. It is hard to overestimate the impact of the simple experiment performed by Dr. Miller. Miller placed methane, ammonia, and hydrogen in a glass container with boiling water. He then zapped it with a spark-discharge device to simulate the lightning that would strike the early earth's atmosphere (supposedly containing these elements). In a few days, amino acids were formed, the building blocks of proteins, part of the basic stuff of life. Presumably these lightning-induced compounds would subsequently evolve upward in the primitive oceans.

The reaction to this single experiment was worldwide. It seemed to illustrate how the scientific world grasps at materialistic straws in order to avoid theistic considerations.

> The response to Miller's experiment within both the scientific community and the general public was extraordinary. For example, Carl Sagan, an astronomer and leader in the search for extraterrestrial life, called Miller's experiment "the single most significant step in convincing many scientists that life is likely to be abundant in the cosmos." Chemist William Day described it as "An experiment that broke the logjam" to show that the first step in the origin of life was not a chance event, but one that had been inevitable. Astronomer Harlow Shapley told a television audience in Chicago in 1959, on the eve of the Darwin Centennial Celebration, that the Miller experiment "assures us of what we had suspected for a long time: that one can bridge the gap between the inanimate and the animate and that the appearance of life is essentially an automatic biochemical development that comes

along naturally when physical conditions are right." In fact, it may be said that Miller's experiments spawned a neovitalism, or belief in the power of self-organization inherent in matter. Biochemical predestination even became a subject for textbooks and [diagrammatic] evolutionary sequences [of life originating from non-life] . . . were generally taken for granted.[1]

But forty years later Miller himself was quoted in *Scientific American* as stating, "The problem of the origin of life has turned out to be much more difficult than I, or most other people, envisioned."[2] One problem is the general consensus that the earth's early atmosphere did not contain methane, ammonia, or hydrogen in significant amounts (also called a reducing atmosphere).

As the late Dr. Wilder-Smith pointed out, the original Miller experiment that is so often stated as evidence that life could arise spontaneously does no such thing. He shows why any polypeptides that would be built up from amino acid molecules would actually be broken down by excess water in the ocean— and therefore that the ocean is the *least* likely place that life could originate. Further, he discusses the fact that the preference for the philosophy of naturalism or materialism is the real reason abiogenesis is accepted, not the scientific data:

> Could biogenesis have occurred spontaneously from amino acids and polypeptides according to the above-mentioned equations [based on the Miller experiments]? Biology text books state nearly unanimously that this is the case. But even a superficial chemical examination of the equations provides a definitive negative reply to this question. How is this possible, when text books practically unanimously teach the contrary? . . . in reactions of this type, synthesis of polypeptides from amino acids does not take place in the presence of excess water. . . . Any amounts of polypeptide which might be formed will be broken down into their initial components (amino acids) by the excess water. *The ocean is thus practically the last place on this or any other planet where the proteins of life could be formed spontaneously from amino acids.* Yet nearly all text books of biology teach this nonsense to support evolutionary theory and spontaneous biogenesis. It requires a very great unfamiliarity with organic chemistry not to take into consideration the above-mentioned facts when proposing postulates for biogenesis . . . or has materialistic neo-Darwinian philosophy overwhelmed us to such an extent that we

forget or overlook the well known facts of science and of chemistry in order to support this philosophy?[3]

He further argues, "Some of these amino acids can, under certain circumstances, be formed in the primeval atmosphere through chance lightning ... But to state, as many experts do, that these amino acids which are formed by chance can be used to build living protoplasm is certainly grossly erroneous in principle, for they are for such purposes, in fact, entirely useless. Without exception all Miller's amino acids are completely unsuitable for any type of spontaneous biogenesis. *And the same applies to all and any randomly formed substances and amino acids which form racemates.* This statement is categorical and absolute and cannot be affected by special conditions."[4]

Chirality

Wilder-Smith proceeds to discuss racemates and the natural phenomenon called chirality, the fact that otherwise chemically identical molecules possess mirror-image structures. (This means that these two mirror-image molecules differ only in their spacial structure, not in chemical analysis.) Chirality is a complete disproof of chance evolution, as Wilder-Smith and other non-evolutionary scientists have pointed out.[5] In order to have the building blocks of life necessary to abiogenesis, the amino acids "must exhibit the correct chirality." In other words, for life to evolve, literally all building blocks—that is the amino acids of living protoplasm—must be of the "L" or levorotatory form. If even a very small amount of amino acid molecules are of the "D" type (or dextrorotatory form), then different proteins are formed that are unsuitable for life's metabolism. In fact, they are often fatal to life.[6] The dilemma is that all the building blocks of life formed by chance are racemates only—half "L" and half "D" forms. This makes them entirely useless for the evolving of life. *"Lightning and chance can, on principle, never produce only pure laevorotatory forms; they produce race-mates only—exactly 50% d-and exactly 50% l-forms—and are therefore unsuitable for life's proteins."*[7]

Present-day science knows absolutely no means by which pure "L" or pure "D" forms can be formed through inorganic random processes. This explains why chance alone can never, absolutely never, produce something like a living cell. Thus, two generations of experiments have only proven the obvious, that laboratory experiments only produce racemates:

> ... It is scientifically erroneous to state that Miller's experiments have made possible the synthesis of life by natural processes (organic chemistry) and chance. Here we are dealing with a misleading half-truth, for Miller, as well as his colleagues after him, only produce racemates which are just as useless for biogenesis as no amino acids at all. . . . For more than 80 years, reputable scientists have attempted in vain to produce optically pure amino acids by random inorganic methods without involving life or other previous present optically active centers in any way. If someone could make progress in this problem, which is fundamental to solving the mystery of biogenesis, he would probably become an immediate candidate for a Nobel prize! For herein lies a major obstacle blocking the scientific credibility of present-day materialistic theories concerning biogenesis. Probably for this reason modern text books often do not even mention this major difficulty of chirality.[8]

In conclusion, "Miller's experiments have little in common with real biogenesis, although text books describe the experiments as if they provided the last link in the chain of evidence for chance biogenesis. To claim that Miller has provided the first step for spontaneous biogenesis involves a willful misleading of the uninformed general public in the interests of biased materialistic philosophy. The facts are purposely concealed in order to render plausible a materialistic philosophy of life."[9]

Worse Problems Today

Today, a generation after the Miller experiments, scientists have far more serious problems to deal with. George Javor is correct in stating that "there is a crisis in the field of chemical evolution. The best efforts of brilliant scientists over the past 40 years have stalled in logical deadends."[10]

One problem concerns the complete lack of evidence for any prebiotic compounds that would allow evolution to occur. If these did exist, they most certainly would be found in great quantities in oceanic sediments. But they are nowhere to be seen.

The first stage on the road to life is presumed to have been the buildup, by purely chemical synthetic processes occurring on the surface of the early Earth, of all the basic organic compounds necessary for the formation of a living cell. These are *supposed* to have accumulated in the primeval oceans, creating a nutrient broth, the so-called "prebiotic soup." In certain specialized environments, these organic compounds were assembled into large macromolecules, proteins and nucleic acids. Eventually, over millions of years, combinations of these macromolecules occurred which were endowed with the property of self-reproduction. Then driven by natural selection ever more efficient and complex self-reproducing molecular systems evolved until finally the first simple cell system emerged.

The existence of a prebiotic soup is crucial to the whole scheme. Without an abiotic accumulation of the building blocks of the cell no life could ever evolve. *If the traditional story* is true, therefore, there must have existed for millions of years a rich mixture of organic compounds in the ancient oceans and some of this material would very likely have been trapped in the sedimentary rocks lain down in the seas of those remote times.

Yet rocks of great antiquity have been examined over the past two decades and in *none of them* has any trace of a biotically produced compound been found. Most notable of these rocks are the "dawn rocks" of western Greenland, the earliest dated rocks on Earth, considered to be approaching 3,900 million years old. . . . *As on so many occasions, paleontology has again failed to substantiate evolutionary presumptions.* Considering the way the prebiotic soup is referred to in so many discussions of the origin of life as an already established reality, it comes as something of a shock to realize that *there is absolutely no positive evidence for its existence.*[11]

Another problem concerns the presence of oxygen in the early atmosphere. Scientists agree this would prohibit evolution because it is thermodynamically impossible that reduced chemical compounds (the building blocks of molecules found in living things) could have arisen in the presence of oxygen.

Scientists have no choice but to continue to maintain that the earth's atmosphere was free of oxygen. Thus, in *Voices for Evolution*, the National Academy of Sciences declares the following in an official statement: "We can, therefore, explain how the early *oxygen-free* earth provided a hospitable site for the accumulation of molecules suitable for the construction of living systems."[12]

Again, biochemists generally agree that the presence of oxygen would, in the words of R. T. Brinkmann of the California Institute of Technology, "preclude biological evolution as presently understood."[13] Yet all the evidence tells us oxygen did exist. The evidence for an early oxidized atmosphere is increasingly so compelling that Henderson-Sellers, Benlow, and Meadows concede that, despite the far-reaching implications, it is "becoming the new orthodoxy."[14]

Biochemical Bias and Chemical Neo-Darwinism

As we will see later, many of those who have studied the probability that life could arise purely by chance recognize that the obstacles are insurmountable. Therefore, they have proposed different ways to circumvent this problem, including biochemical bias and chemical neo-Darwinism. It is true that some molecules are "biochemically biased"—they do have an attraction for others. However, this bias could only overcome chance arrangements if the attraction were great. In some cases this is also true, however, "there are no molecular preferences that are known to produce information like that found in biological DNA and protein."[15]

All that the argument from biochemical bias can reveal is that certain chemicals do have an attraction for one another—*not* how they can order themselves into sequences carrying information. In essence, the small biases that exist can never account for the incredible encyclopedic knowledge stored in the DNA molecule. In fact, if the "letters" of DNA (A, G, C, and T) and amino acids showed strong preferences, then all DNA and protein would have to be the same, which simply isn't true. Further, can anyone explain where this supposed "evolutionary urge" of molecules to become more complex and to code information came from? If it originated in the molecules themselves, where did they get the urge and why have the elements themselves not evolved?

The noted French biochemist and Nobel Prize winner Jacques Monod is correct when he writes that chance alone (not chance plus some teleological evolutionary urge) must be at the edifice of evolution:

> We call these events [mutations] accidental; we say that they are random occurrences. And since they constitute the *only possible source* of modifications in the genetic text, itself the sole repository of the organism's hereditary structures, it necessarily follows that *chance alone* is at the source of *every* innovation, of all creation in the biosphere. Pure chance, absolutely free but blind, at the very root of the stupendous edifice of evolution: this central concept of modern biology is no longer one among other possible or even conceivable hypotheses. *It is today the sole conceivable hypothesis, the only one that squares with observed and tested fact.* And nothing warrants the supposition—or the hope—that on this score our position is likely ever to be revised.[16]

It has been argued that biochemical bias merely explains the building up of biochemicals but that subsequently, mutations and natural selection account for the development of information and more complex organization. The problem is that natural selection, even if it functioned in the manner evolutionists claim, could only hold true when self-reproduction exists. The improved characteristics that natural selection allegedly chooses must be transmitted to the next generation for improvement or evolution. Without reproduction, no improvements can be selected and passed on. Thus, natural selection can't operate on non-reproducing systems. As the leading evolutionist Dobzhansky comments, "Prebiological natural selection is a contradiction of terms."[17]

Evolutionary Origin Impossible

In his monograph on origin of life experiments, Dr. Duane Gish, who holds a Ph.D. in biochemistry from U.C. Berkeley, concluded by noting that an evolutionary origin of life "is impossible."[18] We agree—it is absolutely impossible that life could have originated by chance according to evolutionary theory.

Scientists themselves are perplexed or confused. In their article, "Information and the Origin of Life," Walter L. Bradley and Charles B. Thaxton, authors of *The Mystery of Life's Origin: Reassessing Current Theories*, refer to "Klaus Dose of the

Institute for Biochemistry in Mainz, Germany who asserts that the collective efforts over the past 40 years of scientists have 'lead to a better perception of the immensity of the problem of the origin of life on Earth rather than to its solution. At present all discussions on principal theories and experiments in the field either end in stalemate or in a *confusion of ignorance.*'"[19]

This includes recent approaches by scientists at the Santa Fe Institute of the kind described below. One false argument is that probability calculations against the origin of life are not as convincing as first thought:

> These calculations are supposed to overwhelm our capacity to believe that life could arise spontaneously. But is life really so improbable? Investigations into complexity theory by Stuart Kauffman and other scientists at the Santa Fe Institute indicate otherwise: that spontaneous order may be part and parcel of the universe. . . . [These scientists] argue that life is practically the inevitable result of the laws of physics and chemistry. According to Stuart Kauffman, life bootstrapped itself into existence through autocatalytic sets of chemicals that were in the primordial soup. Kauffman postulates that if a chemical soup has enough different types of compounds, they will begin to act in metabolic ways and be able to reproduce and evolve.[20]

This is more bluff. These scientists won't deal with the real problems involved in abiogenesis because, believing so strongly in evolution, they are incapacitated when it comes to thinking clearly and accepting where the data lead them. Thus, they may indeed devise increasingly complex and, to them, "plausible" scenarios that, in their own minds, justify their faith in evolution. But theorizing of this nature will change nothing, even if it continues to be put forth for hundreds of years with increasingly abstruse form and sophistication. Kauffman's work, and the work of scientists along similar lines, has yet to be validated—and no one should hold their breath that it will be. As we will see later, theories of the self-organization of matter are nonsense of the highest order.

Doomed to Failure

As science discovers more and more of the incredible complexity of life, matters can only deteriorate for an evolutionary explanation of life. "[Robert] Shapiro argues strongly that all current theories are bankrupt and that we need to find a new and more fruitful paradigm to guide our search for a naturalistic explanation for the origin of life."[21] Shapiro is correct—all current theories are indeed bankrupt. But there will be no more fruitful naturalistic paradigm forthcoming to explain life. Why? Everything that science has investigated to date clearly forces us to conclude that the only rational explanation for the origin of life is an infinite God. In other words, life never evolved naturalistically in the first place. This means that the search for *materialistic* explanations is always doomed to failure; all future theories proposed will meet the fate of all past theories. If science is not careful and does not return to rationality and theism, it may by default even be forced into the serpentine labyrinths of occult philosophy in its search for answers to origins.

Regardless, consider that the most brilliant engineers, other scientists, and technologists, who have used the most up-to-date equipment, are unable to create a computer as complex as even a simple amoeba, a single-celled animal. So how believable is it for scientists to almost universally claim that chance—the complete opposite of intelligence—could not only create an amoeba but endless things infinitely more complex—all the varied life forms we see about us, including humanity? Indeed, a fertilized human egg itself, merely the size of a pinhole, has enough information to fill a thousand books, each 500 pages thick, having print so small you would need a microscope to read it. And if we were able to print in books all the DNA information in the entire human body, it has been estimated that they would fill the Grand Canyon 50 times![22]

And it's not just that insurmountable problems are encountered for evolution at the level of the origin of life—they are encountered at virtually *every* level of evolutionary speculation. For example, at the beginning of their important analysis, John W. Oller, Jr. and John L. Omdahl, both first rank scientists in the field of general linguistics and physiology/biophysics respectively, comment that, "The problem of the origin of the human language capacity is not unlike the problem of the origin of life itself."[23] In other words, it is just as impossible, on naturalistic grounds, to account for something so "simple" as the human language capacity as it is to account for the origin of life.

The Genesis account of creation remains—and will always remain—the most credible and logical account of the origin of man, the earth, and the universe. It is more than significant that every theory proposed to date, every attempt to ignore the book of Genesis, has met with failure or encountered serious conflict with established principles of science.

Origin of life experiments cannot explain how life arose— no experiments can. A generation of recent experiments has forced the conclusion that only God can explain the origin of life. But again, committed materialists won't listen to theistic proposals. It only seems fitting then, as theists, for us to illustrate how irrational their commitment to scientific naturalism is. To do this we will use the science of probability to evaluate the odds that life could arise spontaneously from non-life.

The Probability of Life

The laws of probability govern all kinds of daily activities from calculating insurance rates to large purchase orders. The science of probability is one of the most trustworthy disciplines there is. And it has a logical bearing on the issue of origins: "The laws of probability are proven trustworthy. The whole of science and every day practical living is based on the reliability of the probable happening and the improbable not. One need do no more than be consistent with this accepted standard of reality when considering what to believe in relation to the origin of life."[24]

When one reads through the literature on evolution that discusses the probability of the evolution of life, one finds all sorts of euphemisms for the word impossible including "terribly low," "not conceivable," "infinitesimally small," "highly implausible," and "unimaginably small."

It would appear that these terms are used because there is no other choice. To really believe in what is impossible is absurd. Evolutionary scientists do not want to be seen as believers of the absurd.

We have no qualms about using the word "impossible" if it fits. And when considering evolution, no other word is even adequate.

We elsewhere cite George Wald who had concluded that the spontaneous generation of a living organism was impossible. He went on to say that, even so, he chose to believe that spontaneous generation occurred because after all, here we are. As we saw, time was the hero of the plot.

In many ways, time *is* the hero of the plot for the evolutionist. It's even a "deity" of sorts. The evolutionist says that time created life whereas the theist says that God created life. Again, the problem is that time cannot produce miracles. Contrary to Dr. Wald's assertion, time cannot make the impossible inevitable. Even infinite time cannot change an apple into a helicopter or a frog into a prince. To think so is to believe either in absurdities or fairy tales.

Creation Evidence

Further, the fact that we exist doesn't prove evolution occurred, unless one assumes that life *only* originates by evolution. At this point, many evolutionists criticize creation scientists for making the same kinds of assumptions they make. Creationists argue that the fact of the impossibility of evolution indicates the extremely high probability of creation. Evolutionists argue that the fact of life proves the probability of evolution.

But is evolution really so probable? Is it even *possible*?

Remember what we have to do to evolve life. We only have chance and dead matter or lifeless chemicals to start the process. These must make the leap to a small prebiotic molecule (e.g., an amino acid, sugar, nucleic acid base). This molecule must then make an incredible leap to a larger molecule (e.g., a polymer of amino acids). Then there is an even greater leap to the first primitive cell and then the unheard of leap to the first form of complex life such as an eucaryote cell having an organized nucleus bound by a membrane. Then evolution has to produce every living thing.

Bird points out that for the evolution of life, "Such small probabilities are treated as impossibility under statistical rules, in the context of the possible number of events in the entire universe during its entire age."[25]

Even some evolutionists will admit the impossibility of evolution. For example, Ambrose of the University of London writes concerning the emergence of new species, "the probability is so small in terms of the known age of the universe that it is effectively zero."[26]

Creationists and non-evolutionists who have studied probability considerations have long argued, that for all practical purposes, they show evolution to be impossible. What evolutionists don't want to admit is that, even when you adjust for their criticisms of probability calculations, the effect is still to make evolution an impossibility.[27] Let's consider some examples of scientists and researchers who have stated this.

According to Walter James ReMine in his definitive anti-evolutionary text, *The Biotic Message*, "The origin of life by chance in a primeval soup is impossible in probability in the same way that a perpetual motion machine is impossible in probability. . . . A practical person must conclude that life didn't happen by chance."[28]

In "Was Evolution Really Possible?" Moshe Trop, Ph.D., with the Department of Life Sciences, Bar-Ilan University, Ramat Gan, Israel, concludes his discussion by noting that "All calculations made of the probability [that life could evolve by chance, lead to the conclusion that] there could have been *no possibility* of the random appearance of life. . . ."[29]

Probability Calculations

In his article, "The Queen of Science Examines the King of Fools," David J. Rodabaugh, Ph.D., Associate Professor of Mathematics at the University of Missouri, shows that given the amount of time evolutionists claim is necessary, the probability that a simple living organism could be produced by mutations "is so small as to constitute *a scientific impossibility*"—the chance that it could have happened "anywhere in the universe . . . is less than 1 [chance] in $10^{2,999,942}$."[30] A figure like this is termed exponential notation, and is the figure one with almost three million zeros after it. Figures like this are terminal to evolution. (We discuss exponential notation shortly.)

In another article, Dr. Rodabaugh takes the argument to absurd levels to show that "It *is impossible* that evolution occurred." Even giving evolution every conceivable chance and even "assuming that evolution *is* 99.9999% *certain*, then 'evolution [still] has only a 1 in 10^{132} chance of being valid. . . . Therefore, even with the beginning assumption that evolution is *a virtual certainty*, a conditional probability analysis of the fossil record [alone] results in the conclusion that evolution is a demonstrable absurdity.'"[31]

According to the French expert on probability, Emile Borel, his "single law of chance" (1 chance in 10^{50}) beyond which things *never* occur, "carries with it a certainty of another nature than mathematical certainty . . . it is comparable even to the certainty with which we attribute to the existence of the external world."[32] Here we see that even the above one chance in 10^{132} is *no* chance.

Using probability and other calculations, James F. Coppedge, author of *Evolution: Possible or Impossible?*, concludes concerning the origin of left-handed amino acids (the phenomenon of chirality discussed earlier) that, "No natural explanation is in sight which can adequately explain the mystery that proteins use only left-handed components. There is little hope that it will be solved in this way in the future. Even if such a result occurred by chance, life would still not exist. The proteins would be helpless and nonliving without the entire complicated DNA-RNA system to make copies for the future."[33] Indeed, "The odds against the necessary group of proteins being all left-handed 'is beyond all comprehension.'"[34]

As the reader can see, when we apply probability calculations relative to the origin of life, we end up with very large numbers, unimaginably large numbers. And in part, that's the problem. These numbers are so incomprehensible they almost become meaningless. Nevertheless, if evolutionists can use an incomprehensible billions of years of earth history to make evolution *seem* feasible, we can also use incomprehensible numbers to show the absurdity of evolution, even if these numbers do tend to bend the mind at dizzying speeds.

Comprehending Large Numbers

To help the reader understand large numbers, we have prepared a chart of illustrations. Again, these very large numbers are written using exponential notation. Thus, for ease of writing, rather than write out all the zeros in a large number, the number of zeros is placed above the number 10. For example, the figure one million, having six zeros, is written exponentially as 10^6; one billion, with nine zeros, is 10^9; one trillion, with twelve zeros, is 10^{12}, and so on. The kinds of numbers we are dealing with involve hundreds to billions of zeros, depending on what we are trying to calculate and the odds assigned to a given event. (In the calculations below, the odds cited are often skewed vastly in *favor* of evolution. This shows, that even given much better odds than were present, evolution is still impossible.)

To begin, let's show what 10^{50} looks like written out: 100,000,000,000,000,000,000,000,000,000,000,000,000,000, 000,000,000. It would require hundreds of millions of years just to count a number this large.

If we say an event has one chance in 10^{50} of occurring, this is what we refer to. Again, this figure represents Borel's "single law of chance," the odds beyond which things *never* occur. One chance in 10^{50} is an unimaginably small number—it's one chance in 100 trillion, trillion, trillion, trillion. One chance in a billion is an almost infinitely greater chance for an event to occur. If the one billion people in China each bought one lottery ticket, each person's chance of wining would be one in 10^9—one chance in a billion. So how much money do you think an evolutionist would bet on the lottery if the odds of winning were one chance in 10^{50}?

A person would be considered foolish if they bet their entire life savings on even one chance in a thousand—1 in 10^3. The irony is that evolutionists are gambling on an issue far more vital to them than retirement money with literally *infinite* odds against them. They are gambling on the nature of ultimate reality, the odds that materialism is true and theism false. If probability calculations and other considerations relative to prophecy prove Christian theism true[35]—and heaven or hell hang in the balance—one might assume people would be very cautious about the risks they take. Apparently not.

In the chart below, we can see how big exponential numbers truly are. We ask the reader to look over this chart. Ponder its comparisons in order to get a "feel" for the kinds of numbers we are dealing with. Only this will help us realize the kinds of odds against evolution that we are discussing.

Comparison of Exponential Numbers

Comparisons of Time

Seconds in one year = 31.6 million.

Seconds in 15 billion years = 10^{18}.

A picosecond is one-*trillionth* of a second. In 15 *billion* years, there are 10^{30} picoseconds.

Comparisons of Weight

A whale weighs 2,000 tons or 6.4×10^6 ounces.

The earth weighs 5,882,000,000,000,000,000,000 tons or 10^{26} ounces, or 10^{27} grams (one gram is $1/450$ of a pound).

Our Milky Way Galaxy weighs 3×10^{44} grams.

Comparisons of Distance

The distance to the nearest star is 4.3 light years or 40 trillion kilometers or 10^{22} (4×10^{21}) microns (a micron is $1/25,000$ of an inch).

Comparisons of Size

The circumference of the earth is 26,000 miles or 1.6×10^9 inches.

The number of inches across the "known" universe—an estimated 30 billion light years or 192,000,000,000, 000,000 miles—is 10^{27} inches.

The number of grains of sand that would fill one beach is trillions and trillions. Yet 10^{100} grains of sand would fill the *entire universe*.

Comparisons of Measure

Atoms are incredibly small.

One million hydrogen atoms can be lined up, one on top of the other, on the thickness of a single piece of paper. 3,000 *trillion* of them are needed just to cover the period at the end of this sentence. A measly $1/4$ teaspoon of water has 10^{24} molecules, but the estimated number of atoms in the entire universe is "only" 10^{79}.

The total number of electrons and protons in the universe is 10^{80}.

The total number of smallest particles that would fill the universe is 10^{120}.

It takes 2.5×10^{15} electrons, laid side by side, to make one inch. Counting all these electrons at one per second would require 76 million years.

The above chart gives us an indication of really big numbers.

In the material that follows, we are going to discuss the odds of two very "simple" things evolving: 1) a complex molecule and 2) a cell. Remember that thousands and millions of these are needed for more complex life to evolve, even for the simpler forms of life. To begin, consider the following information about molecules:

A single drop of blood has 35,000,000 red blood cells.

A single red blood cell has 280,000,000 hemoglobin molecules, each molecule having 10,000 atoms.

A single human has 27,000,000,000,000 (27×10^{12}) red blood cells.

Again, molecules are so small that $^{1}/_{4}$ teaspoon of water has 10^{24} of them. Molecules vary from the simple to the complex. A simple molecule may consist of only a few bonded atoms, as in water (two atoms hydrogen; one atom oxygen). A complex molecule of protein may have hundreds of amino acids.

The Odds of a Complex Molecule

Noted astronomer Fred Hoyle uses the Rubik cube to illustrate the odds of getting a single molecule, in this case a biopolymer. Biopolymers are biological polymers, i.e., large molecules such as nucleic acids or proteins. In the fascinating illustration below, he calls the idea that chance could originate a biopolymer "nonsense of a high order":

At all events, anyone with even a nodding acquaintance with the Rubik cube will concede the near-impossibility of a solution being obtained by a blind person moving the cubic faces at random. Now imagine 10^{50} blind persons each with a scrambled Rubik cube, and try to conceive of the chance of them all simultaneously arriving at the solved form. You then have the chance of arriving by random shuffling at just *one* of the many biopolymers on which life depends. The notion that not only biopolymers but the operating programme of a living cell could be arrived at by chance in a primordial organic soup here on the Earth is evidently nonsense of a high order.[36]

DeNouy provides another illustration for arriving at a single molecule of high dissymmetry through chance action and normal thermic agitation. He assumes 500 trillion shakings per second plus a liquid material volume equal to the size of the earth. For *one* molecule it would require "10^{243} billions of years." Even if this molecule did somehow arise by chance, it is still only one single molecule. Millions are needed, requiring compound probability calculations for each successive molecule. His logical conclusion is that "it is totally impossible to account scientifically for all phenomena pertaining to life."[37]

Even 40 years ago, scientist Harold F. Blum, writing in *Time's Arrow and Evolution*, wrote that, "The spontaneous formation of a polypeptide of the size of the smallest known proteins seems beyond all probability."[38]

Noted creation scientists Walter L. Bradley and Charles Thaxton, authors of *The Mystery of Life's Origin: Reassessing Current Theories*, point out that the probability of assembling amino acid building blocks into a functional protein is approximately one chance in 4.9×10^{191}.[39] "Such improbabilities have led *essentially all scientists* who work in the field to reject random, accidental assembly or fortuitous good luck as an explanation for how life began."[40] Now, if a figure as "small" as 5 chances in 10^{191} is referenced by such a statement, then what are we to make of the kinds of probabilities below that are infinitely smaller? The mind simply boggles at the wonderful faith of the materialist.

According to Coppedge, the probability of evolving a single protein molecule over 5 billion years is estimated at 1 chance in 10^{161}. This even allows some 14 concessions to help it along which would not actually be present during evolution.[41] Again, this is *no* chance.

Cells and Bacteria

Consider that the smallest *theoretical* cell is made up of 239 proteins. Further, at least 124 different types of proteins are needed for the cell to become a living thing. But the simplest *known* self-reproducing organism is the H^{39} strain of PPLO (mycoplasma) containing 625 proteins with an average of 400 amino acids in each protein.

Yet the probability of the occurrence of the smallest *theoretical* life is only one chance in $10^{119,879}$ and the years required for it to evolve would be $10^{119,841}$ years or $10^{119,831}$ times the assumed age of the earth![42]

The probability of this smallest theoretical cell of 239 proteins evolving without the needed 124 different types of proteins to make up a living cell, i.e., the chance of evolving this "helpless group of *non-living* molecules" in over 500 billion years is one chance in $10^{119,701}$.[43] Dr. David J. Rodabaugh, Associate Professor of Mathematics at the University of Missouri, estimated the more realistic chance that life would spontaneously generate (even on 10^{23} planets) as only one chance in $10^{2,999,940}$.[44]

Even if we are talking about giving evolution every conceivable chance to evolve a single protein molecule or the smallest theoretical cell, the odds are still impossible.[45]

In the 1970s Sir Frederick Hoyle calculated the mathematical probability that a single bacterium could be spontaneously generated was 1 in $10^{40,000}$.

Hoyle confessed what most scientists are, strangely, unwilling to confess, "The likelihood of the formation of life from inanimate matter is one to a number with 40 thousand naughts [zeros after it]. *It is enough to bury Darwin and the whole theory of evolution.* There was no primeval soup, neither on this planet or on any other, and if the beginnings of life were not random they must therefore have been the product of purposeful intelligence."[46]

But a far more realistic "probability" for a single bacterium was given by Harold Morowitz, a Yale University physicist. He calculated that the odds of a single bacterium emerging from the basic building blocks necessary were 1 chance in $10^{100,000,000,000}$.[47]

This number is so large it would require a library of approximately 100,000 books like this just to write it out! Ponder that!

In his book *Origins—A Skeptic's Guide to the Creation of Life on Earth*, Robert Shapiro comments concerning the probabilities calculated by Morowitz, "The improbability involved in generating even one bacterium is so large that it reduces all considerations of time and space to nothingness. Given such odds, the time until the black holes evaporate and the space to the ends of the universe would make no difference at all. If we were to wait, we would truly be waiting for a miracle."[48]

Winning the Lottery, Googols, and Factorials

Again, these numbers are unimaginable. That's why even scientists don't know what to do with them. Consider that a given individual's chance of winning the state lottery is about one in ten million. The odds of winning each successive week involve the multiplication of probabilities so that the odds of winning the lottery every single week of your life from the age of 18 to 99, a period of 80 years, is 1 chance in $4.6 \times 10^{29,120}$. In other words, it is infinitely more likely that you would win the lottery every week of your life consecutively, from the day you were born, without missing even one winning weekly ticket, for 80 years, than it is that we would have the spontaneous generation of a simple bacterium.[49]

Physicist Dr. Howard B. Holroyd refers to the book *Mathematics and the Imagination*, where the authors, Kasner and Newman, name the extremely large number 10^{100}, a "googol." Noting the fact that there could have been, at most, 4.8×10^{38} possible mutations in all the life forms throughout the history of earth, Dr. Holroyd writes, "It is not possible in a googol of operations to select at random, from the possible infinity of forms, the shapes and arrangements of the dextral and sinistral bones of even one mammal. . . . Let us recognize that if a result depends upon a hundred factors, and if the probability of getting each one right is 1 in 10, then the probability of getting the whole 100 right is only one in a googol."[50]

Dr. Holroyd also discusses factorial numbers. A factorial is a number that multiplies each successive number by the next number. So ten factorial would be to multiply $1 \times 2 \times 3 \times 4 \times 5 \times 6 \times 7 \times 8 \times 9 \times 10$. Seventy factorial is around a googol ($1.198 \times$

10^{100}). Sir Arthur Eddington estimated the total number of electrons and protons in the entire universe as approximately 3.145×10^{79}. This is infinitely less than 100 factorial, which equals 9.3×10^{157}. But when it comes to evolution, we are not dealing with 100 factorial but millions times millions factorial. To illustrate, there are 5,000 fibers in the auditory nerve of man that may be connected to the brain in 5,000-factorial ways—and probably only one is correct. The optic nerve has about one million fibers, and these may be connected to the brain in one million factorial ways. The odds they could have been connected correctly by chance cannot even be written out longhand. Holroyd proceeds to show by several other examples how absurd belief in chance evolution is. He points out that the straight hydrocarbon chain $C_{40}H_{82}$ has about 6.25×10^{13} isomers. It would be impossible for the entire human race, working full time for four billion years, just to study all the isomers of this single organic molecule of no great size.[51] (Yet it just happened to evolve by chance!) When we consider there are ten billion cells in the cerebral cortex, and that there are several trillion nerve connections between cells in the brain, it becomes "preposterous beyond words" to believe that all this originated by chance:

> Surely the probability of the whole body is far less than that of any of the internal organs: that of two eyes to send two images over two cables of 1,000,000 conductors each to form one image is less than that of one eye; and surely that of one eye is much less than merely taking the bones of the skeleton and placing them into their proper positions. [—which he calculates as 1 chance in approximately 5.6×10^{388}.][52]

Endless Miracles

The whole point is that the existence of mankind—or of living things generally—isn't just one miracle, it is a succession of endless miracles. Every beneficial combination of factors to produce the simplest mechanism for evolution to occur would require more miracles.

All this and more is why, in the minds of critics, evolution can rationally be classified as one of the "worst superstitions of all time."[53] And it explains why Dr. Holroyd is correct in concluding that evolution is not just physical and mathematical nonsense, "it is logical nonsense as well, for a sound thinker does not assume anything which must be deduced from his theory."[54]

So perhaps now we have some idea of the odds against evolution. Neither words nor figures can adequately convey these odds. But two final illustrations may help.

Texas Silver Dollars

On a cross-country drive, John Weldon recently drove through the great state of Texas and was reminded of an illustration by Professor Don Stoner we used in our book on messianic prophecy.[55] In that book we showed that the odds by chance alone, Jesus would fulfill only eight Old Testament prophecies, was 1 in 10^{17}. To illustrate this, imagine filling the entire state of Texas two feet deep with silver dollars, marking one with an "X," then stirring up all the dollars. Then, blindfold, say, an evolutionist, have him drive anywhere he wished in the state of Texas, then reach down into the silver dollars and pick one out. The odds that he would find the one marked silver dollar are 1 in 10^{17}, or one in one hundred quadrillion, or one in 100 million billion. Now, anyone who has driven through Texas knows how long it takes. If you imagine that as you drive, *everywhere you look*, the land is covered with silver dollars two feet deep, the mind boggles—and yet your field of vision from the road is only an infinitesimal part of Texas.

Yet this number, one chance in 10^{17}, is nothing compared to one chance in $10^{1,000}$, the chance distinguished *evolutionists* give for the formation of a simple precursor to life. Trying to comprehend one chance in $10^{100,000,000,000}$, the chance development of a simple bacterium, would nearly drive one insane. In telling us to believe that such odds are not only conceivable but probable, well-meaning evolutionists would drive us all mad.

Electrons and Gigantic Balls

Consider a final illustration, again of a number infinitely smaller than $10^{1,000}$.

How large is the number one in 10^{157}? 10^{157} contains 157 zeros. Let us try to illustrate the size of this number.

Electrons are incredibly small objects, much smaller than atoms. It would take 2.5 times 10^{15} of them, laid side by side, just to make one inch. Even if we counted four electrons every second and counted day and night, it would still take us 19 million years just to count a line of electrons one-inch long.

But how many electrons are we dealing with in 10^{157} electrons? Imagine building a solid ball of electrons that would extend in all directions from the earth a length of 6 billion light years. The distance in miles of just *one* light year is 6.4 trillion miles. That would be an incredibly big ball! But not big enough to measure 10^{157} electrons.

In order to do that, you must take that big ball of electrons reaching the length of 6 billion light years long in all directions and multiply it by 6×10^{28}! How big is that? It's the length of the space required to store trillions and trillions and trillions of the same gigantic balls and more. In fact, the space required to store all of these balls combined together would just start to "scratch the surface" of the number of electrons we would need to really accurately speak about 10^{157}.

But assuming you have some idea of the number of electrons we are talking about, now imagine marking just one of those electrons in that huge number. Stir them all up. Then appoint an evolutionist to travel in a rocket for as long as he wants, anywhere he wants to go in a 30 billion light year diameter. Tell him to stop and segment a part of space, then take a high-powered microscope and find that one marked electron in that segment. What do you think would be his chances for success? It would be one in 10^{157}.

Again, how small is one chance in 10^{157}? The number 10^{157} can be further illustrated this way. We earlier saw that the number of atoms in the universe was estimated at 10^{78}. You could take these 10^{78} atoms and expand *each one* to the size of our own universe, with each universe having 10^{78} atoms. The total number of atoms in all these 10^{78} universes would be 10^{157}.

Yet we saw that Bradley and Thaxton calculated the chance that one single protein molecule would evolve at about one chance in 10^{191}—odds trillions of times smaller than one chance in 10^{157}.

The odds of finally evolving just one man have been conservatively put at one chance in $10^{10^{12}}$ or one chance in $10^{1,000,000,000,000}$. This is a figure with a *trillion* zeros. If written out in a single line it would extend some 300,000 miles—and circle the earth 24 times. It would require a *million* books like this just to print it! Yet again, beyond one chance in 10^{50}, *no* chance remains—ever, even in all eternity, for an event to occur.

We hope the above material has given the reader at least some small comprehension of the faith of the evolutionist. It is, again, a wonderfully large faith. It is a faith so large it fills the whole universe to produce miracles without end.

12

The Molecules of Melodrama
Molecular Evolution and Its Implications

Evolutionists claim that studies in molecular biology confirm the truth of evolution. Consider two examples: An official statement of the National Academy of Sciences reads: "Very recent studies in molecular biology have independently confirmed the judgments of paleontologists and classical biologists about relationships among lineages and the order in which species appeared within lineages. They have also provided detailed information about the mechanisms of biological evolution."[1]

The National Association of Biology Teachers, also in an official statement, even declares that ". . . effective teaching of cellular and molecular biology *requires* inclusion of evolution."[2]

Darwin's Black Box

Professor Michael Behe is an associate professor of biochemistry at Lehigh University and author of *Darwin's Black Box: The Biochemical Challenge to Evolution*. He makes it clear "I am not a creationist." Although not a creationist, he closes his book with the following words, words that are inspired by the facts of science: "As we reach the end of this book, we are left with no substantive defense against what feels to be a strange conclusion: that life was designed by an intelligent agent."[3] In this chapter our purpose will be to show that if molecular evolution is impossible, evolution beyond that point can hardly be considered factual.

The back cover statement by University of Chicago biochemist Robert Shapiro, author of *Origins: A Skeptic's Guide to the Creation of Life on Earth* says the following of *Darwin's Black Box*. "Michael Behe has done a top-notch job of explaining and illuminating one of the most vexing problems in biology: the origin of the complexity that permeates all of life on this planet. Professor Behe selects an answer that falls outside of science: the original creation of life by an intelligent designer. Many scientists, myself included, will prefer to continue the search for an answer within science. Nonetheless, this book should be on the essential reading list of all those who are interested in the question of where we came from, as it presents the most thorough and clever presentation of the design argument that I have seen."

Peter van Inwagen, Professor of Philosophy at Notre Dame University says, "If Darwinians respond to this important book by ignoring it, misrepresenting it, or ridiculing it, that will be evidence in favor of the widespread suspicion that Darwinism today functions more as an ideology than as a scientific theory. If they can successfully answer Behe's arguments, that will be important evidence in favor of Darwinism." (Back cover.)

Behe's central thesis is given as follows:

> It was once expected that [explaining] the basis of life would be exceedingly simple. That expectation has been smashed. . . . the elegance and complexity of biological systems at the molecular level have paralyzed science's attempt to explain their origins. There has been virtually no attempt to account for the origin of specific, complex biomolecular systems, much less any progress. Many scientists have gamely asserted that explanations are already in hand, or will be sooner or later, but no support for such assertions can be found in the professional science literature. More importantly, there are compelling reasons—based on the structure of the systems themselves—to think that a Darwinian explanation for the mechanisms of life will forever prove illusive.[4]

In other words, Behe argues that the theory of evolution is now and forever impotent to explain the mechanics of life; these are simply far too complex to be accounted for by any naturalistic explanations.

Behe uses the term "black box" to describe a device that does something but whose inner workings are mysterious. Darwin's black box turns out to be something so "simple" as the cell in all its "astonishing complexity of subcellular organic structures."[5]

In the end, Behe argues that the death knell for Darwinism, and all forms of naturalistic evolution, is not just the cell but many other complex biological systems. It was Darwin himself who best understood his own dilemma at this point, "If it could be demonstrated that any complex organ existed which could not possibly have been formed by numerous, successive, slight modifications, my theory would absolutely break down."[6] Darwin's theory breaks down at every point, everywhere we look.

We know today that the cell is one such complicated organ— but, of course, there are innumerable others. Thus, "as the number of unexplained, irreducibly complex biological systems increases, our confidence that Darwin's criterion of failure has been met skyrockets toward the maximum that science allows."[7]

Bombardier Beetles and Blood Clotting

For example, the biochemistry involved in everything from beetles to eye chemistry to blood clotting presents unsolvable dilemmas to the evolutionist: "Both the bombardier beetle's defensive apparatus and the vertebrate eye contain so many molecular components (on the order of tens of thousands of different types of molecules) that listing them—and speculating on the mutations that might have produced them—is currently impossible."[8]

Behe's chapter on blood clotting, "Rube Goldberg in the blood" shows how incredibly complex the phenomenon of "simple" blood clotting really is. Scientists have speculated as to how blood clotting may have evolved, but their speculations have proved futile. In essence, it is impossible to explain blood clotting based on evolutionary theory:

Blood coagulation is a paradigm of the staggering complexity that underlies even apparently simple bodily processes. Faced with such complexity beneath even simple phenomena, Darwinian theory falls silent.

Like some ultimate Rube Goldberg machine, the clotting cascade is a breathtaking balancing act in which a menagerie of biochemicals—sporting various decorations and rearrangements conferred by modifying enzymes—bounce off one another at precise angles in a meticulously ordered sequence until . . . [bleeding stops].[9]

The Cilium and Bacterial Flagellum

Even something as lowly as a cilium presents gigantic problems for evolutionists. But again it is one of only an endless number of entities that do so. A cilium is a structure that beats like a whip and looks like a hair. Cells use them for movement and cleansing. A cilium basically consists of a bunch of fibers that are coated with membranes. The cilium illustrates what is true for virtually every living complex entity: *all* its component parts must be present for it to function at all! Therefore it could never have evolved piecemeal. For example, the cilium *requires* microtubules, a motor, and other things simply to perform one of its major functions, ciliary motion. Behe points out that science cannot even explain how something as simple as the cilium evolved.[10] Yet, for various reasons, the cilium is of special interest to biochemists, biophysicists, molecular biologists and physicians.[11] It has been estimated that there are probably 10,000 papers that have been published about cilia. As a result, one would expect that cilium evolution would be the subject of many papers in the scientific literature. Nevertheless, "In the past two decades, however, only two articles even attempted to suggest a model for the evolution of the cilium that takes into account real mechanical considerations. Worse, the two papers disagree with each other even about the general route such an evolution might take. Neither paper discusses crucial quantitative details, or possible problems that would quickly cause a mechanical device such as a cilium . . . to be useless. . . . The amount of scientific research that has been and is being done on the cilium leads many people to assume that even if they themselves don't know how the cilium evolved, *somebody* must know. But a search of the professional literature proves them wrong. *Nobody knows.*"[12]

Matters get more complex when we consider the "simple" bacterial flagellum, a fascinating biophysical system that has also had thousands of papers published on it. But "here again, the evolutionary literature is totally missing. Even though we are told that all biology must be seen through the lens of evolution, no scientist has *ever* published a model to account for the gradual evolution of this extraordinary molecular machine."[13]

These are only two additional examples to illustrate that evolution cannot finally explain how things evolved—*any* things—and that the more we study living things the weaker the evolutionist's case. In the above cases, what were once seen as extremely simple organisms are now shown to be extremely complex. A cilium alone has over 200 different kinds of proteins while a flagellum is more complex yet. Thus, with just these two entities, biologists and biochemists "have discovered staggering complexity, with dozens or even hundreds of precisely tailored parts. . . . As the number of required parts increases, the difficulty of gradually putting the system together skyrockets, and the likelihood of indirect scenarios plummets. . . . The intransigence of the problem cannot be alleviated; it will only get worse. Darwinian theory has given no explanation for the cilium or the flagellum. The overwhelming complexity of the swimming systems push us to think it may never give an explanation."[14]

In his text, Behe documents why the issue of evolution "must now be argued at the molecular level," in other words, the domain of biochemistry.[15] Essentially, if science cannot explain evolution at the molecular level, it certainly cannot explain it at any other level. Molecular evolution is where evolution "starts" and if it has not happened here it has not happened anywhere.

Machines Made of Molecules

With Michael Denton elsewhere, Behe points out that the cumulative results of science in the last generation prove that life is based on "machines" that are made of molecules. These molecules are amazing to contemplate. Some actually haul cargo from a particular location in the cell to another through "highways" that are made of protein. Other "machines" function as pulleys, ropes, and cables to hold the cell in its proper shape. "Machines turn cellular switches on and off, sometimes killing the cell or causing it to grow. Solar-powered machines capture the energy of photons and store it in chemicals. Electrical machines allow current to flow through nerves. Manufacturing machines build other molecular machines, as well as themselves. Cells swim using machines, copy themselves with machinery, ingest food with machinery. In short, highly sophisticated molecular machines control every cellular process. Thus the details of life are finally calibrated, and the machinery of life enormously complex."[16]

Science's Silence

Secular science has no explanation for any of this: "if you search the scientific literature on evolution, and if you focus your search on the question of how molecular machines— the basis of life—developed, you find an eerie and complete silence. The complexity of life's foundation has paralyzed science's attempt to account for it. . . ."[17] Behe also points out that his survey of 30 biochemistry textbooks used in major universities over the past generation shows that many of them ignore evolution completely. In fact almost half never even mention it and one-fourth mention it three times or less. These texts have 2,500 to 10,000 index entries each. Yet 75 percent of these only mention evolution between zero and three times. This is certainly instructive. The largest number of entries referring to evolution is 22 out of 8,000 total entries, or .0025%.[18] These university texts do not refer to molecular evolution because they have nothing to say about it. Thus,

> the impotence of Darwinian theory in accounting for the molecular basis of life is evident not only from the analyses in this book, but also from the complete absence in the professional scientific literature of any detailed models by which complex biochemical systems could have been produced. . . . In the face of the enormous complexity that modern biochemistry has uncovered in the cell, the scientific community is paralyzed. No one at Harvard

University, no one at the National Institutes of Health, no member of the National Academy of Sciences, no Nobel Prize winner—no one at all can give a detailed account of how the cilium, or vision, or blood clotting, or any complex biochemical process might have developed in a Darwinian fashion. But here we are. Plants and animals are here. The complex systems are here. All these things got here somehow: if not in a Darwinian fashion, then how?[19]

Professor Behe cites noted scientist Lynn Margulis, distinguished University Professor of Biology at the University of Massachusetts as stating that history will finally evaluate neo-Darwinism as "a minor twentieth-century religious sect within the sprawling religious persuasion of Anglo-Saxon biology."[20] At some of her many public talks, she asks the molecular biologists attending her lecture to name a single unambiguous example of new species formation through accumulated mutations. No one has yet accepted her challenge. Behe explains that Margulis is hardly alone in her unhappiness over NeoDarwinism: "Over the past 130 years Darwinism, although securely entrenched, has met a steady stream of dissent both from within the scientific community and from without it."[21] He also cites noted paleontologist Niles Eldredge who stated, "No wonder paleontologists shied away from evolution for so long. It never seems to happen."[22] He then quotes Jerry Coyne with the Department of Ecology and Evolution at the University of Chicago who asserts, "We conclude—unexpectedly—that there is little evidence for the neo-Darwinian view: its theoretical foundations and the experimental evidence supporting it are weak."[23]

Behe argues what we documented earlier. Most scientists accept evolution even though there is little if any evidence for it only because of majority opinion or personal bias:

> If a poll were taken of all the scientists in the world, the great majority would say they believed Darwinism to be true. But scientists, like everybody else, base most of their opinions on the word of other people. Of the great majority who accept Darwinism, most (though not all) do so based on authority. Also, and unfortunately, too often criticisms have been dismissed by the scientific community for fear of giving ammunition to creationists. It is ironic that in the name of protecting science, trenchant scientific criticism of natural selection has been brushed aside.[24]

Behe also shows with specific examples, that despite widespread belief to the contrary, when it gets down to the details, the scientific literature on evolution really has not explained how evolution occurs.

A Strange Absence

The *Journal of Molecular Evolution* (*JME*), established in 1971, is devoted entirely to research that attempts to explain how life evolved at the molecular level. Each month's issue contains about ten scientific papers on various aspects of molecular evolution. That's about 1,000 papers per decade or some 2,500 papers over 25 years. As Behe points out, a survey of 1,000 papers in a given area gives one a fairly good idea of the problems that have either been solved or remain. Yet he argues that this technical scientific journal has explained very little if anything: "In fact, *none* of the papers published in *JME* over the entire course of its life as a journal has ever proposed a detailed model by which a complex biochemical system might have been produced in a gradual, step-by-step Darwinian fashion. . . . How did the photosynthetic reaction center develop? How did intramolecular transport start? How did cholesterol biosynthesis begin? How did retinal become involved in vision? How did phosphoprotein signaling pathways develop? The very fact that none of these problems is even addressed, let alone solved, is a very strong indication that Darwinism is an inadequate framework for understanding the origin of complex biochemical systems."[25]

Behe also provides examples of the kind of articles we would need to find in *JME* in order to begin to solve the problem of molecular evolution. For example, "Twelve Intermediate Steps Leading to the Bacterial Photosynthetic Reaction Center;" "Intermediates in Adenosine Biosynthesis Effectively Mimic Adenosine Itself in ARN Function;" "A Proto-cilium Could Generate a Power Stroke Sufficient to Turn a Cell by Ten Degrees;" and "A Primitive Clot Made of Randomly Aligned Fibers Would Block Circulation in Veins Smaller Than .03 Millimeters." As Behe points out, "Nothing remotely like this has been published."[26]

The reasons such papers are not published is because they *cannot* be published. No scientist anywhere in the world can publish them because they have *no evidence* to write such a paper. Behe points out that attempts to explain such things through evolution "have so far been incoherent" and obviously, "no scientific journal will publish patently incoherent papers, so no studies asking detailed questions of molecular evolution are to be found."[27]

JME is, of course, only one technical journal—there are scores of journals dealing with research in biochemistry and related subjects. Behe wondered if perhaps other journals might have attempted evolutionary explanations. In examining the *Proceedings of the National Academy of Sciences* (PNAS) he discovered that between 1984 and 1994 PNAS published some 20,000 papers, the great majority on the life sciences. During those ten years approximately 400 papers dealt with molecular evolution. We find the same problem here. A great majority of papers are concerned with sequence analysis but never deal with the fundamental question of how evolution might occur. Thus, "No papers were published in PNAS that proposed detailed routes by which complex biochemical structures might have developed. Surveys of other biochemistry journals show the same result: sequences upon sequences, but no explanations."[28]

Behe kept searching. If no answers to how evolution occurs could be found in scientific research journals, then perhaps he could find them in the technical scientific book literature. But books like *The Neutral Theory of Molecular Evolution* by Motoo Kimura or *The Origins of Order* by Stuart Kauffman of the Santa Fe Institute offer no help to Darwinism. Behe next asks, "perhaps in one of the libraries of the world there is a book that tells us how specific biochemical structures came to be." The answer?: "Unfortunately, a computer search of library catalogues shows there is no such book."[29] Nor can we get any assistance by examining the professional scientific meetings attended by scientists. In conclusion, "There has never been a meeting, or a book, or a paper on the details of the evolution of complex biochemical systems."[30]

The reason should be obvious: none of these exist because evolution never occurred. If evolution had occurred, certainly, by now, there would be some evidence for it. Neither the most brilliant scientists alive nor the most prestigious scientific organizations can logically argue with Behe's conclusion:

Molecular evolution is not based on scientific authority. There is no publication in the scientific literature—in prestigious journals, speciality journals, or books—that describes how molecular evolution of any real, complex, biochemical system either did occur or even might have occurred. There are assertions that such evolution occurred, but absolutely none are supported by pertinent experiments or calculations. Since no one knows molecular evolution by direct experience, and since there is no authority on which to base claims of knowledge, it can truly be said that . . . the assertion of Darwinian molecular evolution is merely bluster. "Publish or perish" is a proverb that academicians take seriously. . . . If a theory claims to be able to explain some phenomenon but does not generate even an attempt at explanation, then it should be banished. . . . In effect, the theory of Darwinian molecular evolution has not published, and so it should perish.[31]

Other scientists such as biochemist Shapiro agree with Behe, "There are no detailed Darwinian accounts for the evolution of *any* fundamental biochemical or cellular system, only a variety of wishful explanations."[32] Thus, we arrive at the same conclusion with just about everything else—for example, vesicular transport: "A search of the professional biochemical literature and text books shows that no one has ever proposed a detailed route by which such a system could have come to be. In the face of the enormous complexity of vesicular transport, Darwinian theory is mute."[33]

The immune system: "We can look high or we can look low, in books or in journals, but the result is the same. The scientific literature has no answers to the question of the origin of the immune system."[34]

AMP, one of the building blocks of nucleic acids: "No one has a clue how the AMP pathway developed."[35]

And we could go on and on to the point where, as Professor Behe points out, "Sisyphus himself would pity us."[36] (Sisyphus was the Greek god condemned to eternally roll a large rock up a hill, only to have it roll down each time.)

However, it is not just that journals on molecular biology fail to cite evidence for evolution—evolutionary journals in general cite no evidence.

One example is the standard journal *Evolution* published by the *Society for the Study of Evolution*. This journal began in 1947, over fifty years ago. One would assume that any and all evidence for evolution would have been cited in this journal in over half a century of publication. Indeed, if evidence for evolution can be found anywhere, one would expect it to be found in a journal titled *Evolution*, a journal devoted to evolutionary research and published by the Society for the Study of Evolution.

But where is the evidence? Analyses by Dr. John N. Moore, Professor of Natural Science at Michigan State University, showed that no evidence is offered! An evaluation of over 1,100 articles revealed the subject matter dealt primarily with microevolution and offered no empirical evidence of evolution as generally understood: "In a word, articles in the journal, *Evolution*, do *not* deal with 'evolution,' according to the [standard] definition given above."[37] Thus, "The voluminous collection of articles in the journal . . . is evidence in hand that actual research work is designed to bring forth information about variation and mircoevolutionary changes *within* limits of known types, forms or kinds of plants and animals."[38] Actually, what else could be expected? Evolutionists can only work with what they *have*, which *isn't* evolution as normally understood. Again evolution as normally understood (macroevolution) *has never occurred*.

The Breath of Life

But it gets worse. Evolution cannot explain even the most "basic" of functions such as breathing, sexual reproduction, or consciousness itself.

Even evolutionists like H. S. Lipson will admit that breathing is inexplicable on evolutionary grounds, as we saw in Chapter 9. Concerning sexual reproduction, Isaac Manly, M.D. comments, "One of the most striking examples of a development which could not possibly have evolved is the source of individual minor variation itself. This is the invention and creation of sexual reproduction through which every individual is unique and unlike any other individual."[39]

Concerning consciousness, many noted scientists argue that evolutionary explanations are impotent. Sir Nevill Mott, former Cavendish Professor of Physics at Cambridge University and Nobel Prize winner for physics, writes that, "I believe that there is one 'gap' for which there will never be a scientific explanation, and that is man's consciousness. No scientist in the future, equipped with a super-computer of the twenty-first century or beyond, will be able to set it to work and show that he is thinking about it. This has been argued by my successor as the head of the Cavendish Laboratory at Cambridge, Sir Brian Pippard, in an essay entitled 'The Invincible Ignorance of Science.' . . ."[40]

Sir John Eccles received the Nobel Prize for physiology/medicine. He argues that "the conscious self is not in the Darwinian evolutionary process at all. I think it is a divine creation. . . . And this is a creation, a loving creation. You have to think of it as not just by a Creator who tosses off souls one after the other. This is a loving Creator giving us all these wonderful gifts. . . . I think if people believe that the brain is the creator of all their linguistic expressions and that they are merely passive recipients of the creations of their brain in language, then I don't argue with them. I don't argue with robots."[41]

Professor George Wald received the Nobel Prize for physiology/medicine. He discusses two major problems he views as "ultimately insoluble [in] science." One involves cosmology the other consciousness. Concerning the latter, "Consciousness seems to me to be wholly impervious to science. It does not lie as an indigestible element within science, but just the opposite: Science is the highly digestible element within consciousness. . . ."[42]

It is not merely breathing, sexual reproduction, and consciousness that are and will be forever incapable of explanation according to evolutionary theory, it is virtually everything: the eye, the electric organs of fishes in the deep sea, the orchid *Coryanthes,* the swim bladder of fishes, the human brain, the organ systems in the human body, the tortoise shell, etc., etc.[43] We cited Charles Darwin earlier when he stated in chapter six of his *Origin of Species,* "If it could be demonstrated that any complex organ existed, which could not possibly have been formed by numerous, successive, slight modifications, my theory would absolutely break down."

Again, Darwin's theory breaks down at every point with every created thing. Most scientists familiar with the evidence know it and yet because of their materialism, are forced to continue to accept a bad theory.

About all evolutionists can do in the attempt to deal with such problems is claim that future science will solve the problems or evolution has occurred in great, magnificent, leaps such as Goldschmidt's "hopeful-monster" theory or the more popular "punctuated equilibria" theory. The problem is that an appeal to the future is a hopeless one because the problems can never be resolved: they are already at the point of being irresolvable. The evolution by great leaps also solves nothing and only takes us back to the point of miracle. "Such an appeal to brute luck can never be refuted. Yet it is an empty argument. One may as well say that the world luckily popped into existence yesterday with all the features it now has."[44] Evolutionist and atheist Richard Dawkins is correct in arguing that evolution must be considered an extremely gradual process if it is to be used to explain things like the coming into existence of "complicated, apparently designed objects, like eyes. For if it is not gradual in these cases, it ceases to have any explanatory power at all. Without gradualness in these cases, we are back to miracle, which is simply a synonym for the total absence of explanation."[45]

Creation Evidence

This is where the argument in Behe's book—and many like his, take us—back to the miraculous. The complexity of life simply *cannot* be explained any other way. *All* naturalistic explanations are impotent.

Behe's book goes into this in great detail, showing that complex biological systems or machines could simply never be formed in a gradualistic manner. This includes aspects of DNA replication, photosynthesis, telomere synthesis, electron transport, transcription regulation, and much more. The final story is always the same insult to the materialist: "Even systems that at first glance appear amenable to a gradualistic approach turn out to be major headaches on closer inspection—or when the experimental results roll in—with no reason to expect they will be solved within a Darwinian framework."[46]

We must conclude that if molecular evolution never happened and is impossible, then all subsequent evolution never happened and must be considered impossible.

Is there a more rational conclusion that one can arrive at?

13

The Proof That Poofed
The Fossil Record of Plant
and Animal Evolution

The most important evidence for the theory of evolution is that obtained from the study of paleontology.
—Evolutionist G. A. Kerkut

The last word on the credibility and course of evolution lies with the paleontologist. . . . "
—Evolutionist Sir Gavin de Beer

The only available evidence is that provided by the fossils.
—W. R. Thompson, introduction to *The Origin of Species*[1]

It is generally admitted that the fossil record contains some of the most cogent evidence for the evolutionary story.

Proof of Evolution?

The fossil record has been continually heralded as "proof" of evolution and conceded to offer the only or primary scientific evidence that evolution has really occurred. As the eminent French biologist and zoologist Pierre-P. Grassé correctly points out:

Zoologists and botanists are nearly unanimous in considering evolution as a fact and not a hypothesis. I agree with this position and base it primarily on documents provided by paleontology, i.e., the [fossil] history of the living world. . . .

Naturalists must remember that the process of evolution is re-vealed only through fossil forms. A knowledge of paleontology is, therefore, a prerequisite; only paleontology can provide them with *the evidence of evolution* and reveal its course or mechanisms. Neither the examination of present beings, nor imagination, nor theories can serve as a substitute for paleontological documents. If they ignore them, biologists, the philosophers of nature, indulge in numerous commentaries and can only come up with hypotheses. This is why we constantly have recourse to paleon-tology, the *only true science* of evolution. . . . The true course of evolution is and can *only be revealed* by paleontology.[2]

Thomas Huxley also realized the importance of this issue when he wrote, "*If* it could be shown that this fact [gaps between widely distinct groups] had always existed, the fact would be *fatal* to the doctrine of evolution."[3] Because this sub-ject is so vital, we are going to discuss and document our conclusions in some detail.

Of course, if scientists cannot observe evolution as ever having taken place, because of the immense time periods in-volved,[4] how can they categorically state evolution is a *fact* of science? They attempt to do so by pointing to the fossil record. They believe it provides the critical evidence for evolution by preserving the record of the past that *demonstrates* gradual evo-lutionary change has occurred between the lower and higher life forms.[5]

But even Darwin was very concerned: ". . . [Since] innu-merable transitional forms must have existed, why do we not find them imbedded in countless numbers in the crust of the earth? Why is not *every* geological formation and *every* stratum *full* of such intermediate links? Geology assuredly does not re-veal any such finely graduated organic chain; and this perhaps is the most *obvious* and *gravest objection* which can be urged against my theory."[6] Darwin was right.

Transitions of Necessity

The fact is that the fossil record should produce literally thousands and thousands of legitimate transitional forms. The fact that only a small portion of all plants and animals that have ever existed would be preserved as fossils or that we have only uncovered a relatively small portion of the fossils that exist are not legitimate objections, and evolutionists recognize this. As Dr. Gish states in his valuable refutation of the evolutionary interpretation of the fossil record, "There should not be the slightest difficulty in finding transitional forms. Hundreds of transitional forms should fill museum collections. If we find fossils at all, we ought to find transitional forms. As a matter of fact, difficulty in placing a fossil with a distinct category should be the rule rather than the exception."[7]

Again, Darwin asked, ". . . why if species have descended from other species by insensibly fine gradations, do we not *everywhere* see innumerable transitional forms?" And ". . . the number of intermediate and transitional links, between all living and extinct species *must* have been *inconceivably great.*"[8]

Evolutionists often claim the fossil record *has* provided numerous, indisputable transitional forms. The following citations are official statements by the organizations cited (emphasis added):

National Academy of Sciences
"*Hundreds of thousands* of fossil organisms found in well-dated sequences represent a *succession of forms through time* and manifest *many evolutionary transitions.* . . . There have been so *many discoveries of intermediate forms* between fish and amphibians, between amphibians and reptiles, between reptiles and mammals, and even along the primate line of descent that it is often difficult to identify categorically the line to which a particular genus or species belongs. . . ."[9]

American Institute of Biological Sciences
"The body of knowledge that supports the theory of evolution is ever growing: fossils *continue to be discovered that fill gaps* in the evolutionary tree. . . ."[10]

New Orleans Geological Society
"Creationists, in their charge that the 'gaps' in the fossil record refute evolution, ignore the *hundreds of identifiable transition species* that have been catalogued. Concentrating their criticism only on vertebrate fossil finds, creationists neglect the detailed fossil record of invertebrates, microfauna, and microflora whose evolutionary change over time *is well documented.* That evolution has

occurred is a documented fact, not disputed within the scientific community."[11]

Society of Vertebrate Paleontology
"The fossil record of vertebrates *unequivocally* supports the hypothesis that vertebrates have evolved through time. . . . The hypothesis has been strengthened by *so many independent observations of fossil sequences* that it has come to be regarded as a *confirmed fact,* as certain as the drift of continents through time or the lawful operation of gravity . . . the *evidence* for the *progressive replacement* of fossil forms has been adequate to support the theory of evolution for 150 years . . . the vertebrate fossil record is an excellent set of examples of the patterns and processes of evolution *through time.*"[12]

National Association of Biology Teachers
"The fossil record, which includes *abundant transitional forms* in diverse taxonomic groups, *establishes extensive and comprehensive* evidence for organic evolution."[13]

Such statements are demonstrably false.

No Evidence at All

One hundred and forty years after Darwin, it has become clear that the fossil record does *not* confirm Darwin's hope that future research would fill in the unexpected and extensive gaps in the fossil record. This is conceded by many leading *evolutionary* scientists as the citations below demonstrate. This can only make one wonder about the credibility and perhaps motives of the organizations and individuals who tell us the fossil record is full of demonstrated transitions. Either they are uninformed or engaging in propaganda—and neither involves good science.

Even noted paleontologist Stephen Jay Gould of Harvard points out, "The fossil record with its abrupt transitions offers *no support* for gradual change. . . . All paleontologists know that the fossil record contains *precious little* in the way of intermediate forms; transitions between major groups are characteristically abrupt."[14]

With an estimated 250 million or ¼ *billion* catalogued fossils of some 250,000 fossil species, the problem certainly does not appear to be one of an imperfect record. Many scientists have conceded that the fossil data are sufficiently complete to provide an accurate portrait of the geologic record.[15] University of Chicago professor of geology David Raup also points out the following: "Well, we are now about 120 years after Darwin and the knowledge of the fossil records has been greatly expanded. We now have a quarter of a million fossil species but the situation hasn't changed much. The record of evolution is still surprisingly jerky and, ironically, we have even fewer examples of evolutionary transition than we had in Darwin's time. . . ."[16] This is ironic. Darwin said he had no transitions. Now Raup says, over a century later, that we have even fewer transitions than in Darwin's time.

The truth is that the fossil record is composed *entirely* of gaps, not evidence of evolutionary transitions. Even the claimed transitions, of which there are very few, are all capable of being rationally challenged. This means there isn't even a *single* proven evolutionary transition that exists anywhere in the fossil record. Evolutionary scientists themselves have declared that the fossil record is comprised almost entirely of gaps. How, then, can it logically offer *scientific evidence* and *proof* of evolution? Prior to Dr. Gould's time, Dr. George Gaylord Simpson was one of the world's best-known evolutionists. He was professor of vertebrate paleontology, also at Harvard University, until his retirement.

Simpson thought that the fossil record was almost complete for the larger terrestrial forms of North America and yet "The regular absence of transitional forms is an almost universal phenomenon" among all orders of all classes of animals and analogous categories of plants.[17]

In his book, *The Major Features of Evolution*, he admitted, ". . . it remains true, as every paleontologist knows, that *most* new species, genera, and families and that nearly all new categories above the level of families, appear in the record suddenly and are not led up to by known, gradual, completely continuous transitional sequences."[18]

Simpson had no choice but to accept the systematic gaps in the fossil record. In *Tempo and Mode in Evolution* he also pointed out that not anywhere around the world is there any trace of a fossil that closes the gap between the first horse,

Hyracotherium, and its alleged ancestral order, *Condylarthra*. But he then remarks, "This is true of all thirty-two orders of mammals. . . . The earliest and most primitive known members of every order already have the basic ordinal characters, and in no case is an approximately continuous sequence from one order to another known. In most cases the break is so sharp and the gap so large that the origin of the order is speculative and much disputed." Then later Dr. Simpson declares, "This regular absence of transitional forms is not confined to mammals, but is an almost universal phenomenon, as has long been noted by paleontologists. It is true of almost all orders of all classes of animals, both vertebrate and invertebrate. *A fortiori*, it is also true of the classes, and of the major animal phyla, and it is apparently also true of analogous categories of plants."[19]

If paleontologists have long noted the consistent absence of transitional forms, i.e., the consistent absence of evidence for evolution, one can only wonder why evolutionists have consistently cited the fossil record as evidence for evolution? One can also wonder on what basis, apart from personal preference or bias, Simpson declares that most paleontologists "find it logical, if not scientifically required, to assume that the sudden appearance of a new systematic group is *not* evidence for creation . . ."?[20] Why *isn't* it evidence?

This certainly doesn't explain why Dr. Austin Clark, once curator of paleontology at the Smithsonian Institute in Washington, D.C., wrote in 1928, "Thus so far as concerns the major groups of animals, the creationists seem to have the better of the argument."[21] But this remains true today. In his *Biology, Zoology and Genetics*, Thompson agrees when he writes, "Rather than supporting evolution, the breaks in the known fossil record support *the creation* of major groups with the possibility of some limited variation within each group."[22]

In "The Nature of the Fossil" record, Ager also points out what every informed scientist knows, that "if we examine the fossil record in detail, whether at the level of orders or of species, we find—over and over again—not gradual evolution, but the sudden explosion of one group at the expense of another."[23]

If so, it is not surprising to hear Professor E. J. H. Corner of the Botany Department of Cambridge University say that, although he believes there is evidence for evolution in other fields, ". . . I still think that, to the unprejudiced, the fossil record of plants is in favor of special creation. . . . Can you imagine how an orchid, a duck weed, and a palm have come from the same ancestry, and have we any evidence for this assumption? The evolutionist must be prepared with an answer, but I think that most would break down before an inquisition."[24] Boston University biologist Paul B. Weiss comments, "The first and most important steps of animal evolution remain even more obscure than those of plant evolution."[25]

More of the Same

The complaint of the lack of specific evidence for evolution has been registered for almost every species of plants, animals, insects, birds, fish, etc., known to man.[26]

For example, consider flowering plants or angiosperms. Creationist Dr. Gish has this to say:

> The origin of flowering plants (angiosperms), which Darwin termed "an abominable mystery," is still today, for evolutionists, an abominable mystery. Concerning the problem, Hughes has this to say: "The evolutionary origin of the now dominant land-plant group, the angiosperms, has puzzled scientists since the middle of the nineteenth century. . ."
>
> After describing several attempts to explain why the evidence for the evolutionary origin cannot be found, Hughes says, ". . . with few exceptions of detail, however, the failure to find a satisfactory explanation has persisted and many biologists have concluded that the problem is not capable of solution by fossil evidence. . . ." Beck has stated that, "Indeed, the mystery of the origin and early evolution of the angiosperms is as pervasive and as fascinating today as it was when Darwin emphasized the problem in 1879. . . ."
>
> Flowering plants burst upon the scene in bewildering variety. Forty-three families of the angiosperms abruptly appear with no trace of ancestors or intermediate forms. No wonder evolutionists describe their origin as an abominable mystery.[27]

Other examples include the authority Johansen who observes of the primates, "Modern gorillas, orangutans, and chimpanzees spring *out of nowhere*, as it were. They are here today;

they have no yesterday."[28] Concerning the evolution of reptiles, University of California paleontologist R. A. Stirton points out, "There is no direct proof from the fossil record. . . ."[29]

The late Dr. Pierre-P. Grassé was considered an outstanding scientist of France and was the dean of French zoologists. In his *Evolution of Living Organisms*, he declares of insects, "We are in the dark concerning the origin of insects."[30]

The authority on lungfishes, E. White, reflects, "Whatever ideas authorities may have on the subject, the lungfish, like every other major group of fish that I know, have their origins firmly based on nothing."[31]

Dr. Robert Barnes is an authority of invertebrate zoology. In his book *Invertebrate Beginnings*, he writes . . . "The fossil record tells us almost nothing about the evolutionary origin of phyla and classes. Intermediate forms are non-existent, undiscovered, or not recognized."[32] Thus, Earl L. Core, then chairman of the Department of Biology at West Virginia University, comments, "We do not actually know the phylogenetic history of any group of plants and animals, since it lies in the indecipherable past."[33]

In *Principles of Paleontology*, Dr. David Raup, who was previously the curator of geology at the Field Museum of Natural History in Chicago, and is now professor of geology at the University of Chicago, has also noted the following concerning the mysterious origins of higher plant and animal forms, "Unfortunately, the origins of most higher categories are shrouded in mystery: commonly new higher categories appear abruptly in the fossil record without evidence of transitional forms."[34]

Not One Example

As we saw, many evolutionists claim there are large numbers, even thousands, of demonstrated transitions. But they are wrong. Other evolutionists have told the truth when they have declared there isn't even a *single* proven or significant evolutionary transition. Let's consider examples. In the words of evolutionary scientist Woodruff, the fossil record "fails to contain *a single example* of a significant transition"[35] If so, then we are correct in concluding that the paleontological histories of the plants and animals simply do not exist and should be considered myths. Ichthyologist Dr. Donn Rosen, the late curator of fish at the American Museum of Natural History in New York, noted that evolution has been "unable to provide scientific data about the origin, diversity, and similarity of the two million species that inhabit the earth and the estimated eight million others that once thrived."[36]

It is not that there is nothing that can be *interpreted* as a transitional form such as *Archaeopteryx* (discussed later in this chapter). The issue is whether the interpretation is credible. Does the information we have prove the fossil to be an intermediate form? The answer is always no. But even accepting the legitimacy of some provisional transitions would change nothing. Why? Because such extensive gaps exist where there *must* be intermediate forms if evolution is true. Evolution operates so infinitesimally slow that we should actually expect the fossil record to be composed of almost 100% transitions, since transitionary forms would of necessity occupy almost 100% of geologic "space" and time.

Instead there is nothing at all. No paleontologist in the world disagrees with this fact of extensive gaps.

Paleontologists may believe in evolution, but none can logically deny the fossil record conflicts so badly with Darwin's theory that were this any other subject than evolution, the lack of evidence would be tantamount to a disproof.[37]

Dr. Steven M. Stanley is professor of paleobiology at Johns Hopkins University. He was a recipient of the Schuchert award of the Paleontological Society and has also been awarded a Guggenheim Fellowship. He openly admits, "The known fossil record *fails* to document a single example of phyletic [gradual] evolution accomplishing a major morphologic transition and hence offers no evidence that the gradualistic model can be valid."[38]

The late Luther D. Sunderland was an aerospace engineer with General Electric. He had a long time interest in the creation/evolution issue and assisted the New York State Board of Regents for a study on the manner in which theories of origins should be presented for a revision of the state's Regents Biology Syllabus.

In *Darwin's Enigma: Fossils and Other Problems*, he presents many of the problems of evolution including the fossil record. For example, he interviewed five top paleontologists at leading natural history museums around the world, each having significant fossil collections. Those interviewed were Dr. David Pilbeam, former curator of the Peabody Museum of Natural History at Yale, later Professor of Anthropology at Harvard; Dr. Colin Patterson, Senior Paleontologist at the British Museum of Natural History; Dr. Niles Eldredge, curator of Invertebrate Paleontology at the American Museum in New York City; Dr. David M. Raup, curator of Geology at the Field Museum of Natural History in Chicago; and Dr. Donald Fisher, state paleontologist at the New York State Natural History Museum. "None of the five museum officials could offer a single example of a transitional series of fossilized organisms that would document the transformation of one basically different type to another."[39]

In essence, given the endless textbooks that claim demonstrated transitions, who can argue with Dr. Eldredge when he confessed, "I admit that an awful lot of [misinformation] has gotten into the textbooks as though it were true."[40] Obviously then, "Many statements about prehistoric time, or a presumed fossil record, partake of imaginative narratives."[41]

Thus, the remark of Stephen Jay Gould on Darwin's dilemma remains valid after well over a century, "New species almost always appeared suddenly in the fossil record with no intermediate links to ancestors in older rocks of the same region."[42] Dr. Gould, who remains an evolutionist (though not a Darwinian), goes further and concedes the lack of fossil evidence is the "trade secret" of paleontology: "The extreme rarity of transitional forms in the fossil record persists as the trade secret of paleontology. The evolutionary trees that adorn our textbooks have data only at the tips and nodes of their branches; the rest is inference, however reasonable, not the evidence of fossils. . . . Most species exhibit no directional change during their tenure on earth. . . . In any local area, a species does not arise gradually by the steady transformation of its ancestors; it appears all at once and 'fully formed.'"[43]

Evolutionary Series and Stratomorphic Intermediates

Evolutionists also cite different "series" allegedly showing evolution, as well as what are termed "stratomorphic intermediates." Kurt P. Wise is a young earth creationist who received his Ph.D. in paleontology under Dr. Gould at Harvard University. He points out that different series of fossil species such as the mammal-like reptile series; the horse, elephant, and camel series; and early whales and birds can all seem to offer evidence of evolution. In fact they don't, no more than *stratomorphic intermediates*, which also can *seem* to provide evidence for evolution. These are fossils which are intermediate between the group from which they allegedly descend and the group to which they are ancestral—not only in form but also in their stratigraphic position in the fossil record. In other words, their form and structure is in between that of their ancestors and descendants—they appear to be intermediate forms that could be explained by evolution. Among those cited by evolutionists as stratomorphic intermediate species are the anthracosaurs (those standing between amphibians and reptiles), the phenacodontids (between horses and their alleged ancestors), and mammal-like reptiles that stand between reptiles and mammals. Further, "some fossil genera are stratomorphic intermediates in the group in which they are classified. They are the oldest fossils known in the group and most similar to the group from which they are supposedly descendant. Examples include *Pikaia* among the chordates, *Archaeopteryx* among birds, *Baragwanathia* among lycopods, *Ichthyostega* among the amphibians, *Purgatorius* among the primates, *Pakicetus* among the whales, and *Proconsul* among the hominoids."[44]

But Dr. Wise points out that these apparent intermediates have problems associated with them and in fact can be better explained through the theory of creation. He points out that first, "none of the stratomorphic intermediates have intermediate structures."[45] In other words, while they may appear to be an intermediate organism in form, they are a fully functional organism replete with fully functional structures. *Archaeopteryx* is cited as an example. It is thought to be a transitional form because it has both bird and reptile structures—for example, feathers as well as teeth and four limb claws. But the feathers (several different types), claws, and teeth are all fully functional. So it is not the structures themselves that are intermediate but only their combination that appears intermediate. These are called "mosaic forms" or "chimeras" by Stephen Jay Gould. Wise's point is that these organisms are no more intermediate than any other member of their group and, in fact, there are many such mosaic forms that are alive today, such as the platypus which has a bill like a duck, lays eggs like a reptile, and has hair and produces milk like a mammal. Wise points out that compared to the total number of mosaic forms in the fossil record, "the total list of claimed transitional forms is very small" and, we would add, that's "at best."[46]

The issue this raises is that there is no reason that God, whose love of diversity is obvious, could not have created organisms that could be *interpreted* as transitional by their form or function but which nevertheless were never produced through evolutionary processes. The point is that even among the alleged transitional forms documenting evolution, these could just as easily document creation. If none of the intermediate forms have intermediate structures how can these offer evidence for evolution? Further, "In some cases a series of intermediates cannot even be imagined. More often the imagined intermediates cannot have survived. Transitions from one major group of organisms to another are challenges to the ingenuity of even the most capable macroevolutionist."[47] Wise goes on to point out how divine creation and a global flood are capable of explaining the data that we have in the fossil record. He concludes that the mosaic nature of alleged transitional forms is problematic to the theory of evolution. At the same time stratomorphic intermediates are consistent with the concept of creation and a global deluge.

Evolutionists, of course, have cited what they claim are evidence of transitional forms. But nothing evolutionists have ever cited is proof of a transitional form. Let's take a key example and illustrate why.

Archaeopteryx: Does It Fly or Doesn't It?

Many evolutionary texts have claimed that *Archaeopteryx* is one of the *best* examples of evidence for evolution. This shows how weak the case for evolution is, when over a century of studying *Archaeopteryx* has proven it to be only a bird. As we have seen, creatures such as *Archaeopteryx* or the duckbilled platypus cannot be used as illustrations of legitimate transitional forms. First, they are only found as full, complete forms. Second, they are properly understood as animals that have detectable characteristics of more than one classification group.

Third, one of the recent creationist assessments of *Archaeopteryx* confirms what creationists have said all along about this alleged transition between bird and reptile. Ernest Lutz, Ph.D., after reviewing the evolutionary *claims* about *Archaeopteryx* and examining the *facts* concludes that "there is neither evidence of a lineage from reptiles to *Archaeopteryx* nor from it to any living birds. Further, and also most importantly, natural selection is inadequate as a possible mechanism to explain the descent of *Archaeopteryx*. In view of the evidence, science has oversold the case for *Archaeopteryx* as a transitional form."[48] *Archaeopteryx* as a transition just doesn't fly.

Feduccia (1993) who, among other things, measured the curvature of the footclaws of the three best specimens of *Archaeopteryx* and then compared them with 500 species of existing birds concluded that, "*Archaeopteryx* probably cannot tell us much about the early origins of feathers and flight in true protobirds because *Archaeopteryx* was, in the modern sense, a bird." (p. 793.)[49]

Lutz shows that as early as 1863 *extremely* thorough analysis of *Archaeopteryx* proved it was a bird, and he provides many other examples of both creationists and evolutionists who have said that *Archaeopteryx* should be classified as a bird.[50] The fact is that *Archaeopteryx* could hardly be a half bird if it had wings, was entirely feathered, and flew. Evolutionist Ostrom wrote, "There can be no doubt that *Archaeopteryx* was a true bird" while the creationist Colin Brown also refuted, in detail, arguments that Archaeopteryx was an intermediate form.[51]

Thus, despite all the claims that *Archaeopteryx* is a transitional form between reptile and bird, this is simply not the case. *Archaeopteryx* was a bird.[52] W. E. Swinton, an expert on birds and an evolutionist, is entirely correct when he declares, "There is no fossil evidence of the stages through which the remarkable change from reptile to bird was achieved."[53]

What Dr. Gish says concerning the alleged evolution of birds generally is also true for every category of insect, plant, animal, etc.: "The transitional forms have not been found because they never existed. These facts provide powerful positive evidence for special creation."[54]

All this is why creationist scientists feel justified in doubting that the fossil record provides any evidence at all for evolution. For example, Dr. Kurt Wise, cited earlier, shows that the alleged evidences for evolution in areas including similarity, the fossil record, fossil order, suboptimal improvisations, nested hierarchy of forms, vestigial organs, so-called embryological recapitulation, and biogeography, are either poorly or not at all explained by evolution or better explained by creation.

Our previous discussion of stratomorphic intermediates in the fossil record and the degree of similarity among organisms—the genetic relationship called phylogenies—are good examples of how the *interpretation* of evidence is crucial in the creation/evolution debate. Only one interpretation is correct but both can be interpreted as evidence of creation or evolution. Creation offers a greatly superior explanation for these things.[55]

Hope Springs Eternal

Interested readers may wonder if evolutionary scientists have developed any new theories to explain the embarrassing lack of transitional forms in the fossil record.

Perhaps it was the statements by Darwin concerning the abrupt appearance of higher plant and animal forms which recently sparked a new evolutionary theory. For example, Darwin observed: "Nothing is more extraordinary in the history of the Vegetable Kingdom, as it seems to me, than *the apparently very sudden or abrupt development of the higher plants*."[56] Again, he felt this absence of plant and animal transitions was "the gravest objection" that could be raised against his theory.[57] So what new evolutionary theory has been created to fit the lack of transitional evidence in the fossil record and to explain the "abrupt appearance" of living things that the fossil record undeniably displays?

Niles Eldredge and Stephen J. Gould tentatively proposed the following theory to account for the record as it exists. Rather than accept where the evidence points (creation) they propose "evolutionary" solutions. They suggest that the major gaps should be viewed as real phenomena of nature, an inevitable result of the mechanism of evolution itself. They see evolution taking place in major creative episodes, occurring at different times and places, interspaced with long periods of stability. Thus new species would form over thousands of years rather than hundreds of thousands or millions of years. They call their theory "punctuated equilibria," a somewhat minor version of evolutionary saltationism. In a lesser fashion, these theories returns us to geneticist Richard Goldschmidt's "hopeful monsters" theory, which in Stanley's words, "engender[s] such visions as the first bird hatching from a reptile egg."[58] Some argue this reads more like a fairy tale than modern science.

Gould explains how this idea works in *The Panda's Thumb*, although elsewhere he acknowledges that he and Eldredge do not hold to the exclusive validity of this concept. Nevertheless, they feel their theory is not inconsistent with the evolutionary model and that it helps to explain the systematic gaps in the fossil record—which they believe adequately expresses evolutionary history: "Thus, the fossil record is a faithful rendering of what evolutionary theory predicts, not a pitiful vestige of a once bountiful tale. Eldredge and I refer to this scheme as the model of punctuated equilibria. Lineages change little during most of their history, but events of rapid speciation occasionally punctuate this tranquility."[59] In other words, in order to get new species, evolution drastically speeds up. But this happens so quickly that intermediate forms aren't preserved in the fossil record. Realize that, in part, Gould's concept is an admission that Darwin's theory of very gradual evolution is wrong. Regardless, "For 130 years evolutionists have claimed that they have found evidence for evolution in the fossil record. Despite 'some gaps,' they assured us that the fossil record would eventually become complete. When it became evident that the fossil record we possessed was more than adequate and yet transitions were still not found, new theories were developed to explain the absence. Punctuated equilibria is one of those theories. Here it is important to realize that the theory does not remove the *need* for transitional fossils. It only tells us why those transitions were never found. 'Certainly, the punctuated equilibria theory is unique. It must be the only theory ever put forth in the history of science which claims to be scientific but then explains why evidence for it cannot be found.'"[60]

The fossil evidence is so poor that even the accomplished Swedish botanist and geneticist D. Nils Heribert-Nilsson made the following confession and, for a secular scientist, offered an amazing alternate theory. After 40 years of attempting to find evidence for the theory of evolution, he concluded that the task was impossible and that the theory was even "a serious obstruction to biological research." In his 1200-page magnum opus, *Synthetic Speciation*, he declared the theory "ought to be entirely abandoned," in part because it "obstructs—as has been repeatedly shown—the attainment of consistent results, even from uniform experimental material. For everything must ultimately be forced to fit this speculative theory. An exact biology cannot, therefore, be built up."[61]

After noting that "a close inspection discovers an empirical impossibility to be inherent in the idea of evolution,"[62] he went much farther than Gould, stating his conviction that geologic periods having incredible spurts of biogeneration produced billions of biosyntheses simultaneously. Gametes and other necessary cells and biocatalytic substances literally appeared spontaneously and led immediately to the fully formed end product, such as orchids, elephants, and eagles! Here is his own explanation of why he made such a daring "creationist" conclusion! It was because the empirical *evidence* forced him to it:

> As I have pointed out, there is no discussion among biologists today whether an evolution has taken place or not. The discussion concerns the how, the causation of evolution. No definite answer has been given to this question.
>
> It then becomes necessary to ask: Has there really been an evolution? Are the proofs of its occurrence tenable?
>
> After a detailed and comprehensive review of the facts we have been forced to give the answer: No! *Neither a recent nor a palaeohistorical evolution can be empirically demonstrated.*

If this is the case, all discussions and problems concerning the causation of an evolution lose all interest. Lamarckism or mutationism, monophyletic or polyphyletic, continuity or discontinuity—the roads of evolution are not problems any more. It is rather futile to discuss the digestion or the brain functions of a ghost.

When we have arrived at this standpoint, the evolutionist has the obvious right to ask: What has caused the fundamental differentiation in the world of organisms, the immeasurable variation among animals and plants? That it exists is a fact: you owe us an explanation!

We turn to empirical facts to obtain the answer. They tell us that during the geological history of the earth gigantic revolutions have occurred which at the same time mean *tabula rasa* catastrophes for a whole world of organisms but also the origin of a completely new one. The new one is structurally completely different from the old one. There are no other transitions than hypothetical ones. This origination of biota, which from a geological point of view is sudden as a flaring up I have called emication.

During palaeobiological times whole new worlds of biota have been repeatedly synthesized.

I will be asked: Do you seriously want to make such a statement? Do you not see that the consequences of such a theory are more than daring, that they would be *nearly insane?* Do you really mean to say that an orchid or an elephant should have been *instantaneously created out of non-living material?*

Yes, I do.[63]

Although Heribert-Nilsson rejected Genesis, the evidence still forced him to offer a "secular creation" interpretation—and he was enough of a scientist to do so in spite of the implications. Another scientist who supports Gould's new theory of evolution is Steven M. Stanley, who wrote the following in the preface of his book *The New Evolutionary Timetable: Fossils, Genes, and the Origin of Species*, "The [fossil] record now reveals that species typically survive for a hundred thousand generations, or even a million or more, without evolving very much. We seem *forced to conclude* that most evolution takes place rapidly, when species come into being by the evolutionary divergence of small populations from parent species. After their origins, most species undergo little evolution before becoming extinct."[64]

But what do other scientists think about replacing Darwin's theory of "gradualism" with Stephen J. Gould's "punctuated equilibria"? In essence, not much. It's reminiscent of Ernst Mayr's statement that the "hopeful monsters" theory "is equivalent to believing in miracles."[65] And he's correct.

Denton succinctly explains the problems faced by this approach:

> While [Niles] Eldredge and [Stephen Jay] Gould's model is a perfectly reasonable explanation of the gaps between species (and, in my view, correct), it is doubtful if it can be extended to explain the larger systematic gaps. The gaps which separate species: dog/fox, rat/mouse, etc., are utterly trivial compared with, say, that between a primitive terrestrial mammal and a whale or a primitive terrestrial reptile and an Ichthyosaur; and even these relatively major discontinuities are trivial alongside those which divide major phyla such as molluscs and arthropods. Such major discontinuities simply could not, unless we are to believe *in miracles*, have been crossed in geologically short periods of time through one or two transitional species occupying restricted geographical areas. Surely, such transitions must have involved long lineages including many collateral lines of hundreds or probably thousands of transitional species. . . . To suggest that the hundreds, thousands or possibly even millions of transitional species which must have existed in the interval between vastly dissimilar types were all unsuccessful species occupying isolated areas and having very small population numbers is *verging on the incredible!*[66]

In other words, if evolution is to be considered a true scientific fact, it must be able to explain the origin of developed life forms by recourse to proven methods of evolutionary change. Can it do so? It would seem that most scientists who have examined this subject critically are honest enough to say no, even though they continue to believe in evolution. The problems of natural selection, mutation, and newer theories attempting to explain *how* evolution occurs are, put simply, too expansive to be resolved by current (or even future) knowledge.[67] Indeed, a number of scientists have confessed there is little hope that any conceivable breakthrough in this area will *ever* be forthcoming.[68]

For years evolutionists have stated that the key evidence for evolution is found in the fossil record. Now some are back-tracking, in part due to their debates with creationists in the last twenty years. Anthropologist Vincent Sarich has stated, "No matter what the creationists may pretend, the fossil record is not, and never has been, our major source of information about evolutionary relationships."[69] Try and sell that to the scientific community thirty years ago.

Another example of the *ad hoc* approach, or the tendency to explain away problems rather than deal with them forthrightly, can be seen in the statement of British zoologist and evolution-ist Mark Ridley who claims that ". . . the gradual change of fossil species has *never* been part of the evidence for evolution. . . . In any case, no real evolutionist, whether gradualist or punctuationist, uses the fossil record as evidence in favor of the theory of evolution as opposed to special creation."[70]

One cannot help but wonder if such statements are made because of the frustration or embarrassment evolutionists must feel as they frankly examine the fossil record. The truth was stated by the world renowned entomologist W. R. Thompson in his introduction to Darwin's *Origin of Species*, "The only evi-dence available [for evolution] is that provided by the fossils."[71] So some evolutionists are now denying the fossil record is relevant. What else can they do? It *is* irrelevant—at least for evolution.

Creation Evidence

These more recent views, of course, represent the ignoring of a great deal of significant empirical evidence in the fossil record that provides *scientific evidence* for creation. The evolu-tion model would assume a gradual change of simple forms into more and more complex forms with transitional series linking the different categories and the absence of systematic gaps. On the other hand, the creation model would predict a sudden appearance of highly complex forms in great variety with each created type having complete characteristics and sharp boundaries separating major groups. There would be no transitional forms between distinctly created types.[72]

This is exactly what we find in the fossil record. As Gish remarks:

> [American Museum of Natural History paleontologist] Eldredge admits that "The Cambrian evolutionary explosion is still shrouded in mystery." But creation scientists say, *what greater evidence for creation could the rocks give than this abrupt appearance of a great variety of complex creatures without a trace of ancestors?* Thus we see, right from the beginning, on the basis of an evolutionary scenario, the evidence is directly contradictory to predictions based on evolution but is remarkably in accord with predictions based on creation. *This [Cambrian] evidence alone is sufficient to establish the fact that evolution has not occurred on the earth.*[73]

Conclusion

The most credentialed and brilliant evolutionary paleontologists or scientists cannot logically deny the scientific facts as we have them. The fossil record does *not* support a belief in evolution. As David B. Kitts, professor in the department of geology at the University of Oklahoma, an evolutionist who received his training in vertebrate paleontology under George Gaylord Simpson, comments, "Evolution *requires* intermediate forms between species and paleontology does not provide them. . . ."[74] Again, it doesn't even provide *one* example. Writing in *Science* magazine David Woodruff, in a review of Steven Stanley's *Macroevolution, Pattern and Process*, also writes that the fossil record "fails to contain a single example of a significant transition."[75]

We may close this section with two comments by creationists, both highly relevant.

Isaac V. Manly, M.D., concludes:

> Evolutionists claim their theory is scientific. Where is the science? I can assure the reader the American Kennel Club would not certify an ancestor of your dog based on evidence such as paleontologists present.[76]

In his definitive critique, Dr. Duane Gish concludes the following concerning the complete lack of fossil evidence for an early stage of evolution, from microorganisms to fish or invertebrates to vertebrates:

In the scientific contest between creation and evolution, the controversy is essentially settled at this point. No further discussion of the fossil record is necessary. In fact, no further discussion of any kind is required. *The evidence from the fossil record discussed in this chapter has established beyond any reasonable doubt that evolution has not taken place on the earth.* The evidence is absolutely clear. All of the complex invertebrates appear fully-formed without a trace of ancestors or transitional forms linking one to another. Many millions of years would have been required for their origin by evolutionary processes. Billions times billions of their fossils lie entombed in rocks all over the world, including all kinds of soft-bodied creatures. Even many published reports of the discovery of fossils of microscopic, single-celled, soft-bodied organisms have appeared in scientific journals. If evolution is true, the rocks should contain billions times billions of fossils of the ancestors of the complex invertebrates. *Yet, not one has ever been found.* It is simply physically impossible to have millions of years of evolution, producing a vastly diverse collection of complex invertebrates, without leaving a trace.

Even more convincing, if that can be said, is the total absence of intermediates between invertebrates and fishes, and the total absence of ancestors and transitional forms for each major class of fishes. . . . The rocks should be full of the fossils documenting the transition of some invertebrate into a fish, and a rich fossil record of the various transitional forms should exist linking the various major types of fishes to each other, if evolution is true. . . . *Again, it is physically impossible for millions of years of evolution to take place, producing a great variety of major types of fish, without leaving a trace.*[77]

Please note well the point that Dr. Gish is making. The above summary is from the first chapter of his evaluation of the fossil record concerning the alleged evolution of microorganisms to fish. His point is that if there is absolutely no evidence for evolution at the beginning, then there certainly can be no evidence for evolution *after* the beginning, e.g., from fish to reptiles, reptiles to birds, and on to mammals and man. Gish goes on to point out that fishes, amphibians, reptiles, birds, and mammals are all vertebrates and that proof of the evolutionary origin of vertebrates would correctly be seen as one of the greatest events in all history. Volumes of material would be written containing pictures of various intermediates documenting the step-by-step evolution from one kind into another.

In fact, creationists would admit that the existence of unambiguous transitions would be solid evidence for evolution. With additional confirmation, the entire issue would be settled. "Here would be undoubted proof of the fact of evolution, but what we have instead is a vast void, a total blank. The only thing that evolutionists can offer in an attempt to fill the void is simply pointless speculation, totally devoid of empirical evidence."[78]

Evolutionary speculation *is* "totally devoid of empirical evidence." So what should we make of the following official statement released by the noted scientific organization, the Society for the Study of Evolution?:

> The study of evolution is an empirically based science which employs the scientific process of hypothesis testing. . . . The Society for the Study of Evolution employs a rigorous critical review process to ensure that these procedures are followed—that the empirical data support the conclusions—before a study is accepted as scientific. No hypothesis that cannot be tested empirically is acceptable as scientific to the Society.[79]

In light of such a statement one wonders how this organization can accept evolution, let alone call itself the Society for the *Study* of Evolution.

14

More Monkey Business

Human Evolution and Missing Evidence

The non-scientific public has great faith in what a paleontologist can do with a single bone.

—Bolton Davidheiser, Ph.D.,
Johns Hopkins University[1]

Evolutionists claim that the evidence for human evolution is conclusive and proves that mankind evolved. A National Academy of Sciences official statement reads, "Today, however, there is *no significant scientific doubt* about the close evolutionary relationships among all primates or between apes and humans. The 'missing links' that troubled Darwin and his followers *are no longer missing.*"[2]

The Council for Democratic and Secular Humanism declares in an official statement: "Comparative DNA studies show that humankind shares a common ancestry with the three great apes (orangutan, chimpanzee, and gorilla). Fossil hominid [referring to humans and their evolutionary ancestors] evidence recently found in central East Africa documents the emergence of our species over the past four million years."[3]

As we will see, such statements are, again, demonstrably false. A recent article in *National Geographic* began by correctly pointing out that "Few scientific fields stir debate as intensely as does the search for human ancestors. Strong emotions and deeply held religious beliefs clash against the physical evidence presented by paleoanthropologists" (those who study human fossil remains).[4]

Based on such a statement, one would assume that the physical evidence *itself* clashes with "deeply held religious beliefs." Such an assumption would be wrong. Again, the *interpretation* of the physical evidence is what is at issue. Are evolutionists interpreting the evidence fairly? Clearly, they are not.

As we will see, it is not just in the plant and animal kingdom that the fossil record is woefully inadequate for supplying evidence for evolution. Despite widespread belief to the contrary, the fossil record of mankind is also woefully inadequate to justify belief in evolution.

> Despite 130 years of searching there are no fossils that have convincingly related man to any other species. Most have been conclusively proven false. . . . [Anthropologist Kathleen J.] Reichs [editor of *Hominid Origins*] cited many authorities who disagree about the interpretations of these many [alleged human ancestry] discoveries. Until accurate dating of the finds is possible, she said, "reconstruction of hominid relationships must remain tenuous at best."[5]

The major classifications used to describe the evolutionary ancestors of mankind include the *australopithecines, Homo habilis, Homo erectus (Pithecanthropus), Ramaphithecus,* and *Zinjanthropus.* Cro-Magnon and Neanderthal have also been touted as evolutionary ancestors. These may be subdivided for example, in the *Australopithecus* category, as *A. Aethiopicus, A. boisei, A. robustus, A. afarensis, A. anamensis,* etc.

No Evidence at All

Creationists who have fairly but critically examined the alleged evidence for human evolution have concluded that no such evidences exists. In fact, as we will see later, fossil man, like fossil plants and animals, actually provides very strong evidence for creation. After an extensive evaluation of the evidence Dr. Duane Gish writes, "There is thus no evidence, either in the present world or in the world of the past, that man has arisen from some 'lower' creature. He stands alone as a separate and distinct created type, or basic morphological design, endowed with qualities that sets him far above all other living creatures."[6]

Ramapithecus, Australopithecus, and *Pithecanthropus* have all been heralded as transitional forms between ape and man. The average person on the street probably still believes these classifications represent genuine intermediate forms. But even evolutionists are seriously divided and none of these classifications documents human evolution. For example, "*Ramapithecus* is just one of a long series of creatures that have been suggested at one time or another as 'missing links' but which, when more complete evidence became available, were relegated to the ape family."[7]

Neither is *Australopithecus* evidence of human evolution. The view that the *australopithecines* represent genuine intermediates has been challenged by the famous British anatomist Solly Lord Zuckerman and Dr. Charles Oxnard, formerly director of graduate studies and professor of anatomy at the University of Southern California Medical School. Lord Zuckerman headed a research team for over 15 years that studied the anatomical features of apes, man, monkeys, and the *australopithecine* fossils. Anatomical specimens from hundreds of apes, humans, and monkeys were compared along with almost all available important fossil fragments of *Australopithecus*. Most evolutionists seem to classify *Australopithecus* as a genus of the Hominidae or family of man rather than as a genus of the anthropoid apes. But Zuckerman replies, "I myself remain totally unpersuaded. Almost always when I have tried to check the anatomical claims on which the status of *Australopithecus* is based, I have ended in failure," and he concludes that *Australopithecus* was an ape and as such in no way related to the immediate evolutionary ancestry of man.[8]

Oxnard concludes that *Australopithecus* is actually not related to anything living today either man or ape, but was unique in certain ways. Dr. Gish concludes, "If Oxnard and Lord Zuckerman are correct, certainly *Australopithecus* was neither ancestral to man nor intermediate between ape and man. Oxnard is convinced that the *australopithecines* were unique, not related to anything living today. As we will see later, the research of many others tends to strongly support the conclusions of Lord Zuckerman and Oxnard."[9] With all the other extinct creatures, certainly the *australopithecines* could have been extinct apes that would today, in the hope of finding evidence of human evolution, be considered transitional between man and ape. After careful analysis, Dr. Gish concludes, the *australopithecines* were just this—extinct apes having no genetic relationship to either man or extant apes.[10]

Pithecanthropus or *Homo erectus* (aka Java man; Peking man), according to its discoverer, Dubois, "was not a man, but a gigantic genus allied to the Gibbons...."[11] All the evidence from the fossil record and archeology indicates that the "Cro-Magnon and Neanderthal peoples were human in the same ways that we are human."[12]

One of the definitive works on alleged human evolution from a creationist viewpoint is *Bones of Contention—A Creationist Assessment of Human Fossils* (Baker, 1992) by Professor of Apologetics Marvin L. Lubenow. Lubenow's book illustrates the quandary evolutionists face as they examine the alleged evidence for human evolution and the frequent bias found in the interpretation of data and in dating methods. He cites many examples of how scientists have allowed personal biases in favor of evolution to determine the results of their research and how common circular reasoning is in this field.

Lubenow spent no fewer than 25 years of research in compiling the book and heavily documented it from the most recent scientific sources.

Hominids and Creation

Lubenow begins his book with a statement that will surprise many: "The human fossil record is *strongly supportive of the concept of Special Creation*. On the other hand, the fossil evidence is *so contrary to human evolution* as to effectively *falsify the idea* that humans evolved. This is not the message we hear from a hundred different voices coming at us from a dozen different directions. But the human fossils themselves tell the real story."[13] Indeed, "even when the human fossils are placed on time charts according to the evolutionist's dates for these fossils, the results *do not support* human evolution but conflict with it."[14]

Lubenow's statements may appall evolutionists generally, but those who study human fossils, paleoanthropologists, at least if they investigate these issues openly and interpret data objectively, will discover them to be true.

Lubenow is quite correct when he claims that, "there are no *direct* observations or experiments that can confirm the process of human evolution." And further, if "we assign a value of 10 to Newtonian dynamics and the laws of thermodynamics because of the millions of confirming experiments and observations, what value can we assign to statements regarding human evolution when there is not one direct observation to back them up? The only value to assign to those statements is zero. . . . Studies on living primates—their behavior, genetic makeup, and anatomy—are used to support human evolution. All of these studies are fundamentally flawed. The flaw is known in logic as begging the question. In begging the question, you assume to be true the very thing you are trying to prove."[15]

For example, the sequence we have all seen of human evolution—small primitive stooped creatures slowly becoming modern man is "a very artificial and arbitrary arrangement." Why? Because the fact that human fossils are arranged by evolutionists in an evolutionary sequence hardly proves evolution true. First, the only reason an evolutionary sequence is arranged is *because* evolution is assumed to be true. Second, *"Any series of objects created by humans (or God) can be arranged in such a way as to make it look as if they had evolved when in fact they were created independently by an intelligent being."*[16]

Thus, in order to make human evolution *seem* true, some fossils are excluded by evolutionists when they do not fit into the scheme of evolution. Other fossils are arbitrarily downgraded to make them seem as if they were evolutionary ancestors—when in fact they are true humans. Finally, some non-human fossils are upgraded so that they appear to be human ancestors.[17]

More Doubts

Again, evolutionists generally consider the evidence for human evolution to be a fact beyond dispute. But even leading evolutionary authorities in the field of paleoanthropology disagree with this evidence. Richard Leakey in an AAAS interview said, concerning the study of early man, "I think we are still doing a great deal of guessing."[18]

David Pilbeam commented, "There is no clear-cut and inexorable pathway from ape to human being."[19] As to whether man evolved from chimps, orangutans, or gibbons, he remarks, "The fossil record has been elastic enough, the expectations sufficiently robust, to accommodate almost any story."[20] In a telling statement he writes, "[P]erhaps generations of students of human evolution, including myself, have been flailing about in the dark . . . our database is too sparse, too slippery, for it to be able to mold our theories. Rather, the theories are more statements about us and [our] ideology than about the past."[21]

The late Mary Leakey commented as to constructing evolutionary family trees that, "I do not believe it is [now] possible to fit the known hominid fossils into a reliable pattern."[22]

J. S. Jones and S. Rouhani comment, "The human fossil record is no exception to the general rule that the main lesson to be learned from paleontology is that evolution always takes place somewhere else."[23] "Dobzhansky, Ayala, Stebbins, and Valentine are typical of the technical works: 'at present, the evolutionary sequence *Australopithecus africanus—Australopithecus (or Homo) habilis—Homo erectus—Homo sapiens seems to be the most plausible one.*' Yet this macroevolutionary sequence is not supported by '*any* fossil traces,' according to Zuckerman."[24] Robert Martin is thus correct when he writes, "So one is forced to conclude that there is no clear-cut scientific picture of human evolution."[25] One wonders why, since mankind is by far the most recent of evolutionary adaptations; and would presumably offer the best chance for a series of evidential remains that would document evolution.

Yet Meave Leakey, the noted Kenyan paleoanthropologist concludes that "it may never be possible to say exactly what evolved into what."[26]

In its recent series on human evolution, *National Geographic* magazine, while assuring readers that all scientists agree human evolution is a fact, nevertheless described paleoanthropology as a "contentious field" and pointed out that

"Even within the scientific community debates are passionate."[27]

The debate is passionate because the evidence is equivocal and forces scientists to spend most of their time guessing. Reading the literature proves this. Consider only a few examples from the *National Geographic* series:

> [In contrast to the chart statements given in *National Geographic* above the following quote] Many researchers do not regard *A. aethiopicus*, *H. rudolfensis*, and *H. ergaster* as separate species, combining them instead with *A. boisei*, *H. habilis*, and *H. erectus*, respectively.
>
> One of the great mysteries of paleoanthropology is when, where, and how *Homo* [*habilis, erectus, sapiens*] replaced *Australopithecus*. . . .
>
> Such disagreement over bones is intense.
>
> Other scientists see a much more complex picture, arguing that many of the fossils we call *afarensis* may in fact be something else. Some scientists are now even questioning Lucy's position as the mother of us all [Lucy was a 3.2 million year old partial skeleton of *Australopithecus afarensis*]. . . .
>
> Over dinner we discuss the growing complexity of our view of human origins. Already many scientists are arguing that the tibia she [Leakey] found last year resembles *Homo* more than it does *afarensis*. They suggest that it might be part of another line of hominids. . . .
>
> Tim White of Berkeley . . . thinks this new species is so different from *Australopithecus* that he has created an entirely new genus for it [*ramidus*]. . . . Several of White's colleagues tell me they suspect *ramidus* actually belongs on the chimp lineage; its teeth look too primitive to be on the main line of human evolution.
>
> The fossil record for early *Homo*, however, remains scanty, and specialists argue over how many species existed. . . . New family trees have recently been drawn . . . the early *Homo* family tree is starting to look as bushy as the australopithecine one. . . .
>
> Walker's [divergent] opinion inflames other scientists. . . .
>
> Paleoanthropologists—like philosophers—will no doubt continue to argue about the basic nature of our ancestors.[28]

In light of all this uncertainty, consider the following enlightening statement from *Time* magazine for March 14, 1994,

"Yet despite more than a century of digging, the fossil record remains maddeningly sparse. With so few clues, even a single bone that doesn't fit into the picture can upset everything. Virtually every major discovery has put deep cracks in the conventional wisdom and forced scientists to concoct new theories, amid furious debate."

With all the brazen speculation, one can only wonder why evolutionists like to present the idea to the world that "the fact of human evolution is as established as the fact of gravity." "No one questions human evolution" they say. But again, when one examines the literature in even a cursory fashion, one discovers that evolutionists aren't sure at all. The false *assumption* that human evolution occurred has led them down so many blind alleys that paleoanthropology will never recover until it rejects its false assumption.

Material Problems

One major problem faced by paleoanthropologists is that the materials they must deal with present serious difficulties for establishing human evolution. Lubenow points out that though he had visited most major natural history museums in the U.S. and some overseas, "I have never seen an original human fossil." Nor has the public. He goes on to say that neither have most anthropologists in our universities who teach classes on human evolution. The reason is simple. Because of their extreme value and fragile nature the *original* human fossils are protected and sequestered in climate controlled vaults, so much so that the "total number of people who have access to them is actually fewer than the total number of heads of state—monarchs, presidents, prime ministers, dictators—in the world today."[29] (The lone exception occurred in 1984 when the American Museum of Natural History in New York sponsored its popular "Ancestors" exhibit where over 40 original fossils were brought together for the first time in history for scholars to study and the public to view. Significantly, the real motive for the display was an apparent attempt to counteract the growing "threat" of creationism.[30])

So what do most of us see, when we look at human fossils in museums? What we actually see are casts of the originals. But here is the first problem—the casts are not exact:

> Perhaps the best example of the problem facing paleoanthropology is that many of the scholars who felt that casting technology was now able to provide copies as good as the originals, after studying the originals in the 1984 American Museum exhibition, admitted "that technology still has a long way to go." The crowning blow came at the beginning of the public display. The precision mounts for the original fossils were carefully prepared on the basis of casts supplied in advance. When the original fossils were placed in those mounts, most of them did not fit. No better illustration could be found showing that "casts are no substitute for originals."
>
> Since the original fossils are virtually beyond access even to most who teach in the field of paleoanthropology, and only a few of them are available as reproductions, and reproductions are not recommended in the preparation of scientific papers, and those scientific papers themselves cannot adequately convey differences between fossils, paleoanthropology seems to have a problem. . . . The truth is that paleoanthropology is in the awkward position of being a science that is at least one step removed from the very material upon which it claims to base its findings.[31]

When small specifics of shape and size are crucial, inferior casts are a problem indeed.

A related problem involves the pictorial reconstructions we all see in evolutionary textbooks. Unfortunately, these are largely no more than misleading pictures from artists' imaginations based on the *assumption* of evolution. As Bird writes, "The problem is compounded by misleading pictures, which are merely artist's imaginative portrayals: '[B. Campbell states:] These reconstructions suggest far more knowledge of human evolution than we actually possess. We do not have a complete skeleton of any fossil older than Neanderthal, nor do we have any direct evidence about the extent of hair in these forms. . . Rensberger describes evolution taking place on the artist's palette. . . .' In the view of many paleoanthropologists, the story of human evolution *has been fictionalized* to suit needs other than scientific rigor.'"[32]

The problems of fossil man involved in both reconstruction and genetic/dietary/environmental factors that may affect physiology/bone structure make the interpretation of the data crucial. If erroneous evolutionary presuppositions interpret the data, this can hardly make such interpretations correct. Nor should the fact that we see such things as an alleged three-million-year-old three-foot-high "man-ape" described and classified on the basis of *four* bones. This tells us we should not place our faith in anthropological reconstructions based on an unsubstantiated theory like evolution.[33] In fact, because of its false assumption, the recent history of paleoanthropology indicates its probable future—more confusion. It seems opinions vary widely almost everywhere.

For example, *Ramapithecus* had supposed man-like traits but a living baboon had the same characteristics and some evolutionists called it an ape. *Australopithecus* was first disputed as an hominid because it has distinct ape features. There were two initial species classifications, *africanus* and *robustus,* but there was no general agreement if it was an ape, an ape-man, or a man-ape. *Zinjanthropus* was first discovered by Leaky who said it was a man but later thought it was an ape. Some have continued to claim it is a man even though its brain size and skull are more like an ape. Some claimed that Java man was a human; others say that it is an ape, or an ape-man, or a large gibbon. Little could be said about Peking man because all the fossil material was lost and only doubtful reconstructions remain. Nebraska man was originally erected from one tooth of an extinct pig and declared to have characteristics of a chimpanzee, *Pithecanthropus,* and man. Neanderthal man was for years classified as subhuman but is now classified as human.

A Rich Treasure

We have a very large number of human fossils, paleontologically speaking—literally thousands. This provides a very large amount of evidence concerning human origins. It would certainly seem to be enough to prove human evolution had it occurred.

But, as Professor Lubenow points out, given its richness, the statements by scientists concerning this fossil treasure are inconsistent. We frequently read statements from authorities who study human fossils concerning the very small number of fossils that have been discovered. Lubenow provides examples: *Time* magazine: "Scientists concede that even their most cherished theories are based on embarrassingly few fossil fragments"; *Scientific American*: "The human fossil record is short and scant"; *New Scientist*: "The entire hominid collection known today would barely cover a billiard table"; *Science*: "The primary scientific evidence is a pitifully small array of bones from which to construct man's evolutionary history."[34]

Again, this is just not the case. The human fossil evidence is comparatively abundant. From 1969 to 1976 3,998 hominid fossil individuals were discovered.[35] Since 1976, paleoanthropology has been involved in the most dedicated and successful search for hominid fossils in its history. The famed Olduvai Gorge in Tanzania, East Africa, dubbed "Evolution Headquarters" by *National Geographic,* is alone a treasure house. So far, no one knows exactly how many have been found in this vast search. Lubenow very conservatively estimates it is at least another 2,000 specimens.[36] We would not be too surprised to see a figure of 10,000.

The Real Problem

What the public is unaware of, and what most evolutionists, apparently, do not want to admit, is that the problem is *not* the scanty number of fossils. The real problem is the fact that the fossils we do have *do not fit the evolutionary scenario.* In other words, they do *not* provide evidence for human evolution. *This* is why the fossils are considered to be so few in number. Put simply, as the evolutionist Takahata observes, "There are not enough fossil records to answer when, where, and how *H. sapiens* emerged."[37] Thus, Lubenow declares: "The public is unaware of the rich harvest of hominid fossils we now possess. Although some of the myths I discuss in this book are not the fault of the evolutionists, this one clearly is. It is because they have gone to their public wailing wall and lamented the tragic lack of human fossils."[38] Lubenow points out that when scientists speak of the scarcity of the human fossil record what they are actually saying is "Although there is an abundance of hominid fossils, the bulk of them are either too modern to help me or they do not fit well into the evolutionary scheme. Since we all know that humans evolved, what is so perplexing is the difficulty we are having in finding the fossils that would clearly demonstrate that fact."[39]

The desire to prove evolution causes other serious problems. As the U.C. Berkeley anthropologist White points out, "The problem with a lot of anthropologists is that they want so much to find a hominid that any scrap of bone becomes a hominid bone."[40] This leads us to the conclusion of the anatomist Zuckerman, departmental chairman of the British Advisory Council on Science Policy who writes that "it is legitimate to ask whether much science is yet to be found in this field at all."[41]

The Homo Erectus Key

In his book, Lubenow discusses Neandertal man, archaic *Homo sapiens*, Java man, Wadjak man, the Selenka expedition, *Homo habilis*, *Homo erectus*, and much else. *None* provide evidence for evolution. As an example, consider *Homo erectus*, an absolutely crucial category for evolutionists:

> Java man (*Pithecanthropus* I) was the first of at least 222 similar fossil individuals that have been discovered to date. It would be impossible to exaggerate the importance of this group of fossils known collectively as *Homo erectus*. For the evolutionist, *Homo erectus* is the major category bridging the gap between the australopithecines (which everyone recognizes as nonhuman) and the archaic *Homo sapiens* and Neanderthal fossils (which everyone recognizes as truly human). Thus, *Homo erectus* is indispensable to the evolutionists as *the* transitional taxon. (*Homo habilis* is a flawed taxon that will be given a respectful burial in a later chapter.)
>
> Surprisingly, *Homo erectus* furnishes us with powerful evidence that falsifies the concept of human evolution.[42]

The morphology of *Homo erectus* is clearly not distinct enough to warrant it being classified as a species separate from *Homo sapiens*: "By every legitimate standard applicable, the fossil and cultural evidence indicate that it should be included in the *Homo sapiens* taxon."[43]

But further, the *Homo erectus* fossils clearly are *not* found in the relevant time frame to serve as a legitimate transitional form. In his book, Lubenow includes *Homo erectus* charts that are among the most complete listing of *Homo erectus* fossil morphology to be found anywhere in the scientific literature. When these are compared with other charts in his book, they prove that *Homo erectus* individuals lived side by side with other categories of true humans for the past two million years, according to evolutionist chronology. But what this means is that *Homo erectus could not have evolved* into *Homo sapiens* since they were contemporaries. "That this two-million-year contemporaneousness has been largely camouflaged is a tribute to the skill of evolutionist writers."[44]

This serious misrepresentation—some would argue fraud—concerning the dates of the *Homo erectus* fossil material can be traced squarely to evolutionists' faith in evolution in spite of embarrassing facts to the contrary:

> When people become aware of the massive misrepresentation of the dates for the *Homo erectus* fossil material, they act perplexed. But the factual evidence is so clear that it cannot successfully be challenged. The perplexity usually gives way to the question, Why do evolutionists do this? The answer is obvious. If the date range of all the fossils having a *Homo erectus* morphology were commonly published on a chart as they are in this book, *it would be clear that human evolution has not taken place.* However, it is possible that evolutionists are not being intentionally deceptive. The reason may be deeper and more complex. Because of evolutionists' faith in and commitment to evolution, I believe we are seeing a psychological phenomenon. Evolutionist gives us the dates they want *Homo erectus* to have, the dates they wish *Homo erectus* would have. I suspect it is more a case of self-deception on the part of evolutionists than it is an attempt to deceive others. It indicates how deeply their faith has colored their facts.[45]

The evidence presented in Lubenow's book alone seems tantamount to a disproof of human evolution. For example, he discusses whether there are adequate nonevolutionary explanations for the morphology of Neandertal, *Homo sapiens,* and

Homo erectus. And the answer is clearly yes. "There is a touch of humor in the fact that the nonevolutionary factors that adequately explain this morphology are some of the same factors that evolutionists themselves use to explain *Homo erectus*-like fossils when these fossils mischievously show up in the wrong time frame."[46]

Six Conclusions

Remember, the issue is not the fossils themselves but their interpretation. If we assume evolution, we will interpret the human fossils accordingly, no matter how strained the interpretation. If we do not assume evolution, we will not have the same conclusions and we will interpret the data we do have much more accurately.

In the end, six conclusions are forced upon us by an objective evaluation and interpretation of fossil human data.[47] First, Lubenow points out that fossils which are indistinguishable from modern humans, according to the evolutionary time scale, can be traced all the way back to 4.5 million years ago. This indicates that true humans were on the scene *before* the *australopithecines* (which everyone agrees were not human) appear in the fossil record. Therefore humans *could not have evolved* from the *australopithecines*.

Second, there is no evidence in the fossil record that shows *Homo erectus* evolving from something else or into something else. *Homo erectus* has a consistent morphology throughout its alleged two million year history.

Third, "anatomically modern *Homo sapiens*, Neanderthal, archaic *Homo sapiens*, and *Homo erectus* all lived as contemporaries at one time or another. None of them evolved from a more robust to a more gracile condition."[48]

Fourth, virtually all fossils ascribed to the category of *Homo habilis* are contemporary with *Homo erectus*. In other words, *Homo habilis could not have evolved* into *Homo erectus*.

Fifth, no fossils of *Australopithecus* or any other primate stock in the proper time period can serve as evolutionary ancestors to humans. The only thing the fossil record tells us is that *when ancestral humans first appear in the fossil record they are already fully human.* "It is this abrupt appearance of our ancestors in morphologically human form that makes the human fossil record compatible with the concept of Special Creation."[49] This is true even when we accept the evolutionists' time scale, a time scale that our own research leads us to believe is seriously flawed. Thus, even accepting that the evolutionists' dates for the fossils are accurate, the results still don't support human evolution. In fact, they are "so contradictory to human evolution" that human evolution simply cannot logically be accepted on the basis of the fossil evidence.[50]

Sixth, there is an independent control factor that confirms the above. This is where different types of fossils are found at the same place geographically and the same level stratigraphically. The fact that their morphology is different tells us they should be placed in different evolution categories. The fact that they are found together in the same place and level confirms the lack of evidence of human evolution. Such a situation should not exist if evolution were true.

Creation Evidence

In conclusion, the popular belief expressed by evolutionists, and widely believed by the public, is that the hominid fossil evidence proves human evolution. *Nothing could be further from the truth.* Not only does it not prove human evolution, it actually disproves it and strongly offers evidence for divine creation. As Lubenow points out, "The human fossil evidence is completely in accord with what the Scriptures teach."[51]

How do evolutionists respond to the lack of fossil confirmation for human evolution? Besides being reluctant to admit it, some of them do what they have done with the lack of evidence for plant and animal evolution—they downplay its relevance. They now claim that "the evidence for evolution simply does not depend upon the fossil record."[52] Of course, faced with such embarrassing facts, what else could they say?

One more point must be made. Lubenow shows that the oldest human fossil ever found (KP271) is dated some 4.5 million years ago according to the evolutionary time scale. Significantly, it offers evidence that humans appeared on the scene suddenly, *without* evolutionary ancestors. Although absolute proof is not possible, it can be stated with confidence that *"all* of the scientific evidence points" in the direction that KP271 was a true *Homo sapien* and that there is *no* scientific evidence that opposes it.[53]

This is all that science can say. But if KP271 is human, the theory of human evolution is discredited. And there *should* be nothing wrong with telling students this. The reason why students are *not* told this is because of the anti-naturalistic and creationist implications. "That the oldest human fossil ever found—skimpy as it is—reveals that man was virtually the same 4.5 million years ago (on the evolutionists' time scale) as he is today suggests that humans appeared on the scene suddenly and without evolutionary ancestors. Prior to 4.5 [million years ago] the hominid fossil record is a virtual blank for 10 million years. This supports the idea that humans were created by a supreme being. . . ." Professor Lubenow proceeds to write: "Just for the fun of it, let's grant the evolutionist his point. Let's assume that there is something very bad about telling a student that the oldest human fossil ever discovered supports Special Creation. As bad as that might be, I can think of something even worse. That would be to tell a student that the oldest human fossil ever discovered supports evolution. Because that would be a lie."[54]

Anyone with an open mind, not already philosophically committed to naturalism, who will take the time to read a few quality creationists' books on the subject of human evolution and/or the fossil record will be required to logically conclude that the fossil record provides *no* evidence for evolution.

It is rather startling that merely reading a few scholarly creationist critiques in the areas of alleged evidences for evolution, whether it is the fossil record, thermodynamics, biochemistry, probability theory, or whatever, can undermine confidence in literally scores of evolutionary texts on the same subject.

Certainly this must speak volumes as to the alleged evidences for evolution.

15

Creation, Evolution, and the Universe

Cosmic Evolution and the Big Bang

We saw in Chapter 2 that the theory of evolution is all encompassing, extending far beyond the biological realm. It seeks to explain not only the origin of all life naturalistically but the origin of the entire universe as well. In Chapter 10 we pointed out some of the conceptual difficulties with the idea that nothing created everything. Here we wish to examine the scientific difficulties with cosmogenies—the various scientific theories proposed to explain the creation and evolution of the universe—and show why modern science, in its rejection of theism, is forced to accept things far more difficult to believe.

A Tall Order

Evolution involves a "logical" sequence of events, *all* of which must occur to explain our existence. For example:

1. The universe had to create itself, including our solar system with its planets.
2. On one planet water had to form and life had to arise from non-life in the primitive ocean.
3. Molecular evolution had to happen.

4. The evolution of life generally had to occur—microorganisms, insects, fish, reptiles, birds, mammals, etc.
5. The transition from primates to humanity had to occur.

If evolution didn't occur at any particular level, it could
never have occurred beyond that level. We have seen that evolution never occurred at levels 2, 3, 4, or 5. Merely showing
why it never happened at level two should be sufficient to end
all discussion.

But we want to go back to level one, the very beginning—to
the evolutionary origin of the universe itself. Obviously, if the
universe never created *itself*, it never created *anything*. This is
why the most fundamental question materialists ever ponder is,
"Why is there something rather than nothing?" Apart from
theism, there could only be nothing, which is why the question
is so profound for materialists. In this chapter and Chapter 17
we will show that the fact there is something logically proves
divine creation.

Science and Creation

We should begin by noting that the scientific world clearly
oversteps its bounds when it attempts to make dogmatic statements about creation.

Science has nothing scientific to say about the concept
of creation. Science deals in observation, experimentation, re-
peatability, critical assessment, etc. Science is *incapable* of studying things that happened only once in the past and therefore
science cannot properly comment upon (let alone explain) creation because creation lies outside its proper domain. Science
has no more to do with the events of creation than it has to do
with the events of alleged past lives. Even creation *science* cannot comment on origins at this point, only religious creationism
can. The fact that, in the creation/evolution controversy, so
many scientists have made dogmatic scientific pronouncements
about creation only reveals their misunderstanding of the proper
bounds of science. Science, by its very nature, cannot explain
either the existence of the universe, why the laws of nature exist,
or why the universe is so strikingly ordered. If science cannot

explain the universe, then our only options are no explanation or a personal (theistic) explanation.

Yet, those holding a religious view of origins are ridiculed today while far less credible "scientific" theories are given a respect that greatly exceeds their due. The irony is that when evolutionists teach silliness in the name of science, they demand credibility and respect—and receive it. When theists who have difficulty with nonsense offer more *credible* alternatives that *better* explain the data, much of the scientific world decries them, almost mercilessly, as "ignorant" and "deceived."

It's Humorous

Yet one wonders, for example, if a religious group first proposed Big Bang cosmology, how would evolutionists have reacted?

Consider the following comment of Marilyn vos Savant, listed in *The Guiness Book of World Records* Hall of Fame for "Highest I.Q." Asked what she thought of the Big Bang theory she replied, "I think that if it had been a religion that first maintained the notion that all the matter in the entire universe had once been contained in an area smaller than the point of a pin, scientists probably would have laughed at the idea."[1] Undoubtedly, they would have.

In fact, *we* can't help but chuckle when we read things like the following by eminent U.C. Berkeley astronomer Timothy Ferris in the July 1997 *Astronomy* magazine, "At the start . . . the universe was smaller than a proton."[2]

A Double-Revelation of Equal Validity?

But for us the real question is, if science cannot comment on creation, why have some Christians listened to those who have no authoritative basis upon which to make their pronouncements and adopted evolutionary views?[3] This underscores the common misapplication of the "double-revelation" theory. This theory teaches that God has given us two books, the book of Scripture and the book of nature. The assumption is that these two revelations must agree or harmonize with one another and that what science tells us is true allows the harmonization to occur. The problem occurs when ersatz theories like evolution and the Big Bang are given the status of fact, and then the assumption is applied. Thus, when the "facts" of science are accepted—such as the Big Bang or organic evolution—the assumption is that the Bible must be made to harmonize with the "facts" of science.

This undercuts the authority of Scripture because the Bible must be misinterpreted when it is made to fit a false theory. From such a premise, if a scientific theory contradicts the Bible, assuming Scripture is properly interpreted, then the Scripture must be in error. Since the false scientific theory will not permit a normal interpretation of Scripture, in the end it works out that Scripture cannot be trusted scientifically and thus is considered supreme only in matters of doctrine and ethics. Science becomes supreme in matters of nature. The Bible may tell us the who and why of creation but science must tell us the how and when of creation. But again, if the scientific theory is wrong and if science cannot even properly comment upon creation, this approach is both irrelevant and dangerous. As Marvin L. Lubenow points out, there is a significant difference between the nature of biblical truth and the nature of scientific truth:

> Whether one agrees with it or not, the Bible claims to be truth in the absolute sense, including its statements about nature. On the other hand, philosophers of science are unanimous in recognizing that science does not—in fact, cannot—traffic in absolute truth. All scientific truth is relative. What strange twist of logic would cause us to think that absolute truth and relative truth can be or should be harmonized? In fact, if they could be harmonized, would that not be elevating the relative truth of today to absolute status? Since the average life of a scientific theory is less than 20 years, a harmonization today guarantees a lack of harmony tomorrow. Logic would tell us that a true harmonization cannot take place until Christ returns in glory and all truth is illuminated by the truth of God. Until then, the normal thing is to expect a degree of discord, not harmony. In other words, the basic supposition of the Double-Revelation theory is utterly false.[4]

Put another way, the book of Scripture and the book of nature can only be fully harmonized when all the facts are known.

To now distort the Bible by, for example, teaching that the days of Genesis are geological ages in which evolution occurred, is pure presumption. It is undeniably true that the Bible teaches a supernatural divine creation in six days. Even naturalistic critics and liberal theologians agree this is the literal, normal reading of Genesis. So, if the Bible is God's inerrant word, then for Christians, at least, there should be no creation/evolution controversy. If the Bible teaches special creation, then evolution of any sort, cosmological or biological, is impossible. It is impossible on scientific grounds *because* it is impossible on biblical grounds. God created the universe and gave us His word. His word is not going to mislead us about what God did in creation.

In the following material (and also in Chapter 17) we will show that only God can explain the existence of the universe. So, if theism is *the only* credible alternative, then it should be accepted for that reason. Even by scientists. Again, not only can science not properly comment on origins, the materialistic theories it puts forth to explain the origin of the universe simply aren't credible, despite their scientific popularity. As is true for evolution generally, these theories are far more difficult to believe than the more logical alternative of creation.

How Credible is the Big Bang?

Edward Nelson, Professor of Mathematics at Princeton University, wisely comments as follows, "in my view the big bang theory has been too widely accepted on the basis of insufficient evidence. I am persuaded of this partly by the work of Irving Segal (*Mathematical Cosmology and Extragalactic Astronomy*, NY: Academic Press, 1976; and many articles). Until we have a sound and rigorously established cosmology, it is premature to investigate the origin of the universe. On a metaphysical level, I believe that the origin of the universe is to be found in the free act of its Creator. . . . One of my earliest memories is a feeling of great surprise that there is anything. It still strikes me as amazing. . . . "[5]

Theories that are *demonstrably* true are simply not challenged by competent scientists, let alone leading scientists and Nobel Prize winners. The fact is that the Big Bang theory, in all its glory and forms* has been subject to serious, and we think, fatal critique by reputable scientists, including Nobel Prize winners. A minority of scientists "reject the Big Bang theory entirely" while others are unconvinced by the persuasiveness of the primary evidence.[6] Among scientists who reject the Big Bang theory entirely are Hannes Alfven, a physicist at the Royal Institute of Technology in Stockholm and Nobel Prize recipient; noted astronomer Sir Fred Hoyle, formerly of Cambridge whom noted evolutionist Stephen Jay Gould referred to as an "eminent cosmologist of years past,"; Jayant Narlikar, an astronomer with the Tata Institute of Fundamental Research; and numerous others.[7]

One evolutionist, Vaucouleurs, points out what should be obvious to everyone—that the reliable data are simply far too scant to make the broad origins conclusions science has currently made:

> Nevertheless, *the few facts and figures* which in the past 440 years have been given prominence as particularly relevant to cosmology are still too little understood and often too poorly established or too recently discovered to form a solid basis for a "final" solution. Also we may well still lack some fundamental knowledge of physical laws on the very large (cosmic) scale or on the very small (particle) scale, or both, to even hope for a realistic solution at the present time. . . . Less than 550 years after the birth of what we are pleased to call "modern cosmology," when so few empirical facts are passably well established, when so many different oversimplified models of the universe are still competing for attention, is it, we may ask, really credible to claim, or even reasonable to hope, that we are presently close to a definite solution to the cosmological problem?[8]

We don't think there is a definite solution, not by a long shot. Hannes Alfven, winner of the Nobel prize for physics in 1970 discusses some of the serious problems for Big Bang

---

*For example, in one form the cosmos is created at a specific point in time and expands forever; in another view the universe has no beginning or end but oscillates between an infinite cycle of cosmic deaths and rebirths, similar to Eastern religious belief.

cosmology. Alfven points out that such problems are often ignored or suppressed. In fact, what is true for evolution in general is also true for evolutionary cosmology—because troublesome facts do not fit the accepted theory, the facts are ignored, suppressed, or reinterpreted so that the theory survives at all costs:

> On the other hand, there are an increasing number of observational facts which are difficult to reconcile in the Big Bang hypothesis. The Big Bang establishment very seldom mentions these, and when non-believers try to draw attention to them, the powerful establishment refuses to discuss them in a fair way. . . .
>
> The present situation is characterized by rather desperate attempts to reconcile observations with the hypothesis to "save the phenomena." One cannot avoid thinking of the state under the Ptolemaean Epoch. *An increasing number of ad hoc assumptions* are made, which in a way correspond to the Ptolemaean introduction of more and more epicyles and eccentrics. Without caring very much for logical stringency, the agreement between these *ad hoc* assumptions with the Big Bang hypothesis is often claimed to support the theory.
>
> In reality, with the possible exception of the microwave background condition, *there is not a single [Big Bang] prediction which has been confirmed.*[9]

Scientists tell us that billions of years ago all the matter and energy in the universe were crammed together in a ball of subatomic particles and radiation, the diameter of which has been estimated to be much smaller than just one electron. Its temperature and density were of incredible proportions. Science does not tell us where this entity came from but supposedly it exploded. No one knows why. As it expanded, it cooled sufficiently that hydrogen and helium gas could be formed. These gases expanded outward into the vast stretches of the universe until low temperature and pressure were achieved. Eventually, somehow, stars and galaxies were formed, our solar system was formed and life was formed, including man.

In essence, as if by magic, we go from subatomic particles and radiation to the marvels of the universe and of humanity, including the marvels of the human brain with its 12 billion brain cells and 120 trillion connections.[10] As Gish remarks,

given enough time and luck, science tells us, subatomic particles and radiation, left entirely to themselves, finally become
people! It's really a fairy tale for materialists. A nice story, but
that's it. Perhaps this is where the following view of man originates. J. D. Bernal, a Professor of x-ray crystallography gave the
following definition of life, "Life is a partial, continuous,
progressive, multiform, and continually interactive self-
realization of the potentialities of atomic electron states."[11] But
really now, is that all man is? Would the good professor supply
this reductionist description to his own son or daughter?

Regardless, the truth is we have *no* idea of what happened
at the moment of creation, or any way to determine what
physical laws may or may not have existed. This makes *everything* speculative. Robert Oldershaw, writing in *New Scientist*
observes, "In the light of all these problems, it is astounding
that the Big Bang hypothesis is the only cosmological model
that physicists have taken seriously."[12]

The Big Bang survives for two reasons: 1) other theories
have even more problems and 2) the only alternative is *supernatural* creation. One of the nation's leading astronomers, Geoffrey Burbridge remarks, "Big Bang cosmology has become a
bandwagon of thought that reflects faith as much as objective
truth. . . . This situation is particularly worrisome because
there are good reasons to think the Big Bang model is seriously
flawed."[13]

Rather than discard the theory, one may expect that *ad hoc*
explanations will become both more sophisticated and more
strained. So, what are some of the problems with the Big Bang?
Every aspect of the Big Bang, all the way up to humanity, is
fraught with intractable problems. Below we consider several.

Problem One: The Mystery of the "Egg" and Its Explosion

As Dr. Gish points out, the origin of the cosmic "egg" is a
complete mystery:

> Why should it have been there at all? The First Law [of thermo-
> dynamics] tells us that the total quantity of energy in the universe
> is a constant. If one holds to the belief that these natural laws are
> all there is and all there ever has been, then it must be accepted
> that the cosmic egg could not have come into being from nothing.

If even a single atom cannot come into being from nothing, surely the matter and energy equivalent to that presently existing in the universe could not have come into being from nothing. Where did all this mass/energy come from? How long did it sit there before it exploded? What caused it to explode? But why worry about these little problems while playing games? And all of this is just a game. George Abell tells us, "We are playing games—cosmology is the best sport of all, because it is the ultimate game."[14]

Thus, "the first law of thermodynamics rules out a Big Bang that brings matter into existence, as Narlikar and Padmanabhan point out: The conservation of energy—one of the most cherished principles of physics—is violated in the Big-Bang model . . . it is impossible for matter to come into existence without violating energy conservation. It is customary to water down this difficulty by statements like 'the laws of physics break down at a singularity'; however the essential truth remains the same. . . ."[15]

Why should the laws of physics break down at the singularity of the Big Bang? Can any scientist convincingly explain why? And what on earth caused the matter-energy to be so infinitely concentrated in the cosmic egg? Some kind of unknown force that no one can explain. Further, what happened before the Big Bang? No one knows. There are no physical principles that allow for such a concentration and no known basis for it to explode, which essentially "invalidate[s] the Big Bang theory."[16]

Problem Two: The Needed Precision and Inexplicable Results of the Explosion

A greater problem is the need for the incredibly fine tuned accuracy of the characteristics of the explosion which would result in ordered galaxies, solar systems, planets, and moons:

Simply put, a compacted universe was the ultimate black hole, and black holes may not be exploding today and certainly do not produce galaxies, stars, planets, and other complexity.

Moreover, the problem that the expansion must be incredibly "tuned to an accuracy of 1 part in 10^{50}" is summarized by Lake: "What we find from this is that the initial data (expansion rate and density), specified at a time 10^{-39} seconds after the Bang, have to be tuned to an accuracy of 1 part in 10^{50}, even though p is so poorly known today. . . .

Leslie affirms the need for a precise expansion rate: ". . . Reduction by *one part in a million million* at an initial stage would seemingly have led to recollapse in under 100,000 years and before temperatures had fallen below 10,000 degrees. Equivalently tiny increases would have had similarly huge results. Even as matters stand it is hard to see how galaxies could have formed in a universe which is flying apart so fast—and an early speed increased by one thousandth would quickly have led to a thousand-fold increase. (b) Again, very slight reductions in the smoothness with which matter is distributed . . . would apparently have multiplied the primeval heat billions of times with disastrous effect."[17]

Explosions are anything but accurate and certainly not accurate to such incredible degrees. Burbridge states, "Probably the strongest argument against a Big Bang is that when we come to the universe in total and the large number of complex condensed objects in it [e.g., galaxies, stars], *the theory is able to explain so little*."[18] Again, "an explosion merely throws matter apart, while the Big Bang has mysteriously produced the opposite effect, with matter clumping together in the form of galaxies."[19]

Cosmologists face intractable problems if they attempt to explain the origin of the universe, galaxies, solar systems, and planets on evolutionary principles. Galaxies alone spin so fast that they ought to fly apart. Clusters and super clusters of galaxies are linked together gravitationally in patterns estimated to stretch more than a half billion light years. The Big Bang explosion cannot account for this. Further, recent observations of extremely distant quasars, apparently close to the edge of the universe, indicate stars are clustering in galaxies much earlier than had been thought possible.

Evolutionary cosmologists and astrophysicists cannot explain how, in an exploding universe, matter could ever become concentrated into the intricate systems we see. For example, the M13 globular star cluster contains an estimated one million suns. About 100 such star clusters are known and they apparently surround our galaxy on all sides. "When the distribution of these objects is plotted, it is found that they form a nearly spherical system and that the center of this system is identical with the center of our galaxy."[20]

The intricate formation of moons that orbit planets, planets that orbit stars, stars and galaxies that cluster, etc., simply *cannot* result from an explosion like the Big Bang. Noted astronomer Fred Hoyle tells us why:

> This persistent weakness has haunted the Big Bang theory ever since the 1930s. It can probably be understood most easily by thinking to begin with of what happens when a bomb explodes. After detonation, fragments are thrown into the air, moving with essentially uniform motion. As is well-known in physics, *uniform motion is inert*, capable in itself of doing nothing. It is only when the fragments of a bomb strike a target—a building for example— that anything happens. . . . But in a single Big Bang there are no targets at all, because the whole universe takes part in the explosion. There is nothing for the expanding material to hit against, and after sufficient expansion, the whole affair *should go dead.* . . . [E]ven though outward speeds are maintained in a free explosion, *internal motions are not.* Internal motions die away adiabatically, and the *expanding system becomes* inert, which is exactly why the Big Bang cosmologies lead to a universe that is dead and done with almost from its beginning.[21]

The conditions that must exist for galaxies, etc., to form after a Big Bang explosion are so improbable as to nullify the possibility they occurred through an explosion of this sort. Rather than forgo the Big Bang, however, scientists offer strained theories or interpretations of data to "explain how" the Big Bang could have produced galaxies, or they ignore contrary evidence altogether.

Problem Three: Red Shift Interpretation

To illustrate that important evidence is being ignored, Bird points out that astronomer Halton Arp had produced significant data to undermine the current interpretation of the red-shift phenomenon in support of the Big Bang cosmology.

The red shift, interpreted through the Doppler effect, involves the shift or change of a spectrum of light toward longer, that is redder, wavelengths. Scientists generally believe the red shifts result from the expansion of the universe, but alternate interpretations are equally or more credible. Here is yet another case of the evolutionary tail wagging nature's dog—assumptions of evolution forcing interpretation of data into an evolutionary, in this case Big Bang, model.

Arp and Sulentic had completed a massive study involving 260 companion galaxies. They discovered that the red shifts of these companion galaxies systematically and significantly differed. Further:

> Earlier, Arp had tabulated "24 main galaxies and 38 discordant red shift companions," and had published a catalog of hundreds of discordant red shifts. His assessment of why his Herculean research has been "ignored" is as follows: "This important result has largely been ignored by astronomers because it does not fit in with the current theoretical framework. . . . "[22]

Arp's data requires the conclusion that red shifts are not universally applicable as distance indicators and thus not evidence for a Big Bang cosmology.

The prominent astronomer Burbidge concurs that these extremely important results obtained by Arp, as well as other scientists, now provide strong evidence that red shifts can *not* be accurately interpreted as being accurate measures of distance and age. Again, this evidence is simply ignored by evolutionary cosmologists. Burbidge recalls, "If this evidence is presented to any gathering of scientists who are not astronomers, as I have done on a number of occasions, it is accepted without any real debate. But among the professionals, *it is largely ignored. . . .* Perhaps because astronomers, knowing that *their subject in this area already rests on rather shaky foundations* as far as hard-proven evidence is concerned, cannot face up to the opening of Pandora's box in extragalactic astronomy."[23]

Burbidge goes on to point out that despite the consensus among astronomers as to their interpretation of the red shifts, "the evidence is there" that seriously questions it "and if we are really searching for the truth, we ignore it at our intellectual peril."[24]

In his critique of the Doppler effect, Vincent A. Ettari writes that the red shift appears to be related "to the type of radiation the object emits, rather than its distance" and therefore that "few red shifts are actually Doppler in nature." In addition, "due to the vagueness and seemingly contradictory nature of the recorded data, a red shift/distance relationship has never been successfully calculated, leaving the so-called 'Hubble constant' undetermined and indefensible as a theoretical construct. Thus, the Doppler explanation must be abandoned, leaving the 'Big Bang' evolutionary cosmology without any supporting evidence."[25]

The difficulties with the red shift time/distance interpretation is one reason why those who attempt to mix a Genesis cosmology with the Big Bang theory are faced with formidable problems. One problem is discussed by Professor Marvin Lubenow as follows:

> In all forms of the Big Bang model, all matter was initially concentrated at one point. The Big Bang explosion propelled this matter outward in all directions. . . . After the Big Bang, time increases in direct proportion to distance. Vast distances translate to immense time or age. To say that a galaxy is ten billion light-years distant is also to say that it is ten billion years old.
>
> However, in the Genesis cosmology there is no relationship between time and distance. When God spoke the universe into existence with the power of his word, it was fully developed immediately. In the beginning (T=O), the distance (D) was already immense. *Distance is not a measure of time or age because there is no time-distance relationship.* This is why the mixing of a Genesis creation concept with the Big Bang time scale produces absurdities.
>
> One of the fallacies of the Big Bang cosmology is based upon this time-distance relationship. Because the light from distant galaxies appears to be red shifted, astronomers believe that the universe is expanding. Although the idea of an expanding universe is just one of several possible interpretations of the red shift of light, this expansion in itself is not necessarily unbiblical. What is unbiblical is the extrapolation of this expansion backward 15 billion years to an alleged Big Bang. [26]

Professor Lubenow points out that the validity of the extrapolation can be put to a test. Looking back out in space we look back in time. Had the universe been expanding for 15 billion years we would expect that there would be a difference in the spacial density of the galaxies. In other words, the galaxies that are far out should be closer together than galaxies close to our own local Milky Way system, since they are closer to the Big Bang in time. But the fact is *we do not see these differences* "even when measured within the parameters of the Big Bang cosmology." Lubenow quotes authority Sir Bernard Lovell, the one who basically pioneered radio astronomy, as admitting that "we do not find any change even in what we call the spatial density of the galaxies." In other words, the number of galaxies in a given volume of space is the same in the region of our own local galaxy as it is at the distance of four billion light years. What this means is that if the universe *is* expanding, it has not been expanding very long, presumably indicating a recent creation.[27]

Problem Four: The Background Radiation

Another example of scientists ignoring hard facts for preferred theories deals with a problem that is stressed by Hoyle and others such as Woody and Richards, who argue if there were ever a Big Bang explosion, the microwave background radiation should be somewhere between 10 and 1,000 times more powerful than it is. Thus, despite the widespread claims that background radiation offers proof of the Big Bang, in fact it "does not prove but disproves the Big Bang theory and invites alternative explanations."[28] Woody and Richards conclude with the following dismal fact concerning scientific objectivity, "The latest data differ by so much from what theory would suggest as to *kill the Big Bang cosmologies*. But now, because the scientific world is emotionally attracted to the Big Bang cosmologies, the data are ignored."[29]

No less an authority than Alfven points out that the "claim that this radiation lends strong support to hot Big Bang cosmologies is without foundation." He says that if we examine the background radiation "without any preconceived ideas" we do not find it convincing at all. It involves tremendous leaps of faith: "Is there any other field of science where such an extrapolation in one jump is accepted without very strong proof?"[30]

Unfortunately, because preferential theories so entirely dominate modern science, one does not need to look far to find example after example of the misuse of data to support a particular belief. There is no doubt that red shift occurs or that background microwave radiation exists—the issue is what they actually mean. If the Big Bang theory is assumed, then the data will be interpreted to fit the theory. The data should be left to interpret itself. The truth is there are major problems in using either of these primary lines of evidence (red shift, background radiation) as support for the Big Bang. When one looks at the data objectively, one is forced to a contrary conclusion as Burbidge points out, "I believe that if one attempts to evaluate this evidence objectively *there is still no really conclusive evidence in favor of such a [Big Bang] universe.*"[31]

In fact, concerning the red shift, discordant red shift results should actually *require* a different explanation because the data are too strong to ignore. In the words of Arp:

> It cannot be stressed too strongly, however, that these discordant red shifts are not discovered in just one or two isolated cases that have no relation to each other. But *in every case* we can test—large clusters, groups, companions to nearby galaxies, companions to middle-distance galaxies, companions linked by luminous filaments, galaxies interacting gravitationally, chains of galaxies—in every conceivable case, we come out with the same answer: the same discordant red shifts for the same general class of younger, fainter galaxies. . . . [32]

In conclusion, even if the red shift did accurately reflect a proportional recession, this "expansion tells one virtually nothing about initial cosmic states," and "[e]specially . . . does not imply the singularly dense superpositioned state used in the Big Bang model."[33]

Other Problems

Beyond the above, there are other serious problems with the Big Bang cosmology which make this theory even more difficult to accept. Four of the more well-known problems involve: 1) why such little anti-matter exists in the universe; 2) how galaxies could have formed in the allotted time span; 3) the isotropic nature of the universe; and 4) the "flatness" problem or why the mass of the universe is so proximate to the critical value necessary to close the universe.[34] Then there are a half dozen additional problems, including the necessity of amazingly precise relations between the four universal forces (the strong and weak nuclear forces, electromagnetism, and gravity). These also rule out a Big Bang cosmology.

In fact, so many objections have been raised against the Big Bang that we find texts with bold titles like Eric Lerner's *The Big Bang Never Happened* (1991). Thus, other models have been proposed. One significant model is that of creationist J. K. West, Ph.D., with the Advanced Materials Research Center, Department of Materials Science and Engineering, University of Florida, Alachua. West presents technical evidence that the universe may be stable and not expanding: "In recent literature, there has been a significant number of objections and problems presented concerning the Big Bang. In this work, a non-expanding polytropic model of the universe is presented that can account for many of the observations previously attributed to the Big Bang and some observations that cannot be explained if the Big Bang did occur."[35]

The Big Bang explosion theory would seem to be ruled out. And the oscillating Big Bang theory is just as dead since it declares that matter and energy are eternal. If this were true, hydrogen would have been consumed at some point in the infinite past. The existence of unconsumed hydrogen rules out an eternal universe.[36] In addition, significantly, "The proofs against the oscillating universe model destroys this scientific foundation of Hinduism, Buddhism, and their New Age derivatives. The proofs against the eternal existence of the cosmos translate into the impossibility of pantheism and all of its daughter faiths insofar as they include the notion of an eternal past."[37]

Because of the above difficulties, different scientists have concluded that the Big Bang cosmology in any form is not credible. Allen argues that "the Big Bang is not needed" while Bondi tells us that the theory has "been disproved by present day empirical evidence."[38] Hoyle concludes that a "number of serious difficulties have to be ignored, swept under the rug, difficulties which indeed it may never be possible to resolve from within this particular theory. . . . I have little hesitation in saying that as a result a sickly pall now hangs over the Big Bang theory. As I have mentioned earlier, when a pattern of facts becomes set against a theory, experience shows that it rarely recovers."[39]

Of course, the death of a favored theory is usually slow and agonizing. Committed Big Bang believers will not accept the above evidence since it "can't" disprove what "must" be true. If most scientists accept the Big Bang cosmology because it fits their personal preference for a naturalistic cosmology, problems with the theory are ignored simply because there are no alternatives. Science is again reduced to preference.

In conclusion, naturalistic speculation concerning the origin of the universe and life in it will come and go and never be definitive. The Bible now, and always, will give us the only truly believable account of origins.

In light of this, perhaps it should surprise no one that even leading scientists are now turning to theism as the only possible *reasonable* explanation for origins. In our final section we will offer a brief introduction and then sufficient examples to document this.

Cosmogenies, Science, and Silence

An examination of all the different theories put forth, both past and present, to explain the origin of the universe and the solar system prove one thing: scientists will never, no matter how much they search and speculate, be able to explain the origin of the universe. It is simply beyond human capacity. Astronomer George Mulfinger observes, "No system of evolutionary cosmogeny once it has been given an adequate length of time to demonstrate its worth, has survived."[40] Lemaitre's Primeval Atom Hypothesis (1927), Gamow's Big Bang Hypothesis (1947), Hoyle's Steady State Theory (1948), Alfven's Ambiplasma Hypothesis (1965) all fall short of explaining the data. So do newer inflationary theories of the Big Bang and the more incredible, almost mystical concepts such as the super-string theory. (The super-string theory is that vibrating "strings," trillions of times smaller than protons, created the universe.)

What scientist H. Jeffreys declares concerning theories of the origin of the solar system is equally true concerning theories of galaxy formation and the origin of the universe itself: "To sum it up, I think that all suggested accounts of the origin of the Solar System are subject to serious objections. The conclusion in the present state of the subject would be that *the system cannot exist.*"[41] This conclusion is true. Naturalistically, they cannot exist. Only God can explain them.

Again, because science is forced to begin with nothing, it only has *nothing* to work with and this can never explain or produce anything. Guth and Steinhardt, writing in *Scientific American* for May 1984, find it tempting to "speculate that the entire universe evolved from literally nothing."

But as Varghese correctly comments, "No scientific theory, it seems, can bridge the gulf between absolute nothingness and a full-fledged universe (or fledgling universes). This ultimate origin question is a metascientific question—one which science can ask but not answer."[42] Further:

> That there has to be an explanation is evident to the scientific mind. But it is equally evident that this explanation cannot be verified or falsified with scientific tools if it involves absolute nothingness at any point. . . . Theoreticians at the cutting-edge of cosmology have tried to overcome the obstacles to explanations of the Big Bang in scientific terms by probing the ultimate and the fundamental laws and mechanism behind the processes detected by the experimentalists. The most influential approaches to this level of explanation include the Oscillating Universe hypothesis and the Quantum Gravity, Vacuum Fluxuation, and Inflationary Universe models.[43]

None of these theories even comes close to explaining the origin of the universe. And the best scientists know it. For those who doubt it, we now present sufficient documentation and, in light of the presumptions of many scientists who consider themselves experts on creation, while belittling creationist "know nothings," we belabor the point.

Noted Professor Eugene P. Wigner, winner of the Nobel Prize for physics and Emeritus Professor of Physics at Princeton University writes, "The origin of the universe is a mystery for science, surely for the present. It is a disturbing mystery."[44]

William Stoeger (Ph.D., astrophysics, Cambridge) points out, "In other words, any physical model of the universe—even though it be the definitive unified field theory—will apparently not be able to account intelligibly for the existence of the universe by itself."[45]

Professor Frederick C. Robbins, M.D. in Pediatrics from Harvard Medical School and Nobel Prize winner for physiology/medicine, writes, "No matter how deeply we probe scientifically, I doubt if we will be able to discover the ultimate answers."[46]

Professor Jeffrey I. Steinfield, Ph.D. in Chemistry, Harvard University, currently Professor of Chemistry at Massachusetts Institute of Technology, remarks that modern theories may be just as useless as long disproven medieval myths: "I have become convinced that, at some level, physical reality must be more complex than our conscious minds are able to comprehend. Is it not possible that most (or perhaps all!) of the currently fashionable cosmological constructs, such as 'super strings,' 'folded dimension,' 'worm holes,' 'pocket universes,' and so on, might be just as fanciful as the cosmology of medieval scholasticism, with its angels, crystal spheres, and *primum mobile*?"[47]

Professor John Erik Fornaess, Professor of Mathematics at Princeton University, writes, "Where matter came from is also unknown. It is also unknown where consciousness came from. . . . We don't have any idea where the basic ingredients of the universe came from."[48]

Professor Sir Nevill Mott, winner of the Nobel Prize for physics comments that "I am far from believing that science will ever give us the answers to all our questions."[49]

Professor Louis Neel, also winner of the Nobel Prize for physics writes frankly, "The progress of science, no matter how marvelous it appears to be, does not bring science closer to religion but it leads to dead ends and shows our final ineptitude at producing a rational explanation of the universe."[50]

Science and God: A Warming Trend?

If the reader is currently enamored with the authority of science in the sphere of origins, let him or her read the last comment again. Not only do the most brilliant of scientists agree that science is impotent in the face of ultimate issues, they now realize these issues are ultimately answered only by theism.

The above subheading headlined a "News and Comment" article in *Science* magazine for August 15, 1997. The author pointed out some interesting facts, for example, the Society of Ordained Scientists currently numbers about 3,000 worldwide and a 1997 poll conducted by Edward Larson of the University of Georgia, Athens, revealed that 40 percent of working physicists and biologists have strong religious beliefs.

There is indeed a warming trend of science to religious ideas. Consider some examples:

Professor Charles H. Townes, Nobel Prize winner in physics writes, "In my view, the question of origins seems always left unanswered if we explore from a scientific view alone. Thus, I believe there is a need for some religious or metaphysical explanation if we are to have one."[51]

Professor Werner Arber, winner of the Nobel Prize for physiology/medicine, writes concerning the vast complexity of molecular biology, "How such already quite complex structures may have come together, remains a mystery to me. The possibility of the existence of a Creator, of God, represents to me a satisfactory solution to this problem. . . . I know that the concept of God helped me to master many questions in life; it guides me in critical situations, and I see it confirmed in many deep insights into the beauty of the functioning of the living world."[52]

Indeed, the facts of science themselves now lead many brilliant scientists to posit a scientific need for God in order to explain the existence of the universe and life in it. A dozen illustrations can be offered. As Professor Christian B. Anfinsen, Ph.D. in biochemistry Harvard University and Nobel Prize winner for chemistry writes, "I think only an idiot can be an atheist."[53] Anfinsen, and many others like him, apparently now share the same sentiments as those of the Psalmist, "The fool has said in his heart there is no God."

Professor Henry Margenau, Emeritus Eugene Higgins Professor of Physics and Natural Philosophy, Yale University, and former president of the American Association for the Philosophy of Science writes, "Theories like the Big Bang, black holes, quantum theory, relativity, and the Anthropic Principle have introduced science to a world of awe and mystery that is not far removed from the ultimate mystery that drives the religious impulse. . . . What, then, is the answer to the question concerning the origin of the innumerable laws of nature? I know only one answer that is adequate to their universal validity: they were created by God."[54]

Ulrich J. Becker, Professor of Physics at Massachusetts Institute of Technology and member of the Research Council of Europe in Geneva, Switzerland, writes, "How can I exist without a creator? I am not aware of any compelling answer ever given."[55]

Robert A. Naumann, Professor of Chemistry and Physics at Princeton University, writes, "The existence of the universe requires me to conclude that God exists."[56]

Dr. Arno Penzias, winner of the Nobel Prize for physics, writing in "Creation Is Supported by All the Data So Far" declares:

> Astronomy leads us to a unique event, a universe which was created out of nothing, one with the very delicate balance needed to provide exactly the conditions required to permit life, and one which has an underlying (one might say "supernatural") plan. Thus, the observations of modern science seem to lead to the same conclusions as centuries-old intuition.[57]

Professor Arthur L. Schawlow, J. G. Jackson-C. J. Wood Professor of Physics at Stanford University, argues, "It seems to me that when confronted with the marvels of life and the universe, one must ask why and not just how. The only possible answers are religious. . . . I find a need for God in the universe and in my own life."[58]

Professor Wolfgang Smith, Ph.D. in Mathematics, Columbia University and Professor of Mathematics at Oregon State University, writes, "To me personally nothing is more evident, more certain, than the existence or reality of God. I incline in fact to the view that the existence of God constitutes indeed the only absolute certainty, even as he (or it) constitutes, in the final analysis, the only true or absolute Existent. . . ."[59]

Professor Walter Thirring, currently Director for the Institute for Theoretical Physics and Professor at the University of Vienna, believes that "scientists who devote their lives to exploring the *harmonia mundi* [harmony of the world] cannot help seeing in it some divine plan."[60]

Thomas C. Emmel, Ph.D. in Population Biology, Stanford University, and currently Professor of Zoology at the University of Florida, Gainesville, declares, "To me, the concept of God is a logical outcome of the study of the immense universe that lies around us. My readings in science and my professional pursuit of science have simply confirmed further to me that there are ultimate questions that we as scientists cannot answer. . . . To me, God exists as the Supreme Being who started this creation that we call the universe. . . . The evidence is all too pervasive for me to think otherwise."[61]

Professor P. C. C. Garnham, M.D., D.Sc., recipient of the Darling Medal and Prize and the Bernhard Noct Medal among others, currently Emeritus Professor of Medical Protozoology at the University of London, writes, "By faith and by appreciation of scientific necessity, God must exist."[62]

Professor Roger J. Gautheret, former Professor of Cell Biology at the Paris Facility of Science and former President of the Academy of Sciences, Paris, concludes, "I believe that notions such as infinite space and time, matter, structure, and order which govern the universe suggest the intervention of a spirit which has established the universe and its laws. Reflection on these subjects cannot avoid the notion of God."[63]

The above statements come from some of the leading scientists in the world. As the back cover of the book containing their statements declares, "Stranger and more momentous than the strangest of scientific theories is the appearance of God on the intellectual horizon of contemporary science. From Einstein, Planck, and Heisenberg, to Margenau, Hawking and Eccles, some of the most penetrating modern minds have needed God in order to make sense of the cosmos." We had space to quote only a few of these 60 leading scientists, including 24 Nobel Prize winners, as to their views on the existence of God. Of course, it should never be considered strange that God should appear on the intellectual horizon of science. He never left it; He was only voted out of consideration by materialists, many of whom now recognize they were wrong.

What must be obvious by now is that no Christian ever need be intimidated in stating their belief in the distinctly biblical God or in His Son Jesus Christ when some of the leading scientists—indeed leading thinkers in all disciplines—have openly declared their faith in theism.

The Bible and the Big Bang

What must also be evident is that science cannot tell us how the universe came to be. Even though the Big Bang theory is without basis, many scientists who are Christians have unfortunately made a Big Bang cosmology the model for the proper interpretation of Genesis.

The Big Bang, like evolution, is widely accepted by Christians today, no doubt because of its popularity. In fact, one prominent and highly influential evangelical scientist is so enamored with the Big Bang theory he required us to delete a one paragraph criticism of it (in an appendix!) before he would distribute the book to his extensive organization membership. This is unfortunate, indeed, when even Christian scientists become censors of alternate viewpoints to prevailing dogmas.

Christians should never interpret Genesis through the eyes of some scientific cosmogenic theory. When the theory goes, as it will, the Bible is only discredited for "harmonizing" with a false theory. As we have said before, the Bible stands alone, and stands on its own, as having the most *believable* view of origins ever put forth. It needs no help from speculation, naturalistic or otherwise.

In fact, returning to the Big Bang for a moment, there are sufficient number of physical impossibilities in Big Bang cosmology to require the need to invoke the miraculous. (We saw this was also true in the theory of evolution.) Paul C. W. Davis wrote the following concerning how we might be able to accept the Big Bang in light of all its problems. All we need do is accept miracles! "So far it has been supposed that the shuffling process is random. But how do we know that the universe which emerged from the Big Bang was truly chaotic so that subsequent collisions and interactions between subatomic particles are overwhelmingly likely to disintegrate in the order which may appear? If *the miracle* of the Big Bang included *miraculously* organized subatomic arrangements too, then random shuffling would have to be replaced by organized rearrangement."[64]

Davis refers to the "*miracle* of the Big Bang" and to "*miraculously* organized subatomic arrangements." Of course one can have a Big Bang if one invokes the miraculous. But there is no way to account for it naturalistically. And if we are going to invoke the miraculous in the Big Bang, why shouldn't Christians, at least, simply accept the straightforward account in Genesis?

Again, many Christians believe God used the Big Bang to create the universe and even that it fits perfectly with Genesis. Astronomer Hugh Ross is probably best known for this view but there are many others such as science writer Fred Heeren who writes that "Modern science's most favored theory of beginnings, the Big Bang theory . . . harmonizes with the Bible."[65]

To the contrary, biblically speaking, is there anything to suggest that God did *not* use the Big Bang event to create the universe? In fact there is. The Scriptures teach that God directly created the universe, not that He indirectly created it through some incredibly dense cosmic egg with the propensity to explode and then expand for billions of years. In Job 9:8 we read, "*He alone* stretches out the heavens. . . ." God alone created the heavens. And, He also didn't scatter them randomly as the Big Bang model would demand because "He is the Maker of the Bear and Orion, the Pleiades and the constellations of the south. He performs wonders that cannot be fathomed, miracles that cannot be counted" (Job 9:9,10). Thus, "the universe was formed at God's command" for "he spoke and it came to be" (Hebrews 11:3; Psalm 33:9).

Anyone who reads Genesis 1 will clearly see that God made all the specifics of creation in six literal days by immediate divine command, not some lengthy cosmological process. Consider a few examples.

> And God said, "Let there be light," and there was light. . . . And there was evening and there was morning—the first day (Genesis 1:3,5).
>
> And God said, "Let there be an expanse between the waters.". . . God called the expanse "sky." And there was evening, and there was morning—the second day (Genesis 1:6,8).
>
> Then God said, "Let the land produce vegetation." . . . And it was so. . . . And there was evening and there was morning—the third day (Genesis 1:11,13).
>
> And God said, "Let there be lights in the expanse of the sky to separate the day from the night, and let them serve as signs to mark seasons and days and years.". . . And it was so. . . . God

made two great lights—the greater light to govern the day and the lesser light to govern the night. He also made the stars. . . . And there was evening, and there was morning—the fourth day (Genesis 1:14-16,19).

And God said, "Let the water teem with living creatures, and let birds fly above the earth across the expanse of the sky." So God created the great creatures of the sea and every living and moving thing with which the water teems, according to their kinds, and every winged bird according to its kind. . . . And there was evening, and there was morning—the fifth day (Genesis 1:20,21,23).

[God made the living creatures of the land and man]—"and it was so.". . . And there was evening, and there was morning—the sixth day (Genesis 1:24,30).

Does this sound anything at all like the Big Bang? The plain meaning of Genesis chapter one is that God directly, instantaneously, created all things in six days. His comments afterward, "And God saw that it was good" simply do not allow for billions of years for cosmological evolutionary processes to intervene before God can finally declare what He has made good.

God's question to Job, "Where were you when I laid the earth's foundation?" is a question that scientists, Christian or otherwise, who are enamored with the Big Bang theory, should ask themselves. Where were they when God created the heavens and the earth and everything in them? Isn't it just a bit presumptuous to claim that God did *not* do it the way He says He did when they weren't even there to know for sure?

16

Additional Evidence and Issues

Selection, Thermodynamics, the Dating Game, Geology, and Life on Mars

In this chapter we will briefly examine several additional issues and alleged evidences relating to evolution, including mutation and natural selection, the second law of thermodynamics, the age of the earth, the geological column, and life from Mars.

The Evolutionary Mechanism: Mutation and Natural Selection

Evolution claims to operate through beneficial mutations and natural selection. According to Darwin, evolution happens when an organism is confronted by a changing environment. Some organisms in a population become better adapted for survival than others, partly because of beneficial mutations, incredibly rare events that alter an organism and allow it to improve. Natural selection involves the survival of those organisms best adapted to their environment; those less adapted die out. The best adapted transmit then their improved genetic characteristics and populations evolve upward. On the surface,

273

it seems to make sense—that billions of years could produce sufficient mutations to allow things to slowly change and improve so that all life evolves upward. But as we will see, it actually doesn't make sense at all.

Perceptually, many things in life initially seem true but aren't—the sun rising and setting; the distant water of a mirage in a hot desert, etc. Explanations that can seem to make sense, but are false, are also not unusual—consider certain psychoanalytic interpretations, critical naturalistic theories to explain Jesus' empty tomb; explanations for why a given treatment works in certain New Age holistic health practices, etc. Natural selection is one such theory that on the surface seems to make sense but when examined critically breaks down.

Darwin himself considered that the idea of evolution was unsatisfactory unless its mechanism could be explained. For evolution to occur, obviously, there must be some mechanism of change. Again, mutations produce the change needed for evolution to advance; natural selection, through genetic recombination (the formation of new genetic combinations in offspring), selects the best aspects of change for life to progress and evolve. Natural selection is the evolutionary process through which the life that is best adapted to local environments leave more surviving offspring—and thus spread their favored traits through populations, insuring greater adaptation and survival.[1]

The leading evolutionists Dobzhansky, Ayala, Stebbins, and Valentine summarize the postulated basis of evolutionary change: "...In a nutshell, the [neo-Darwinian synthesis] theory maintains that mutation and sexual recombination furnish the raw materials; that natural selection fashions from these materials genotypes and gene pools; and that, in sexually reproducing forms, the arrays of adaptively coherent genotypes are protected from disintegration by reproductive isolating mechanisms."[2] Whether we are considering the three major postulated mechanisms of evolution—mutation, natural selection, and genetic recombination—or other factors such as migration and isolation and genetic drift, none of these is adequate to explain how evolution could occur.

There are variations on the concept of the mechanisms of evolution and how they work, but they all boil down to the fact that somehow things must mutate or change and somehow they must improve. As *Voices for Evolution* tells it, "The one constant [throughout evolutionary history] has been the process of change itself—of mutation and natural selection, the hammer and anvil by which nature has sculpted her handiwork into the imperfectly beautiful and intricate web of life that now covers the planet."[3] But one of the greatest myths of evolution is the myth of change.

The truth is that today we still know nothing about how an alleged evolution would work. Mutations cannot account for the kinds of changes necessary, since the vast majority of mutations are either neutral or harmful. Natural selection is tautological and has been critiqued to death by both creationists and evolutionists.[4]

The problem with genetic recombination is that it merely redistributes existing genetic material among different individuals but it makes no change in it. The evolutionist Savage declares that it "cannot be regarded as an evolutionary force, since it never changes gene frequencies."[5]

The Problem with Mutations

The evolutionist Mayr wrote, "It must not be forgotten that mutation is the ultimate source of all genetic variation found in natural populations and the only new material available for natural selection to work on."[6] The noted evolutionist Dobzhansky comments that, "The process of mutation is the only known source of the new materials of genetic variability, and hence of evolution."[7]

Again, the difficulty is that mutations cannot account for evolutionary change. H. J. Muller won the Nobel Prize for his work on mutations. He observes correctly that, "It is entirely in line with the accidental nature of mutations that extensive tests have agreed in showing the vast majority of them detrimental to the organism . . . good ones are so rare that we can consider them all bad."[8] In *Mankind Evolving*, Dobzhansky comments, "Yet we have to face a peculiar fact, one so peculiar that in the opinion of some people it *makes nonsense* of the whole biological theory of evolution: although the biological theory calls for incorporation of beneficial genetic variants (via mutations) in the living populations, a vast majority of the mutants observed in any organism are detrimental to its welfare."[9] The world-famous French evolutionist Grassé was also correct when he wrote, "No matter how numerous they may be, mutations do not produce any kind of evolution."[10]

Not only are the vast majority of mutations detrimental (or neutral), mutations are also extremely rare. George Gaylord Simpson argues that even with extremely favorable conditions, the probability of just *five* mutations in the same nucleus would be one chance in 10^{22} and the event would occur only once in 274 billion years. He concludes, ". . . unless there is an unknown factor tremendously increasing the chance of simultaneous mutations, such a process has played no part whatever in evolution."[11]

Adaptive mutations, such as the resistance of insects to pesticides, changes in a moth's wing color, or adaptation of soil bacteria to new nutrients also offer no evidence for evolution. These changes are intraspecies events. They originate from already existing genes and constitute an innate capacity to respond to the environment. They are not random evolutionary mutations, nor do they add new information or capacity to the gene pool. This and more has been discussed by biophysicist Lee Spetner, who has published in prestigious journals that include *Nature, Journal of Theoretical Biology* and the *Proceedings of the Second International Congress on Biophysics*. In *Not by Chance! Shattering the Modern Theory of Evolution* (Judaica, 1997) he thoroughly refutes the Darwinian reliance on mutations and natural selection, as does Professor Michael Behe in *Darwin's Black Box*.

What do evolutionists do with the difficulty? Basically, they ignore it. We elsewhere cited George Wald who concluded that even though the spontaneous generation of a living organism was impossible, he still believed that we are here as a result of spontaneous generation. Dobzhansky, after discussing the harmful effects of mutations writes in a similar vein, "This is not inconsistent with the recognition that useful mutations *did occur* in the evolutionary line which produced man, for other-wise, obviously, mankind *would not be here.*"[12]

In other words, even though there is no evidence whatsoever that mutations could be responsible for evolutionary changes, beneficial mutations must have occurred because mankind exists! But we think Dobzhansky was correct earlier when he wrote that evolution's reliance on mutations "makes nonsense of the whole biological theory of evolution."

The Problem with Natural Selection

Natural selection faces similar difficulty. Evolutionists make statements like the following concerning natural selection. Sir Julian Huxley argues, "So far as we know, not only is natural selection inevitable, not only is it an effective agency of evolu-tion, it is the *only effective agency* of evolution."[13] Sir Gavin De Beer comments that "it is selection, not mutations, that controls evolution."[14] Leading evolutionists such as Dobzhansky and Mayr agree that natural selection "remains the fundamental process directing evolutionary change."[15]

Yet there are so many problems facing natural selection, even evolutionists aren't sure what to do with the theory. Dar-win himself was troubled by it. In his various sections cri-tiquing natural selection, Bird cites dozens of evolutionists who have serious doubts about the relevance and/or validity of the theory. This is so in spite of the fact that *there is no evolution without it.* Thus: "Natural selection has received the most widespread and vehement criticism (by evolutionists) as being nonexplanatory and tautologous...."[16] Natural selection is described by evolutionists as: "extremely improbable"; "impos-sible"; "may be an illusion", etc.[17]

Many other scientists, biologists included, have argued that natural selection simply has no evidence in its support. As Har-vard trained lawyer and non-creationist Norman MacBeth wrote in his *Darwin Retried*, "[George Gaylord] Simpson says that some students ascribe almost no importance to [natural selection], while others believe it is the only really essential factor in evolution. Stebbins laments that because the 'adaptive' nature of certain traits cannot be easily seen or proved, a number of reputable biologists argue that it does not exist, thus virtually denying natural selection." MacBeth then remarks, "A process that operates invisibly, with an intensity that cannot be observed and with no ability to explain specific problems, an impersonal process that is continually given personal qualities—this sets my teeth on edge."[18]

Of course, evolutionists still accept natural selection because they have little choice. As MacBeth points out, evolutionists will concede they cannot measure it, observe it, or define it and will admit that it has tautological elements but "will nevertheless defend it with their heart's blood."[19]

W. R. Bird observes that biologists have attacked the concept of natural selection because "it does not provide an adequate mechanism to bring about macroevolution ultimately from one or more first living cells to all existing life."[20] Further, "The different attack on natural selection by several dozen philosophers and biologists, in published articles, is [based on the fact] that it is unfalsifiable, untestable, tautologist or nonexplanatory, or all three, as discussed in full later."[21] For example, physician H. S. Hamilton discusses a number of difficulties that "plague evolutionary theories with respect to the eye and which natural selection acting on chance mutational change cannot explain. Natural selection has been termed a tautology, even by some evolutionists, and while it may have some validity in minor genetic variation it is totally powerless in macroevolution. It is evident that present concepts of organic evolution have not and cannot account for the remarkable design and ability of the organs of vision from the light-sensitivity of the amoeba to the perfection of the eagle's eye."[22]

Apparently in response to the many criticisms of natural selection, the concept has undergone revision. Not openly, but seemingly by "subterfuge." According to the evolutionist Rosen: "If the theory of natural selection as formulated by Darwin is tautological, and if the neo-Darwinists have retreated from the criticism of this tautology by redefining natural selection in more esoteric terms (population genetics or ecological genetics)—even though it still does not explain either the appearance of evolutionary novelties or evolutionary diversity—

then biologists might appear to an onlooker to have rejected modern synthetic evolutionary theory but practiced a subterfuge to retain it as the orthodox position."[23]

In other words, a fruitful imagination solves all kinds of problems, as also recognized by the California Academy of Sciences: "Prior to the fundamental contribution of Darwin in 1859, there seemed to be no way to explain the remarkable adaptations of organisms *except in terms of a miracle*. With the discovery and recognition of natural selection, this argument was shown to depend upon a pre-Darwinian *failure of the human imagination* to find testable, scientific explanations for the origin and diversity of life."[24] And, as N. Takahata observes, "Even with DNA sequence data, we have no direct access to the processes of evolution, so objective reconstruction of the vanished past can be achieved only by *creative imagination*."[25]

Of course, there is no doubt that minor limited changes do occur in the natural world. This may be termed natural selection at the microevolutionary level. But to extrapolate such change to macroevolution is a logical impossibility, since there is simply no evidence for it and the postulated mechanisms are impotent. The evolutionist Patterson argues, "There's no doubt at all that natural selection works—it's been repeatedly demonstrated by experiment. But the question of whether it produces new species is quite another matter. No one has ever produced a new species by means of natural selection, no one has never got near it, and most of the current argument in neo-Darwinism is about this question. . . ."[26]

Creationist Jerry Bergman, Ph.D. writes that there is more here than meets the eye:

> Natural selection would not evolve upward—for example, bacteria into humans—but at best would evolve simple bacteria into better adapted bacteria, or flies into better adapted flies. The fossil record shows no evidence of anything beyond this. No clear example has ever been found of a lower, clearly less adapted animal in the fossil record which can be shown to be evolutionarily related to a similar, or advanced type of an animal living today. . . . The easy-to-grasp and compelling natural selection argument is used to help explain all biological data, but it may actually

explain very little. Human life consists of many activities which are mentally pleasurable. Walking in forests, listening to music, creating poems, doing scientific research, aesthetic enjoyment of nature, and myriads of other activities are often not related in the least to survival or adaptation in the Darwinian sense. . . . Music in its many variations is loved the world over, and yet certain music preferences have not been shown to increase reproduction rates or to facilitate survival. Many, if not almost all of our most rewarding activities, "peak experience producers," are not only unexplainable by this theory, but contradict it.[27]

But in fact, some biologists not only deny that natural selection occurs at the macroevolutionary level, they argue that it has no relevance even at the microevolutionary level. "Other biologists carry the point further to deny that natural selection is supported by any evidence at all, whether at the macroevolutionary or even microevolutionary level. Grassé, whose 'knowledge of the living world is encyclopedic' according to Dobzhansky, simply finds 'not one single sure datum': 'The role assigned to natural selection in establishing adaptation, while speciously probable, is based on not one single sure datum. Paleontology . . . does not support it; direct observation here and now of the genesis of a hereditary adaptation is nonexistent, except, as we have stated, in the case of bacteria and insects preadapted to resist viruses or drugs.'"[28]

The bottom line is that there is simply no way that mutations and natural selection could have produced the entire world of life, even with endless periods of time. In 1980, 150 leading evolutionists of both of the dominant evolutionary schools, neo-Darwinism and punctuated equilibria, met in Chicago to attempt to grapple with the problems involved in the mechanism of evolution. "[They] came away without any agreement on any viable mechanism to explain how macroevolution could occur."[29] Indeed, according to evolutionist Colin Patterson, in the words of Phillip E. Johnson, today "Darwin's theory of natural selection is under fire and scientists are no longer sure of its general validity."[30] (Cf. 31-34)

Darwin was right—if we can't explain how evolution occurs, even 140 years later, the theory must be considered unsatisfactory.

The Second Law of Thermodynamics

There has been much discussion between creationists and evolutionists concerning the applicability of the second law of thermodynamics as it relates to the issue of origins. Does it make evolution impossible, as the creationists maintain, or are there ways around the problem, as evolutionists maintain? A proper understanding of thermodynamics and the theory of evolution as it relates to the origin of the universe and the origin of life reveals that cosmically and biologically evolution is not just improbable, it is basically impossible.

In laymen's terms, the second law of thermodynamics teaches that everything in the universe is running down, or going from a state of more useful energy to less useful energy. It tells us what we all know from experience, that, sooner or later, everything deteriorates and falls apart.

The second law teaches that systems will lead to their most probable state, the most random state, and that systems will increase entropy which is a measure of the availability of energy to do useful work. Increasing entropy means less availability. In other words, all systems lead to increasing disorder, for all things are running down. Everything finally wears out—objects, plants, animals, man.

The second law is perhaps the most pertinent for evolution/creation considerations. The difficulty is that almost everything having to do with evolution—whether the origin of the universe or the evolution of life—contradicts the second law. If we start with the supposed Big Bang of the universe, we have an initial violent explosion shot out in all directions. As anyone knows, anytime you have an explosion, there is increasing disorder until the force of the explosion is dissipated and everything stops. Explosions do not produce incredible systems of complexity, order, and design, but the Big Bang theory teaches that as this explosion moved out, things became infinitely ordered—planets formed, of vastly different size, composition, and appearance (some 1/10 the size of the earth; some 1,000 times its size; some with braided rings; some solid; some gaseous, etc.), all kinds of moons came to orbit planets, suns of infinite variety formed, solar systems formed, galaxies formed, startling clusters of suns and galaxies formed, etc. (A recently discovered star is apparently so gargantuan that it would fill all space between the sun and Mars!)

Again, we don't think most evolutionists have fairly considered the problems involved in this scenario. After a "cosmic egg" as small as a proton exploded, the result was this beautiful universe we know, with planets rotating stars, stars rotating in their own systems, and galaxies rotating with all kinds of incredibly complex entities such as quasars and black holes. How an initial explosion of gases and extremely dense matter could ever have produced something like our incredibly beautiful and complex planet earth, with its perfectly synchronized oceans, atmosphere, plant and animal life, etc., is impossible to fathom.

Thus, when we consider the origin of life on the earth, we find the same problems presented by the second law that we find with the Big Bang and its galaxy formation, planet formation, star formation, etc. Everything that has supposedly evolved, whether in space or on earth, evolves to an increasingly ordered and complex state of existence. The second law says that, left to its own, this kind of increasing order would never have occurred.

Any scientist who fairly applies the second law of thermodynamics to the possibility of evolution must logically conclude that evolution has not occurred.[35] Thaxton, Bradley, and Olsen's *The Mystery of Life's Origin*, for example, contains three devastating chapters on the second law as it relates to evolution. According to Dr. Duane Gish, an authority in the creation/evolution controversy, "This is the finest critique of origin-of-life theories by creation scientists."[36]

Evolutionists, of course, have responses to creationists' arguments. Evolutionists reason that, since evolution is true, and the second law is true, somehow they must be reconcilable. And so rather than accepting a disproof of their theory, they go to great lengths to make it reconcilable with the second law.

Again, science is forced to fit a bad theory because of bad assumptions. Hampered by their own philosophical premises, scientists really have little choice except to end up doing bad science. Dr. Gish responds to the evolutionists' critiques of creationists' applications of the second law of thermodynamics as follows:

In many cases, evolutionists have simply brushed aside the challenges of creation scientists to evolution based on thermodynamics, by resorting to tactics similar to those employed by Patterson—charging creation scientists with incompetence, and suggesting absurd examples of apparent circumventions of the Second Law by evolution, such as tornadoes, crystallization, ram pumps, batteries, and fertilized eggs developing into adult animals, and employing the old closed-system, open-system argument. The most vitally important questions, however, they have failed to answer—how the universe, an isolated system, could transform itself from chaos and simplicity into order and complexity, when the Second Law tells us this is impossible; how the natural laws and processes now destroying the universe could also create it; and how the incredibly complex internal organization of a living cell could create itself in spite of all the work that had to be done to create the enormous amount of information required to specify that organization. It is strange that evolutionists believe that random, blind, chance natural processes have managed to create this universe and man, with his incredible brain, in spite of the Second Law, but man, an open-system with a steady flow-through of energy, equipped with the most complex machinery in the universe and endowed with that incredible brain, cannot devise a way to circumvent the Second Law—and live forever![37]

Violations of the second law are only theoretically possible —none are known to exist. In fact, chemist Harry Bent calculated that on the basis of the second law, the chance of a *reversal* of entropy so that one single calorie could be completely converted into work is equal to the odds that a group of monkeys randomly hitting typewriter keys could "produce Shakespeare's works 15 quadrillion times in succession without error."[38]

Open Versus Closed Systems

Let's cite one example of an evolutionist argument against the creationist application of the second law to evolution. Evolutionists argue the law applies only to closed systems where there is no incoming energy and that because we have the sun's energy coming to the earth (thus, an open system), the second law is not applicable to the evolution of life on earth. As the

National Association of Biology Teachers argues in an official statement: "Evolution does not violate the second law of thermodynamics; producing order from disorder is possible with the addition of energy, such as from the sun."[39] In other words, the second law does not apply to *open* systems. As the New Orleans Geological Society argues in another official statement: "Thermodynamics does in fact show that entropy reversals can and do occur in an a biological system that is open with respect to energy input, which is the case for the biosphere of the earth."[40]

Nevertheless, the fact is the second law is always tested in open systems and always proves true. Further, there is no such thing as a perfectly closed system. The idea that the sun's incoming energy might somehow counteract the second law temporarily to allow evolution confuses quantity of energy with the quality or abilities of energy. The issue is not whether energy was available, but could life arise by the input of energy that existed? The problem is that the sun's energy per se has no quality that endows it with the ability to organize and order molecules into life. Further, in the beginning there would be no means to capture and utilize the energy of the sun—no chlorophyll, DNA, etc. Also, the second law teaches that whatever energy was present, it would be dissolved and lost, not upgraded and improved.

Evolutionists are wrong when they claim evolution is possible because the second law is not applicable to open systems:

> Ross of Harvard chastises those who argue that the second law does not apply to open systems:
>
>> Please be advised that there are *no known violations* of the second law of thermodynamics. Ordinarily the second law is stated for isolated systems, *but the second law applies equally well to open systems*. However, there is somehow associated with the field of far-from-equilibrium phenomenon [open systems] the notion that the second law of thermodynamics fails for such systems. It is important to make sure that this error does not perpetuate itself.
>
> The effect of the second law of thermodynamics under classical theory is to make biochemical evolution "highly improbable,"

according to Nobel Prize laureate Prigogine and others: The probability that at ordinary temperatures a macroscopic number of molecules is assembled to give rise to the highly ordered structures and to the coordinated functions characterizing living organisms is *vanishingly small* . . .

The revision of the second law under nonequilibrium [open] thermodynamic theory, as it applies to open systems such as those in which life would have arisen, is alleged to solve the problem of present specified complexity requiring greater rather than less past complexity. However, that problem of thermodynamic entropy "will not go away nor will the biological evidence to the contrary," according to Yockey . . .

Many researchers state that among thermodynamic laws "the second law applies equally well to open systems," and that the concept is in "error" that "the second law of thermodynamics fails for [nonequilibrium or open] systems."[41]

The technical treatments of this issue by creationists responding to technical evolutionist argument prove in detail that evolutionists are wrong and creationists right.[42]

As is so often true, the evolutionist is in the position of having to cite the disclaimer that future research will resolve current problems while he resorts to theoretical speculation that violate what we know as fact today.

If the second law of thermodynamics forces us to conclude that a Cadillac could not form spontaneously from a heap of scrap metal even if the pile were an open system, it certainly must force us to conclude that far greater miracles, including the spontaneous formation of life, will never occur.

The Age of the Universe: Not Quite So Settled

The fact that most scientists believe in an old earth should not be considered proof the earth is billions of years old. Most scientists also believe in evolution. If science has lied about the fact of evolution, why should anyone uncritically accept what science also tells us about the earth's age?

Concerning the alleged evidences cited for an old earth, scientists of a young earth persuasion, with equally impressive academic credentials and research capacities in different aspects of the sciences, have evaluated and critiqued the old earth evidence, and supplied evidence for a young earth. Again, the interpretation of the data is the key issue. The same data can be interpreted either way, depending on one's assumptions.

Stephen R. Schrader, Associate Professor of Hebrew and Old Testament, Liberty University, Lynchburg, Virginia summarizes the conclusions of his own study on this issue: "The arguments used to support an old-earth stance are not as airtight and intimidating as its proponents would like to imagine and in each case are open to serious challenges based upon the given data in light of a biblical model."[43]

In "The Age of the Earth," Frederic R. Howe, emeritus professor of systematic theology at Dallas Theological Seminary, is quite correct when he points out that the major factual data can be logically placed into a young earth model, and further, that old earth creationists sometimes engage in faulty argumentation with their young earth colleagues:

> It is vital to know that concerning the main lines of evidence for an older earth, advocates of the young-earth model, with equally impressive credentials and research in various scientific disciplines, respond with equally feasible lines of evidence for a young earth. . . . In summary, many lines of evidence are used, from essentially the same realms as those used by old-earth model advocates (including astronomical, radiometric, and nonradiometric areas) to enable young-earth theoreticians to present a cogent and reasonable framework for earth history. . . . [Also] it becomes apparent when studying the literature that some old earth proponents engage in faulty argumentation when they underestimate the credibility and scientific expertise of the young-earth contenders.[44]

This is why it is so regrettable to find Christians thinking they must *insist* that the earth is billions of years old and that young earth creationists are distorting science, leading people away from God, and hindering their salvation.[45]

In Don Stoner's book, *A New Look at an Old Earth* we read, "the young-earth position is *incompatible* with the scientific evidence. . . . Scientists can *easily* determine how old God's creation is . . . there is no escaping the antiquity of the earth. It is billions of years old. The scientific evidence is *very clear*."[46]

If the actual scientific facts for an old earth *were* so clear and unquestionable, would thousands of creation scientists world-wide be able to maintain intellectual credibility in their *own* minds, let alone rationalize in good conscience the serious moral implications of leading others astray?

Dr. Eugene F. Chaffin, Associate Professor of Physics, in his "A Young Earth?—A Survey of Dating Methods," concludes his article by noting that despite Stoner's claim, "very reasonable defenses can be made" for a young age of the earth.[47]

Evidence for Recent Creation

In *The Biblical Basis for Modern Science*, scientist Henry Morris lists 68 different global processes, most of which indicate a relatively recent creation. These are based on certain assumptions: 1) zero initial "daughter" components, 2) a closed system, and 3) a uniform rate. About 20 of these processes give ages of less than 100,000 years, obviously a vastly insufficient time for evolution to occur. (The wide variety found, from 1,750 years to 500,000,000 years, is suggestive of the tentative nature of dating methods generally.)

The fact that young ages are thrown out by evolutionists as *necessarily* inaccurate, based on evolutionary presuppositions of needed old ages, is hardly proof that the old dates are valid or that the young dates are invalid. In fact, there are dozens of different indicators of an earth no older than 20,000 years.[48] No one can declare that it is a scientific fact that the earth is billions of years old.

As physicist Thomas Barnes argues, "It takes but one proof of a young-age limit on the earth, the moon, or the sun to refute the whole gamut of evolution. There are many proofs. Lord Kelvin gave two young-age proofs that have never really been falsified. . . . There is much more evidence of a young-age of the earth, moon, and sun now than at the time of Kelvin. . . . There is no lack of scientific evidences of a young-age for the earth, moon, sun and some of the other astronomical bodies. There is no lack of sound physical theories upon which to found those proofs."[49]

In his article "On Stellar Structure and Stellar Evolution," Bruce Briegler points out that, "observational data does not require an old universe. Given all the observational data it is not known for certain how old stars are. In a fashion analogous in earth history, evolutionary astronomers have *interpreted* the observational data consistently with the philosophical view of slow, naturalistic origins of stellar systems."[50]

Even one of the world's leading solar astronomers, evolutionist John Eddy, actually stated that there isn't "much in the way of observational evidence in astronomy to conflict with" a very young age for the sun and earth—less than 7,000 years.[51]

Part of his reasoning came from 25 years of experiments on solar neutrinos whose results have led to "a crisis" for evolutionary time spans, and a possible confirmation of a recent creation. Not surprisingly, most evolutionists won't even talk about this research because of its implications.[52]

Consider also the mitochondrial DNA analysis of living persons conducted by evolutionists[53] and the polonium halo research of the creationist physicist Robert Gentry, which give very young ages for man and the creation respectively.[54] Gentry is the world's foremost authority on polonium halos. His research, which apparently indicates the earth is less than 10,000 years old, has never been falsified, though for 20 years he has challenged evolutionists to do so—with specific, testable experiments.[55] Gentry's challenge is for evolutionary scientists to perform a few crucial experiments that would disprove his thesis. No one has been able to. "The evolutionary scenario views granites—a widely distributed rock type that contains polonium halos—as having formed countless thousands of times during the course of earth history. If this is true, then it certainly should be possible to synthesize a small, hand-sized piece of granite or a 10 cm wide crystal of biotite in a scientific laboratory. Thus, I have invited (Gentry 1979, 1984, 1986) my scientific colleagues who believe these rocks formed naturally to confirm their view by experimental demonstration. But my 9-year-old invitation (Gentry 1979) for them to produce such specimens has produced only silence. This is not surprising. *The parentless polonium halos in these rocks provide unique evidence that they did not form by natural processes.*" And, "I will likewise relinquish any claim for primordial ^{218}Po halos when coercive evidence (not just plausibility arguments) is provided for a conventional origin. . . . I will consider my thesis to be *doubly falsified* by these synthesis of a biotite which contains just one ^{218}Po halo (some of my natural specimens contain more than 10^4 Po halos/cm.^{3}) . . ."[56]

Gentry's work is so startling in its implications for an instant young creation, that evolutionists, and some creationists, have taken serious note of his work and subjected it to vigorous critique. But Gentry's work continues to withstand the test of time and apparently he has successfully answered his critics.[57]

If the exact age of the earth is scientifically unknowable, this is not to say that the scientific *facts* (as opposed to evolutionary interpretations and speculations) are not weighted toward a recent creation. They seem to be. As Henry Morris says, "The real facts of science, as distinguished from various evolutionary interpretations imposed on those facts, all point to the recent special creation of all things, not long ages of evolutionary uniformitarianism. . . . [Further] the overwhelming biblical evidence for literal-day creationism has still not been refuted. . . ."[58]

In a review of Marvin L. Lubenow's *Bones of Contention—A Creationist Assessment of Human Fossils*, Michael J. Oard comments, "From my reading of historical science, I believe the manipulation of the many 'independent' dating methods to arrive at a consistent result is common. I believe it includes the manipulation of rocks, fossils, and radiometric dates to bolster a consistent geological column. . . . [Citing Lubenow] 'The radioactive dating methods are a classic example of self-deception and circular reasoning. . . . In the dating game, evolution always wins.' "[59]

A Moot Point?

In one sense, the issue of the age of the universe as far as evolution is concerned is something of a moot point. If there is no hard scientific evidence for evolution, if in fact there is sufficient scientific evidence against evolution tantamount to a disproof, then a young age of the universe as a startling disproof of evolution is irrelevant. Evolution is already disproved by the facts of science. On the other hand, if there are legitimate scientific and other reasons to doubt the credibility of the age dating methods, and if these methods are characteristically employed as evidence for evolution in a begging-the-question fashion, then the age of the earth is clearly relevant. If the age of the earth is 10,000 to 20,000 years, then the question of whether or not evolution has occurred must certainly be settled. Professor Marvin Lubenow comments:

> The age of the earth and the sun is foundational to the creation/ evolution issue. A recent creation demands a supreme being who created the universe. A recent creation also destroys *any* possibility of evolution. But that is not all. The scientific area may be one of the least important areas this issue impacts. The age of the earth and the sun have profound implications in theology, philosophy, anthropology, and ethics, to name just a few areas. In fact, there are few areas of life that would be untouched. That's why it is such an emotional issue. It is also a political one; jobs have been lost over it.[60]

Radioactive Dating

For now, we simply wish to examine some of the scientific problems with the current radiometric age dating methods. It must first be noted that the prior assumption is that evolution is a fact and therefore the rocks to be dated *must* exhibit great ages. On a billion year old planet, for example, it is *impossible* to find only rocks that are 20,000 years old. If one assumes the earth is billions of years old, and if the methodology one uses in radiometric dating are capable of fitting this assumption, then obviously the results are going to be skewed toward the billions of years "necessary" for evolution to occur.

Although some argue that creationist literature in the dating game currently lags behind its evolutionary colleagues in sophistication, this is hardly unexpected considering the relative age, size, and funding of the two parties. Evolutionists have had 140 years compared to creationists' 20. Regardless, we think enough significant creationist re-evaluation of the age dating methods—including radiocarbon, uranium thorium lead, rubidium strontium and others—has been done to *legitimately* cast doubt upon the great ages that these methods reveal. The Institute for Creation Research, the Creation Research Society, and other creationist organizations, and even a few evolutionists, have produced critiques of these methods which show their flawed assumptions.

As Dr. Wilder-Smith points out, "Finally one is forced to admit that our dating methods by means of radioactivity provide us with little really reliable data as to the enormous time spans required for evolution according to Darwin. It is relatively easy for any biological or inorganic material to simulate a great age—or no age at all!"[61]

Let's see some reasons why this is so.

In introducing our subject we need to remember certain basic facts and to give a brief explanation of how radiometric dating works.

First, we should keep in mind that documented history dates back only a few thousand years. Written history is about 5,000 years old and archeological data can at most extend things another 5,000 to 10,000 years.

Second, even if the earth were five billion years old, this doesn't even scratch the surface of the time necessary for evolution to occur. However, five billion years does make evolution *seem* possible simply because of the incomprehensibility of billions of years.

Third, none of the common radioactive age-methods are capable of empirical verification. For example, no one has watched uranium decaying for millions of years to make sure the rate was constant.

Fourth, dozens of dating methods exist, but evolutionists choose those methods whose assumptions yield the great ages necessary to allow evolution.

The radioactive methods work as follows. The parent component, such as uranium, is gradually changed into the daughter component, such as lead, and the current relative amounts of each are considered to be an index of the time since the initial formation of the material.

Necessary Assumptions

All these methods are based on certain assumptions, and all the assumptions are incapable of proof, and cannot be tested.

In fact, in most cases the assumptions would seem to be unreasonable.[62]

Some of the assumptions of the methods include the following:

1. The assumption of a closed system, i.e., that no outside factor can have affected the concentration of the parent or daughter element, as this would bias the results. The addition or subtraction of material would change the resulting age. But can evolutionists truly believe they are dealing with a closed system for millions or billions of years?

2. The assumption that the material must *initially* have contained no daughter component, since otherwise it would need a corresponding correction to account for this. But no one was present when the material was formed, and daughter elements could have been already present in the creation. Certainly when Adam was created he was created with the appearance of age. When Jesus made wine at the wedding in Cana it was apparently truly aged since it was said to be the best of the wine, yet it also was newly created. In other words, in His miracles God has created "aged" items that are without age. For whatever reason, this may have been true in creation. In addition, daughter elements could also have been incorporated along the way through natural processes.

3. Another assumption is that the decay rate must always have been the same. But how do we know this? For example, say we have ten grams of pure metallic rubidium-87. Its half-life is estimated at 47 billion years. Now, if nothing in the next 47 billion years changes its rate of decay, then five grams of rubidium-87 will remain and five grams of strontium-87 will remain. After 94 billion years, 2.5 grams of rubidium-87 will exist and 7.5 grams of strontium-87 will exist.

To illustrate the problem here, let's say we have an ice tray with water and we want to find the size of the ice cube and the time it took to melt. In order to do this, we have to assume certain things and know certain things. We must know the rate of melting and assume the rate of melting was constant. We must assume that no water was added at any point and that no evaporation occurred and that no water was in the tray originally. If we know all this, then we can calculate the size of the cube and the time it took to melt.

Going back to our example of rubidium-87, if we find a sample containing five grams of rubidium-87 and five grams of strontium-87 then, and only then:

1. if the decay was constant
2. if there were ten grams of rubidium-87 to begin with and
3. if there were no additions or subtractions of either rubidium-87 or strontium-87, we could say that the sample was 47 billion years old.

Not So Reliable as Assumed

It becomes evident that the accuracy of certain assumptions are essential to the billion year dates found in these dating methods. Further, even though these methods are continually being refined, they involve many inaccuracies and difficulties, which make them suspect. When we find such anomalies as new wood from growing trees dated by the carbon 14 method at 10,000 years, or living snail shells dated at 2,300 years, or 200-year-old lava flows dated by potassium-argon at 3 billion years, or moon rocks dated between 2 million to 28 billion years, it's obvious that these methods are not necessarily that reliable.[63] Even if we argue that snails had eaten old material or that the lava brought up aged substances, such explanations do not solve the problems with these methods.

Dr. Melvin A. Cook received his Ph.D. in Physical Chemistry from Yale University. In reviewing the six uranium-thorium-lead methods, the radiocarbon method, potassium-argon and rubidium-strontium methods he concludes as follows, "They may be further summarized by the simple statement that there are really *no reliable* long-time radiological 'clocks,' and even the short-time radiocarbon 'clock' is in serious need of repair."[64] Similarly, throughout its more than 30-year history the journal of the *Creation Research Society* has had many articles revealing the unreliability of these methods.

Dr. Morris further shows why the radiocarbon, uranium-lead, potassium-argon, and rubidium-strontium methods must all be considered flawed.[65] And even geochronologists who use these methods recognize there are flaws. As an article in *Industrial Research and Development* points out, "There has been in recent years the horrible realization that radiodecay rates are *not as constant as previously thought*, nor are they *immune to environmental influences*. And this could mean that the atomic clocks are reset during some global disaster and events which brought the Mesozoic to a close may not be 65 million years ago but, rather, within the age and memory of man."[66] That eliminates about 65 million years!

In the end, such methods tell us nothing definitive about the age of the earth or the universe.[67] "We may conclude that dates obtained by radiometric means are interesting geophysical exercises but prove nothing as far as the age of the earth is concerned."[68]

Thus, evolutionary scientists, generally, have blinders on when they examine the radiometric dating results. These results *must* produce large ages and that is that. The fact that these methods can be *made* to produce vast ages does *not* mean those ages are legitimate. Evolutionists have only made these dating methods the "servants of evolution," rather than applying them scientifically and judiciously. For example, A. Hayatsu admitted, "In conventional interpretation of K-Ar (potassium argon) age data, it is *common* to discard ages which are substantially too high or too low compared with the rest of the group or with other available data such as the *geological time scale*. The discrepancies between the rejected and the accepted are *arbitrarily* attributed to excess or loss of argon."[69]

Lubenow's important study of the famous fossil skull, KNM-ER 1470 discovered by Richard Leaky's team in 1972, is only one of many additional examples: "This case study clearly reveals that the radiometric dating methods are not independent confirmations of evolution and an old earth, nor are the various dating methods independent of each other. These dating methods are, instead, 'faithful and obedient servants' of evolution."[70] And:

A very popular myth is that the radioactive dating methods are an independent confirmation of the geological time scale and the concept of human evolution. . . . The methods appear so impressive that many creationists have accepted them as evidence that the earth is very old. Perhaps the best way to expose this myth for what it is—science fiction—is to present a case study of the dating of the East African KBS TUFF strata and the famous fossil KNM-ER 1470, as recorded in the scientific journals, especially the British journal *Nature*.[71]

Part of Lubenow's conclusion is that, as one would expect, since great ages are a necessity, the data are actually *manipulated* to conform to the great ages. Obviously, this is done in full sincerity, but "it is manipulation nonetheless":

The study of the ten-year controversy in the dating of the KBS TUFF is tremendously revealing. Whereas the public is lead to believe that these dating methods are highly objective and accurate, the scientific literature itself reveals that they are highly subjective. There is no question that rock samples are often manipulated to give the desired results. There is also no question that this manipulation is done in the utmost sincerity and with the noblest motives. But it is manipulation nonetheless. The "bad" material must be removed to allow the "good" material to be dated. But there is no way of knowing for sure which material is "good" and which is "bad." . . . The literature suggests that even if radiometric dating were valid in concept (which it is not), the practical manner of selecting rock samples that can be proven pure and uncontaminated requires an omniscience that is beyond the ability of mortal humans. The radioactive dating methods are a classic example of self-deception and circular reasoning. It is another of the myths of human evolution. Naeser et al. have said it well: "The accuracy of any age can only be guessed at, in that we do not know the true age of any geological sample."[72]

A final consideration for Christians on this issue is whether the biblical genealogies point to a young earth.

Several genealogies begin with Adam who clearly, biblically, is the first man created on day six of a six-day-old universe. The genealogies extend to Old or New Testament individuals, the dates of which are known. The problems with alleging vast gaps in the genealogies, such as in Genesis chapters 5 and 11, 1 Chronicles 1-4, Luke 3, and Matthew 1 is that it becomes difficult to insert total gaps of more than a few thousand years. For example, it would require a gap of 100 generations—that is ten omissions for every listed individual in the account in Genesis 5—just to move human history back some 16,500 years.[73] If 90 percent of the links in a genealogy are omitted, what is the point of a genealogy?

The most natural way to read the genealogies is that they are intending to give a simple line of descent. Gaps may exist, but not millions of years of gaps. On what biblical or other legitimate basis can tens of thousands, hundreds of thousands, or millions of years of gaps be posited between the individuals given in these records?

In part, this may explain why "almost all of the early Christian expositors believed in a young earth, a fact attested to by [old earth promoter] Young himself. This view was held on the basis of biblical exegesis alone, since 'the prevailing view among the Greeks, the Egyptians, the Babylonians, and other advanced nations of the world at the time, was that the world was very old, probably eternal.' Young also shows that the Church writings of the medieval and Reformation periods likewise adhered to a young earth, literal creation days, and a worldwide flood."[74]

Allegedly a major problem for creation is the ancient features of the earth and the inability of a recent creation theory to explain features like the Grand Canyon that supposedly took millions of years to form. But nothing in science or Scripture is contrary to the concept that the earth's geography today results entirely from how it was originally created, catastrophism (e.g. the Flood), and normal geophysical processes. Science doesn't know enough to say otherwise. Scientifically, no geographical features of the earth can be said to require billions of years to explain when we don't have sufficient information to know the features and conditions of the earth on day seven of creation or after Noah's Flood. It could be quite similar to what we see now. Only the unjustified assumption of evolutionary uniformitarianism demands billions of years. Assuming the truth of creation, the Flood, etc., then a period of 10,000 to 20,000 years should be sufficient to explain the earth's geophysical characteristics.

The Geological Column

Evolutionary texts present the geological column as a fact of geology and proof of evolution. The geologic timetable spreads life out over some two billion years, placing the simplest and smallest organisms at the beginning of life—making them the oldest—and moves progressively upwards to the most complex organisms, as the youngest and most recent.

Unfortunately, the only evidence for this scheme is found in the mind of the evolutionist and the paper on which the chart is drawn. The complete succession of fossils as portrayed by the geologic timetable exists nowhere. As Brown Monnett and Stoval declare in their *Introduction to Geology*:

> Whatever his method of approach, the geologist must take cognizance of the following facts. . . . There is no place on the earth where a complete record of the rocks is present. . . . To reconstruct the history of the earth, scattered bits of information from thousands of locations all over the world must be pieced together. The results will be at best only a very incomplete record. If the complete history of the earth is compared to an encyclopedia of 30 volumes, then we can seldom hope to find even one complete volume in a given area. Sometimes only a few chapters, perhaps only a paragraph or two, will be the total geological contribution of a region; indeed, we are often reduced to studying scattered bits of information more nearly comparable to a few words or letters.[75]

Then how do geologists arrive at the geologic timetable when the record of the earth does not show it? By the means we have so often seen—assuming that evolution is true and applying circular reasoning.

We noted earlier, that one of the primary "evidences" for evolution is the fossil record. Here the simpler or earlier fossils are believed to exist in the "older" rocks. The circular reasoning can be seen as follows: the *age* of the rocks is determined by the index fossils they contain. The ages assigned to the index fossils is determined by their stage of evolution. So the stage of evolution of the fossils determines the geological age of the rocks; the geological age of the rocks in turn determines the sequences of the fossils; the sequence of the fossils in the rocks in turn demonstrates evolution.[76]

As Bill Crofut and Raymond M. Seaman of Catholic Creation Ministries state:

> Our personal view, after nearly a decade of reading, research, and correspondence is that the geological column will only provide evidence for evolution for those who approach the empirical evidence with the idea that evolution is a fact. Of course, the evolutionists with whom we are familiar, would probably deny such accusation, but a ranking evolutionist geologist seems to have substantiated the claim: "Paleontologists often claim that fossils tell us something. But fossils, by themselves, tell us nothing: not even that they are fossils. . . . When a paleontologist concludes that he is dealing with a fossil and by implication with an organism, he already knows a great deal about that organism. He knows that the plants and animals which he encountered in the geologic past will have the characteristics required of them by the theory which he has presupposed in order to reach them."[77]

Again, strata are *dated* by the fossils they contain. For example, trilobites found in the Cambrian strata date the Cambrian strata based on evolutionary assumption that trilobites fit in a particular order of evolution from the less complex to the more complex. The fossil age is then determined by the rock stratum in which the trilobite was found, again based on evolutionists' assumptions, i.e., that the deeper the stratum the older the life. Consider the following example.

Let's say we find a fossil clam, and we ask, "When would this clam fossil have evolved?" Since evolution is assumed to be true, that life progresses from the simple to the complex, and the clam is less complex than the crab but more complex than the trilobite, it must logically be placed between the two. The stratum is dated accordingly. As more fossils are found, we must place them accordingly on a time scale chart denoting simplicity to complexity. In the end, the evolutionist uses this chart as proof of evolution.

The problems are that fossils are not always found in proper evolutionary, geologic succession. The assumption of evolution alone is used to arrange the sequence of fossils—which is circular reasoning, not proof of evolution.

Since the arrangement of fossils is arbitrary, based on the false assumption of evolution, the geological column cannot be used to demonstrate evolution or vast ages. Even if there were a perfect evolutionary geologic succession to be found, the succession would only show relative positions of fossils in the stream of time. But apart from evolution, the fact that clams are placed above trilobites says nothing about the amount of time between them, or about their age in an absolute sense. Regardless, the geological column is suspect because of the faulty reasoning it employs.

Let's back up and walk through the reasoning used to arrive at the geologic timetable. First, it is assumed that since life is here, life evolved. Then, if life evolved and all natural events are proceeding today essentially as they have throughout history (uniformity), then the deeper the strata in the earth, the older its age. It follows also that the older the strata, the more primitive (simple) assemblage of organisms it should portray.

Assuming these "truths," fossils are gathered from around the world (no complete succession being found in any one place) and assembled in a progressive order from simple to complex on a chart. Time is then allotted to the various divisions of the geologic chart on the assumption that the earth is billions of years old—it must be, of course, because evolution would take that long to occur. The fossils are spread in a reasonable (evolutionary) order throughout the assumed antiquity of life's existence, then substantiation and more exact dates are determined on the basis of measuring strata thicknesses and radioactive elements. Strata thickness are dated upon the assumption that strata were laid down in the past at the same rate as today: about one foot every 5,000 years. Radio datings (based on a set of assumptions that likewise assume uniformity) that fit the preconceived order of the geologic column are accepted as accurate and advanced as corroborative proof of the order of the column. Those radio dates not fitting the "correct" order of the strata are rejected. (The time allotments to the geological column were assigned before radio dating techniques.) If any contradictions to the preconceived order of the column are found, i.e., radioactive datings showing a "wrong" age, or fossils out of "correct" sequences, these contradictions are explained away. For example, if the radioactive dates do not coincide with the order, this "anomaly" is accounted for by simply arguing that the radio date was in error; if fossils are found

out of sequence, this is explained on the basis of geological fault-
ing, folding, thrusting and intense erosion whether or not there is
evidence for such.[78]

Further, it is important to note that the geologic column
was first devised by *creationist* scientists who had no problem
interpreting it in light of *creationist* assumptions. In fact, they
saw it as *nonsupportive* of evolution. It was only after Darwin
that evolutionists began to *reinterpret* the geologic record along
evolutionist lines. The truth is that the fossil sequence does not
at all require an evolutionary explanation:

> Many macroevolutionists suggest that, even if the specific fossil
> record for particular organisms does not compel or support belief
> in biological macroevolution or Darwinism, the general fossil
> sequence for all organisms does prove macroevolution and a
> Darwinian mechanism. Whatever their interpretation of the
> geological column, however, modern discontinuitist scientists
> disagree on powerful historical grounds that the fossil sequence
> requires either macroevolution or Darwinism.
>
> Those historical grounds, as many evolutionists concede such
> as Glenister and Witzke, are that "[b]oth the stratigraphic col-
> umn and our general understanding were thus developed empiri-
> cally and without any reference to evolutionary assumption," by
> scientists who nearly all found the geological record consistent
> with the theory of creation and nonsupportive of the theory of
> evolution:
>
>> With the exception of the Ordovician (established later to re-
>> solve a dispute over the boundary between Cambrian and Sil-
>> urian), *all intervals were proposed prior to publication of
>> Darwin's Origin of Species in 1859.* The Tertiary preceded the
>> *Origin* by a full century. Components of the time scale were
>> established on the basis of objective data, primarily super-
>> position (observed stratigraphic succession) and fossil con-
>> tent. This "wonderful order and regularity with which nature
>> has disposed of these singular productions (fossils) and as-
>> signed to each its class and peculiar strata" *were recognized as
>> early as 1796 by William Smith, the father of stratigraphy.* At
>> about the same time, the noted French biologists Georges
>> Cuvier and Alexandre Brongniart arrived independently at
>> comparable conclusions. . . . Both the stratigraphic column
>> and our general understanding of fossil successions were

thus developed empirically and without any reference to evolutionary assumption. In fact, *Cuvier* was a leading catastrophist who *emphatically denied that evolution has occurred.* The sequence of geologic periods was reasonably well established in 1841. It was not until several decades later that scientists rather suddenly began to recognize the [alleged] evolutionary thread connecting successive assemblages of fossils.[79]

In essence, the geologic column can offer no proof of evolution when it can so easily be interpreted in a nonevolutionary fashion.

The Genesis Flood

Finally, although the interpretation of the data are not without some problems, what the geological column *does* offer is evidence of a worldwide flood, as early and contemporary creationists argue. In his publication, *Catastrophes in Earth History*, geologist Steven A. Austin, Ph.D., cites some 250 publications involving the work of almost 350 authors to show that, "Modern geology contains a rich body of research and speculation that directly challenges the theory that the earth evolved to its present configuration only by gradual processes."[80] This book, along with the classic by Henry Morris and John Whitcomb, *The Genesis Flood*, offers persuasive evidence that catastrophism, not uniformitarianism, is the best explanation for the present features of the earth. Neither explain all the data, but catastrophism explains more than evolution.

To illustrate, in his *Grand Canyon: Monument to Catastrophe* (1994), Austin shows how a creationist/flood interpretation is superior to an evolutionary/uniformitarian model. This magnificent canyon has long been offered by evolutionists as proof of uniformitarianism. In other words, how could a canyon of such size as this be formed rapidly? Austin shows how. In the words of Dr. Emmett L. Williams, who declares the book "a monument to creationist scholarship," "Interpretations based on creationist assumptions and observations related to catastrophic events are offered. Every scientific fact is explained within a Flood model. A creationist geological timetable for the canyon is shown on page 58. . . . Austin has performed a valuable service in placing the division of the rocks of the Grand Canyon within a creation-week-Flood-framework."[81]

Evolutionists often claim that creation isn't science because it has no scientific models or predictive ability concerning its theories. We have addressed this briefly in this volume and will in more detail elsewhere. But for now we may note the following examples to counter such claims. Walter Brown is the author of *In the Beginning*. He has a Ph.D. in mechanical engineering from the Massachusetts Institute of Technology and in the words of a reviewer of his book he "unveils what this writer believes to be the closest model to the actual Genesis Flood that any creationist has ever assembled. . . . Brown's Hydroplate Theory is elegant in its parsimony and explanatory power. Brown has been refining this theory for the last 15 years and the theory has gotten little exposure in the creationist literature. It presents itself as the unified field theory of the earth sciences. It also has more predictive power than any model available."[82]

One particularly fascinating illustration of creationist research, again relative to the biblical flood and its implications, is now being conducted by Dr. Carl Baugh at the Creation Evidence museum in Glen Rose, Texas. The reults are significant enough that NASA invited him to speak before its scientists and engineers on the scientific (if not creationist) implications. As with all research, the results must be considered tentative until further confirmation.

In the world's first byperbaric biosphere, Dr. Baugh has simulated (not duplicated) the pre-flood atmosphere by 1) doubling the atmospheric pressure; 2) increasing the earth's magnetic field tenfold; 3) slightly increasing the oxygen ratio; 4) increasing the carbon dioxide ratio tenfold; and 5) eliminating ultraviolet radiation, dominating with pink light. In a personal conversation with John Weldon in December 1997, Dr. Baugh revealed that the results so far are startling:

- Third generation fruit flies have tripled their adult life-span.
- First generation pacu piranha have tripled their growth rate from 4 inches to 19 inches in a matter of months.

- First generation snake venom actually alters its molecular structure.

Creationist research worldwide, though terribly underfunded, is nevertheless proving its value even to some skeptics.

Models and research like this are why open-minded evolutionists are increasingly interested in catastrophic models. To illustrate, John MacKay made a presentation to the Association of Geological and Earth Sciences at Oxford University in Britain on the evidence for Noah's flood, titled, "An Evening at Oxford: Evidence for Noah's Flood." In this presentation, a collection of slides was given which showed that the "physical evidence of a catastrophic flood event is staggering."[83]

Henry M. Morris's conclusion after 40 years of research into civil engineering, geology, Genesis, and the Genesis flood is that the entire geological column had to be formed rapidly:

> All of this adds up to the fact that there is no real evidence for the geological ages except evolution, and no real evidence for evolution except the geological ages. In any other field of science, such a system would be flagrant circular reasoning. There is, therefore, no real evidence that the entire geological column (to the extent that it actually exists) could not have been formed in a single worldwide complex of catastrophes extending over a relatively short duration of time, finally comprising a unique hydraulic/volcanic/tectonic cataclysm. This, of course is also what the Bible teaches. . . . The deposition of the entire column—whether or not it is believed to represent the geological ages—proceeded from bottom to top (Proterozoic through Tertiary) with no worldwide interruption in its deposition. That being true (and it is), and if also every deposit has been formed very rapidly (as the neo-catastrophists now recognize), then it follows as day follows night that *the entire column was formed rapidly!* If all formations represent local catastrophes, as acknowledged now by Ager and most other active geologists, then they must all be interconnected and essentially continuous, forming the tremendous record of a global hydraulic/volcanic/tectonic cataclysm—nothing less than the great Flood of the Bible!

One can, of course, find many difficulties in applying Flood geology to the entire geological column. These become especially troublesome in trying to correlate all the local columns of the world with each other and all within the context of one global Flood. . . . [However] The Flood was unique in size, in scope, in complexity and in duration—not to mention its control by divine providence, possibly even miraculous in some degree—so much so that it cannot really be compared with later geological processes—not even other major geological catastrophes. To say that such-and-such a local geological formation or sequence cannot be assimilated in a Flood explanation is to say more than one can prove. We cannot know all that was happening during the Flood year, and it is spiritually presumptuous to think we can. . . . It is better to leave some geological problems for further study than to let uniformitarian pseudo-science and our own limited understanding dictate our biblical interpretations.[84]

Biblical Testimony for a Universal Flood

In light of the clear statements in Genesis chapters six through nine and elsewhere in Scripture, the arguments often put forth for a local Mesopotamian flood simply aren't convincing. In Genesis 6:13, God specifically said that the earth had become *"filled* with violence." Thus, the entire earth had been populated from its original parents, Adam and Eve. Articles by creationists in the *Creation Research Society Quarterly* and other literature have shown that the earth could easily be populated worldwide in a few thousand years.[85]

Regardless, it simply isn't possible to derive a local flood from statements like the following:

They rose greatly on the earth, and all the high mountains under the entire heavens were covered. The waters rose and covered the mountains to a depth of more than twenty feet (Genesis 7:19,20).

The waters flooded the earth for a hundred and fifty days (Genesis 7:24).

Every living thing that moved on the earth perished—birds, livestock, wild animals, all the creatures that swarm over the earth, and all mankind. Everything on dry land that had the breath of life in its nostrils died. Every living thing on the face of the earth was wiped out; men and animals and the creatures that move along the ground and the birds of the air were wiped from the earth. Only Noah was left, and those with him in the ark (Genesis 7:21,23).

I establish my covenant with you: Never again will all life be cut off by the waters of a flood; never again will there be a flood to destroy the earth (Genesis 9:11).

If all the hills and mountains under the whole heaven were covered to a depth of 20 feet, then the whole earth had to be covered with water. The ark would have floated freely over the mountains of the pre-flood world. (See also Genesis 6:7,12,13; 7:4; 8:21; 9:11-15.)

When the cities and towns in America, or other places in the world, receive extremely heavy rains for only a few days, they have serious flood problems. According to Genesis, the waters prevailed on the earth for 150 days. Based on the descriptions that *"all the springs* of the *great deep* burst forth" and "the *floodgates* of the heavens were opened," (Genesis 7:11,12) this was unlike any other rainstorm that has ever been.

Clearly, according to Scripture, every living thing on the earth died. Only Noah and his family survived.

In addition, if the flood had been local, Noah and his family could have easily migrated to a different location. There would have been no need to go through the lengthy and difficult process of building an ark the size Noah built. But God specifically said the purpose of the ark was to keep Noah alive on the earth (Genesis 6:19,20). This can only be understood in light of a universal flood that would have left nowhere to go. Noah had to enter the ark because there would be no land on which to live.

Further, in Genesis 9:11, God promised there would never be a flood to destroy the earth again. How could this be just a local flood, when there have been centuries of destructive local floods around the world? It seems God would have broken His covenant promise. Why put a rainbow in the sky as a covenant to all humanity that He would never again destroy the earth with a flood, if the flood waters only concerned a fraction of the earth? (See Genesis 9:11-17.)

Actually, the rainbow is tantamount to disproof of a local flood and proof of a worldwide flood. God said His covenant with Noah was also "for all generations to come" and that He would never again "destroy all life" by a flood: "I have set my rainbow in the clouds, and it will be the sign of the covenant between me and the earth" and further, "this is the sign of the covenant I have established between me and all life on the earth" (Genesis 9:12-17).

Every nation and all the peoples on earth experience rainbows. If Noah's flood was a minor local flood that did not cover the whole planet, the above verses make no sense. Why would God display rainbows to the entire world as a covenant to all people that he will never again bring a local flood in Mesopotamia? In essence, the universality of rainbows only makes sense if God is telling people around the world that He will never flood the entire earth again. Again, the rainbow is a covenant "for *all* generations to come" and between God and "*all* life on earth," so that no one anywhere on earth, anytime, ever need to worry about divine judgment by flood. Therefore, the rainbow must be proof that at one time the entire world was flooded, just as Genesis describes.

It is pointed out that universal language is used non-literally elsewhere in Genesis, e.g., 41:54,57. Does this require the conclusion that the universal language used in Genesis chapters six through nine is not to be taken literally? No. One has to consider the much larger number of statements and descriptions regarding the Flood, as well as the Apostle Peter's comment in 2 Peter 3:6. Here, even the *NIV Study Bible* footnote (which seem to favor a local flood in its Genesis 6:17 comment) asserts that, "The Apostle Peter, however, seems to assume that the flood and its devastation were universal and total, except for Noah and his family."[86]

Universal language aside, one has a hard time getting around the specific descriptions in Genesis. Would torrential rain for 40 days and nights be necessary for a local flood? Would an ark to put the animals in be necessary? Would the flood waters remain for almost a year with a local flood? The problems seem too great to maintain a local flood theory. Think carefully: What exactly was God trying to convey when He wrote the following words?

> For forty days the flood kept coming on the earth, and as the waters increased they lifted the ark high above the earth. The waters rose and increased greatly on the earth, and the ark floated on the

surface of the water. They rose greatly on the earth, and all the high mountains under the entire heavens were covered. The waters rose and covered the mountains to a depth of more than twenty feet. Every living thing that moved on the earth perished—birds, livestock, wild animals, all the creatures that swarm over the earth, and all mankind. Everything on dry land that had the breath of life in its nostrils died. Every living thing on the face of the earth was wiped out; men and animals and the creatures that move along the ground and the birds of the air were wiped from the earth. Only Noah was left, and those with him in the ark. The waters flooded the earth for a hundred and fifty days (Genesis 7:17-24).

Certainly if "the birds of the air were wiped from the earth" the waters had to be everywhere and cover all land. In addition, after it stopped raining, it says the water receded *steadily* from the earth. But look how long it took. *After* it stopped raining, at *the end of the 150 days*, "the water had gone down, and on the seventeenth day of the seventh month the ark came to rest on the mountains of Ararat. The waters continued to recede until the tenth month, and on the first day of the tenth month the tops of the mountains became visible" (Genesis 8:3-5).

How could this be a local flood when waters receded for five full months *after* the rain stopped and only *then* "the tops of the mountains became visible"? According to Genesis 8:14, it was over *a year* after the flood began that "the earth was completely dry." Genesis 8:6-12 tells us that prior to this, Noah sent out a raven and a dove to see if they would find dry land. "But the dove could find no place to set its feet because there was water all over the surface of the earth; so it returned to Noah in the ark" (Genesis 8:9). Doves and ravens can fly great distances. Perhaps, like seagulls, they could rest on the water and fly again. Regardless, had this been a local flood, they would eventually have found dry land.

Finally, there are significant scientific evidences for a global flood.[87] And most cultures *around the world* have written traditions of a universal flood. How does such a cultural consensus arise if there has only been a local flood to destroy the inhabitants of Mesopotamia? Why do people in India, China, and all around the globe have universal flood traditions? The logical answer is because the whole world was flooded, just as geological evidence indicates. (If 70 percent of the earth is currently under water, the idea that it was once 100 percent covered with water should not be considered impossible.)

Life from Mars?

In 1996 the world was told about the discovery of supposed lifelike forms on the planet Mars through a meteorite found on earth. Despite the almost instantaneous worldwide broadcasting of this news with great excitement, we and most other creationists were skeptical. The reason for our skepticism was that the assumption of finding life was based on the evolutionary theory that such life evolved naturalistically which, as we have seen, is an impossibility. And if it is impossible, the only other option is for God to have created such life. But there seems little reason for God to do so. (This has not prevented all sorts of nonsense being proposed—as Barbara Yost wrote in the *Arizona Republic* (August 1997): "The Garden of Eden might have been located on the Red Planet. Adam and Eve might have been Martians. They might have been bacteria. Apple-eating, serpent-fearing, sin-committing bacteria.")

There is no evidence that any form of naturalistic exobiogenesis has ever occurred. We are convinced that this will remain true with the latest "findings" from Mars. While it is true that astrochemists have identified some 100 molecules in outer space, this is hardly unexpected given the composition of material in outer space.

The truth is that outer space, as everyone knows, is extremely hostile to life. The fact that many scientists who reject the idea that life on earth has evolved are now looking to outer space—despite the fact that they encounter the very same problems—only shows how intractable is the problem of an evolutionary origin to life anywhere. As George Javor writes, "Increasing numbers of evolutionary scientists are accepting now the concept of 'panspermia,' that life evolved elsewhere in space and was imported accidentally or purposefully to the earth. . . . [This] pushes the problem out of the realm of experimentation and gives up on suggesting how life could have come about. But it is also a stubborn clinging to the notion that somehow matter can self-organize into living matter—if not on this earth, then elsewhere in the universe. What we know about living matter makes it clear that this cannot happen."[88]

Finally, many other alleged evidences for evolution are now proven wrong. One false idea is called "embryonic recapitulation," the idea that the preborn child undergoes the stages of evolution in its own development. Another is the concept of vestigial organs. This is based on the false idea that some organs are useless evolutionary remnants or vestigials, rather than organs created with a purpose and, therefore, always functional. At one time or another some 150 organs were held to be vestigial. Today almost all of them have known functions. Among humans, the fact that millions of unneeded appendectomies and tonsillectomies may have occurred simply because evolutionists convinced everyone they were useless organs is a small testimony to the cost of a bad idea.[89]

In conclusion, the alleged evidences for evolution may properly be considered at home in *Alice in Wonderland*. In that fantasy world, as the Red Queen said, "six impossible things can be believed before breakfast."

But to be fair, we should not forget there are also problems with creation. We simply don't have enough scientific data or information about the past to solve all problems. Creation science is, after all, only in its infancy. Undoubtedly, it will continue to grow and expand. What we can know with certainty is that there are no final problems because creation is based not only on scientific data but on the Word of God.[90]

17

The Ultimate Con?

The Religious Faith of Scientific Naturalism

Most evolutionists bristle when someone tells them that their belief in evolution is "a religious faith" or "a religion." In their own minds, the distinctions between science and religion are so concrete they hardly find the assertion fathomable. The book cited earlier, *Voices for Evolution*, illustrates this with an official statement from the North Carolina Academy of Science: "We totally reject the concept, put forth by certain pressure groups, that evolution is itself a tenet of religion."[1]

However, if evolution were not a faith in the power of matter and potentially a religious ideology, we would not find philosophers of religion, philosophers of science, lawyers who specialize in religious issues, and evolutionary scientists themselves saying that evolution *is* potentially religious or a religion. "Those concurring that evolution too often involves religious faith include Midgley in the recent book *Evolution as a Religion*, Lipson, Jaki, Patterson, MacBeth, and Jastrow."[2]

In his *Darwin Retried*, lawyer Norman MacBeth states flatly, "Darwinism itself has become a religion."[3] Is he correct? Yes and no, but mostly yes. What is interesting about this issue is the similarity between evolution and creation regarding their scientific and religious natures.

Evolution or Creation: Science and Religion

Evolution can be either a science or a religion and so can creation. On the one hand, both evolution and creation can be scientific and nonreligious. As leading lawyer W. R. Bird points out, "The definition of religion is as elusive a holy grail as the definition of science. However, under most of the attempts to snare it, the theory of evolution and the theory of abrupt appearance [a theory roughly parallel to creation] are equally non-religious. The reason is that both theories consist of affirmative scientific arguments based on empirical data, and neither theory necessarily involves a concept of creation or of a creator."[4]

And ". . . neither the theory of evolution nor the theory of abrupt appearance constitutes such an 'ultimate concern' or religious belief system as required by those philosophical definitions or legal definitions."[5] Bird shows that both evolution and abrupt appearance lack most or all of the characteristics of religion as given in *Encyclopedia of Philosophy, Encyclopedia Britannica,* etc., and do "not substantially meet any of the prevailing philosophical definitions."[6] Further, despite evolutionist denials, "The theory of abrupt appearance instead consists of empirical evidence and scientific interpretations, without any reference to or reliance on religious texts and doctrines. Recognition of the scientific evidence supporting the theory of abrupt appearance can be and has been based entirely on nonreligious grounds, as several agnostic scientists and philosophers demonstrate. The concept of a God or creator is not a part of that scientific evidence, and thus is not a part of the theory when properly defined, as discussed later."[7]

Bird's extensive discussion of "abrupt appearance" involves a nonreligious creationist view that is *fully* scientific. But even creation per se *can* be scientific: "Not only is the theory of abrupt appearance testable, but even the scientific theory of creation is testable. Quinn observes that '[c]reation-science as defined in [the Arkansas law even] clearly satisfies these conditions' of testability and falsifiability. Laudan similarly acknowledges its testability (while also strongly opposing the theory of creation)" and "The theories of evolution and of abrupt appearance are not religious, under the prevailing definitions of religion offered by philosophers of religion, theologians, and judges. Even the theory of creation can be nonreligious under those standards, although it is a more difficult case to access."[8]

No one argues that creation is solely a scientific theory. But what most evolutionists won't concede is the frequently religious nature of their own beliefs or that creation itself can be fully scientific.

Evolution as Religion

In the following material, we are going to show that evolution is a religious belief requiring "infinitely" more faith than creationism. In fact, what it requires is not legitimate faith at all. As we illustrated in Chapters 4 and 5, evolutionists frequently refer to Christian faith as being irrational and nonevidential. Actually, the shoe is on the other foot. It is evolution that requires a blind faith and, as such, it is the antithesis of biblical faith.[9] In order to show this we will, of necessity, reintroduce one or two of our earlier discussions, although with new material and in a different format.

To begin, faith is a tenet of religion and there is absolutely no doubt that evolution requires faith—plenty of faith. Consider some examples. First, W. R. Bird cites numerous evolutionists who recognize the need for faith or argue that evolution is a religion:

> Macroevolution must be accepted as "an act of faith" because it is "not a scientifically ascertained fact," in Scott's view; and is "a matter of personal faith" and an "article of faith," in Rifkin's estimation. . . . Matthews finds Darwinism a "faith," although a satisfactory one; and Bateson found it to require "extraordinary acts of faith. . . ." Midgley concludes that the "belief in future events does seem to be religious," with reference to "the escalator view of evolution" of "steady, careful progress." Darwinism "has virtually become a religion itself" in Leith's view, and many examples of its "religion in reverse" are cited by MacBeth and others.
>
> Within the field of biochemical evolution, Yockey concludes that current theories are "based on faith" because of insuperable information content problems: "it is concluded that belief in currently accepted scenarios of spontaneous biogenesis is based on faith, contrary to conventional wisdom."
>
> Kerkut also finds that biochemical evolution is "a matter of faith." . . . Others write that "faith in science" can be a religion,

and that to many scientists, in fact, "pure science has become the new religion." The prevalent intellectual attitude of science "is continuous with a typically religious view of the physical world."[10]

Elsewhere Bird lists comments of those evolutionists who believe evolution is a religion:

> Lipson calls evolution "a scientific religion," Jaki terms it "a creed . . . with scientists committed to document the all-purpose role of natural selection," Midgley writes of "evolution as a religion," MacBeth concludes that "Darwinism has itself become a religion," and Conklin said that for many biologists evolution "is an object of genuinely religious devotion. . . ."[11]

In *Growth of Ideas*, Julian Huxley and British evolutionist Jacob Bronowski write that, "A religion is essentially an attitude to the world as a whole. Thus evolution, for example, may prove as powerful a principle to coordinate man's beliefs and hopes as God was in the past."[12]

The noted philosopher and historian of science Marjorie Grene observes that, "It is as a religion of science that Darwinism chiefly held, and holds man's minds. . . . [It is] preached by its adherents with religious fervor. . . ."[13]

The senior paleontologist at the British Museum of Natural History, Colin Patterson, has written that, "Just as pre-Darwinian biology was carried out by people whose faith was in the Creator and His plan, post-Darwinian biology is being carried out by people whose faith is in, almost, the deity of Darwin."[14]

When it comes to the particulars of evolutionary theory, faith is required in each case, and evolution has other religious aspects as well. Evolutionary theory has its own creator "gods" (time, chance, matter, natural selection), its own faith *in the miraculous*, its own creeds, altars, and heresies. Darwin himself referred to "my deity, Natural Selection."[15] Leading evolutionist Pierre-P. Grassé states in his *Evolution of Living Organisms*: "We repeatedly hear that chance is all powerful. Statements are insufficient. Evidence must be produced. . . . Directed by all-powerful selection, chance becomes a sort of providence, which, under the cover of atheism, is not named but which is secretly worshipped."[16]

Randy L. Wysong, D.V.M., an instructor in human anatomy and physiology, observes in *The Creation-Evolution Controversy*:

Evolution can be thought of as sort of a magical religion. Magic is simply an effect without a cause, or at least a competent cause. "Chance," "time," and "nature" are the small gods enshrined at evolutionary temples. Yet these gods cannot explain the origin of life. These gods are impotent. Thus, evolution is left without competent cause and is, therefore, only a magical explanation for the existence of life. And, like other cultures practicing magic, evolution has its witchdoctors. But their dance is not performed in the glimmer of bonfires, rather, it is performed in the various temples found on campuses around the world, in subsidized research institutions and in the light cast by spark discharge tubes.

Is it not fairy tales that spin wild yarns of physical transforma-tions—mice into horses, gingerbread into men, children into spiders? Of course, it is not the fairy's word or a witch's spell that causes evolutionary transformation, it is the intellectually accept-able power of the stardust of the time-chance-nature deity.

Those who doubt, who lack faith in the rights of the evolution-ary high priests are fitting only for exorcism: the exorcism of the spirit of an open mind, and the possession by the spiritual dogma: "Since life is here, life evolved."

Evolutionists attribute to time, chance and nature the capaci-ties that creationists attribute to God.[17]

Evolution not only requires faith in general but faith in virtually every area it cites as evidence:

Evolution requires plenty of faith: a faith in L-proteins ˌleft-handed molecules] that defy chance formation; a faith in the formation of DNA codes which if generated spontaneously would spell only pandemonium; a faith in a primitive environment that in reality would fiendishly devour any chemical precursors to life; a faith in experiments [on the origin of life] that prove nothing but the need for intelligence in the beginning; a faith in a primitive ocean that would not thicken but would only hopelessly dilute chemicals; a faith in natural laws including the laws of thermody-namics and biogenesis that actually deny the possibility for the spontaneous generation of life; a faith in future scientific revela-tions that when realized always seem to present more dilemmas to the evolutionists; faith in probabilities that tenuously tell two stories—one denying evolution, the other confirming the creator, faith in transformations that remain fixed; faith in mutations and natural selection that add to a double negative for evolution; faith in fossils that embarrassingly show fixity through time, regular absence from transitional forms and striking testimony to a world-wide water deluge; a faith in time which proves only to promote degradation in the absence of mind; and faith in reductionism that ends up reducing the materialist arguments to zero and enforcing the need to invoke the supernatural creator.

The evolutionary religion is consistently inconsistent. Scientists rely upon the rational order of the universe to make accomplishments, yet the evolutionist tells us the rational universe had an irrational beginning from nothing. Due to lack of understanding about mechanisms and structure, science cannot even create a simple twig. Yet the evolutionary religion speaks with bold dogmatism about the origin of life.[18]

In addition, religious support for evolution has been lengthy and consistent among religious humanism, theological liberalism, and related views, as Bird documents extensively, and its consistency with religion generally is also evident.[19]

In conclusion, there is little doubt that evolution, especially in the manner in which it is held and defended today, is *just as much* a religious faith as a science. Indeed, "Religious devotion . . . is probably the reason why severe methodological criticism employed in other departments of biology has not yet been brought to bear on evolutionary speculation, Conklin of Princeton wrote and Smith of Syracuse University reiterates."[20]

We will pursue this idea in greater detail and see just how *much* faith evolution requires its adherents to muster. As we will discover, it is an impossibly large amount, immeasurably greater than a theist's faith in a creator. And many evolutionists, in their more rational moments, will concede this on a variety of levels, as we will also discover.

The God of Nothing?

However, to begin, we should observe again that evolutionists often argue *there is no need* for belief in a creator to explain the natural world. As noted evolutionist George Gaylord

Simpson declared, "There is neither need nor excuse for postulation of nonmaterial [i.e., divine] intervention in the origin of life, the rise of man, or any other part of the long history of the material cosmos."[21]

C. D. Darlington of Oxford University wrote, "We owe to the *Origin of Species* the overthrow of the myth of creation, especially the dramatic character of the overthrow."[22]

But as we documented earlier, the ideas that everything has come from nothing, and that life came from nonlife, are virtually impossible to hold as rational tenets. Consider a few refreshers which underscore that evolution is not just a faith, but, in contrast to Christianity, an *irrational* faith. This is recognized by leading scientists: Roy Abraham Varghese and others have pointed out that the idea that everything that exists came to be *without* a cause involves an implicit contradiction and is a notion that is ultimately incoherent.[23]

Professor H. D. Lewis, Chairman of the Royal Institute of Philosophy and first President of the International Society for Metaphysics, puts it as follows. He argues that the idea that everything has come from nothing "is a notion we just cannot accept, *not because* of any religious background or upbringing, but as ordinary sensible beings. *Ex nihilo nihil fit* [from nothing nothing comes] was said long ago, and seems as unavoidable for us as for those who pondered these things earlier. . . . I can only put it to you that, if you reflect, you just cannot, independently of any further implications, accept the idea of a totally random springing into being out of nonbeing."[24]

Professor William Stoeger, who received a Ph.D. in astrophysics from the University of Cambridge, writes, "Now, in the case where there is not a necessary being, then absolute nothingness will remain absolute nothingness 'forever.' There is no intelligible way in which this nothingness can yield something—existence, something existing."[25]

Of course, this is exactly what evolutionists argue. God is deliberately removed and Nothing becomes the *necessary* source of Everything. This constitutes a far greater miracle than creation.[26]

Evolutionists won't concede it, but their theory requires a faith in the miraculous exceedingly beyond anything a Christian believes.

"I THINK YOU SHOULD BE MORE EXPLICIT HERE IN STEP TWO."

A Miracle Either Way

"To me every hour of the light and dark is a miracle. Every cubic inch of space is a miracle" (Walt Whitman).

After discussing aspects of design in nature Darwin himself stated, "To admit all this is as it seems to me, to enter into the realms of miracle and to leave those of Science."[27]

At least here, Darwin was correct. Both evolution and creation require miracles—the only issue is which of the miracles is believable and which is not.

As modern science increasingly uncovers the indescribable complexity of the living world but fails to explain the nature of abiogenesis (that life can originate from nonlife), the miraculous nature of all theories of origins is made evident. The term miracle is no longer properly restricted to creationist belief. This is true whether we are considering cosmology or biology. As the famous psychiatrist M. Scott Peck observed in *The Road Less Traveled* (1978, p. 264): "The most striking feature of the processs of physical evolution is that it is a miracle. Given what we understand of the universe, evolution should not occur; the phenomenon should not exist at all."

It's not as if earlier eras could not conclude the same thing. Current discoveries have made the miraculous nature of life logically undeniable. But Einstein himself viewed the high degree of order throughout the universe as a "miracle:" "This is the single "miracle" that is strengthened more and more with the development of our knowledge."[28] And this has proved true.

In the material below we will cite nine examples, all but one from evolutionists or non-creationists, to show that leading scientists now concede that our existence requires a belief in the miraculous.

In terms of cosmologies, Heinz Pagels, a pioneer in the Vacuum Fluxuation theory of the origin of the universe, offers the following description. To our way of thinking, this is tantamount to speaking of miracles:

> The nothingness "before" the creation of the universe is the most complete void that we can imagine—no space, time, or matter existed. It is a world without place, without duration or eternity, without number—it is what the mathematicians call "empty set." Yet this unthinkable void converts itself into the plenum of existence. . . .[29]

Professor Vera Kistiakowsky, Professor of Physics at the Massachusetts Institute of Technology remarks, "For me, the whole process is miraculous, from the formation of the first complex molecules to the evolution of human intelligence" and "the exquisite order displayed by our scientific understanding of the physical world calls for the divine."[30]

Professor Henry Margenau, Emeritus Eugene Higgins Professor of Physics and Natural Philosophy at Yale University and former President of the American Association for the Philosophy of Science, writes:

What is the origin of the laws of nature? For this I can find only one convincing answer: they are created by God, and God is omnipotent and omniscient. In my latest book (*The Miracle of Existence*) I called Him "the Universal Mind" and suggested that every human soul is a part of Him. . . . Science needs religion in order to account for its origin and its successes. I discussed this view with Einstein when I did research at the Institute for Advanced Study at Princeton in 1932 and remember his comment: "The discovery of a fundamental, verified law of nature is an inspiration of God."

There is a common belief that science rejects miracles. But what, in precise terms, is a miracle? . . . The existence of man, indeed of the entire universe, has long been regarded as a miracle, incomprehensible without assuming the existence of a Creator who is omnipotent and omniscient. . . . God created the universe out of nothing in an act which also brought time into existence. Recent discoveries . . . are wholly compatible with this view.[31]

Nobel prize winning biochemist Dr. Francis Crick commented, "An honest man, armed with all the knowledge available to us now, could only state that in some sense, the origin of life appears at the moment to be almost a miracle, so many are the conditions which would have had to have been satisfied to get it going."[32]

Robert E. D. Clark (Ph.D. organic chemistry, Cambridge) remarks, "If complex organisms ever did evolve from simpler ones, the process took place contrary to the laws of nature and must have involved what may rightly be termed the miraculous."[33] Wigner, after showing the impossibility of forming a self-reproducing unit concludes that life is ". . . a miracle from the point of view of the physical scientist."[34] In *Information Theory and Molecular Biology* (1992), Hubert Yockey argues that the chance formation of a single molecule of iso-l-cytochrome c requires a miracle.

Fred Hoyle's research partner, Chandra Wickramasinghe, also noted, "Contrary to the popular notion that only creationism relies on the supernatural, evolutionism must as well, since the probabilities of random formation of life are so tiny as to require a 'miracle' for spontaneous generation tantamount to a theological argument."[35] In recent years, many noted scientists have declared of the origin of life, "the whole process is miraculous" as the earlier mentioned text, *Cosmos, Bios, Theos* illustrates. So let's briefly look deeper into this idea that belief in evolution is essentially a belief in miracles.

Limited Options

Mark Eastman, M.D. and Chuck Missler point out that when you boil down all the materialistic arguments for the origin of the universe, there are only two alternatives:

1. that matter is infinitely old, i.e., eternal.
2. that matter appeared out of nothing at a finite point in the past.

They point out, "There is no third option."

These authors proceed to cite evidence to show that matter cannot be eternal, including evidence from physics, such as proton decay, and evidence from the first and second laws of thermodynamics which "provide some of the strongest evidence for a finite universe."[36]

Everyone agrees that matter does exist, so we have to explain its existence somehow. If matter cannot be infinitely old—and the scientific evidence is so strong at this point as to make this conclusion inevitable—then our only option is that matter appeared in the universe out of nothing at a finite point in the past.

Of course, as we saw, if we begin with the Big Bang and an extremely small amount of dense matter, which some dub the "cosmic egg," the problem is not resolved. The origin of the "cosmic egg" is a matter of intense debate as well it should be. Where did such an egg originate? Did it exist forever? If not, where did it come from? Either it existed forever, which is impossible, or it appeared out of nothing at a finite point in the past, which is impossible. And how could something the size of a proton produce the billions and trillions of suns and galaxies in our universe, let alone life? Isn't this irrational faith in "a god of the gaps" involving miracles without number? Materialistically, there is no explanation, nor will there be. Thus, such scenarios are not only unscientific and irrational, they are impossible, as we have seen in Chapters 10 and 15 and will further document herein.

What is more amazing is that the scientific world and general public have accepted this infinitely implausible scenario for the origin of the universe over an infinitely more probable one—creation by an infinite God.

In the creation/evolution debate, one must recognize that whether you begin with a materialistic or a theistic origin for the universe, both are miracles. Again, it's only a question of which miracle is more credible. As Eastman and Missler state:

> The creationist's model begins with an infinitely intelligent, omnipotent, transcendent Creator who used intelligent design, expertise or know-how to create everything from the sub-atomic particles to giant redwood trees. Was it a miracle? Absolutely!
>
> The atheist's [i.e., materialistic] model begins with an even more impressive miracle—the appearance of all matter in the universe from nothing, by no one, and for no reason. A supernatural event. A miracle! However, the atheist does not believe in the outside or transcendent "First Cause" we call God. Therefore, the atheist has no "natural explanation" nor "supernatural explanation" for the origin of space-time and matter. Consequently the atheistic scenario on the origin of the universe leaves us hanging in a totally dissatisfying position. He begins his model for the universe with a supernatural event. This supernatural event, however, is accomplished without a supernatural agent to perform it.[37]

Many religions, especially Eastern religions, believe in the idea of an infinite, eternal universe. Unfortunately, this has serious implications for their doctrine of God. If the universe is infinite and eternal, then by definition there can be nothing else. As a result, even God becomes immanent within the universe, an occupant of it rather than an infinite, transcendent being beyond it. "Therefore, God could not dwell in eternity. He could not exist before time and space began. And because God is confined to the universe, He is subject to its laws. Therefore, God becomes either a product of the universe or the universe itself."[38]

It's beyond the scope of this book to discuss the problems of a solely immanent, pantheistic God; however, they are anything but small as seen in the religious, social, and moral consequences in those cultures which espouse pantheism. Regardless, if there is now virtual proof that the universe is not infinite and that it has not existed eternally, the logical conclusion is that pantheism is a scientific impossibility because it would equate God with an infinite, eternal universe.

A Return to Common Sense

Nevertheless, the current crisis in evolution and the lack of alternate theories other than divine creation are, thankfully, encouraging even materialistic scientists to consider God and religious ideas concerning the origin of the universe. Thus: "The evidence for a finite, decaying, and finely-tuned universe has led many to conclude that there must be a Mind behind it all. Remarkably, many of these men are professed atheists who have been forced by the weight of 20th-century discoveries in astronomy and physics to concede the existence of an intelligent Designer behind the creation of the universe."[39]

For example, Paul Davies was once a leader for the atheistic, materialistic worldview. He now asserts of the universe, "[There] is for me powerful evidence that there is something going on behind it all. . . . It seems as though somebody has fine-tuned nature's numbers to make the Universe. . . . The impression of design is overwhelming." Further, the laws of physics themselves seem "to be the product of exceedingly ingenious design."[40]

Even noted atheist Professor Antony Flew, one of the best known promoters of atheism in the English speaking world, comments in response to a paper by Professor H. D. Lewis, Chairman of the Royal Institute of Philosophy and first President of the International Society for Metaphysics:

> Notoriously, confession is good for the soul. I will therefore begin by confessing that the Stratonician atheist has to be embarrassed by the contemporary cosmological consensus. For it seems that the cosmologists are providing a scientific proof of what St. Thomas contended could not be proved philosophically; namely, that the universe had a beginning.[41]

Professor Steven L. Bernasek, Professor of Chemistry at Princeton University, remarks, "I believe in the existence of God. His existence is apparent to me in everything around me, especially in my work as a scientist."[42]

Noted orthopedist Dr. R. Merle d'Aubigne writes, "If I am asked: Do you believe in God? I answer 'yes'. I cannot deprive myself of the feeling of an entity supporting the Good and the Beautiful . . . [the feeling] is quite strong."[43]

Astronomer George Greenstein observed, "As we survey all the evidence, the thought instantly arises that some supernatural agency—or, rather Agency—must be involved. Is it possible that suddenly, without intending to, we have stumbled upon scientific proof of the existence of a Supreme Being? Was it God who stepped in and so providentially crafted the cosmos for our benefit?"[44]

Theoretical physicist Tony Rothman acknowledges, "When confronted with the order and beauty of the universe and the strange coincidences of nature, it's very tempting to take the leap of faith from science into religion. I am sure many physicists want to. I only wish they would admit it."[45]

Actually, science has been so touched with religion recently that even many prominent scientists are talking about "knowing" the mind of God through scientific discovery. The theoretical physicist who is frequently held out as the successor to Einstein, Stephen Hawking, noted in his *A Brief History of Time* that our goal should be to "know the mind of God." Einstein himself once stated, "I want to know how God created this world. . . . I want to know His thoughts, the rest are details." [46]

In *Infinite in All Directions* , physicist Freeman Dyson writes that in attempting to formulate some statement of the ultimate purpose of the universe "the problem is to read God's mind."[47]

What scientists will discover, if they wish, is that if they brought the same degree of objectivity and effort they do in their scientific investigations to the study of Christian evidences, they *could* literally read God's mind—in the Bible. Science at best only gives us hints. To really know the one true God, one must read His revelation in Scripture.

All this is exactly what Romans 1:20 teaches—that the creation itself provides evidence that is clearly seen and understood concerning God's existence. "For since the creation of the world God's invisible qualities—his eternal power and divine nature—have been *clearly seen*, being *understood* from what has been made, so that men are *without excuse*" (emphasis added).

Statements like the above could be multiplied many times over. They prove beyond a doubt that the doing of the best science by some of the most brilliant scientific minds leads us back, not to dead matter, but to a living God. At the very least, we may accept the following statement without qualification:

> In the case of the origin of the universe and life on earth, as we have seen, there are only two possible explanations—chance or design. In each case a balanced examination of twentieth-century scientific evidence has led a number of world authorities to conclude that appealing to chance is akin to faith in supernatural miracles! In effect, to believe that the universe "just happened," the skeptic must place as much faith in arbitrary and purposeless laws of physics and chance chemistry as the Christian does in the God of the Bible.[48]

But again, it is not as if the materialist and the theist are actually exerting *equal* amounts of faith. To the contrary, the materialist's faith is far greater. Let's see just how much faith is needed.

Faith Beyond Reason: More on Probability

Dr. Harry Rimmer (SC.D., D.D.) was allegedly one of only 12 men around 1940 capable of understanding Einstein's theory of relativity. He was precisely correct when he wrote the following: "I fail to see how the natural man can scoff at the faith of a Christian who believes in one miracle of creation, when the unbeliever accepts multiplied millions of miracles to justify his violation of every known law of biology and every evidence of paleontology, and to cling to the exploded myth of evolution."[49]

The esteemed late Carl Sagan and other prominent scientists have estimated the chance of man evolving at roughly 1 chance in $10^{2,000,000,000}$.[50] This is a figure with two billion zeros after it and would require about 2,000 books to write out. This number is so infinitely small it is not even conceivable. So, for argument's sake, let's take an infinitely more favorable view toward the chance that evolution might occur.

What if the chances are only 1 in 10^{1000} the figure that a prestigious symposium of evolutionary scientists used computers to arrive at? This figure involved only a mechanism necessary to abiogenesis and not the evolution of actual primitive life. Regardless, this figure is also infinitely above Borel's single law of chance—(1 chance in 10^{50})—beyond which, put simply, events never occur.[51] Not even *one* chance remains.

On April 25 and 26, 1962, a scientific symposium was held at the Wistar Institute of Anatomy and Biology in Philadelphia, Pennsylvania, in which some of the most distinguished evolutionist scientists gathered, including:

Dr. Niels Barricelli: Department of Genetics, University of Washington, Seattle, Washington

Dr. William Bossert: Computation Laboratories, Harvard University, Cambridge, Massachusetts

Dr. J. L. Crosby: Department of Botany, University of Durham, Durham, England

Dr. Murray Eden: Professor of Electrical Engineering, Massachusetts Institute of Technology, Cambridge, Massachusetts

Dr. Loren C. Eiseley: Professor of Anthropology and History of Science, University of Pennsylvania, Philadelphia, Pennsylvania

Dr. Ralph O. Erickson: Professor of Botany, University of Pennsylvania, Philadelphia, Pennsylvania

Dr. Sidney Fox: 1114 Waverly Road, Tallahassee, Florida

Dr. Alex Fraser: Professor of Genetics, University of California, Davis, California

Dr. Walter Goad: Los Alamos Scientific Laboratory, Los Alamos, New Mexico

Dr. Martin Kaplan: WHO, Geneva, Switzerland

Dr. H. B. D. Kettlewell: Department of Zoology, Oxford University, Oxford, England

Dr. A. W. Kozinski: Department of Medical Genetics, University of Pennsylvania, Philadelphia, Pennsylvania

Dr. Wilton M. Krogman: Department of Physical Anthropology, University of Pennsylvania, Philadelphia, Pennsylvania

Dr. Michael Lerner: Department of Genetics, University of California, Berkeley, California

Dr. Richard C. Lewontin: Professor of Zoology, University of Chicago, Chicago, Illinois

Dr. Ernst Mayr: Museum of Comparative Zoology, Harvard University, Cambridge, Massachusetts

Sir Peter Medawar: National Institute for Medical Research, London, England

Dr. Paul S. Moorhead: The Wistar Institute, Philadelphia, Pennsylvania

Dr. Charles Price: Department of Chemistry, University of Pennsylvania, Philadelphia, Pennsylvania

Dr. Marcel Schützenberger: Professor of Mathematics, University of Paris, Paris, France

Mr. Arthur Shapiro: Department of Botany, University of Pennsylvania, Philadelphia, Pennsylvania

Dr. Stanislaw Ulam: Los Alamos Scientific Laboratories, Los Alamos, New Mexico

Professor C. H. Waddington: Institute of Animal Genetics, Edinburgh, Scotland

Dr. George Wald: Professor of Biology, Harvard University, Cambridge, Massachusetts

Dr. Eberhard Wecker: Institute for Virology, University of Wurburg, Wurburg, Germany

Dr. V. F. Weisskopf: Professor of Physics, Massachusetts Institute of Technology, Cambridge, Massachusetts

Dr. Conway Zirkle: Professor of Botany, University of Pennsylvania, Philadelphia, Pennsylvania

At the beginning of this Symposium, which was entitled, "Mathematical Challenges to the neo-Darwinian Interpretation of Evolution," the Chairman, Sir Peter Medawar of the National Institute for Medical Research in London, England, stated the reasons why they had gathered:

> . . . the immediate cause of this conference is a pretty *widespread sense of dissatisfaction* about what has come to be thought of as the accepted evolutionary theory in the English-speaking world, the so-called neo-Darwinian Theory. . . . These objections to current neo-Darwinian theory *are very widely held among biologists generally;* and we must on no account, I think, make light of them. The very fact that we are having this conference is evidence that we are *not* making light of them.[52]

In his paper, "Inadequacies of Neo-Darwinian Evolution as a Scientific Theory," Dr. Murray Eden, Professor of Electrical Engineering at MIT, emphasized the following: "It is our contention that if 'random' [chance] is given a serious and crucial interpretation from a probabilistic point of view, the randomness postulate is *highly implausible* and that an adequate scientific theory of evolution must await the discovery and elucidation of new natural laws, physical, chemical, and biological."[53]

In "Algorithms and the Neo-Darwinian Theory of Evolution," Marcel P. Schutzenberger of the University of Paris, France, calculated the probability of evolution based on mutation and natural selection. Like many other noted scientists, he concluded that it was "not conceivable" because the probability of a chance process accomplishing this is zero: ". . .there is *no chance* ($<10^{-1000}$) to see this mechanism appear spontaneously and, if it did, *even less* for it to remain. . . .Thus, to conclude, we believe there is a *considerable gap* in the neo-Darwinian Theory of evolution, and we believe this gap to be of such a nature that it *cannot be bridged within the current conception of biology.*"[54]

Evolutionary scientists have called just 1 chance in 10^{15} "a virtual impossibility."[55] So, how can they believe in something that has less than 1 chance in 10^{1000}? After all, how small is 1 chance in 10^{1000}? It's *very* small—1 chance in 10^{12} is only one chance in a trillion.

We can also gauge the size of 1 in 10^{1000} (a figure with a thousand zeros) by considering the sample figure 10^{171}. How large is this figure? First, consider that the number of *atoms* in the period at the end of this sentence is approximately 3,000 trillion. Now, in 10^{171} years an amoeba could actually transport *all the atoms, one at a time*, in six hundred thousand, trillion, trillion, trillion, trillion, trillion, *universes*, each universe the size of ours, from one end of the universe to the other (assuming a distance of 30 *billion* light years) going at the dismally slow traveling speed of *1 inch* every *15 billion years.*[56] The amoeba *could do all this* in 10^{171} years. Yet this figure of 1 chance in 10^{171}, quite literally, cannot even scratch the surface of 1 chance in 10^{1000}— the "chance" that a certain mechanism necessary to the beginning of life might supposedly evolve. Again, who can believe in such miracles—something whose odds are 1 "chance" in 10^{1000}, 1 "chance" in $10^{2,000,000,000}$, or even far beyond this? As we saw earlier, Yale University physicist Harold Morowitz once calculated the odds of a single bacteria reassembling its components, after being superheated to break down its chemicals into their basic building blocks, at 1 chance in $10^{100,000,000,000}$.[57] And, in fact, when you add up all the different odds for all the millions of miracles necessary for evolution, the actual "chances" that life could evolve probably couldn't even be adequately *expressed* mathematically.

Please note that in exponential notation, every time we add a single number in the exponent, we multiply the number itself by a factor of *ten*. Thus, 1 chance in 10^{172} is *ten times* larger than 1 chance in 10^{171}. One chance in 10^{177} is *one million times* larger than 1 chance in 10^{171}. And 1 chance in 10^{183} is *one trillion* times larger than 1 chance in 10^{171}. So where do you think we end up with odds like 1 chance in $10^{100,000,000,000}$? In fact, the dimensions of the entire known universe can be packed full by 10^{50} planets—but the odds of probability theory indicate that evolution would not occur on even a single planet.[58]

Still a Chance?

This kind of probability "progression into absurdity" is the very reason Borel devised his single law of chance—to show that beyond a certain point some things will *never* happen. For example, what are the odds that elephants will ever evolve into helicopters? There are none, no matter how much time we allow for the event to occur.

On occasion, the argument we are making here is sometimes misunderstood. Dr. Weldon's uncle 'Sam' once heard a minister deliver a sermon in church regarding the odds against life originating by chance. The minister was stating that, based on probability considerations, it was "mathematically impossible" that the universe was created by chance. The minister greeted Sam after the service and asked him what he thought of the argument. Sam replied that he had two serious problems with it. The first was that even if there was one in a zillion chances that the universe was created by chance, then the conclusion that it was mathematically *impossible* for the universe to originate by chance was not valid. Even one chance in a zillion is still *1* chance and therefore mathematically possible. The second objection was that if there are an infinite number of opportunities for an event to occur then the odds could increase infinitely so that sooner or later the event would occur.

But this misses the whole point behind Borel's single law of chance. Once we arrive at a certain point in probability considerations, *no* chance remains *regardless* of the amount of opportunities that are present. Anything beyond 1 chance in 10^{50} is not 1 chance in 10^{50} but 0 chance in 10^{50}. And, as we have seen, the "chance" of evolution occurring is infinitely beyond this. Probability considerations are important and do offer valid conclusions in the creation/evolution debate. They tell us there is *no* chance evolution will ever occur even if the universe is infinitely old.

Evolutionists respond the only way they can. They say that given enough time even the impossible becomes possible. Nobel prize-winning biologist George Wald of Harvard University once wrote, "One only has to concede the magnitude of the task to concede the possibility of the spontaneous generation of a living organism is impossible. Yet here we are—as a result, I believe, in spontaneous generation."[59]

Wald proceeds to discuss what he means by "impossible." Not unexpectedly, he claims that the word "is not a very meaningful concept."[60] He goes on to say that, in terms of originating life, "Time is in fact the hero of the plot. The time with which we have to deal is of the order of two billion years. What we regard as impossible on the basis of human experience is meaningless here. Given so much time, the 'impossible' becomes possible, the possible probable, and the probable virtually certain. One has only to wait: time itself performs the miracles."[61]

Oh? Given probability considerations, on what logical basis does Dr. Wald go from the impossible to the "virtually certain"? Wald is arguing as a committed materialist who has great faith in the magical powers of matter. Even though evolution is impossible, it really can't be impossible because after all, here we are. Later he states, "We can be certain that, given time, all these things [necessary to evolution] must occur. Every substance that has ever been found in an organism displays thereby the finite probability of its occurrence. Hence, given time, it should arise spontaneously. One only has to wait."[62]

We are dealing with word games: the impossible is really possible, an event is conceded as impossible so we invoke infinite time and material to make it "possible."

Dr. Wald himself has stated that a 99.999 percent probability is "almost inevitable."[63] A little calculation shows that

Wald's initial statement that spontaneous generation was impossible is far closer to the truth than he himself proceeds to argue in his own chapter.

The word impossible is defined in the dictionary as, "*Not possible*, unable to be done or to exist" and "*not capable* of coming into being or occurring." Also, we don't have infinite time, we only have a few billion years even by evolutionists' calculations, and these calculations themselves are suspect. Nor do we have anywhere near infinite material; it was quite finite and limited. If an event is truly impossible, then it will never occur *by definition* even *given* infinite time and material. ". . . [A]s Saki wisely observed: Those who use 'chance' to argue that 'anything is possible' have reached the antithesis of science, whose laws are based upon the assumption that some things occur and others do not."[64] Evolutionists should reconsider the following statement from a standard evolutionary text on the origin of life, *The Origin of Prebiological Systems*, edited by Sidney W. Fox:

> A further aspect I should like to discuss is what I call the practice of infinite escape clauses. I believe we developed this practice to avoid facing the conclusion that the probability of self-reproducing state is zero. This is what we must conclude from classical quantum mechanical principles as Wigner demonstrated (1961).[65]

Sir John Eccles, winner of the Nobel Prize and one of the foremost brain scientists in this century speaks of 1 chance in $10^{10,000}$ as being "infinitely improbable," noting that "materialists solutions fail to account for our experienced uniqueness" and that therefore "we are constrained to attribute uniqueness of the psyche or soul to a supernatural spiritual creation. . . . We submit that no other explanation is tenable. . . ."[66]

We are constrained to ask, What kind of logic deduces that the infinitely more complex things in nature resulted from *chance* when all the *facts* and *evidence* we possess concerning every *single* man-made object in existence says these much simpler objects had to result from intelligence, plan, and design? If the "simple" objects *demand* intelligence, how do the infinitely more complex objects not demand it?

Placed into a more practical setting, 1 chance in 10^9 is 1 chance in a billion. If a horse had only 1 chance in a billion of placing first, how much money would an evolutionist bet on it? Would he or she bet even a dollar? If not, should anyone gamble their personal convictions about reality, let alone destiny, on the basis of "1" chance in $10^{100,000,000,000,000}$ (1 chance in 10 to the trillionth power)? (At 5,000 zeros per page, per 200 page book, this figure would require over one *million* books just to write out! Imagine walking into a university library and realizing that every book was filled with zeroes, from beginning to end. This illustrates the odds of evolution being true.

Further, if, in ultimate terms, there are only two possible answers to the question of origins, then the disproving of one should logically prove the other. If A or B is the only possible explanations of an event, and A is disproved, only B can be considered the cause. If the chances of evolution occurring are, e.g., "1" in $10^{1,000,000,000,000,000}$, then the chance of creation occurring would have to be its opposite—the odds being 99.9 (followed by one trillion more 9's). Again, George Wald of Harvard has stated that a 99.995 percent probability is "almost inevitable."[67] Then what of 99.999999999999999 (plus one trillion more 9's)—the "chance" that creation has occurred?

Thus, it is not surprising to hear famous astronomer Sir Fred Hoyle, originator of the Steady State theory of the origin of the universe, concede that the chance that higher life forms might have emerged through evolutionary processes is comparable with the chance that a "tornado sweeping through a junk yard might assemble a Boeing 747 from the material therein."[68] As he ponders the magnificence of the world about him, even the outstanding French biochemist and Nobel Prize winner Jacques Monod admits in his *Chance and Necessity*: "One may well find oneself beginning to doubt again whether all this could conceivably be the product of an enormous lottery presided over by natural selection, blindly picking the rare winners from among numbers drawn at utter random. . . . [Nevertheless although] the miracle [of life] stands 'explained'; it does not strike us as any less miraculous. As Francois Mauriac wrote, 'What this professor says is far more incredible than what we poor Christians believe.' "[69]

Although Monod believes that life arose by chance, he freely admits the chances of this happening *before* it occurred were virtually zero: "The riddle remains, and in so doing masks the answer to a question of profound interest. Life appeared on earth: what, *before the event* were the chances that this would occur? The present structure of the biosphere far from excludes the possibility that the decisive event occurred only once. Which would mean that its a priori probability was virtually zero."[70]

The Myth of Chance

A number of scientists have expressed their belief that evolution is a myth. In the following section we are going to amplify this idea by concentrating on the myth of chance and what faith in chance does to science. In *Not a Chance: The Myth of Chance in Modern Science and Cosmology*, theologian and apologist R. C. Sproul points out that mythology was practiced not only by pre-modern cultures. It occurs in every culture and has even intruded significantly into the realm of science, such as in the spontaneous generation theory of evolution (that all life arose from dead matter solely by chance). He shows that the concept of chance—something happening totally without cause—is *impossible*. The *Macmillan Dictionary for Students* (1984) defines impossible as, "not capable of coming into being or occurring; not possible" and "not acceptable as truth."

And yet modern science argues that the universe and all life in it arose solely by chance. Again, in the words of Nobelist Jacques Monod, ". . . chance *alone* is at the source of every innovation, of all creation in the biosphere. Pure chance, absolutely free but blind, [is] at the very root of the stupendous edifice of evolution. . . ."[71]

Sproul argues persuasively that, for science and philosophy to continue in fruitful fashion, the modern penchant for chance must be abandoned once and for all. If not, the stakes are not insignificant—the very possibility of doing science lies in the balance. Essentially, when logic and empirical data are neglected or neutralized in the doing of science then "mythology is free to run wild."[72]

When modern science assigns the origin of the universe and all life in it to pure, random chance it does an incalculable disservice to science, because it "reduces scientific investigation not only to chaos but to sheer absurdity. Half of the scientific method is left impaled on the horns of chance. The classical scientific method consists of the marriage of induction and deduction, of the empirical and the rational. Attributing instrumental causal power to chance vitiates deduction and the rational. It is manifest irrationality, which is not only bad philosophy but horrible science as well. Perhaps the attributing of instrumental power to chance is the most serious error made in modern science and cosmology. . . . If left unchallenged and uncorrected, [it] will lead science into nonsense. . . . Magic and logic are not compatible bedfellows. Once something is thought to come from nothing, something has to give. What gives is logic."[73]

Chance can explain nothing because chance itself is nothing: "chance has no power to do anything. It is cosmically, totally, consummately impotent. . . . It has no power because it has no being."[74] One of the most inviolate and oldest laws of science is *Ex nihilo nihil fit*—"Out of nothing, nothing comes." When scientists ascribe absolute power to nothing, they are engaging myths. Here, chance is the "magic wand to make not only rabbits but entire universes appear out of nothing."[75]

To illustrate, consider again the Nobel laureate and Harvard professor Dr. George Wald who stated concerning the evolution of life, "Given so much time, the 'impossible' becomes possible, the possible probable, and the probable virtually certain. One only has to wait: time itself performs the miracles."[76]

Time is indeed the hero of the plot in the modern evolutionary storybook. Professor Abdus Salam, winner of the Nobel Prize for Physics, comments that one reason the Big Bang occurred ten billion years ago was that "it takes about that long for intelligent beings to evolve. . . ."[77]

Sir John Eccles, winner of the Nobel prize in Physiology /Medicine comments in a similar fashion, "You cannot make life out of hydrogen and helium, and that was the original stuff. You have to have the time for the creation of all the extraordinary elements that are necessary for living existence, and so you will have to have, shall we say, something like 10,000 million years from the Big Bang. . . ."[78]

Time, of course, is not the hero and cannot perform miracles. To argue otherwise violates the laws of science, logic, and common sense. Regardless, how did the universe exist *forever* and then do in time (i.e., create life) what it had not done *forever*?

More Magic

Sproul comments:

> Here is magic with a vengeance. Not only does the impossible become possible; it reaches the acme of certainty—with time serving as the Grand Master Magician.
>
> In a world where a miracle-working God is deemed an anachronism, he is replaced by an even greater miracle-worker: time or chance. I say these twin miracle workers are greater than God because they produce the same result with so much less, indeed infinitely less, to work with.
>
> God is conceived as a self-existent, eternal being who possesses inextricably the power of being. Such power is a sufficient cause for creation. Time and chance have no being, and consequently no power. Yet they are able to be so effective as to render God an anachronism. At least with God we have a potential miracle-worker. With chance we have nothing with which to work the miracle. Chance offers us a rabbit without a hat and—what's even more astonishing—without a magician.[79]

As scientist A. E. Wilder-Smith puts it: "Present-day biology has also discovered a magic wand which solves all biological and chemical problems with one wave of the wand. Does the origin of the most complicated machinery of a protein molecule need explanation? Do we need to explain how optical isomers are formed? Do we wish to know why the wings of certain butterflies are decorated with eagle's eyes? The magic wand called chance and natural selection will without exception explain all of these miracles. It explains the origin of the most complicated biological machine—the enzymatic protein molecule. The explanation is fabulous—machines are formed of their own accord, spontaneously, just as the waving of a magic wand would demand. The same wand explains the billions of teleonomical electrical contacts in the brain. It explains the almost infinitely complicated wiring of the computer called the brain."[80]

Further, to argue as modern science does that the universe "exploded into being" billions of years ago requires the belief that the universe exploded from *nonbeing* into being. Since science has proven that matter cannot be eternal, this phrase must be taken literally. (Technically this would also be true for the "cosmic egg.") But to do so requires more faith in magic and is, in effect, a faith in self-creation, which, as Sproul shows, is something logically impossible. Thus,

> We can hardly resist the inference that that which exploded, since it was not yet in being, was nonbeing, or nothing. This we call self-creation by another name. This is so absurd that, upon reflection, it seems to be downright silly. It is so evidently contradictory and illogical that it must represent a straw-man argument. No sober scientist would really go so far as to suggest such a self-contradictory theory, would they? Unfortunately, they would and they do. This raises questions about the soberness of the scientists involved. But generally these are not silly people who make such silly statements. Far from it. They number some of the most well-credentialed and erudite scholars in the world, who make a prophet out of Aristotle when he said that in the minds of the brightest men often reside the corner of a fool. In other words, brilliant people are capable of making the most foolish errors. That is understandable, given our frailties as mortals. What is not so understandable are the ardent attempts people make to justify such foolishness.[81]

Of course, there is much more going on here than poor science. In Romans 1:18-25 we are told that the unregenerate suppress the truth of God as Creator. Here the truth is suppressed by the rejection of the laws of science such as the law of causality, the law of noncontradiction, and the law of biogenesis (that life arises only from life). That the *rejection* of scientific principles, laws, and reasoning should be so forcefully employed in *defense* of what is inherently irrational and impossible (the creation of the universe from nothing), is surely a commentary on the condition of modern origins science.

A Sin Against God

However, because God has created us as rational creatures, it may even be argued that sin against reason is a sin against

God. Scientists should *know* better. And, generally, in their rational moments they do. They know the universe didn't arise from literally nothing. They suppress the truth when they try and make it seem as if it did. *That* is the sin. Most scientists, it seems, prefer to disguise their belief in magic by making the idea of chance origins appear scientific and rational. Why? Because they do not like the consequences of having to seriously consider the implications of a Creator God.

God as the Only Option

But in the end, a Creator God is our only logically *possible* explanation for origins. How do we know this? In order to answer this question, we must first make one assumption that is crucial to almost everything else. Dr. Sproul has pointed out the necessity of not only assuming the validity of the laws of logic but the necessity of adhering to them. Without this, even science is impossible and must end up teaching nonsense, as it does now in the area of origins.

To argue the validity of logic *is* an assumption, but an absolutely necessary one. If logic has no validity, even the words used to argue against logic have no meaning:

> To say anything intelligible, positive or negative, about logic requires that the words we use in the assertion or denial have intelligible meaning. If the words we use can mean what they mean and they're contrary, then they mean nothing and our words are unintelligible.
>
> Philosopher Ronald H. Nash writes: "Strictly speaking, the law of noncontradiction cannot be proved. The reason is simple. Any argument offered as proof for the law of noncontradiction would of necessity have to assume the law as part of the proof. Hence, any direct proof of the law would end up being circular. It would beg the question."
>
> Nash is correct in his analysis. But again we remember that any attempt to refute the law of noncontradiction also requires one to assume the law being refuted.
>
> When I declare that the law of noncontradiction is a necessary assumption, I mean that without it all other assumptions about anything become impossible. To challenge this assumption makes science an excuse in absurdity. Again, the scientific method itself must be discarded.

> People do challenge and deny the law of noncontradiction, but they do so selectively. They deny it when it suits them. . . . Although most people I've met who argue against logic will readily admit to or even glory in the irrationality of it, they will protest if you label their position *absurd*. They want irrationality without absurdity—a difficult request to fulfill.[82]

Put another way, "How do we know that the real is rational? We don't. What we do know is that if it isn't rational, we have no possible way of knowing anything about reality. That the real is rational is an assumption. It is the classical assumption of science. Again, it is a *necessary* assumption for science to be possible. If the assumption is valid and reality is rational and intelligible, then the falsifying power of logic can play a major role in scientific inquiry."[83]

In other words, if we reject the laws of logic, we reject everything and all knowledge becomes impossible. But if we accept the laws of logic, as we must, then this leaves us only *one* valid option for explaining the origin of the universe—creation by God. Let's see why.

Only Four Options

As Sproul points out, there are really only four options to consider for the origin of the universe: 1) that the universe is an illusion—it does not exist; 2) that it is self-created; 3) that it is self-existent and eternal by itself; and 4) that it was created by something self-existent. He further argues out that there are no other options: "Are there are options I've overlooked? I've puzzled over this for decades and sought the counsel of philosophers, theologians, and scientists, and I have been unable to locate any other theoretical options that cannot be subsumed under these four options."[84] For example, the idea of spontaneous generation inherent to naturalistic evolution is the same as option 3, self-creation; philosopher Bertrand Russell's concept of an infinite regress, an infinite series of finite causes, is simply a camouflaged form of self-creation disguised to infinity.

Dr. Sproul proceeds to show that the first three options concerning the origin of the universe *must* logically be eliminated as rational options.

Option 1 must be eliminated for two reasons. First, if the universe is an illusion, the illusion must somehow be accounted for. If it's a false illusion then it isn't an illusion; if it's a true illusion then someone or something must be existing to have the illusion. If this is the case then that which is having the illusion must either be self-created, self-existent, or caused by something ultimately self-existent, so therefore, *everything* is not an illusion.

The second reason for eliminating option 1 is that if we assume the illusion is absolute (that nothing exists), including that which is having the illusion, then there is no question of origins even to answer because literally nothing exists. But if something exists, then whatever exists must either be self-created, self-existent, or created by something that is self-existent.

The problem with option 2, self-creation, is that "it is formally false. It is contradictory and logically impossible."[85] In essence, self-creation requires the existence of something before it exists: "For something to come from nothing it must, in effect, create itself. Self-creation is a logical and rational impossibility. . . . For something to create itself it must be *before* it is. This is impossible. It is impossible for solids, liquids, and gases. It is impossible for atoms, and subatomic particles. It is impossible for light and heat. It is impossible for God. Nothing anywhere, anytime, can create itself."[86] Sproul points out that an entity can be self-existent and not violate logic but it can't be self-created. Again, when scientists claim that 15 to 20 billion years ago "the universe exploded into being" what are they really saying? If it exploded from nonbeing into being then what exploded?

Sproul summarizes his reasoning in six points. First, chance is not an entity. Second, non-entities are powerless because they have no being. Third, to argue that something is caused by chance attributes instrumental power to nothing. Fourth, something caused by nothing is self-created. Fifth, the idea of self-creation is irrational and violates the law of noncontradiction. Sixth, to retain a theory of self-creation requires the rejection of logic and rationality.[87] While the concept of self-creation can be believed, it cannot be argued rationally. It is as rationally inconceivable as a round square or a four-sided triangle.[88]

The problem with option 3, that the universe is self-existent and eternal, is that the discoveries of modern science force us to reject it. And there are other problems.

Again, how did the universe exist *forever* and then do in time (i.e., create life) what it had not done *forever*? Are all parts of the cosmos self-existent and eternal or only some parts? If we say all parts, that includes ourselves and every single man-made item that exists. But we know these *cannot* be self-existent and eternal. Cars, watches, chairs, and all people were brought into existence at some point in time. If we say some parts of the material cosmos are self-existent and that they created other parts, we have essentially transferred the attributes of a transcendent God to the self-existent, eternal parts of the universe and thereby rejected our own assumption of materialism. Besides, it *simply* is not rational to argue that matter created life.

All the laws of science, logic, and common sense show that life does not originate from non-life.

Finally, if there were ever a "time" when nothing existed, what would exist now? Clearly, nothing would exist—unless we argue something can come from nothing—more magic which places us back at self-creation, a logical impossibility. So if something exists now, then *something* is self-existent, and it must be either God or matter. If it *can't* be matter, and it *can't*, then it must be God.[89]

Sproul continues to point out that the remaining concept of a self-existent reality i.e., God, is not only logically possible it is logically *necessary*:

> There must be a self-existent being of some sort somewhere, or nothing would or could exist. A self-existent being is both logically and ontologically necessary. . . . We have labored the *logical* necessity of such being. Yet it is also necessary ontologically. An ontologically necessary being is a being who cannot not be. It is proven by the law of the impossibility of the contrary. A self-existent being, by his very nature must be eternal. It has no antecedent cause, else it would not be self-existent. It would be contingent.[90]

After logically demonstrating option 4 as the only reasonable option available in the realm of the debate over origins, Sproul also shows that the classic arguments by Kant and Hume against the cosmological argument are invalid. Indeed, Kant and Hume are vastly overrated by skeptics, and, in fact their theories are actually antithetical to science. For example, Roy Abraham Varghese comments as follows:

> Jaki, Meynell, and a number of other thinkers have repeatedly demonstrated that the Humean and Kantian theories of knowledge used against theistic arguments cannot be accepted uncritically because they fly in the face of the key assumptions underlying the scientific method. [Bertrand] Russell himself once said, "Kant deluged the philosophical world with muddle and mystery, from which it is only now beginning to emerge. Kant has the reputation of being the greatest of modern philosophers, but to my mind he was a mere misfortune." Additionally, Kant's attempt to identify the cosmological argument with the ontological argument has often been effectively derailed, most notably in A. E. Taylor's *Theism*.[91]

In sum, based upon the law of non-contradiction and its extension, the law of causality, Sproul demonstrates that we have no other *rational* option than option 4, that the universe was *created* by something that is self-existent, i.e., God.[92] But it is also a necessary and practical conclusion that this God be personal, not impersonal. "Can there be an impersonal cause of personality ultimately?"[93] No. Put another way, since there cannot be a scientific explanation for the universe, either there is a personal explanation (God) or no explanation. Of course, many people today prefer the idea that God is impersonal, whether we have the Brahman of Hinduism, some other form of pantheism, or the essentially illogical "deification" of matter as in naturalistic evolution. (Again, if the universe is created, then pantheism is impossible for this would mean God was created.)

The reason for this preference for impersonality is evident. If God is impersonal, we are off the hook and accountable to no one. The concept of an impersonal origin is attractive because it allows us to think we escape moral responsibility to a personal God. We can live as we wish and do what we want. Biblically, of course, and often practically, this is the ultimate exercise in self-delusion.

Sproul concludes by stating, "Chance as a real force is a myth. It has no basis in reality and no place in scientific inquiry.

For science and philosophy to continue the advance in knowledge, chance must be demythologized once and for all."[94]

If the results of a recent Gallup poll reported on a CNN "factoid" are correct, only 9 percent of Americans believe that life on earth arose by chance. This would seem to imply that most Americans are better informed about origins than most scientists. Of course, most Americans also believe in evolution; they simply believe God used the evolutionary processes to create life. The reasoning is that, if life exists, it is much more reasonable to think it came from God than from nothing, regardless of the process. At this point, unfortunately, most Americans have also bought into the second level of modern scientific myth-making, the garnering of scientific data in such a manner as to make evolution *seem* possible. In other words, if chance is rejected, and we assume God used the process of evolution to create life, then all the "evidence" scientists *claim* for evolution "must" be valid. Biblically, however, it is impossible that God could have used the process of evolution,[95] and this explains why its claimed evidences are found to be non-existent.

In conclusion, once we have God on board, it is simply a matter of logically employing Christian evidences to prove that the Christian God is the one true self-existent being, as we have done in *Ready with an Answer*. Indeed, what other rational, comprehensive, convincing worldviews do we have as options? Apart from Christianity, there are none.[96] For example, Eastern religions are philosophically self-refuting and nihilistic; modern materialism/secularism/atheism/humanism is bankrupt philosophically, morally, and in most other ways, as demonstrated by a number of modern philosophers and theologians.[97] Polytheism, deism, pantheism, panentheism, and other worldviews are also inadequate or logically deficient.[98] Only Christianity survives the tests of logic, rationality, and empirical, historical verification as a comprehensive worldview.

Epilogue

"Have we not all one Father? Did not one God create us?" (Malachi 2:10)

The state seal and motto of Hawaii is one reflected in the teachings of the Bible: *Ua mau ke ea o ka aina ka pono.* ("The life of the land is perpetuated in righteousness." Cf., Proverbs 14:34; Isaiah 32:17,18).

The Bible also teaches, "No lie comes from the truth" (1 John 2:21). Perhaps if as a nation, we once again tell the truth in an area so crucial as origins—a topic overflowing with implications for personal meaning in life, absolute moral values, and the welfare of society—the life of our land will be healed and again perpetuated in righteousness.

For well over a century, evolutionary theory has undermined or eliminated belief in the biblical God, robbing Him of the glory He alone is due, giving it instead to chance and an alleged immanent power in His creation. History clearly demonstrates how severe the consequences of idolatry are.

Considering how we have robbed God, only biblical creationism with its logical implications can rescue us from even more wrath to come.

> The wrath of God is being revealed from heaven against all the godliness and wickedness of men who suppress the truth by their wickedness, since what may be known about God is plain to them, because He has made it plain to them. For since the creation of the world God's invisible qualities—His eternal power and divine nature—have been clearly seen, being understood from what has been made, so that men are without excuse. For although they knew God, they neither glorified Him as God nor gave thanks to Him, but their thinking became futile and their foolish hearts were darkened. Although they claimed to be wise, they became fools and exchanged the glory of the immortal God. ... They exchanged the truth of God for a lie, and worshipped

and served created things rather than the Creator—who is forever praised. Amen. (Romans 1:18-25)

The good news is that it is possible for anyone to come to know the eternal God who created them by receiving Jesus Christ as their Lord and Savior. As Jesus said in John 17:3, "This is eternal life to know Thee the only true God and Jesus Christ whom Thou hast sent" (NASB).

If you desire to know the one true God who created you— and loved you enough to send His own Son to die for your sins—you may do so by saying the following prayer.

Lord Jesus Christ, *I humbly acknowledge* that I have sinned in my thinking, speaking, and acting, that I am guilty of deliberate wrongdoing, that my sins have separated me from Your Holy presence, and that I am helpless to commend myself to You.

I firmly believe that You died on the cross for my sins, bearing them in Your own body and suffering in my place the condemnation they deserved.

I *have thoughtfully counted the cost of following You.* I sincerely repent, turning away from my past sins. I am willing to surrender to You as my Lord and Master. Help me not to be ashamed of You.

So now I come to You. I believe that for a long time You have been patiently standing outside the door knocking. I now open the door. Come in, Lord Jesus, and be my Savior and my Lord forever. Amen. (Taken from John Scott, *Becoming a Christian,* Downer's Grove, IL: InterVarsity, 1950, p. 25.)

Recommended Reading

There are hundreds of books by researchers and scientists who have rejected the modern theory of evolution strictly on scientific grounds. Others reject the theory of evolution as it is currently formulated but present other evolutionary theories (usually less plausible). Many of the books listed below are not by creationists.

Ambrose, E. C., *The Nature and Origin of the Biological World* (1982).

Andrews, E. H. and W. J. Ouweneel, eds., *Concepts in Creationism* (Nutley, NJ: Presbyterian and Reformed Publishing, 1986).

Austin, Steven A., *Catastrophes in Earth History: A Source Book of Geologic Evidence, Speculation and Theory* (Institute for Creation Research, 1984).

Bergman, Jerry and George Howe, *"Vestigial Organs" Are Fully Functional* (Creation Research Society Books, Monograph series no. 4, 1990).

Berlinski, David, "The Deniable Darwin," *Commentary,* June 1996. See also responses, especially Berlinski's in *Commentary,* September 1996.

Bird, W. R., *The Origin of Species Revisited: The Theories of Evolution and Abrupt Appearance,* 2 vol. (New York: Philosophical Library, 1991).

Buell, J. and V. Hearn, *Darwinism: Science or Philosophy?* Proceedings of a Symposium on "Darwinism: Scientific Inference or Philosophical Preference?" held on March 1992 and pub. 1994 (Richardson, TX: Foundation for Thought and Ethics, 1994).

Camp, Ashby L., *The Myth of Natural Origins: How Science Points to Divine Creation* (Tempe, AZ: Ktisis Publishing, 1994).

Cohen, I. L., *Darwin Was Wrong: A Study in Probabilities* (Greenvale, NY: New Research Publications, 1984).

Coppedge, James, F., *Evolution Possible or Impossible?* (Grand Rapids: Zondervan, 1973).

Davis, P. and D. H. Kenyon, *Of Pandas and People: The Central Question of Biological Origins,* 2nd ed. (Dallas: Haughton Publishing Company, 1993).

Denton, Michael, *Evolution: A Theory in Crisis* (Rockville, MN: Woodbine House, 1986).

Fix, W. R., *The Bone Peddlers: Selling Evolution* (New York: MacMillan, 1984).

Frair, W. and P. W. Davis, *A Case for Creation,* 3d ed., 1983, CRS Books, 6801 N. Highway 89, Chino Valley AZ 86323, 1983).

Geisler, Norman L. and J. Kirby Anderson, *Origin Science: A Proposal for the Creation-Evolution Controversy* (1987).

Gentry, Robert V., *Creation's Tiny Mystery* (1986).

Gish, Duane, *Evolution: The Fossils Still Say No!* (El Cajon, CA: Institute for Creation Research, 1995).

—————, *Teaching Creation Science in Public Schools* (El Cajon, CA: Institute for Creation Research, 1995).

Grassé, Pierre-P., *The Evolution of Living Organisms.* (New York: Academic, 1977).

Herbert, D., *The Key to Understanding Origins* (London, Ontario N6E 1G3 Canada: Hersil Publishing, 1993).

Heribert-Nilsson, N., *Synthetische Artbildung, Grundlinien Einer Exakten Biologie,* 2 vols. (Lund, Sweden: Gleerup, 1953).

Himmelfarb, Gertrude, *Darwin and the Darwinian Revolution* (Garden City, NY: Doubleday, 1959).

Hitching, Francis, *The Neck of the Giraffe: Darwin, Evolution, and the New Biology* (New Haven, NY: Ticknor and Fields, 1982).

Hoyle, Fred and Chandra Wickramasinghe, *Evolution from Space* (New York: Simon & Schuster, 1981).

Johnson, Phillip P., *Darwin on Trial* (Downers Grove, IL: InterVarsity, 1991).

—————, *Defeating Darwinism: By Opening Minds* (Downer's Grove, IL: InterVarsity, 1997).

————, *Reason in the Balance: The Case Against Naturalism in Science, Law, and Education* (Downer's Grove, IL: InterVarsity Press, 1995).

Keane, G. J., *Creation Rediscovered* (Doncaster Vic. Australia: Credis Pyt Ltd., P.O. Box 451, 1991).

Kerkut, G. A., *Implications of Evolution* (Elkins Park, PA: Franklin Book Company, 1960).

Lemoine, Paul, ed., *Encyclopedia Francaise* in introduction: "De L' Evolution?" in 5 Encyclopedie Francaise 06-6.

Lester, Lane P. and Raymond G. Bohlin, *The Natural Limits to Biological Change* (Waco, TX: Word, Inc., 1984).

Løvtrup, Søren, *Darwinism: The Refutation of a Myth* (New York: Croom Helm, 1987).

Lubenow, Marvin L., *Bones of Contention: A Creationist Assessment of Human Fossils* (Grand Rapids: Baker Book House, 1992).

MacBeth, Norman, *Darwin Retried: An Appeal to Reason* (Boston: Gambit, 1971).

McCann, L. J., *Blowing the Whistle on Darwinism* (Lester J. McCann, College of St. Thomas, St. Paul, MN 55215).

McIver, T., *Anti-Evolution: An Annotated Bibliography* (Baltimore, MD: Johns Hopkins University Press, 1988).

Milton, Richard, *Shattering the Myths of Darwinism* (Rochester, VT: Park Street Press, 1997).

Moorhead P. S., and M. M. Kaplan, eds., *Mathematical Challenges to the Neo-Darwinian Interpretation of Evolution* (Philadelphia: Wistar Institute Press, 1967).

Morris, H. M. and G. E. Parker, *What Is Creation Science?* rev. ed. (El Cajon, CA: Institute for Creation Research, 1987).

Morris, John D., *The Young Earth* (San Diego: Master Books, 1994).

Morris, Henry M. and John D. Morris, *Modern Creation Trilogy:* vol. 1 *Scripture and Creation;* vol. 2 *Science and Creation;* vol. 3 *Society and Creation* (Santee, CA: Institute for Creation Research, 1986).

Oxnard, C. E., *Fossils, Teeth and Sex: New Perspectives on Human Evolution* (Seattle: University of Washington Press, 1987).

Paley, W., *Natural Theology* (Houston: St. Thomas Press, 1972, reprint).

Parker, G., *Creation: Facts of Life* (Green Forest, AR: Master Books, 1994).

Pearcey, N. R. and C. B. Thaxton, *The Soul of Science: Christian Faith and Natural Philosophy* (Wheaton, IL: Crossway Books, 1994).

Pitman, W., *Adam and Evolution* (Grand Rapids: Baker Book House, 1984).

Re Mine, W. J., *The Biotic Message: Evolution Versus Message Theory* (St. Paul, MN: St. Paul Science Publishers, 1993).

Rifkin, Jeremy, *Algeny* (New York: The Viking Press, 1983).

Rybka, Theodore W., *Geophysical and Astronomical Clocks* (American Writing and Publishing Co., 1993).

Sermonti, Giuseppe and Roberto Fondi, *Dopo Darwin: Critica All' Evoluzionismo* (1980).

Shute, Evan, *Flaws in the Theory of Evolution* (Nutley, NJ: Craig Press, 1971).

Slusher, Harold S. and Steven G. Robertson, *The Age of the Solar System* (Santee, CA: Institute for Creation Research, 1982).

Spetner, Lee M., *Not By Chance! Shattering the Modern Theory of Evolution* (Brooklyn, NY: The Judaica Press, 1997).

Taylor, I. T., *In the Minds of Men: Darwin and the New World Order,* 3d ed. (Toronto, Canada: TFE Publishing, 1991).

Taylor, G., *The Great Evolution Mystery* (1983).

Thaxton, Charles B., Walter L. Bradley and Roger L. Olsen, *The Mystery of Life's Origins: Reassessing Current Theories* (Dallas: Lewis and Stanley, 1984).

Thompson, B., *The Scientific Case for Creation,* rev. ed. (Montgomery, AL 36117-2752: Apologetics Press (230 Landmark Drive), 1995).

Proceedings of the International Conference on Creationism, various volumes for the years 1986, 1990, 1994, published the following years by the Creation Science Fellowship, Pittsburgh, PA.

Vernet, M., *Revolution en Biologie* (1969)

Wilder-Smith, A. E., *The Natural Sciences Know Nothing of Evolution* (San Diego, CA: Master Books, 1981).

——————, *The Scientific Alternative to Neo-Darwinian Evolutionary Theory: Information Sources and Structures* (Costa Mesa, CA: TWFT Publishers, 1987).

Williams, Emmett L., ed., *Thermodynamics and the Development of Order* (Creation Research Society Books, Monograph series no. 1, 1981).

Wise, Kurt P., "The Fossil Record: The Ultimate Test Case for Young-Earth Creationism," *Opus: A Journal for Interdisciplinary Studies,* 1991–92, pp. 17–29.

Woodmorappe, John, *Studies in Flood Geology: A Compilation of Research Studies Supporting Creation and the Flood* Santee, CA: Institute for Creation Research, 1993).

——————, *Studies in Flood Geology* and *Noah's Ark: A Feasibility Study* (Santee, CA: Institute for Creation Research, 1993 & 1995).

Wysong, R. L., *The Creation Evolution Controversy: Implications, Methodology and Survey of Evidence—Toward a Rational Solution* (East Lansing, MI: Inqiry Press, 1976).

Yockey, Hubert, *Information Theory and Molecular Biology* (1992).

Journal

Creation Research Society Quarterly, St. Joseph, MN.

Notes

Note to the Reader: Due to the temporary loss of the author's library, some citations are incomplete or, in rare cases, absent. We apologize for this situation. Full references are given only at the first citation.

PREFACE

1. Michael Denton, *Evolution: A Theory in Crisis* (Bethesda, MD: Adler & Adler Publishers, Inc., 1986), p. 358.
2. J. Rostand, "LaMonde et la Vie," October 1963, p. 31 from V. Long, "Evolution: A Fairy Tale for Adults," *Homiletic and Pastoral Review*, Vol. 78 (1978), no. 7, pp. 27–32.
3. The National Center for Science Education, Inc., *Voices for Evolution*, rev. edition Molleen Matsumura (ed.) (Berkeley, CA: The National Center for Science Education, Inc., 1995), p. 20. This is a compilation of official statements by leading scientific, religious, educational, and civil liberties organizations containing their views on science, evolution, and creation.
4. Ibid., p. 37.
5. Arthur L. Schawlow, "One Must Ask Why and Not Just How?" in Henry Margenau and Roy Abraham Varghese, *Cosmos, Bios, Theos: Scientists Reflect on Science, God, and the Origins of the Universe, Life, and Homo Sapiens* (La Salle, IL: Open Court, 1994), p. 105.
6. Simone de Beauvoir, "A Conversation About Death and God," *Harper's* magazine, February 1984, p. 39.
7. Aldous Huxley, *Ends and Means: An Inquiry into the Nature of Ideals and into the Methods Employed for Their Realization* (New York: Harper & Brothers, 1937), p. 303.
8. For detailed documentation, see our *Ready with an Answer* (Eugene, OR: Harvest House, 1997).
9. Ibid.

CHAPTER 1—THE BIG GAMBLE

1. George Gaylord Simpson, "The World into Which Darwin Led Us," *Science*, Vol. 131 (1960), p. 970, from W. R. Bird, *The Origin of Species Revisited: The Theories of Evolution and of Abrupt Appearance*, Vol. 1 (New York: Philosophical Library, 1989), p. 139, emphasis added.
2. Ayala and Valentine, *Evolving* (Benjamin/Cummings Publishing Co., Inc.).

3. Marvin L. Lubenow, *Bones of Contention: A Creationist Assessment of Human Fossils* (Grand Rapids, MI: Baker, 1992), pp. 187–89.

4. Deborah Erickson, "Blood Feud," *Scientific American*, June 1990, p. 17, from Ibid., p. 188.

5. Personally seen by John Weldon on cable television, "The Internet Cafe" January or February 1997.

6. Charles S. Nicoll, Sharon M. Russell, "Animal Rights Literature," *Science*, May 26, 1989, p. 903; and Bartell Nyberg, *Denver Post*, Dec. 6, 1987 from Lubenow, *Bones* p. 188.

7. Lubenow, *Bones*, p. 188.

8. Jacque Monod, *Chance and Necessity* (New York: A.A. Knopf, 1971), p. 112.

9. Jacques Monod, *Chance and Necessity* (New York: Vintage Books, 1972), pp. 112–13.

10. J. W. Burrow, introduction in J. W. Burrow, ed., *Charles Darwin, The Origin of Species by Means of Natural Selection* (Baltimore, MD: Penguin, 1974), p. 43.

11. Cf., Francis A. Schaeffer and C. Everett Koop, *Whatever Happened to the Human Race?* (Old Tappan, NJ: Flemming H. Revell, 1979).

12. William Provine, "Scientists, Face It! Science and Religion Are Incompatible," *The Scientist*, 5 September 1988, p. 10 from Henry Morris, *The Long War Against God: The History and Impact of the Creation/Evolution Conflict* (Grand Rapids, MI: Baker, 1989), p. 112.

13. "Interview with Jacques Monod," John C. Hess, *New York Times*, March 15, 1971, p. 6 from Francis Schaeffer, *Back to Freedom and Dignity* (Downer's Grove, IL: InterVarsity Press, 1972), p. 13.

14. Leslie Paul, *The Annihilation of Man* (New York: Harcourt Brace, 1945), p. 154 from Arthur Custance, Doorway Paper #29, "A Framework of History" (Ottowa, Canada: 1968), III. Dr. Custance's series was published in ten volumes titled *The Doorway Papers* (Grand Rapids, MI: Zondervan Publishers).

15. J. D. Bernal, *The Origin of Life* (New York: Universe Books, 1967), p. xv, cf., p. 168, cited by Donald England, *A Christian View of Origins* (Grand Rapids, MI: Baker, 1972), p. 35.

16. W. R. Bird, *The Origin of Species Revisited: The Theories of Evolution and of Abrupt Appearance*, Vol. 1 (New York: Philosophical Library, 1989), p. 8.

17. Cited in *World* magazine Nov. 22, 1997; see John Ankerberg, John Weldon, *The Facts on Creation and Evolution* (Eugene, OR: Harvest House, 1993), pp. 35–36.

18. Will Durant, "Are We in the Last Stage of a Pagan Period?" *Chicago Tribune*, Syndicate, April, 1980, from Morris, *Long War*, p. 149.

19. Ravi Zacharias, *Can Man Live Without God?* (Dallas: Word, 1994); Henry Morris, *The Troubled Waters of Evolution* (San Diego: Creation Life Publishers, 1974). Also, Morris, *Long War*.

20. Respectively, Ionesco is cited in Martin Esslin, *Theatre of the Absurd* (New York: Doubleday, 1961), p. xix; Theodore Dreiser, "What I Believe," *The Forum*, vol. 82, 1929, p. 320; Albert Camus, *The Rebel* (New York:

Vintage, 1956), p. 47; Donald Kalish, cited in "What (If Anything) to Expect from Today's Philosophers," *Time*, January 7, 1966, p. 24; Nietzsche, in Os Guinness, *The Dust of Death* (Downer's Grove, IL: InterVarsity, 1973), p. 24; Hegel, preface to *Lectures on the Philosophy of History* cited by Walter Kaufman, *Nietzsche: Philosopher, Psychologist, Anti-Christ* (New York: Vintage, 3rd edition, 1968), p. 142, footnotes; Henry Miller cited in H. R. Rookmaaker, *Modern Art and the Death of a Culture* (Downer's Grove, IL: InterVarsity, 1971), p. 146; Timothy Leary, *The Politics of Ecstasy* (New York: World, 1968), p. 321; Andy Warhol cited in Clark Pinnock, *Live Now Brother* (Chicago: Moody Press, 1972), p. 18; Eric Fromm, "Alienation Under Capitalism" in Ed Josephson, *Man Alone* (New York: Dell, 1964), p. 59.

21. Robert E. D. Clark, *Darwin: Before and After* (Chicago: Moody Press, 1967), p. 96.

22. Ibid.

23. Alexander Soltzenitzen, *Warning to the West* (New York: Firrar Straus & Grioux, 1977), p. 129.

24. In Marshall and Sandra Hall, *The Truth: God or Evolution?* (Nutley, NJ: Craig Press, 1974), p. 100.

25. Quoted by Arthur Koestler, "Beyond Reductionism" (London: Hutcheson, 1969), p. 403 from Arthur Custance, Doorway Paper #21, "Is Man an Animal?" (Ontario, Canada: Brockville, 1972) p. 2, see note 14. According to the *Encyclopedia of Philosophy* (Paul Edwards, ed-in-chief) Vol. 3, New York: Macmillan 1972, p. 98, "The Impact of Darwin's theory of natural evolution produced naturalistic echoes of Hegelian historical relativism and the utilitarian 'survival of the fittest' doctrine of Herbert Spencer (1820–1903), the Marxist philosophy of class conflict, and the cultural elitism of Nietzsche."

26. Sir Arthur Keith, *Evolution and Ethics* (New York: G. P. Putnam's Sons, 1947), pp. 69–70.

27. Ibid., p. 15.

28. Ibid.

29. Ibid., pp. 71, 76.

30. Jacques Barzun, *Darwin, Marx, Wagner: Critique of a Heritage* (Garden City, NY: Doubleday, 1958), p. 92.

31. The International Christian Crusade, *Evolution: Science Falsely So-Called* (Toronto, Ontario, Canada) 18th edition, p. 94, No. 12, emphasis added.

32. Friedrich von Bernhardi, *Germany and the Next War*, cited in Hofstadter, *Social Darwinism*, p. 197 from Morris, *The Long War Against God*, p. 74.

33. Keith, *Evolution and Ethics*, pp. 149–50.

34. Ibid., pp. 28–29, 230.

35. Henry Morris, *Long War*, p. 79; cf. Benno Muller-Hull, *Murderous Science: Elimination by Scientific Selection of Jews, Gypsies and Others in Germany 1933–1945* (New York: Oxford University Press, 1988) for documentation of the role played by German evolutionary scientists in Nazi racial policies.

36. Translated from the German *Anatomie Dermenschlichen Destruktivitat* from A. E. Wilder-Smith, *The Natural Sciences Know Nothing of Evolution* (San Diego, CA: Master Books, 1981), p. 148, emphasis added.

37. K. J. Hsu, *Journal of Sedimentary Petrology*, Vol. 56, Sept. 1986, p. 730 cited by Morris, *Long War*, p. 77.

38. Gasman, *Scientific Origins*, p. 168 from Morris, *Long War*, see Note to Reader.

39. In *Creation Research Society Quarterly*, Sept. 1990, p. 73, citing p. x, 155 of Larry Azar, *Twentieth Century in Crisis: Foundations of Totalitarianism*.

40. Adolph Hitler, *Mein Kampf* (New York: Reynal and Hitchcock, 1940), pp. 397, 603, 406, cf., 396, 601, 392, 84, 406–419; R. E. D. Clark, *Darwin: Before and After* (Chicago: Moody, 1967), p. 116; Jacques Barzun, *Darwin, Marx and Wagner*, p. 15.

41. Cf. A. E. Wilder-Smith, *Man's Origin, Man's Destiny: A Critical Survey of the Principles of Evolution and Christianity* (Wheaton, IL: Harold Shaw, 1970), pp. 187–92.

42. Clark, *Darwin: Before and After*, p. 115.

43. In Barzun, *Darwin, Marx, and Wagner*, pp. 15–16.

44. Clark, *Darwin: Before and After*, pp. 116–17.

45. Cf. Ibid., p. 117.

46. Ibid., p. 115.

47. Cited in Donald B. DeYoung, book review, *Creation Research Society Quarterly*, Sept. 1990, p. 73, citing pp. x, 155, and 180 of Azar's book.

48. Jerry Bergman, "Nineteenth Century Darwinism and the Tasmania Genocide," *Creation Research Society Quarterly*, March 1996, p. 190.

49. Burrow, intro to *Charles Darwin*, p. 45; J. Barzun, *Darwin, Marx, and Wagner*, p. 8; cf. q.v. "Darwinism," *Encyclopedia of Philosophy*, Vol. 2, p. 304.

50. In David Jorafsky, *Soviet Marxism and Natural Science* (New York: Columbia University Press, 1961), p. 12 from Morris, *Long War*, p. 84.

51. Marshall and Sandra Hall, *The Truth*, pp. 139–140.

52. Burrow, *Charles Darwin*, p. 45.

53. Morris, *Long War*, pp. 84–85.

54. John P. Koster, Jr., *The Atheist Syndrome* (Brentwood, TN: Wolgemuth & Hyatt, 1989), pp. 168–179; Hall and Hall, *The Truth*, pp. 140–142.

55. A. E. Wilder-Smith, *Man's Origin—Man's Destiny*, pp. 192–195.

56. In Marshall and Hall, pp. 150–51.

57. Koster, *Athiest*, p. 142.

58. Ibid., pp. 187–89.

CHAPTER 2—THE WORLD AS WE KNOW IT

1. Sir Julian Huxley, *Essays of a Humanist* (New York: Harper & Row, 1964), p. 125.

2. As cited in the *Los Angeles Times*, December 31, 1972, p. 26. The original reference is Ernst Mayr, "The Nature of the Darwinian Revolution," *Science*, Vol. 176, 2 June 1972, p. 981.

3. A. E. Wilder-Smith, *The Natural Sciences Know Nothing of Evolution* (San Diego, CA: Master Books, 1981), p. 5.
4. James Moore, *Darwin: The Life of a Tormented Evolutionist* (New York: Warner, 1991), p. xxi.
5. Bird, *Origin . . . Revisited,* Vol. 1, p. 1.
6. H. S. Lipson, "A Physicist Looks at Evolution," *Physics Bulletin,* Vol. 31 (1980), p. 136.
7. Theodosius Dobzhansky, *Mankind Evolving: The Evolution of the Human Species* (New York: Bantam, 1970), p. 1.
8. Ibid., p. xi.
9. Henry Morris, *The Long War Against God: The History and Impact of the Creation/Evolution Conflict* (Grand Rapids, MI: Baker, 1989), p. 20.
10. Ibid., p. 21.
11. Robert B. Downs, *Books That Changed the World* (New York: New American Library/Mentor, rev. 1983), pp. 276, 286–87.
12. Michael Denton, *Evolution: A Theory in Crisis* (New York: Adler & Adler, 1985), p. 358.
13. Michael Pitman, *Adam and Evolution* (London, Rider & Co., 1984), pp. 9–10, introduction.
14. Francis A. Schaeffer, *How Should We Then Live?: The Rise and Decline of Western Thought and Culture* (Old Tappan, NJ: Revell, 1976), p. 389.
15. In Morris, *Long War,* p. 112.
16. In Ibid., p. 20.
17. Timothy Leary, *The Politics of Ecstasy* (New York: Paladin, 1970), p. 293.
18. In Morris, *Long War,* p. 19.
19. In Ibid., p. 132.
20. In Ibid., p. 22, emphasis added.
21. Ibid., p. 150.
22. Morris, *Long War,* p. 18.
23. Huxley, *Ends and Means,* p. 303.

Chapter 3—Seeing Things Differently

1. The National Center for Science Education, Inc., *Voices for Evolution,* p. 119.
2. J. P. Moreland, *Christianity and the Nature of Science: A Philosophical Investigation* (Grand Rapids, MI: Baker, 1989), p. 21.
3. See e.g., ibid., passim and Bird, *Origin . . . Revisited,* Vol. 2.
4. Moreland, *Christianity,* pp. 21–42.
5. Ibid., pp. 17–138; Bird, *Origin . . . Revisited,* Vol. 2, pp. 9–175.
6. Robert K. Barnhart with Sol Steinmetz, managing editor, *The American Heritage Dictionary of Science* (Boston: Houghton Mifflin Co., 1986), q.v. "Hypothesis," "Theory," "Law."
7. Ibid., p. 663.
8. Ibid.
9. Ibid.

10. Ibid., p. 353.
11. Ibid.
12. Bird, Vol. 2, p. 14.
13. Ibid., pp. 15–16; cf. Vol. 1, passim.
14. William Broad and Nicholas Wade, *Betrayers of the Truth: Fraud and Deceit in the Halls of Science* (New York: Simon & Schuster, 1982), p. 16.
15. The National Center for Science Education, Inc., *Voices for Evolution* p. 39.
16. New Orleans Geological Society in ibid., p. 61, cf., p. 119.
17. R. L. Wysong, *The Creation/Evolution Controversy* (East Lansing, MI: Inquiry Press, 1976), p. 44.
18. Bird, *Origin . . . Revisited,* Vol. 2, p. 9.
19. Ibid., pp. 20–22.
20. Ibid., p. 14.
21. M. C. La Follette (ed.), *Creationism, Science and the Law: The Arkansas Case* (Cambridge, MA: The MIT Press, 1983), p. 66, article by Larry Lauden, cf., J. T. Cushing, C. F. Delancy, and G. M. Gutting (eds.), *Science and Reality* (Notre Dame, IN: University of Notre Dame Press, 1984) cited by Duane T. Gish, *Creation Scientists Answer Their Critics* (El Cajon, CA: Institute for Creation Research, 1993), p. 45.
22. See e.g., The National Center for Science Education, Inc., *Voices for Evolution,* pp. 2–5, 111.
23. Gish, *Creation Scientists Answer,* p. 71.
24. Ibid., p. 107.
25. A. E. Wilder-Smith, *The Natural Sciences Know Nothing of Evolution* (San Diego: Master Books, 1981), p. 133.
26. Gish, *Creation Scientists Answer,* p. 32, emphasis added.
27. Paul Ehrlich, L. C. Birch in *Nature,* Vol. 214, (1967) p. 352 cited in ibid., p. 37.
28. Gish, *Creation Scientists Answer,* p. 37.
29. Ibid.
30. Willem J. Ouweneel, "The Scientific Character of the Evolution Doctrine," *Creation Research Society Quarterly,* September 1971, p. 109.
31. Ibid., pp. 109–115.
32. Robert T. Clark, James D. Bales, *Why Scientists Accept Evolution* (Grand Rapids, MI: Baker, 1976), pp. 29–95; Ankerberg and Weldon, *The Facts on Creation vs. Evolution,* pp. 25–42.
33. Apostolos Ch. Frangos, "The Correct Approach to Scientific Theories," *Creation Research Society Quarterly,* June 1991, p. 18.
34. Edward O. Dodson and George F. Howe, *Creation or Evolution: Correspondents on the Current Controversy* (Ottawa: University of Ottawa Press, 1990), p. 143.
35. Gareth J. Nelson, Preface in Bird, *The Origin of Species Revisited,* Vol. 1, p. xii.
36. Kurt P. Wise, "The Origin of Life's Major Groups" in J. P. Moreland (ed.), *The Creation Hypothesis: Scientific Evidence for an Intelligent Designer* (Downer's Grove, IL: InterVarsity, 1994), p. 223.

37. Bird, *Origin . . . Revisited,* Vol. 1, p. xi.

38. Author's copy unavailable. From a book review by Wes Harrison in *Creation Research Society Quarterly,* March 1997.

39. Jerry Bergman, Book Reviews, "God's Own Scientists: Creationists in a Secular World," *Creation Research Society Quarterly,* Sept. 1995, p. 115.

40. Christopher P. Toumey, *God's Own Scientists: Creationists in a Secular World* (Rutgers University Press, 1994), pp. 143–44 cited in ibid., p. 116

41. Neal C. Gillespie, *Charles Darwin and the Problem of Creation* (Chicago: University of Chicago Press, 1979), pp. 1–18, 40–66, 146–57. Gillespie showed how Darwin redefined science in such a way as to make creationist dissent impossible.

42. Marvin L. Lubenow, "Progressive Creationism: Is It a Biblical Option?" in *Proceedings of the Third Creation Science Conference,* August 15–18, 1976 (Caldwell, Idaho, Bible Science Association, 1976), p. 67.

43. Jerry Bergman, "Book Review: Dictionary of Science and Creationism," *Creation Research Society Quarterly,* March 1992, p. 172.

44. Introduction in Bolton Davidheiser, *Evolution and the Christian Faith* (Nutley, NJ: Presbyterian and Reformed Publishing Company, 1969).

45. Francis Darwin (ed.), *The Life and Letters of Charles Darwin,* Vol. 2 (D. Appleton & Co., 1888), p. 124, in Clark and Bales, *Why Scientists Accept Evolution,* p. 145, cf., pp. 37–42.

46. Merrill Unger, *Demons in the World Today* (Tyndale, 1972), p. 149.

47. In Sol Tax (ed.), *Evolution After Darwin,* Vol. 3 (Chicago, IL: University of Chicago Press, 1960), p. 45.

Chapter 4—It Must Be True (Science Says So)

1. The National Center for Science Education, Inc., West Virginia Academy of Science, *Voices for Evolution,* p. 81.

2. Michael Ruse in *Darwinism Defended* (1982), p. 58, emphasis his from Bird, *Origin . . . Revisited,* Vol. 2, p. 128.

3. Robert T. Clark, James D. Bales, *Why Scientists Accept Evolution,* pp. 29–95.

4. Lewontin, "Evolution/Creation Debate: A Time for Truth," *BioScience,* Vol. 31, p. 559 (1981) from Bird, *Origin . . . Revisited,* Vol. 2, p. 129.

5. The National Center for Science Education, Inc., *Voices for Evolution,* pp. 38–39.

6. Ibid., p. 42.

7. Ibid., p. 67.

8. Ibid., p. 74.

9. Ibid., p. 78.

10. Ibid., p. 128.

11. Ibid., p. 22.

12. Ibid., p. 151.

13. Ibid., p. 31.

14. Ibid., p. 33.

15. Ibid., p. 148.

16. Ibid., passim.
17. Pierre-P. Grassé, *Evolution of Living Organisms: Evidence for a New Theory of Transformation* (New York: Academic Press, 1977), p. 3, emphasis added.
18. Cited in Bird, *Origin . . . Revisited,* Vol. 1, p. 141.
19. Theodosius Dobzhansky, *Mankind Evolving: The Evolution of the Human Species* (New York: Bantam, 1970), pp. 5–6, emphasis added.
20. George Gaylord Simpson, *The Meaning of Evolution* (New York: Bantam, 1971), pp. 4–5, emphasis added.
21. Ibid., p. 4.
22. The National Center for Science Education, Inc., *Voices for Evolution,* p. 56.
23. T. Dobzhansky, F. Ayala, G. Stebbins & J. Valentine, *Evolution* (1977), p. 8 in Bird, *Origin . . . Revisited,* Vol. 2, p. 160.
24. Everett C. Olson, *The Evolution of Life* (New York: The New American Library, 1966), p. xii, emphasis added.
25. Douglas J. Futuyama, *Science on Trial* (New York: Pantheon Books, 1983), back cover quotation, in Marvin L. Lubenow, *Bones of Contention—A Creationist Assessment of Human Fossils* (Grand Rapids, MI: Baker, 1992), p. 206.
26. Carl Sagan, *Cosmos* (New York: Random House, 1980), p. 27, emphasis added.
27. Konrad Lorenz, *Intellectual Digest,* February 1974, p. 62, emphasis added.
28. Rene Dubos, *American Scientist,* March 1965, p. 6 in Morris, *Long War,* p. 20, emphasis added.
29. Richard Goldschmidt, *American Scientist,* January 1952, p. 84 in Morris, *Long War,* p. 24, emphasis added.
30. Julian Huxley in Sol Tax (ed.), *Issues in Evolution* (Chicago, IL: University of Chicago Press, 1960), p. 41 from Morris, *Long War,* p. 322, emphasis added.
31. In Davidheiser, *Evolution and the Christian Faith,* p. 165.
32. Ibid.
33. Ibid.
34. Ibid.
35. Ibid.
36. Ibid.
37. Ibid., emphasis added.
38. Ibid., emphasis added.
39. Ibid., emphasis added.
40. Ibid.
41. Clark and Bales, *Why Scientists Accept,* p. 5, emphasis added.
42. Ibid.
43. Morris, *Long War,* p. 32.
44. Arthur Custance, "Evolution: An Irrational Faith" in *Evolution or Creation? Vol. 4—The Doorway Papers* (Grand Rapids, MI: Zondervan, 1976), pp. 173–74.

45. Ibid., pp. 174–75.
46. Ibid., p. 179.
47. Richard Miltons, *Shattering the Myth of Darwinism* (1977), extensive geological research reveals how evolution "totters atop a shambles of outdated and circumstantial evidence" that "in any less controversial field would have been questioned long ago" (press release).

CHAPTER 5—TRUTH IN ADVERTISING

1. Cf., Phillip E. Johnson, *Reason in the Balance: The Case Against Naturalism in Science, Law, and Education* (Downer's Grove, IL: InterVarsity, 1995).
2. Gregg Easterbrook, "Science and God—A Warming Trend?" *Science*, August 15, 1997, p. 893.
3. Arthur Custance, *Evolution or Creation?* pp. 172–73.
4. Ibid., p. 172.
5. Isaac V. Manly, M.D., *God Made: A Medical Doctor Looks at the Reality of Creation* (Joplin, MO: College Press, 1994), pp. 13, 116.
6. Ibid., p. 52.
7. Ibid., p. 143.
8. Johnson, *Reason*, pp. 11–12.
9. Bethell, "Darwin's Mistake," *Harper's* magazine, February 1976, pp. 70, 72 in Bird, *Origin . . . Revisited*, Vol. 1, p. 136.
10. Easterbrook, "Science and God," p. 890.
11. The National Center for Science Education, Inc., *Voices for Evolution*, p. iv.
12. Ibid., p. x.
13. Ibid., p. 16.
14. Ibid., pp. 24–25.
15. Ibid., p. 37.
16. Ibid., p. 46.
17. The National Center for Science Education, Inc., *Voices for Evolution: Addendum*, rev. edition, 1995, p. 19.
18. The National Center for Science Education, Inc., *Voices for Evolution*, p. 130.
19. Ibid., p. 159.
20. The National Center for Science Education, Inc., *Voices for Evolution: Addendum*, p. 11.
21. The National Center for Science Education, Inc., *Voices for Evolution*, p. 162.
22. J. P. Moreland (ed.), *The Creation Hypothesis*; Bird, *Origin . . . Revisited*, Vols. 1 & 2, passim; Norman L. Geisler, J. Kirby Anderson, *Origin Science: A Proposal for the Creation-Evolution Controversy* (Grand Rapids, MI: Baker, 1987); Henry M. Morris, Gary E. Parker, *What Is Creation Science?* (San Diego, CA: Creation Life, 1982).
23. Bird, *Origin . . . Revisited*, Vol. 1, p. 6.

24. See the discussion in Henry M. Morris, Gary E. Parker, *What Is Creation Science?*

25. See the biography note in Bird, *Origin . . . Revisited,* Vol. 1, p. xvi.

26. Dean Kenyon in the introduction to Morris and Parker, *What Is Creation Science?*, p. 3.

27. Ibid., p. 3.

28. Bird, *Origin . . . Revisited,* Vol. 1, p. 44.

29. Ibid., p. 45.

30. Bird, *Origin . . . Revisited,* Vol. 2, pp. 104–07.

31. A. E. Wilder-Smith, *A Basis for a New Biology* (Einigen/Schweiz: TELOS-International, 1976) and his *Scientific Alternative to Neo-Darwinian Evolutionary Theory: Information, Sources and Structures* (Costa Mesa, CA: TWFP Publishers, 1987), cf., p. v.

32. Dennis Dubay, "Evolution/Creation Debate," *Bioscience,* Vol. 30, January 1980, pp. 4–5.

33. Available from the Institute for Creation Research, Santee, CA.

34. Gish, *Creation Scientists Answer,* p. ix.

35. Ibid., p. vi.

36. Ibid., p. 63.

37. Bird, *Origin . . . Revisited,* Vol. 1, p. 8.

38. The National Center for Science Education, Inc., *Voices for Evolution* p. 74.

39. Ibid., p. 160.

40. Ibid., p. 41.

41. Ibid., pp. 154–55.

42. Ibid., p. 20.

43. Ibid., p. 35.

44. Ibid., p. 78.·

45. Ibid., pp. 140, 142.

46. Ibid., p. 168.

47. Ibid., p. 130.

48. Ibid., p. 169.

49. Ibid., p. 124.

50. Ibid., p. 73.

51. Ibid., p. 139; addendum, p. 4; see also Karl Wessel in *Commentary,* Sept. 1986, p. 11.

52. The National Center for Science Education, Inc., *Voices for Evolution,* pp. ix, x.

53. Ibid., p. 166.

54. Ibid., pp. 40, 48, 73, 50, 51, 170, 172, 118 and addendum, p. 6.

55. Ibid., p. 81.

56. Ibid., p. 119.

57. Ibid., p. 136.

58. Russell L. French, preface in Bird, Vol. 2, p. xviii.

59. The National Center for Science Education, Inc., *Voices for Evolution,* p. 38.

60. Ibid., p. 174.
61. Ibid., p. 51.
62. Ibid., p. 54.
63. Ibid., p. 59.
64. Ibid., pp. 61, 63.
65. Ibid., p. 65.
66. Ibid., p. 161.
67. Ibid., p. 75.
68. Ibid., p. 74.
69. Ibid., p. 82.
70. Ibid., p. 128.
71. Ibid., p. 168.
72. Ibid., p. 171.
73. See Recommended Reading.
74. The National Center for Science Education, Inc., *Voices for Evolution*, pp. 48.
75. Ibid., p. 33.
76. Ibid., p. 159.

CHAPTER 6—PROFESSIONAL OBJECTIVITY AND THE POLITICS OF PREJUDICE

1. Broad and Wade, *Betrayed*, p. 20.
2. Ibid., pp. 19–20.
3. Bird, *Origin . . . Revisited*, Vol. 2, pp. 135–36.
4. Søren Løvtrup, *Darwinism: The Refutation of a Myth* (New York: Croom Helm, 1987), p. 352 in Bird, *Origin . . . Revisited*, Vol. 1, p. 150.
5. Bird, *Origin . . . Revisited*, Vol. 2, p. 5.
6. R. J. Rushdoony, *The Mythology of Science* (Nutley, NJ: Craig Press, 1968), p. 13.
7. Ibid.
8. The National Center for Science Education, Inc., *Voices for Evolution* p. 4.
9. Strike, "The Status of Creation-Science: A Comment on Siegel and Hahn," *Phi Delta Kappan*, Vol. 63 (1982), pp. 555–56 in Bird, *Origin . . . Revisited*, Vol. 2, pp. 403–04.
10. Arno Penzias, "Creation Is Supported by All the Data So Far" in Margenau and Varghese (eds.), *Cosmos, Bios, Theos: Scientists Reflect on Science, God, and the Origins of the Universe, Life, and Homo Sapiens* (LaSalle, IL: Open Court, 1994), p. 80.
11. G. G. Simpson, *Tempo and Mode in Evolution* (New York: Columbia University Press, 1944), p. 105 in Duane Gish, *Evolution: The Fossils Still Say No!* (El Cajon, CA: Institute for Creation Research, 1995), pp. 333–34, emphasis added.
12. Tom Bethell, in *Commentary*, Sept. 1996, p. 20, and in *The American Spectator*, July 1994, p. 17, last citation from Gish, *Evolution: The Fossils Still Say No!*, p. 13.

13. Wilder-Smith, *Scientific Alternative,* pp. iii–iv.
14. Cited in Jerry Bergman, "The Professor Dean Kenyon Case," *Creation Research Society Quarterly,* Dec. 1994, pp. 186-88.
15. Jerry Bergman, *The Criterion* (Richfield, MN: Onesimus Publishers, 1984), passim.
16. Ibid., p. vii.
17. Ibid., pp. vii–viii.
18. Ibid., p. v.
19. Morris, *Long War,* p. 323.
20. Institute for Creation Research, *Acts and Facts,* December 1989, pp. 2–3.
21. Bergman, *The Criterion,* p. xi.
22. Ibid., p. xiii, xv.
23. Michael J. Behe, *Darwin's Black Box: The Biochemical Challenge to Evolution* (New York: The Free Press, 1996), p. 250, emphasis added.
24. Bergman, *The Criterion,* p. xi.
25. Ibid., p. 54.
26. Ibid., pp. 33, 53.
27. Ibid., p. 14.
28. Ibid., p. 15.
29. Ibid., pp. 36–40; Robert V. Gentry, *Creation's Tiny Mystery* (Knoxville, TN, Earth Science Associates, 1986), pp. 5, 99–111.
30. Gentry, *Creation's Tiny Mystery,* p. 7.
31. ibid., pp. 5–6.
32. Ibid., pp. 44–48, 63–73; Bird, *Origin . . . Revisited,* Vol. 1, pp. 419–432.
33. Ibid., pp. 221–304.
34. Ibid., pp. 73–86.
35. Ibid., p. 86.
36. The examples that follow were taken from Bergman, *The Criterion,* pp. 4–11, 20–24.
37. Bergman, *The Criterion,* pp. 13–14.
38. Ibid,. p. 18.
39. Ibid., p. 19.
40. Ibid., pp. 29–30.
41. Ibid., pp. 45–46.
42. Ibid., pp. 59–72.
43. Ibid., p. 72.
44. Ibid., pp. 56–57.
45. Ibid., pp. 11–12.
46. Ruse, "The Ideology of Darwinism," in E. Geissler and W. Scheler (eds.), *Darwin Today* (1983), pp. 233, 255 in Bird, *Origin . . . Revisited,* Vol. 2, p 54.
47. Bird, *Origin . . . Revisited,* Vol. 2, p. 391.
48. Ibid., p. 401.
49. Ibid., p. 400.
50. Bergman, *The Criterion,* p. 7.

51. Ibid.
52. Ibid., p. 28.

CHAPTER 7—THE RETREAT FROM GOOD SCIENCE

1. Phillip E. Johnson, Foreword in Moreland (ed.), *The Creation Hypothesis*, p. 7.
2. Basil Willey, "Darwin's Place in the History of Thought," M. Banton (ed.) in *Darwinism and the Study of Society* (Chicago: Quadrangle Books, 1961) in Stephen C. Meyer, "The Methodological Equivalence of Design and Descent: Can There Be a Scientific 'Theory of Creation'? Moreland (ed.), *Creation Hypothesis*, p. 69.
3. Raymond Grizzle, "Some Comments on the 'Godless' Nature of Darwinian Evolution, and a Plea to the Philosophers Among Us," *Perspectives on Science and the Christian Faith*, Vol. 45 (1993), p. 176 in Meyer, "Methodological Equivalent," Moreland (ed.), *Creation Hypothesis*, p. 69.
4. Nancey Murphy, "Phillip Johnson on Trial: A Critique of His Critique of Darwin," *Perspectives on Science and the Christian Faith*, Vol. 45, no. 1 (1993), p. 33 in Meyer, "Methodological Equivalent," Moreland (ed.), *Creation Hypothesis*, p. 69.
5. Cf., Moreland (ed.), *Creation Hypothesis*, pp. 7–65. A good summary is given in Michael J. Wilkins & J. P. Moreland (eds.), *Jesus Under Fire* (Grand Rapids, MI: Zondervan, 1995), pp. 8–10.
6. Wilder-Smith, *Scientific Alternative*, p. III.
7. Denton, *Evolution*, p. 326.
8. Wilder-Smith, *Scientific Alternative*, p. iv.
9. Ibid., second emphasis added.
10. Bird, *Origin . . . Revisited*, Vols. 1 and 2; cf., Vol. 1, p. 45.
11. Denton, *Evolution*, p. 348, emphasis added.
12. Ibid.
13. Ibid., p. 349.
14. Ibid., emphasis added.
15. Ibid.
16. Wilder-Smith, *Scientific Alternative*, p. I.
17. Denton, *Evolution*, p. 358.
18. Ibid.
19. H. Butterfield, *Origins of Modern Science*, 1957, p. 199 cited in Denton, *Evolution*, p. 351.
20. Denton, *Evolution*, pp. 351–352.
21. Ibid., p. 75.
22. In ibid.
23. Ibid., p. 76.
24. P. Feyerabend, *Beyond the Edge of Certainty*, 1965, p. 176 from Denton, *Evolution*, p. 77.

25. Morris, *Long War*, pp. 109–20.
26. Theodosius Dobzhansky, *Heredity, Race and Society* (1952), p. 63, emphasis added in Wysong, *The Creation/Evolution Controversy*, p. 40.
27. Aldous Huxley, *Ends and Means* (London: Chatto & Windus, 1946), pp. 270, 273.

CHAPTER 8—THE RETREAT FROM GOD

1. Robert E. D. Clark, *Darwin: Before and After* (Chicago: Moody Press, 1967), p. 62.
2. Ibid., p. 63.
3. Charles Darwin, J.W. Burrow (ed.), *The Origin of Species* (Baltimore, MD: Penguin Books, 1974), p. 205.
4. Ibid., p. 234.
5. Ibid., p. 435.
6. Ibid., p. 217.
7. Ibid., p. 292.
8. Ibid., p. 315.
9. Ibid., p. 440.
10. Ibid., p. 66.
11. Clark, *Darwin: Before and After*, 87.
12. Francis Darwin (ed.), *Charles Darwin: Life and Letters*, Vol. 2, pp. 232, 229.
13. Cf., Clark, *Darwin: Before and After*, p. 88.
14. Clark, *Darwin: Before and After*, p. 89.
15. Ibid.
16. Francis Darwin (ed.), *Life and Letters*, Vol. 1, p. 285, rrom Clark and Bales, *Why Scientists Accept*, p. 38.
17. Clark and Bales, *Why Scientists Accept*, pp. 38–39.
18. Clark, *Darwin: Before and After*, p. 93.
19. Leslie Paul, *The Annihilation of Man* (New York: Harcourt Brace, 1945), p. 154.
20. Darwin, *Origin*, p. 43.
21. Clark and Bales, *Why Scientists Accept*, p. 45 citing Francis Darwin (ed.), *Charles Darwin: Life and Letters*, Vol. 2, p. 124.
22. Clark, *Darwin: Before and After*, p. 85.
23. Robert E. Kofahl, "Correctly Redefining Distorted Science: A Most Essential Task," *Creation Research Society Quarterly*, Dec. 1986, p. 113.
24. Lubenow, *Bones*, pp. 191–92.
25. Clark Pinnock, *Set Forth Your Case* (Chicago: Moody Press, 1967), p. 38.
26. Greg Bahnsen in *The Challenge of Design*, p. 87.
27. Taken from R. Clyde McCone, "Three Levels of Anthropological Objection to Evolution," in the *Creation Research Society Quarterly*, March 1973, p. 208.

28. Wernher von Braun, preface in *Creation: Nature's Designs and Designer* (Mountain View, CA: Pacific Press Publishing Association, 1971), p. 6. This is a compendium by leading scientists.

29. Sol Tax (ed.), *Evolution of Man*, p. 2 in Clark and Bales, *Why Scientists Accept*, p. 93.

30. Clark and Bales, *Why Scientists Accept*, p. 94; cf. pp. 55–56, 70–87.

31. Ibid., p. 108.

32. Ibid., p. 88.

33. Louis T. More, *The Dogma of Evolution* (Princeton University Press, 1925), p. 117, emphasis added in Clark and Bales, *Why Scientists Accept*, p. 93.

34. Clark and Bales, *Why Scientists Accept*, p. 90.

35. In ibid., p. 94.

36. Ibid.

37. Ibid., p. 69.

38. Ibid., p. 92.

39. *Scientific American*, May 1959, p. 66.

40. In Sol Tax (ed.), *Evolution After Darwin*, Vol. III (University of Chicago Press, 1960), p. 45.

41. Clark and Bales, *Why Scientists Accept*, p. 91.

42. E.g., Bolton Davidheiser, *Evolution and Christian Faith*, pp. 302–13.

43. E.g., Bird, *The Origin of Species Revisited*, Vols. 1 & 2; Clark and Bales, pp. 98–105; Davidheiser, *Evolution and the Christian Faith*, pp. 302–13.

44. Clark and Bales, *Why Scientists Accept*, p. 89.

45. Ibid., p. 5.

46. Cf., Karl Popper, *Unended Quests: An Intellectual Autobiography*, rev. edition (London: Fontana/Collins, 1976), pp. 168–69.

47. In Norman L. Geisler, *Creator in the Courtroom—"Scopes 2": The 1981 Arkansas Creation/Evolution Trial* (Milford, MI: Mott Media, 1982), p. 151.

48. Sir Francis Crick, *Life Itself: Its Origin and Nature* (New York: Simon & Schuster, 1981), p. 88.

49. Loren Eiseley, *The Immense Journey* (New York: Time, Inc., 1962), p. 144, cf., 199.

50. Isaac Newton, *Mathematical Principles of Natural Philosophy*, in *The Great Books of the Western World*, Vol. 34 (Chicago: Encyclopedia Britannica, 1952), p. 369.

51. Robert Jastrow, *God and the Astronomers* (New York: Norton, 1978), pp. 115–16.

CHAPTER 9—EVOLUTION, LOGIC, AND INCREASING DOUBTS

1. The National Center for Science Education, Inc., *Voices for Evolution*, p. 56.

2. Ibid., p. 166.

3. Manly, *God Made*, pp. 114–15.
4. Dodson and Howe, *Creation or Evolution*, p. 143.
5. Kurt P. Wise, "The Origin of Life's Major Groups" in Moreland (ed.), *Creation Hypothesis*, p. 232.
6. Cited in Phillip E. Johnson, *Darwin on Trial* (Downer's Grove, IL: Inter-Varsity, 1991), p. 10.
7. Ibid.
8. For example, Dean H. Kenyon (Ph.D. biophysics, Stanford) is professor of biology and coordinator of the general biology program at San Francisco State University. He is coauthor of *Biochemical Predestination*, a standard work on the origin of life, and a former evolutionist. He has extensively reviewed the scientific case for creation and accepts it as legitimate as do hundreds of other established scientists (H. M. Morris, G. E. Parker, *What Is Creation Science?* [San Diego: Creation Life, 1982] iii–v; cf., Bird, *Origin . . . Revisited*, I, xv–xvi). On the other hand, the religious and unscientific nature of evolutionary theory has been pointed out in the following articles by creationists in *The Creation Research Society Quarterly:* William J. Ouweneel, "The Scientific Character of the Evolution Doctrine," Vol. 8, No. 2; Randall Hedtke, "The Divine Essence in Evolutionary Theorizing—An Analysis of the Rise and Fall of Evolutionary Natural Selection, Mutation, and Punctuated Equilibria as Mechanisms of Megaevolution," Vol. 21, No. 1; John N. Moore, "Retrieval System Problems with Articles in 'Evolution,'" Vol. 10, No. 2; Glenn W. Wolfram, "Evolution, Science and Religion," Vol. 12, No. 2; Raymond C. Telfar, II, "Should Macroevolution Be Taught As Fact?"; Vol. 10, No. 1; Ralph E. Ancil, "On the Importance of Philosophy in the Origins Debate," Vol. 22, No. 3; Gary L. Schoephlin, "On Assumptions and Their Relation to Science," Vol. 9, No. 2; John N. Moore, "An Estimate of the Current Status of Evolutionary Thinking," Vol. 18, No. 4; Arthur Jones, "The Nature of Evolutionary Thought," Vol. 8, No. 1; W. R. Bird, "Expostulated Evidence for Macroevolution and Darwinism: Darwinian Arguments and the Disintegrating Neo-Darwinian Synthesis—Part II," Vol. 25, No. 2; John N. Moore, "Educational Column—Properly Defining 'Evolution,'" Vol. 23, No. 3; Robert E. Kofahl, "Correctly Redefining Distorted Science: A Most Essential Task," Vol. 23, No. 3.
9. Karl Popper, *Unended Quest: An Intellectual Autobiography* (Great Britain: Fontana/Collins, 1976, rev.), pp. 168–69.
10. E.g., cf., Denton, *Evolution* 308–44; in his survey of the evidence, R. L. Wysong observes that evolution itself requires faith and lists some of the problems (see chapter 17 of this book).
11. Bird, *Origin . . . Revisited*, Vols. 1 and 2, who cites almost exclusively non-creationists; also see the technical reports and publications of the Institute for Creation Research in Santee, California and the Creation Research Society in St. Joseph, Missouri; also see the Recommended Reading.
12. See Recommended Reading.

13. A. J. Hoover, *Don't You Believe It* (Chicago, IL: Moody Press, 1982).
14. Lubenow, *Bones*, p. 25.
15. Norman MacBeth, *Darwin Retried* (Boston: Gambit, 1971).
16. Summarized by Lubenow; *Bones*.
17. To illustrate, W. R. Bird is a summa cum laude graduate of Vanderbilt University and the Yale Law School who argued the major case on the origins issue before the U.S. Supreme Court. He is a member of the most prestigious legal organization, the American Law Institute, and has published articles on origins in the *Harvard Journal of Law and Public Policy* and the *Yale Law Journal*. He is also listed in the most selective directory, *Who's Who in the World*, and several others. In *The Origin of Species Revisited*, 2 vol., NY Philosophical Library, 1993, he documents how evolutionary scientists are increasingly questioning the validity of standard evolutionary theory. This book was prepared utilizing the research amassed for the 1981 Supreme Court case over the issue of origins. (Aguillard, et. al., v. Edwards, et. al., civil action No. 81–4787, Section H, U.S. District Court for the Eastern District of Louisiana, *Brief of the State in Opposition to ACLU Motion for Summary Judgment*, c., 1984, W. R. Bird.) Attorneys for the defendant gathered thousands of pages of information from hundreds of evolutionary scientists who, collectively, had expressed reservations from most scientific fields, in most areas of evolutionary thinking.
18. Klein, Preface to L. Sunderland, *Darwin's Enigma* (1985), p. 5 in Bird, *Origin . . . Revisited*, Vol. 2, p. 399.
19. McLean V. Arkansas, Bd. of Educ., 529 F. Supp. 1255, 1272 (E.D.Ark. 1982); G. Skoog, "Coverage of Evolution in Secondary School Biology Textbooks: 1900–1982," at 12 (unpublished ms. October 16, 1982) from Bird, *Origin . . . Revisited*, Vol. 2, pp. 394–95.
20. Bird, *Origin . . . Revisited*, Vol. 2, p. 517.
21. In Ronald Bailey, "Origin of the Specious: Why Do Neo-Conservatives Doubt Darwin?" *Reason*, July 1997, p. 24.
22. B. Leith, *The Descent of Darwin: A Handbook of Doubts About Darwinism* (1982), pp. 10–11 in Bird, *Origin . . . Revisited*, Vol. 1, p. 3, emphasis added.
23. Wolfgang Smith, "The Universe Is Ultimately to Be Explained in Terms of a Metacosmic Reality" in Margenau and Varghese (eds.), *Cosmos, Bios, Theos*, p. 113.
24. Merle d'Aubigne, "How Is It Possible to Escape the Idea of Some Intelligent and Organizing Force?" in Margenau and Varghese (eds.), *Cosmos, Bios, Theos*, p. 158.
25. Sir John Eccles, "A Divine Design: Some Questions on Origins" in Margenau and Varghese (eds.), *Cosmos, Bios, Theos*, p. 163.
26. Harry Rubin, "Life, Even in Bacteria, Is Too Complex to Have Occurred by Chance" in Margenau and Varghese (eds.), p. 203.
27. M. Bowden, *The Rise of the Evolution Fraud (An Exposure of Its Roots)* (San Diego: Creation Life Publishers, 1982), pp. 216, 218.

28. Ibid.
29. Ibid.
30. Pierre-P. Grassé, *The Evolution of Living Organisms* (New York: Academic Press, 1977), p. 202.
31. Hsu, reply, *Geology*, Vol. 15 (1987), p. 177; Hsu, "Darwin's Three Mistakes," *Geology*, Vol. 14, pp. 532–34 (1986) in Bird, Vol. 2, p. 516.
32. Lemoine, *Introduction: De L'Evolution?* in 5 Encyclopedie Francaise 06–6 (P. Lemoine, ed., 1937), emphasis added, in Bird, *Origin . . . Revisited*, Vol. 1, p. 151.
33. Julio Garrido, "Evolution and Molecular Biology," *Creation Research Society Quarterly*, Dec. 1973, p. 167.
34. Ibid., p. 168.
35. Ibid.
36. Howard Byington Holroyd, "Darwinism Is Physical and Mathematical Nonsense," *Creation Research Society Quarterly*, June 1972, p. 5.
37. R. Clyde McCone, "Three Levels of Anthropological Objection to Evolution," *Creation Research Society Quarterly*, March 1973, p. 209.
38. Róger Haines, Jr., "Macroevolution Questioned," *Creation Research Society Quarterly*, Dec. 1976, p. 169.
39. G. A. Kerkut, *Implications of Evolution* (Pergammon Press, 1960), pp. 150–53.
40. Ibid., p. 150.
41. Gish, *Creation Scientists Answer*, p. ix.
42. See Note to the Reader. Dr. Morris may be contacted at the Santee, CA Institute for Creation Research in confirmation.
43. See the discussion in chs. 7, 8.
44. Bird, *Origin . . . Revisited*, Vol. 1, p. 486.
45. Cf., Ibid., pp. 487–89 for a summary of most of these.
46. D. Futuyama, *Science on Trial* (1983), p. 198 in Bird, *Origin . . . Revisited*, Vol. 2, p. 167.
47. George Wald, "The Origin of Life" in *Physics and Chemistry of Life* (1955), p. 3 in Bird, *Origin . . . Revisited*, Vol. 2, p. 167.
48. Original references cited in Bird, *Origin . . . Revisited*, Vol. 2, pp. 172–73.
49. In ibid., p. 168.
50. Ibid.
51. Henry Morris, *Long War*, p. 32.
52. Henry M. Morris, *The Biblical Basis for Modern Science* (Grand Rapids, MI: Baker, 1984), pp. 130–31.
53. E. J. H. Corner, "Evolution" in Anna M. MacLeod and L. S. Cobley (eds.), *Contemporary Botanical Thought* (Chicago: Quadrangle Books, 1961), pp. 97.
54. H. S. Lipson, "A Physicist Looks at Evolution," *Physics Bulletin*, Vol. 31 (1980), p. 138.
55. A. Thompson, *Biology, Zoology and Genetics: Evolution Model vs. Creation Model* (1983), p. 76 cited in Bird, *Origin . . . Revisited*, Vol. 1, p. 49; Thompson does not regard the creation theory as scientific.

56. Austin Clark, "Animal Evolution," *Quarterly Review of Biology*, Vol. 3, p. 539, cf., p. 523 in Bird, *Origin . . . Revisited*, Vol. 1, p. 50.

57. Bird, *Origin . . . Revisited*, Vol. 1, p. 102.

58. Fred Hoyle, Chandra Wickramasinghe, *Evolution from Space* (1981), p. 130 in Bird, *Origin . . . Revisited*, Vol. 1, p. 82.

59. Evan V. Shute, "Evolution in the Glare of New Knowledge," *The Summary*, Dec. 1969, p. 2.

60. Phillip E. Johnson, "Controversy," *Commentary*, September 1996, p. 22.

CHAPTER 10: THE GREATEST MAGIC IN THE WORLD

1. Victor J. Stenger, "The Face of Chaos," *Free Inquiry*, Vol. 13, no. 1 (Winter 1992/93), p. 13 in Fred Heeren, *Show Me God: What the Message from Space Is Telling Us About God*, rev. edition (Wheeling, IL: Daystar Publications, 1997), p. 118.

2. Interview with Arno Penzias in Heeren, *Show Me God*, p. 156

3. H. Bondi, *Cosmology* (1968), p. 144 ("It should be clearly understood that the creation here discussed is the formation of matter not out of radiation but *out of nothing*."); F. Hoyle, *The Nature of the Universe* (1950), p. 125 in Bird, *Origin . . . Revisited*, Vol. 1, p. 26.

4. Interview with John Mather in Heeren, *Show Me God*, pp. 119–20.

5. Guth and Steinhardt, "The Inflationary Universe," *Scientific American*, May 1984, pp. 116, 128, see also Tryon, "What Made the World?" *New Scientist*, March 8, 1984, pp. 14, 16. ("In 1973, I proposed that our Universe had been created spontaneously from nothing [*ex nihilo*], as a result of established principles of physics.") in Bird, *Origin . . . Revisited*, Vol. 1, p. 25.

6. Interview with Alan Guth in Heeren, *Show Me God*, p. 174.

7. Heeren, *Show Me God*, pp. 170–71, cf., notes 3 and 5.

8. Ibid., p. 174, cf., Bird, *Origin . . . Revisited*, Vol. 1, p. 26.

9. The National Center for Science Education, Inc., *Voices for Evolution*, pp. ix–x.

10. Isaac Asimov, "What Is Beyond the Universe?" *Science Digest*, April 1971, p. 69 in Heeren, *Show Me God*, pp. 118–19.

11. Heeren, *Show Me God*, p. 120.

12. Herman J. Eckelmann, "Some Concluding Thoughts on Evolutionary Belief" in John Warwick Montgomery (ed.), *Evidence for Faith: Deciding the God Question* (Dallas: Probe Books, 1991), pp. 344–45.

13. Tipler, *How to Construct a Falsifiable Theory in Which the Universe Came into Being Several Thousand Years Ago*, Philosophy of Science Association, pp. 873, 893–94 (1984) in Bird, *Origin . . . Revisited*, Vol. 2, p. 464.

14. Martin Heidegger, *Was Ist Metaphysik?* in John Warwick Montgomery, *The Suicide of Christian Theology* (Minneapolis, MN: Bethany, 1965), pp. 332–33.

15. Andrei Linde, "The Self-Reproducing Inflationary Universe," *Scientific American*, Nov. 1994, p. 53 in Heeren, *Show Me God*, p. 174.

CHAPTER 11—ALPHABET SOUP AND WINNING THE LOTTERY

1. Walter L. Bradley, Charles B. Thaxton, "Information and the Origin of Life" in Moreland (ed.), *Creation Hypothesis*, pp. 173–74.
2. Ibid., p. 175.
3. A. E. Wilder-Smith, *The Natural Sciences Know Nothing of Evolution* (San Diego: Master Books, 1981), pp. 13–14.
4. Ibid., p. 16.
5. In "Probability and Left-Handed Molecules," (*Creation Research Society Quarterly*, Dec. 1971); James F. Coppedge shows that the probability of *Mycoplasma Hominis* H39, the smallest known living entity, having all left-handed amino acids, is one chance in $10^{68,400}$ and shows why it is impossible to explain stereo-selectivity on the basis of chance alone. Cf., Bird, *Origin . . . Revisited*, Vol. 1, pp. 309–11.
6. Wilder-Smith, *Natural Sciences*, p. 19.
7. Ibid., p. 20.
8. Ibid., pp. 21–22.
9. Ibid., pp. 22–23.
10. Cited in Jerry Bergman, "A Review of Exobiogenesis Theories," *Creation Research Society Quarterly*, March 1995, p. 213.
11. Denton, *Evolution*, pp. 260–61, emphasis added.
12. The National Center for Science Education, Inc., *Voices for Evolution*, p. 59.
13. "Theoretical Blow to the Origin of Life," *New Scientist*, 19, February 1970, p. 344; cf., Bird, *Origin . . . Revisited*, Vol. 1, pp. 328–329.
14. Henderson-Sellers, Benlow, and Meadows, "The Early Atmosphere of the Terrestrial Planets," p. 21, *Quarterly Journal of the Royal Astronomical Society*, pp. 74, 81 (1980) from Bird, *Origin . . . Revisited*, Vol. 1, p. 329.
15. R. L. Wysong, *The Creation Evolution Controversy* (East Lansing, MI: Inquiry Press, 1976), p. 124.
16. Jacques Monod, *Chance and Necessity* (New York: Vintage, 1972), p. 112.
17. Cited in Wysong, *Creation Evolution Controversy*, p. 127.
18. Duane Gish, *Speculations and Experiments Related to the Origin of Life: A Critique* (San Diego: Institute for Creation Research, 1972).
19. Bradley and Thaxton "Information and the Origin of Life" in Moreland (ed.), *Creation Hypothesis*, p. 176, emphasis added.
20. Ronald Bailey, "Origin of the Specious," *Reason*, July 1997, p. 26.
21. Bradley and Thaxton in Moreland (ed.), *Creation Hypothesis*, p. 196. On the Sante Fe Institute and Stuart Kauffman see David Berlinski's comments in *Commentary*, September 1996, p. 34.
22. Mark Eastman, Chuck Missler *The Creator Beyond Time and Space* (Costa Mesa: TWFT, 1996), p. 68.
23. John W. Oller, Jr. and John L. Omdahl, "Origin of the Human Language Capacity: In Whose Image?" in Moreland (ed.), *Creation Hypothesis*, p. 238.
24. Dr. Monty Kester, "Is Organic Evolution Reasonable?" in *Science at the Crossroads: Observation or Speculation? Proceedings of the 1983 National*

Creation Conference, Minneapolis, Minnesota, Bible Science Association 1985, p. 107.

25. Bird, *Origin . . . Revisited*, Vol. 1, p. 80.

26. E. Ambrose, *The Nature and Origin of the Biological World* (1982), p. 142 [This is assuming natural selection did not increase the probability, which would not happen, as Bird discusses in Section 3.3(a).] In Bird, *Origin . . . Revisited*, Vol. 1, p. 79.

27. Cf., Bird, *Origin . . . Revisited*, Vol. 1, pp. 306–08ff.

28. Walter James ReMine, *The Biotic Message*, p. 257, cited in Wayne Friar, Book Review, *Creation Research Society Quarterly*, Dec. 1994, p. 163.

29. Moshe Trop, "Was Evolution Really Possible?" *Creation Research Society Quarterly*, March 1975, p. 187, emphasis added.

30. David J. Rodabaugh, "The Queen of Science Examines the King of Fools," *Creation Research Society Quarterly*, June 1975, p. 14, emphasis added.

31. David J. Rodabaugh, "Mathematicians Do It Again," *Creation Research Society Quarterly*, Dec. 1975, pp. 173–75, emphasis added.

32. Cited in James Coppedge, *Evolution: Possible or Impossible?* (Grand Rapids, MI: Zondervan, 1973), p. 260.

33. James F. Coppedge, "Probability and Left-Handed Molecules," *Creation Research Society Quarterly*, Dec. 1971, p. 172.

34. Ibid., p. 171.

35. See John Ankerberg, John Weldon, *Ready with an Answer* (Eugene, OR: Harvest House, 1997), especially pp. 220–28.

36. Fred Hoyle, *The Big Bang in Astronomy*, p. 527, emphasis added.

37. Cited in Evan Shute, *Flaws in the Theory of Evolution* (Nutley, NJ: Craig Press, 1971), pp. 23–24.

38. Harold F. Blum, *Time's Arrow and Evolution*, 3rd ed. (Princeton, NJ: Princeton University Press, 1968), p. 158.

39. Walter L. Bradley and Charles B. Thaxton, "Information and the Origin of Life" in Moreland (ed.), *Creation Hypothesis*, p. 190.

40. Ibid., emphasis added; cf., William A. Dembski, "Reviving the Argument from Design: Detecting Design Through Small Probabilities," *Proceedings of the Biennial Conference of the Association of Christians in the Mathematical Sciences*, Vol. 8, (1991), pp. 101–45.

41. Coppedge, *Evolution: Possible or Impossible?* cf., Paul A. Zimmerman, "The Spontaneous Generation of Life," Walter Lammerts (ed.), *Scientific Studies in Special Creation* (Nutley, NJ: Presbyterian & Reformed, 1971); Gary E. Parker, "The Origin of Life on Earth," *Creation Research Society Quarterly*, Sept. 1970; and A. E. Wilder-Smith, *The Creation of Life—A Cybernetic Approach to Evolution* (Harold Shaw, 1970).

42. Coppedge, *Evolution: Possible or Impossible?* p. 114.

43. Ibid.

44. David J. Rodabough, "The Queen of Science," p. 15.

45. See Coppedge, *Evolution: Possible or Impossible?* for an extended discussion.

46. Cited in *Nature*, November 12, 1981, p. 105, emphasis added.
47. Cited in Eastman, Missler, *The Creator Beyond*, p. 61.
48. Robert Shapiro, *Origins—A Skeptics Guide to the Creation of Life on Earth* (1986), p. 128.
49. Eastman and Missler, *Creator Beyond*, p. 61.
50. Howard Byington Holroyd, "Darwinism Is Physical and Mathematical Nonsense," *Creation Research Society Quarterly*, June 1972, pp. 6, 9.
51. Ibid., p. 10.
52. Ibid., p. 12.
53. Ibid., p. 13.
54. Ibid., p. 12.
55. John Ankerberg, John Weldon, *The Case for Jesus the Messiah* (Chattanooga, TN: Ankerberg Theological Research Institute, 1992).

CHAPTER 12—THE MOLECULES OF MELODRAMA

1. The National Center for Science Education, Inc., *Voices for Evolution* pp. 57–58.
2. Ibid., p. 142, emphasis added.
3. Michael Behe, *Darwin's Black Box: The Biochemical Challenge to Evolution* (New York: The Free Press, 1996), p. 252.
4. Ibid., p. x.
5. Ibid., p. 15.
6. Charles Darwin, J. W. Burrow (ed.), *The Origin of Species* (Baltimore, MD: Penguin Books, 1974), p. 219; Darwin went on to say, "But I can find out no such case," a typical rationalization not infrequent in his writings which refused to treat the problems of evolution seriously.
7. Behe, *Darwin's Black Box*, p. 40.
8. Ibid., p. 41.
9. Ibid., p. 97.
10. Ibid., pp. 62–69.
11. Ibid., p. 67.
12. Ibid., pp. 68–69, last emphasis added.
13. Ibid., p. 72.
14. Ibid., p. 73.
15. Ibid., p. xii.
16. Ibid., pp. 4–5.
17. Ibid., p. 5.
18. Ibid., p. 182.
19. Ibid., p. 187.
20. Ibid., p. 26.
21. Ibid.
22. Ibid., p. 27.
23. Ibid., p. 29.
24. Ibid., p. 30.

25. Ibid., p. 176.
26. Ibid.
27. Ibid., p. 177.
28. Ibid., p. 178.
29. Ibid.
30. Ibid., p. 179.
31. Ibid., pp. 185–86.
32. *The New York Times*, October 29, 1996, p. 15, emphasis added.
33. Behe, *Darwin's Black Box*, pp. 115–16.
34. Ibid., p. 138.
35. Ibid., p. 159.
36. Ibid., p. 139.
37. John N. Moore, "Retrieval System Problems with Articles in 'Evolution,'" *Creation Research Society Quarterly*, Sept. 1973, p. 116.
38. Ibid., pp. 116–17.
39. Manly, *God Made*, p. 77.
40. Sir Nevill Mott, "Science Will Never Give Us the Answers to All Our Questions" in Henry Margenau and Roy Abraham Varghese (eds.), *Cosmos, Bios, Theo*, p. 66.
41. Sir John Eccles, "A Divine Design: Some Questions on Origins" in Margenau and Varghese (eds.), *Cosmos, Bios, Theos*, p. 164.
42. George Wald, "Life and Mind in the Universe" in Margenau and Varghese (eds.), *Cosmos, Bios, Theos*, p. 218.
43. Manly, *God Made*, p. 77.
44. Behe, *Darwin's Black Box*, p. 40.
45. R. Dawkins, *River Out of Eden* (New York: Basic Books, 1995), p. 83 in ibid., p. 40.
46. Behe, *Darwin's Black Box*, p. 160.

CHAPTER 13—THE PROOF THAT POOFED

1. G. A. Kerkut cited in Henry Morris, "Sedimentation and the Fossil Record: A Study in Hydraulic Engineering," in Walter Lammerts (ed.), *Why Not Creation?* (Nutley, NJ: Presbyterian & Reformed, 1970), p. 119; Sir Gavin de Beer, *Science* 143:1311 (1964); W. R. Thompson in *The Origin of Species*, 1956 p. 14.
2. Grassé, *Evolution of Living Organisms*, pp. 3–4, 204.
3. Thomas Huxley in *Three Lectures on Evolution* (1882), 619 from Bird, *Origin . . . Revisited*, I, p. 59.
4. "These evolutionary happenings are unique, unrepeatable, and irreversible. It is as impossible to turn a land vertebrate into a fish as it is to effect the reverse transformation. The applicability of the experimental method to the study of such unique historical processes *is severely restricted before all else by the time intervals involved, which far exceed the lifetime of any human experimenter*," Theodosius Dobzhansky, *American*

Scientist, 45, 388, 1957, as cited in Stephen Jay Gould, *Wonderful Life: The Burgess Shale and the Nature of History* (New York: W. W. Norton, 1985), p. 3, emphasis added.

5. The National Center for Science Education, Inc., *Voices for Evolution*, e.g., pp. 33, 56, 62, 78–79, 141.
6. Charles Darwin, J. W. Burrow (ed.), *Origin of Species*, pp. 206, 292; cf., pp. 313–316, emphasis added.
7. Gish, *Evolution: The Fossils Still Say No!* p. 42.
8. Darin, Burrow (ed.), *Origin of Species*, pp. 206, 292, cf., pp. 313–16.
9. The National Center for Science Education, Inc., *Voices for Evolution*, p. 56.
10. Ibid., p. 33.
11. Ibid., p. 62.
12. Ibid., pp. 78–79.
13. Ibid., p. 141.
14. Stephen Jay Gould, "The Return of Hopeful Monsters," *Natural History*, June–July, 1977, pp. 22, 24, emphasis added.
15. See e.g., Bird, *Origin . . . Revisited,* I, pp. 48, 59 citing Stanley, Gould, Eldredge, Kitts and Tattersall. See Steven M. Stanley, *Macroevolution: Pattern and Process* (San Francisco: W. H. Freeman, 1979), pp. 1, 4–9, 23, 74, 84, 88–98.
16. David Raup, "Conflicts Between Darwin and Paleontology," *Field Museum of Natural History Bulletin*, January 1979 at 22, 25 from Bird, *Origin . . . Revisited*, Vol. 1, p. 48.
17. G. Simpson, *The Major Features of Evolution* (1953), 143 and G. Simpson, *Tempo and Mode in Evolution* (1944), p. 107 from Bird, *Origin . . . Revisited*, Vol. 1, pp. 49, 57.
18. George Gaylord Simpson, *The Major Features of Evolution* (New York: Columbia University Press, 1965), p. 360, emphasis in original. Simpson went on to state that these discontinuities did not require a belief in special creation.
19. G. G. Simpson, *Tempo and Mode in Evolution* (New York: Columbia University Press, 1944), pp. 105, 107, cited in Gish, *Evolution—The Fossils Still Say No!* pp. 333–34.
20. Simpson, *Major Features of Evolution*, p. 360 in Gish, *Evolution—The Fossils Still Say No!* p. 336, emphasis added.
21. Austin Clark, "Animal Evolution," *Quarterly Review of Biology*, Vol. 3, 539 from Bird, *Origin . . . Revisited*, Vol. 1, p. 50.
22. A. Thompson, *Biology, Zoology and Genetics: Evolution Model vs. Creation Model*, 2 (1983), p. 76, emphasis added, from Bird, *Origin . . . Revisited*, Vol. 1, p. 49.
23. Derek V. Ager, "The Nature of the Fossil Record," 87, *Proceedings of Geological Association* 133 (1976) from Bird, *Origin . . . Revisited*, p. 51.
24. E. J. H. Corner "Evolution" in A. M. MacLeod and L. S. Cobley, eds., *Evolution in Contemporary Botanical Thought* (Chicago, IL: Quadrangle Books, 1961), at 95, 97 from Bird, *Origin . . . Revisited*, Vol. 1, p. 234.

25. Paul B. Weiss, *The Science of Biology* (McGraw Hill, 1963), p. 732 from Davidheiser, *Evolution and the Christian Faith*, p. 303.
26. For examples, cf., Bird, *Origin . . . Revisited*, Vol. 1, passim and Davidheiser, *Evolution and Christian Faith*, pp. 302–09.
27. Gish, *Evolution—The Fossils Still Say No!* p. 337.
28. D. Johansen, M. Edey, *Lucy: The Beginnings of Humankind*, p. 363 (1981); cf., N. Eldedge and I. Tattersall, *The Myths of Human Evolution*, pp. 7–8 (1982) from Bird, *Origin . . . Revisited*, Vol. 1, p. 55.
29. R. A. Stirton, *Time, Life and Man*, John Wiley and Sons, 1957, p. 416 from Davidheiser, *Evolution and the Christian Faith*, p. 307.
30. Grassé, *Evolution of Living Organisms*, p. 30.
31. White, "Presidential Address: A Little on Lungfishes" 177, *Proceedings of the Linnean Society*, 1, 8 (1966) in Bird, *Origin . . . Revisited*, Vol. 1, p. 62.
32. Robert Barnes, book review of *Invertebrate Beginnings, Paleobiology*, 6(3), 1980, p. 365.
33. Earl L. Core, et al., *General Biology*, 4th ed., (John Wiley and Sons, 1961), p. 299 from Davidheiser, *Evolution and the Christian Faith*, p. 309.
34. David Raup and Steven M. Stanley, *Principles of Paleontology* (San Francisco: W. H. Freeman, 1978), p. 372.
35. Woodruff, "Evolution: The Paleobiological View," *Science*, Vol. 208 (1980), p. 716, emphasis added cf., Bird, *Origin . . . Revisited*, Vol. 1, pp. 58–59.
36. Donn Rosen, "Evolution: An Old Debate With a New Twist," in *St. Louis Post Dispatch*, 17 May 1981, quoted by James E. Adams; cf. references in Bird, *Origin . . . Revisited*, Vol. 1, p. 536.
37. Gish, *Creation Scientists Answer*, 234–42; Gish, *Evolution the Fossils Still Say No!* passim.
38. Steven M. Stanley, *Macroevolution: Pattern and Process* (San Francisco: W. H. Freeman & Co., 1979), p. 39; cf., pp. 47, 62.
39. Luther D. Sunderland, *Darwin's Enigma: Fossils and Other Problems* (Santee, CA: Master Books, 1984), p. 88.
40. Ibid., p. 78.
41. John N. Moore, "Was Evolution Involved in the Process of Creation?" in Ronald F. Youngblood (ed.), *The Genesis Debate: Persistent Questions About Creation and the Flood* (Grand Rapids: Baker, 1990), p. 106.
42. Stephen Jay Gould, "Evolution's Erratic Pace," *Natural History*, May, 1977, p. 12.
43. Ibid., p. 14.
44. Kurt P. Wise, "The Origin of Life's Major Groups" in J. P. Moreland (ed.), *Creation Hypothesis*, p. 227.
45. Ibid.
46. Ibid.
47. Ibid., p. 228.
48. Ernest Lutz, "A Review of Claims about *Archaeopteryx* in the Light of the Evidence," *Creation Research Society Quarterly*, June 1995, p. 18.
49. Ibid., p. 19.

50. Ibid.
51. Ibid.
52. For more information see Gish, *Evolution—The Fossils Still Say No!* pp. 129–41.
53. W. E. Swinton in A. J. Marshall (ed.), *Biology and Comparative Physiology of Birds*, Vol. 1 (New York: Academic Press, 1960), p. 1, cited in Gish, *Evolution—The Fossils Still Say No!*, p. 140.
54. Gish, *Evolution—The Fossils Still Say No!*, p. 145.
55. Cf., Wise, pp. 212–18.
56. Francis Darwin (ed.), *The Life and Letters of Charles Darwin* (New York: Johnson Reprint, 1969), Vol. 3, p. 248. Apparently emphasized in the original.
57. Charles Darwin, *The Origin of Species* (ed: J. W. Burrow), p. 292.
58. Stanley, *Macroevolution*, p. 35.
59. Stephen J. Gould, *The Panda's Thumb: More Reflections in Natural History*, (New York: W. W. Norton & Co., 1980), 184–185 and Grassé, p. 24.
60. Lubenow, *Bones*, p. 182.
61. Nils Heribert-Nilsson, *Synthetische Artbildung* (Lund, Sweden: CWK Glerups, 1953), p. 11.
62. Ibid., pp. 1142–43.
63. Ibid., pp. 1239–40.
64. Steven M. Stanley, *The New Evolutionary Timetable: Fossils, Genes, and the Origin of Species* (New York: Basic Books, 1981), p. xv.
65. Ernst Mayr, *Populations, Species and Evolution*, p. 253 (Harvard University Press, 1970) in Bird, *Origin . . . Revisited*, Vol. I, p. 177 (cf., Bird, pp. 168–177).
66. Michael Denton, *Evolution: A Theory in Crisis*, pp. 193–94. See also Stanley, *Macroevolution*, pp. 122–23.
67. E.g., cf., the citations in Bird, *Origin . . . Revisited*, Vol. 1, pp. 155–290 (cf., pp. 134–55).
68. Cf., Coppedge, *Evolution: Possible or Impossible?*, p. 113, passim.
69. V. Sarich in W. J. Bennetta (ed.), "Scientists Decry Slick New Packaging of Creationism," *The Science Teacher*, 1987, Vol. 54, p. 41, reported in Bill Crofut and Raymond M. Seaman, "Evolutionism: Bones and Stones of Contention" in *Creation Research Society Quarterly*, June 1990, p. 35.
70. M. Ridley, *New Scientist*, Vol. 90, p. 830 (1981) cited in Gish, *Evolution—The Fossils Still Say No!* p. 352.
71. W. R. Thompson, Introduction, Charles Darwin, *The Origin of Species* (New York: Dutton: Every Man's Library, Series No. 811, 1956), p. 14.
72. Summarized from Gish, *Evolution—The Fossils Still Say No!* p. 43.
73. Gish, *Evolution—The Fossils Still Say No!* p. 69.
74. D. B. Kitts, *Evolution*, Vol. 28, p. 467 (1974), cited in Gish, *Evolution—The Fossils Still Say No!* p. 347, emphasis added.
75. D. S. Woodruff, *Science*, Vol. 208, p. 716 (1980) cited in Gish, *Evolution—The Fossils Still Say No!* p. 350.
76. Manly, *God Made*, p. 171.

77. Gish, *Evolution—The Fossils Still Say No!* p. 81.
78. Gish, ibid., p. 81, cf., p. 42.
79. The National Center for Science Education, Inc., *Voices for Evolution,* p. 75.

CHAPTER 14—MORE MONKEY BUSINESS

1. Davidheiser, *Evolution and the Christian Faith,* p. 326.
2. The National Center for Science Education, Inc., *Voices for Evolution,* p. 58, emphasis added.
3. Ibid., p. 167.
4. Rick Gore, "The Dawn of Humans: The First Steps," *National Geographic,* Feb. 1997, p. 72.
5. Manly, *God Made,* pp. 158–59, 168.
6. Gish, *Evolution—The Fossils Still Say No!* p. 331.
7. Ibid., p. 232.
8. Zuckerman, *Beyond the Ivory Tower* (New York: Taplinger, 1970), p. 77 in ibid., p. 239.
9. Gish, *Evolution—The Fossils Still Say No!* p. 241.
10. Ibid., p. 279.
11. Dubois, "On the Fossil Human Skulls Recently Discovered in Java and *Pithecanthropus Erectus,*" *Man,* Vol. 37 (1937), pp. 1, 4–5 in Bird, *Origin . . . Revisited,* Vol. 1, p. 231.
12. Lubenow, *Bones,* p. 235.
13. Ibid., p. 7, emphasis added.
14. Ibid., p. 8, emphasis added.
15. Ibid., p. 19.
16. Ibid., p. 21.
17. Ibid.
18. Richard Leakey, "The Search for Early Man," cassette tape produced by the American Association for the Advancement of Science, Washington, D.C., 1973, cited in Lubenow, *Bones,* p. 24.
19. David Pilbeam, "Rearranging Our Family Tree," *Human Nature,* June 1978, p. 40 in Lubenow, *Bones,* p. 182.
20. Pilbeam, p. 45 in ibid.
21. Pilbeam, "Book Review of Leakey's Origins," *American Scientist,* Vol. 66 (1978), pp. 378–79 in Bird, *Origin . . . Revisited,* Vol. 1, p. 226.
22. Mary Leakey, *Disclosing the Past* (Garden City, NY: Doubleday & Co., 1984), p. 214 in Lubenow, *Bones,* p. 182.
23. J. S. Jones and Esta Rouhani, "How Small Was the Bottleneck?" *Nature,* Feb. 6, 1986, p. 449 in Lubenow, *Bones,* p. 182.
24. S. Zuckerman, *Beyond the Ivory Tower* (1970), p. 64 in Bird, *Origin . . . Revisited,* Vol. 1, p. 226, emphasis added.
25. Robert Martin, "Man Is Not an Onion," *New Scientist,* Aug. 1977, p. 285 in Lubenow, *Bones,* p. 182.

26. Gore, "Dawn of Humans," p. 88.
27. Ibid., p. 72.
28. Ibid., pp. 87, 77, 80, 88, 96–97, respectively.
29. Lubenow, *Bones*, p. 13 (original citations provided).
30. Ibid., p. 14.
31. Ibid., p. 17.
32. Bird, *Origin . . . Revisited*, Vol. 1, pp. 226–27, emphasis added.
33. Cf., the *National Observer*, February 16, 1974, p. 10.
34. Lubenow, *Bones*, p. 31.
35. Ibid., p. 29.
36. Ibid., p. 32.
37. Takahata, "A Genetic Perspective on the Origin and History of Humans," *Annual Review of Ecology & Systematics*, 1995, p. 355.
38. Lubenow, *Bones*, p. 31.
39. Ibid., p. 32.
40. Bird, *Origin . . . Revisited*, Vol. 1, p. 228.
41. S. Zuckerman, *Beyond the Ivory Tower* (1970), p. 64 in Bird, *Origin . . . Revisited*, Vol. 1, p. 228.
42. Lubenow, *Bones*, p. 120.
43. Ibid.
44. Ibid., p. 121.
45. Ibid., p. 127, emphasis added.
46. Ibid., pp. 121, 124.
47. Ibid., pp. 178–79.
48. Ibid., p. 178.
49. Ibid., p. 179.
50. Ibid.
51. Ibid., p. 183.
52. In ibid., p. 181.
53. Ibid., p. 57.
54. Ibid., p. 58.

CHAPTER 15—CREATION, EVOLUTION, AND THE UNIVERSE

1. *Parade* magazine, Feb. 4, 1996, p. 7.
2. Timothy Ferris, "Inflating the Cosmos," *Astronomy*, July 1997, p. 40.
3. Lubenow, *Bones*, p. 245.
4. Ibid., pp. 245–46.
5. Edward Nelson, "A Feeling of Great Surprise That There Is Anything," in Margenau and Varghese (eds.), *Cosmos, Bios, Theos*, pp. 76–77.
6. Bird, *Origin . . . Revisited*, Vol. 1, p. 437.
7. Ibid.
8. Vaucouleurs, "The Case for a Hierarchical Cosmology," *Science*, Vol. 167 (1970), p. 1203 in Bird, *Origin . . . Revisited*, Vol. 1, p. 439.

9. H. Alfven, "Cosmology: Myth or Science?" 5 *Journal of Astrophysics and Astronomy* (1984), pp. 79, 90 in Bird, *Origin . . . Revisited*, Vol. 1, pp. 439–40.

10. Gish, *Creation Scientists Answer*, pp. 153–54.

11. Bernal, *The Origin of Life*, p. xv; cf., p. 168 cited by Donald England, *A Christian View of Origins*, p. 35.

12. Robert Oldershaw, "What's Wrong with the New Physics?" *New Scientist*, Dec. 22/29, 1990, p. 59 in Henry M. Morris, "The Bust," *Back to Genesis*, May 1994, p. b.

13. Geoffrey Burbridge, "Why Only One Big Bang?" in *Scientific American*, February, 1992, p. 120 in Morris, "The Bust," ibid.

14. Gish, *Creation Scientists Answer*, pp. 155–56.

15. Narlikar and Padmanabhan, "Creation-Field Cosmology: A Possible Solution to Singularity, Horizon, and Flatness Problems," *Physical Review*, Vol. 32 (1985), p. 1928 in Bird, *Origin . . . Revisited*, Vol. 1, p. 459.

16. Bird, *Origin . . . Revisited*, p. 460.

17. Ibid., pp. 460–61; the statement by Lake is from Lake, "Windows on a New Cosmology," *Science*, Vol. 224 (1984), pp. 675, 678.

18. Burbidge, "Was There Really a Big Bang?" *Nature*, Vol. 233 (1971), pp. 36, 40 in Bird, *Origin . . . Revisited*, Vol. 1, p. 462.

19. F. Hoyle, *The Intelligent Universe* (1983), pp. 184–85 in Bird, *Origin . . . Revisited*, Vol. 1, p. 462.

20. *Astronomy*, July 1997, p. 25, advertisement.

21. Hoyle, "The Big Bang in Astronomy," p. 92; *New Scientist* (1981), pp. 521, 523 emphasis added in Bird, *Origin . . . Revisited*, Vol. 1, pp. 417–18.

22. Arp, "Further Examples of Companion Galaxies with Discordant Redshifts and Their Spectral Peculiarities," *Astrophysical Journal*, Vol. 263 (1982), p. 54; H. Arp and B. Madore, *Catalogue of Southern Peculiar Galaxies and Associations* (1977) in Bird, *Origin . . . Revisited*, Vol. 1, pp. 445–46.

23. Burbidge, "Redshifts and Distances," *Nature*, Vol. 286 (1980), p. 307 in ibid., p. 448.

24. Ibid.

25. Vincent A. Ettari, "Critical Thoughts and Conjectures Concerning the Doppler Effect and the Concept of an Expanding Universe—Part 1," *Creation Research Society Quarterly*, Dec. 1988, p. 146.

26. Lubenow, *Bones*, pp. 210–11.

27. Ibid., p. 211.

28. Bird, Vol. 1, p. 454.

29. Hoyle, "Big Bang in Astronomy," pp. in Bird, *Origin . . . Revisited*, Vol. 1, p. 454; cf., Schoonover, "Big Bang Theory Fizzles," *Fusion*, March/April 1979.

30. Alfven, *Cosmology: Myth or Science?* No. 5 *Journal of Astrophysics and Astronomy* (1984), pp. 79, 91 in Bird, *Origin . . . Revisited*, Vol. 1, p. 453.

31. Burbidge, "Was There Really a Big Bang?" 39 in Bird, *Origin . . . Revisited*, Vol. 1, p. 442.

32. Arp, "Evidence for Discordant Redshifts" in G. Field (ed.), *The Redshift Controversy* (1973), pp. 15, 54–55 in Bird, *Origin . . . Revisited,* Vol. 1, p. 444.

33. Allen, "The Big Bang Is Not Needed," 6 *Foundations of Physics* (1976), p. 59 in Bird, *Origin . . . Revisited,* Vol. 1, p. 452.

34. Bird, *Origin . . . Revisited,* Vol. 1, p.458.

35. Abstract, J. K. West, "Polytropic Model of the Universe," *Creation Research Society Quarterly,* Sept. 1994, p. 78.

36. Bird, *Origin . . . Revisited,* Vol. 1, pp. 458–59.

37. Hugh Ross, "Astronomical Evidences for a Personal, Transcendent God" in Moreland (ed.), *Creation Hypothesis,* p. 152.

38. See Allen above; Bondi, letter, *New Scientist,* Vol. 87 (1980), p. 611 in Bird, *Origin . . . Revisited,* Vol. 1, p. 464.

39. Fred Hoyle, *The Intelligent Universe: A New View of Creation and Evolution* (1983), pp. 179, 186 in Bird, *Origin . . . Revisited,* Vol. 1, p. 464.

40. George Mulfinger, "Theories of the Origin of the Universe" in Walter Lammerts (ed.), *Why Not Creation?* (Nutley, NJ: Presbyterian and Reformed, 1970), p. 39; cf., his "Examining the Cosmogenies—A Historical Review" in ibid.

41. H. Jeffreys, *The Earth: Its Origin, History and Physical Constitution,* p. 359 (5th edition, 1970), p. 359 in Bird, *Origin . . . Revisited,* Vol. 1, p. 417.

42. Varghese, introduction in Margenau and Varghese (eds.), *Cosmos, Bios, Theos,* p. 11.

43. Ibid., p. 6.

44. Eugene P. Wigner, "The Origin of the Universe Is a Disturbing Mystery for Science" in Margenau and Varghese (eds.), *Cosmos, Bios, Theos,* p. 131.

45. William Stoeger, "The Origin of the Universe in Science and Religion" in Margenau and Varghese (eds.), *Cosmos, Bios, Theos,* p. 258.

46. Frederick C. Robbins, "I Have Very Little in the Way of Belief in a Concrete God" in Margenau and Varghese (eds.), *Cosmos, Bios, Theos,* p. 196.

47. Jeffrey I. Steinfield, "A Deeper Connectivity Than the Mechanical Models of Our Current World View May Comprehend" in Margenau and Varghese (eds.), *Cosmos, Bios, Theos,* p. 212.

48. John Erik Fornaess, "Where Matter and Consciousness Came From is Unknown" in Margenau and Varghese (eds.), *Cosmos, Bios, Theos,* pp. 40–41.

49. Sir Nevill Mott, "Science Will Never Give Us the Answers to All Our Questions" in Margenau and Varghese (eds.), *Cosmos, Bios, Theos,* p. 65.

50. Louis Neel, "Our Final Ineptitude at Producing a Rational Explanation of the Universe" in Margenau and Varghese (eds.), *Cosmos, Bios, Theos,* p. 73.

51. Charles H. Townes, "The Question of Origin Seems Unanswered if We Explore from a Scientific View Alone" in Margenau and Varghese (eds.), *Cosmos, Bios, Theos,* p. 123.

52. Werner Arber, "The Existence of a Creator Represents a Satisfactory Solution" in Margenau and Varghese (eds.), *Cosmos, Bios, Theos,* pp. 142–43.

53. Christian B. Anfinsen, "There Exists an Incomprehensible Power with Limitless Foresight and Knowledge" in Margenau and Varghese (eds.), *Cosmos, Bios, Theos,* p. 139.

54. Henry Margenau, "The Laws of Nature Are Created by God" in Margenau and Varghese (eds.), *Cosmos, Bios, Theos,* pp. 57–59.

55. Ulrich J. Becker, "Who Arranged for These Laws to Cooperate so Well?" in Margenau and Varghese (eds.), *Cosmos, Bios, Theos,* p. 29.

56. Robert A. Naumann, "Religion and Science Both Proceed from Acts of Faith" in Margenau and Varghese (eds.), *Cosmos, Bios, Theos,* p. 72.

57. Arno Penzias, "Creation Is Supported by All the Data So Far" in Margenau and Varghese (eds.), *Cosmos, Bios, Theos,* p. 83.

58. Arthur L. Schawlow, "One Must Ask Why and Not Just How" in Margenau and Varghese (eds.), *Cosmos, Bios, Theos,* p. 105.

59. Wolfgang Smith, "The Universe Is Ultimately to Be Explained in Terms of a Metacosmic Reality" in Margenau and Varghese (eds.), *Cosmos, Bios, Theos,* p. 117.

60. Walter Thirring, "The Guidance of Evolution Lets God Appear to Us in Many Guises" in Margenau and Varghese (eds.), *Cosmos, Bios, Theos,* p. 119.

61. Thomas C. Emmel, "The Creative Process May Well Be What We Observe, Deduce, and Call Evolution" in Margenau and Varghese (eds.), *Cosmos, Bios, Theos,* p. 171.

62. P. C. C. Garnham, "At Some Stage in Evolution, God Created the Human Soul," in Margenau and Varghese (eds.), *Cosmos, Bios, Theos,* p. 173.

63. Roger J. Gautheret,"A Spirit Which Has Established the Universe and Its Laws" in Margenau and Varghese (eds.), *Cosmos, Bios, Theos,* p. 176.

64. In Morris, *The Biblical Basis for Modern Science, Cosmos, Bios, Theos,* p. 193, emphasis added.

65. Heeren, *Show Me God,* p. 139.

CHAPTER 16—ADDITIONAL EVIDENCE AND ISSUES

1. For a good critique see Lane P. Lester and Raymond G. Bohlin, *The Natural Limits to Biological Change* (Grand Rapids, MI: Zondervan/Probe, 1984).

2. T. Dobzhansky, F. Ayala, G. Stebbins and J. Valentine, *Evolution* (1977), p. 129 in Bird, *Origin . . . Revisited,* Vol. 1, p. 156.

3. The National Center for Science Education, Inc., *Voices for Evolution,* pp. 73–74.

4. For example see Norman MacBeth, *Darwin Retried* (Gambit, 1971), pp. 40–67, 134–42 or Bird, *Origin . . . Revisited,* Vol. 1, pp. 158–67; Bergman, "Some Biological Problems of Natural Selection Theory," *Creation Research Society Quarterly,* Dec. 1992; see also ch. 9, note 8, Hedtke.

5. J. Savage, *Evolution* (1977, 3rd edition), p. 73 in Bird, *Origin . . . Revisited,* Vol. 1, p. 167.

6. In Wysong, p. 267.

7. Ibid., cf., the original citations and references in Wysong, *Creation/Evolution Controversy*, Vol. 1, p. 165.

8. In Wysong, *Creation/Evolution Controversy*, p. 265.

9. Theodosius Dobzhansky, *Mankind Evolving* (New York: Bantum, 1970), p. 143, emphasis added.

10. Grassé, *The Evolution of Living Organisms*, pp. 87–88.

11. In Wysong, *Creation/Evolution Controversy*, p. 272.

12. Dobzhansky, *Mankind Evolving*, p. 146.

13. Cited in MacBeth, *Darwin Retried*, pp. 40–41, citing *Evolution in Action* (Mentor), p. 35, emphasis added.

14. In Hall and Hall, *The Truth*, p. 23.

15. T. Dobzhansky, F. Ayala, G. Stebbins and J. Valentine, *Evolution* (1977), pp. 32, 504; Mayr, Prologue in E. Mayr and W. Provine (eds.), *The Evolutionary Synthesis* (1980), pp. 1, 24 in Bird, *Origin . . . Revisited*, Vol. 2, p. 89.

16. Bird, *Origin . . . Revisited*, Vol. 2, p. 89.

17. Bird, *Origin . . . Revisited*, Vol. 1, pp. 150–67, and Vol. 2, p. 559.

18. Norman MacBeth, *Darwin Retried* (Gambit, 1971), pp. 42, 46.

19. Ibid., p. 134.

20. Bird, *Origin . . . Revisited*, Vol. 1, p. 159.

21. Ibid.

22. H. S. Hamilton, "The Eye: By Chance or Intelligence?" in *Creation Research Society Quarterly*, March 1991, pp. 143–44.

23. Rosen, "Darwin's Demon," *Systematic Zoology*, Vol. 27 (1978), pp. 370, 372 in Bird, *Origin . . . Revisited*, Vol. 1, p. 160.

24. The National Center for Science Education, Inc., *Voices for Evolution*, pp. 40–41, emphasis added.

25. N. Takahata, "A Genetic Perspective on the Origin & History of Humans," *Annual Review of Ecology & Systematics*, 1995, p. 344, emphasis added.

26. Leith, "Are the Reports of Darwin's Death Exaggerated?" *The Listener*, Vol. 166 (1981), pp. 390–91 in Bird, *Origin . . . Revisited*, Vol. 1, p. 161.

27. Jerry Bergman, "Some Biological Problems of Natural Selection Theory," *Creation Research Society Quarterly*, Dec. 1992, p. 157.

28. Grassé, *The Evolution of Living Organisms*, p. 84.

29. Lewin, "Evolutionary Theory Under Fire," *Science*, Vol. 210 (1980), p. 883 in Bird, *Origin . . . Revisited*, Vol. 1, p. 156.

30. Phillip E. Johnson, *Darwin on Trial* (Downer's Grove, IL: InterVarsity, 1991), pp. 9–10.

31. George Gaylord Simpson, *The Meaning of Evolution* (New York: Bantam, 1971), p. 208.

32. In Hall and Hall, *The Truth*, p. 23.

33. Ibid.

34. Bill Crowfut and Raymond M. Seaman, "Panorama of Science," *Creation Research Society Quarterly*, March 1991, p. 136.

35. A good example is the text by leading creationist scientists, C. B. Thaxton, W. L. Bradley, and R. L. Olsen, *The Mystery of Life's Origin: Reassessing Current Theories* (New York: Philosophical Library, 1984). Also see the many articles in the *Creation Research Society Quarterly* and other creationist books available from the Institute for Creation Research in San Diego or the Creation Research Society in St. Joseph, Missouri, especially Emmett Williams (ed.), *Thermodynamics and the Development of Order* (Kansas City, MO: Creation Research Society Books, 1981) and Gish, *Speculations and Laboratory Experiments Related to Theories on the Origin of Life: A Critique* (San Diego: Creation Life Publishers, 1972).

36. Gish, *Creation Scientists Answer*, p. 207.

37. Ibid., pp. 205–06.

38. Wysong, *Creation/Evolution Controversy*, p. 253.

39. The National Center for Science Education, Inc., *Voices for Evolution* p. 141.

40. Ibid., p. 63.

41. Ross, letter, *Chemical and Engineering News*, July 7, 1980, p. 4; Prigogine, Nicolis and Babloyantz, "Thermodynamics of Evolution," *Physics Today*, November 1972, p. 23 in Bird, *Origin . . . Revisited*, Vol. 1, pp. 315–17, first emphasis added.

42. E.g., Gish, *Christian Scientists Answer*, pp. 405–440; cf., 151–208, 219, 245, 387–404; see also note 35 in this chapter.

43. Stephen R. Shrader, "Was the Earth Created a Few Thousand Years Ago? (Yes)" in Youngblood (ed.), pp. 72–73.

44. Frederic R. Howe, "The Age of the Earth" in Roy B. Zuck (gen. ed.), *Vital Apologetic Issues: Examining Reasons and Revelation in Biblical Perspective* (Grand Rapids, MI: Kregel, 1995), pp. 109, 113, 119; cf., Recommended Reading.

45. See e.g., Don Stoner, *A New Look at an Old Earth* (Eugene, OR: Harvest House, 1997), pp. 16, 20–21.

46. Ibid., p. 19, emphasis added.

47. Dr. Eugene F. Chaffin, "A Young Earth?—A Survey of Dating Methods" in *Creation Research Society Quarterly*, Dec. 1987, p. 115, cf., his reference list.

48. Wysong, *Creation/Evolution Controversy*, pp. 158–97.

49. Thomas G. Barnes, "The Dilemma of a Theistic Evolutionist: An Answer to Howard Van Till," in *Creation Research Society Quarterly*, March 1987, Vol. 23, no. 4, p. 167.

50. Bruce Briegler, "On Stellar Structure and Stellar Evolution," *Creation Research Society Quarterly*, Sept. 1993, p. 76, emphasis added.

51 Raphael G. Kazmann, "It's About Time: 4.5 Billion Years," *GeoTimes*, Sept. 1978, p. 18 in Lubenow, *Bones*, p. 205. Lubenow points out: "A careful study of the recording of the session confirms that Kazmann has quoted John Eddy accurately" (Lubenow, p. 283).

52 Lubenow, *Bones*, pp. 207–10.

53. *Creation Research Society Quarterly*, March 1995, p. 23.
54. Gentry, *Earth's Tiny Mystery*.
55. Robert V. Gentry, "Response to Wise," *Creation Research Society Quarterly*, March 1989, p. 178.
56. Gentry's first statement comes from Robert V. Gentry, "Response to Wise," *Creation Research Society Quarterly*, March 1989, p. 178; his second comment is from Gentry, *Polonium Halos* 61E.O.S. [*Trans. Am. Geophysical U.*] 514 (1980) cited in Bird, *Origin . . . Revisited*, Vol. 1, p. 431.
57. See, e.g., Kurt P. Wise, "Radioactive Halos: Geological Concerns" and Robert V. Gentry, "Response to Wise" in *Creation Research Society Quarterly*, March 1989, pp. 171–79.
58. Morris, *Biblical Basis*, pp. 125–26.
59. Michael J. Oard, *Creation Research Society Quarterly*, March 1994, p. 224 citing Lubenow, *Bones*, pp. 265, 266.
60. Lubenow, *Bones*, p. 207.
61. Wilder-Smith, *The Natural Sciences Know Nothing of Evolution*, p. 122.
62. Morris, *Biblical Basis*, p. 264.
63. Wysong, *Creation/Evolution Controversy*, Chapter 10, pp. 151–79, 354.
64. Melvin A. Cook, "Radiological Dating and Some Pertinent Applications of Historical Interest: Do Radiological 'Clocks' Need Repair?" Walter M. Lammerts (ed.), *Scientific Studies in Special Creation* (Nutley, NJ: Presbyterian and Reformed, 1971), p. 79; see also Melvin A. Cook, *Prehistory and Earth Models* (London: Max Parish & Co. Limited, 1966).
65. Morris, *Biblical Basis*, pp. 260–69.
66. Frederick B. Jueneman, "Secular Catastrophism," *Industrial Research and Development*, June, 1982, p. 21, emphasis added in Morris, *Biblical Basis*, p. 266.
67. Morris, *Biblical Basis*, pp. 265–69.
68. Ibid., p. 269.
69. A. Hayatsu, "K-Ar Isochron Age of the North Mountain Basalt, Nova Scotia," *Canadian Journal of Earth Sciences*, No. 16 (8):973–975, emphasis added in Richard D. Lumsden, "Error and Worse in the Scientific Literature," *Creation Research Society Quarterly*, Dec. 1992, p. 128.
70. Lubenow, *Bones*, p. 9.
71. Ibid., p. 247.
72. Ibid., pp. 264–65.
73. James A. Borland, "Did People Live to Be Hundreds of Years Old Before the Flood?" in Youngblood (ed.), *Genesis Debate*, p. 178.
74. Youngblood (ed.), *Genesis Debate*, pp. 74–75.
75. In Wysong, *Creation/Evolution Controversy*, p. 350.
76. Taken from Morris, *Biblical Basis*, p. 312.
77. Crofut and Seaman, "Evolution: Factual or Fanciful?" in *Creation Research Society Quarterly*, Sept. 1990, p. 59, citing D. B. Kitts, "Paleontology and Evolutionary Theory," *Evolution*, Vol. 28, p. 458 (1974).
78. From Wysong, *Creation/Evolution Controversy*, chapter 20.
79. Bird, *Origin . . . Revisited*, Vol. 1, pp. 185–86.

80. Steven A. Austin, *Catastrophes in Earth History* (El Cajon, CA: Institute for Creation Research, 1984), p. 2.

81. Emmitt L. Williams, Book Review, *Creation Research Society Quarterly*, Dec. 1994, p. 160.

82. *Creation Research Society Quarterly*, Sept. 1996, p. 114. The publisher is Center for Scientific Creation, Phoenix, AZ, 1995.

83. *Creation Research Society Quarterly*, Video Review, Dec. 1994, p. 166.

84. Henry Morris, "The Geologic Column and the Flood of Genesis," *Creation Research Society Quarterly*, June 1996, pp. 54–57.

85. See also information from the Institute for Creation Research, Santee, California.

86. NIV Study Bible notes on Genesis 6:17.

87. See Henry Morris' *The Genesis Flood*, Austin's *Catastrophes in Earth History*, John Warwick Montgomery's *The Search for Noah's Ark*.

88. Cited in Jerry Bergman, "A Review of Exobiogenesis Theories," *Creation Research Society Quarterly*, March 1995, p. 213.

89. Cf., the scholarly refutation by Drs. Jerry Bergman and George Howe, *"Vestigial Organs" are Fully Functional—A History and Evaluation of the Vestigial Organs Origins Concept*, Creation Research Monograph Series, No. 4 (Kansas City, MO: Creation Research Society Books, 1990).

90. For an illustration see "Bill Yake, 'Objections from Science to Global Flood'" and the response in letters to the editor (*Creation Research Society Quarterly*, June 1995, pp. 12, 21–24).

CHAPTER 17—THE ULTIMATE CON?

1. The National Center for Science Education, Inc., *Voices for Evolution*, p. 68.

2. Bird, *Origin . . . Revisited*, Vol. 2, p. 130.

3. MacBeth, *Darwin Retried*, pp. 126–27.

4. Bird, *Origin . . . Revisited*, Vol. 2, p. 177.

5. Ibid., p. 185.

6. Ibid.

7. Ibid., p. 185.

8. Ibid., pp. 107, 187.

9. Cf., John Ankerberg, John Weldon, *Ready with an Answer*.

10. Bird, *Origin . . . Revisited*, Vol. 2, p. 282.

11. Ibid., p. 52.

12. Julian Huxley and Jacob Bronowski, *Growth of Ideas* (Englewood Cliffs, NJ: Prentice Hall, 1968), p. 99 in Gish, *Creation Scientists Answer*, p. 31.

13. Marjorie Grene, *Encounter*, November 1959, p. 49 in Gish, ibid., p. 31.

14. Colin Patterson, *The Listener*, October 8, 1981, Vol. 106, pp. 390–92. (*The Listener* is a publication of the British Broadcasting Corporation) in Gish, ibid., p. 31.

15. J. Moore, *The Post-Darwinian Controversies* (1979), p. 344, cf., 109, 314–15; Grene, "The Faith of Darwinism," *Encounter*, November 1959, p. 48 in Bird, *Origin . . . Revisited,* Vol. 2, p. 210.

16. Grassé, *Evolution of Living Organisms*, p. 107.

17. Wysong, *Creation/Evolution Controversy,* pp. 418–19.

18. Ibid., p. 419; cf., Denton, *Evolution*, 308–44.

19. Bird, *Origin . . . Revisited,* Vol. 2, pp. 251–319.

20. Ibid., p. 252.

21. In Phillip E. Johnson, *Darwin on Trial*, p. 114.

22. *Scientific American*, May 1959, p. 66.

23. Roy Abraham Varghese, introduction in Margenau and Varghese (eds.), *Cosmos, Bios, Theos*, p. 17.

24. H. D. Lewis, "The Existence of the Universe as a Pointer to the Existence of God" in Margenau and Varghese (eds.), *Cosmos, Bios, Theos*, pp. 228–29.

25. William Stoeger, "The Origin of the Universe in Science and Religion" in Margenau and Varghese (eds.), p. 260.

26. See the discussion in chapters 10, 11, and later in this chapter.

27. Richard E. Leaky, *The Illustrated Origin of Species by Charles Darwin*, abridged and introduced by Richard E. Leaky (New York: Hill & Wang, 1979), p. 129 in Manly, *God Made*, p. 65.

28. Albert Einstein, *Lettres a Maurice Solovine* (1956), pp. 114–15 in Bird, *Origin . . . Revisied,* Vol. 1, p. 402.

29. In Roy Abraham Varghese, "Introduction" in Margenau and Varghese (eds.), *Cosmos, Bios, Theos*, p. 9.

30. Vera Kistiakowsky, "The Exquisite Order of the Physical World Calls for the Divine" in Margenau and Varghese (eds.), *Cosmos, Bios, Theos*, pp. 52–53.

31. Henry Margenau, "The Laws of Nature Are Created by God" in Margenau and Varghese (eds.), *Cosmos, Bios, Theos*, pp. 61–62.

32. Francis Crick, *Life Itself: Its Origin and Nature* (New York: Simon & Schuster, 1981), p. 88.

33. Victoria Institute 1943, p. 63 in Bowden, *The Rise of the Evolution Fraud*, pp. 218.

34. In Wysong,*Creation/Evolution Controversy,* p. 131.

35. Cited in Norman L. Geisler, *Creator in the Courtroom—"Scopes 2": The 1981 Arkansas Creation/Evolution Trial* (Milford, MI: Mott Media, 1982), p. 151.

36. Eastman, Missler, *Creator Beyond,* pp. 11–12. See especially Alexander Vilenkin, "Did the Universe Have a Beginning?" CALT-68-1772DOE Research and Development Report, California Institute of Technology, Pasadena, November 1992.

37. Eastman, Missler, *The Creator Beyond*, p. 17.

38. Ibid., p. 207.

39. Ibid., p. 27.

40. Paul Davies, *The Cosmic Blueprint: New Discoveries in Nature's Creative Ability to Order the Universe* (New York: Simon & Schuster, 1988), p. 203

and Paul Davies, *Superforce: The Search for a Grand Unified Theory of Nature* (New York: Simon & Schuster, 1984), p. 243 in Hugh Ross, "Astronomical Evidences for a Personal, Transcendent God" in Moreland (ed.), *Creation Hypothesis*, p. 164.

41. Antony Flew, "Response to Lewis" in Margenau and Varghese (eds.), *Cosmos, Bios, Theos*, p. 241.

42. Steven L. Bernasek, "The Mechanism of the World and the Why of It" in Margenau and Varghese (eds.), *Cosmos, Bios, Theos*, p. 151.

43. R. Merle d'Aubigne, "How Is It Possible to Escape the Idea of Some Intelligent and Organizing Force?" in Margenau and Varghese (eds.), *Cosmos, Bios, Theos*, p. 159.

44. George Greenstein, *The Symbiotic Universe: Life and Mind in the Cosmos* (New York: William Morrow, 1988), pp. 26–27 in Meyer, "Methodological Equivalence," in Moreland (ed.), *Creation Hypothesis*, pp. 67–68.

45. Tony Rothman, "A 'What You See Is What You Beget' Theory," *Discover*, May 1987, p. 99 in Eastman and Missler, *Creator Beyond*, p. 28.

46. Cited in Varghese, "Introduction" in Margenau and Varghese (eds.), *Cosmos, Bios, Theos*, p. 2.

47. In ibid., p. 21.

48. Ibid., p. 156.

49. Harry Rimmer, *The Magnificence of Jesus* (Grand Rapids, MI: Eerdmans, 1943), p. 116.

50. Carl Sagan, F. H. C. Crick, L. M. Muchin in Carl Sagan, ed., *Communication with Extraterrestrial Intelligence* (CETI) (Cambridge, MA: MIT Press), pp. 45–46.

51. Emile Borel, *Probabilities and Life* (New York: Dover, 1962), Chs. 1 and 3. Borel's cosmic limit of 10^{200} changes nothing.

52. Paul S. Moorehead and Martin M. Kaplan (eds.), *Mathematical Challenges to the Neo-Darwinian Interpretation of Evolution*, Wistar Institute Symposium Monograph Number 5 (Philadelphia, PA: The Wistar Institute Press, 1967), p. xi, third emphasis in original.

53. Murray Eden, "Inadequacies of Neo-Darwinism Evolution as a Scientific Theory" in ibid., p. 109.

54. Marcel P. Schutzenberger, "Algorithms and the Neo-Darwinian Theory of Evolution" in Moorehead and Kaplan (eds.), *Mathematical Challenges*, p. 75; cf., Bird, *Origin . . . Revisted*, Vol. 1, pp. 79–80; for reasons why natural selection would not modify randomness and decrease these probabilities, see Bird, *Origin . . . Revisted*, Vol. 1, pp. 158–65.

55. J. Allen Hynek, Jacque Vallee, *The Edge of Reality* (Chicago, IL: Henry Regenery, 1975), p. 157.

56. Coppedge, *Evolution: Possible or Impossible?*, pp. 118–20.

57. Cited in Eastman, Missler, *Creator Beyond*, p. 61.

58. Cf., Frank B. Salisbury, "Natural Selection and the Complexity of the Gene," *Nature*, Vol. 24, October 25, 1969, pp. 342–343 and James Coppedge, Director, Center for Probability Research and Biology, Northridge, California, personal conversation; cf., Coppedge, *Evolution: Possible or Impossible?* passim.

59. George Wald, "The Origin of Life" in Editors of Scientific American, *The Physics and Chemistry of Life* (New York: Simon & Schuster, 1955), p. 9.

60. Ibid., p. 10.

61. Ibid., p. 12.

62. Ibid., p. 15.

63. Ibid., p. 12.

64. Gary A. Parker, "The Origin of Life on Earth," *Creation Research Society Quarterly*, Sept. 1970, p. 101.

65. Sidney W. Fox (ed.), *The Origins of Prebiological Systems* (New York: Academic Press, 1965), p. 45.

66. Sir John Eccles, Daniel N. Robinson, *The Wonder of Being Human: Our Brain and Our Mind* (Boston: Shambhala/New Science Library, 1985), p. 43.

67. George Wald, *The Physics and Chemistry of Life* (New York: Simon & Schuster, 1955), p. 12.

68. Sir Fred Hoyle, "Hoyle on Evolution," *Nature*, Vol. 294, November 12, 1981, p. 105.

69. Jacques Monod, *Chance and Necessity: An Essay on the Natural Philosophy of Modern Biology* (New York: Vintage, 1971), pp. 138–39.

70. Jacques Monod, *Chance and Necessity;* Coppedge, *Evolution: Possible or Impossible;* cf. the following: Cohen, *Darwin Was Wrong: A Study in Probabilities;* Denton, *Evolution,* pp. 308–327; John M. Andresen, "Notes on the Use of Statistics in the Debate of Creation vs. Evolution," *Creation Research Society Quarterly,* 1980, 160–62; Moshe Trop, "Was Evolution Really Possible?" *Creation Research Society Quarterly,* March 1975, pp. 183–87; Howard Byington Holroyd, "Darwinism Is Physical and Mathematical Nonsense," *Creation Research Society Quarterly,* June 1972, 5–13; Charles B. Thaxton, Walter L. Bradley, Roger L. Olsen, *The Mystery of Life's Origin: Reassessing Current Theories* (New York Philosophical Library, 1984); Julio Garrido, "Evolution and Molecular Biology," *Creation Research Society Quarterly,* Dec. 1973, pp. 166–69; Larry Butler, "A Problem of Missing Links at the Ultimate Primary Stage of Evolution," *Creation Research Society Quarterly,* Dec. 1969, p. 128; David J. Rodabaugh, "Mathematicians Do It Again," *Creation Research Society Quarterly,* Dec. 1975, pp. 173–75.

71. Monod, *Chance and Necessity,* pp. 112–13, emphasis added.

72. R. C. Sproul, *Not a Chance: The Myth of Chance in Modern Science & Cosmology* (Grand Rapids, MI: Baker, 1994), p. xiv; cf., R. J. Rushdoony, *The Mythology of Modern Science.*

73. Ibid., pp. 10–11.

74. Ibid., p. 6.

75. Ibid., p. 9.

76. Wald, "Origin of Life" in *Physics and Chemistry of Life,* pp. 9, 12.

77. Abdus Salam, "Science and Religion: Reflections on Transcendence and Secularization" in Margenau and Varghese (eds.), *Creation/Evolution Debate,* p. 100.

78. John Eccles, "A Divine Design: Some Questions on Origins" in Margenau and Varghese (eds.), *Creation/Evolution Debate*, p. 161.
79. Sproul, *Not a Chance*, pp. 14–15.
80. Wilder-Smith, *Natural Sciences Know Nothing of Evolution*, p. 26
81. Sproul, *Not a Chance*, pp. 15–16.
82. Ibid., pp. 145–46.
83. Ibid., p. 156.
84. Ibid., pp. 157–58.
85. Ibid., p. 158; cf., pp. 12ff.
86. Ibid., p. 12.
87. Ibid., pp. 12–13.
88. Ibid., p. 173.
89. Ibid., pp. 159–60; see also Richard Swieburne's trilogy, esp. *The Existence of God.*
90. Ibid., pp. 185–86.
91. In Varghese, "Introduction" in Margenau and Varghese (eds.), *Creation/ Evolution Controversy*, p. 16.
92. Sproul, *Not a Chance*, p. 192.
93. Ibid., p. 190.
94. Ibid., p. 214.
95. See our *Ready with an Answer*, pp. 166–68.
96. Cf., our *Ready with an Answer* and companion volume *Knowing the Truth about Salvation.*
97. Stuart C. Hackett, *Oriental Philosophy* (Madison, WI: The University of Wisconsin Press, 1979); David L. Johnson, *A Reasoned Look at Asian Religions* (Minneapolis: Bethany, 1985); R. C. Sproul, *Lifeviews* (Old Tappan, NJ: Revell, 1986); David Ehrenfeld, *The Arrogance of Humanism* (New York: Oxford University Press, 1978); Ravi Zacharias, *Can Man Live Without God?* (Dallas: Word, 1994); R. C. Sproul, *If There's a God Why Are There Atheists?* (Wheaton, IL: Tyndale, 1978); Johnson, *Reason in the Balance*; Norman L. Geisler, William Watkins, *Perspectives: Understanding and Evaluating Today's Worldviews* (San Bernandino, CA: Here's Life Publishers, 1984); John Warwick Montgomery, "Is Man His Own God?" in John Warwick Montgomery (ed.), *Christianity for the Toughminded* (Minneapolis: Bethany, 1975).
98. Norman Geisler, et al., *Perspectives.* Creationism: Is It a Biblical Option?," *Proceedings of the Third Creation-Science Conference* (Caldwell, Idaho: Bible Science Association, (1976) and Marvin L. Lubenow, *Bones of Contention: A Creationist Assessment of Human Fossils* (Grand Rapids, Mich: Baker, 1992), Ch. 20.

Sequential Index

This brief index is intended to help readers find the approximate locations of major themes sequentially by chapter.

Chapter 1: evolutionary kin and animal rights; meaning in life; materialist vs. Christian worldview; despair; evolutionary ethics; Naziism and communism.

Chapter 2: influence of the *Origin of Species*; influence outside science; evolution and religion.

Chapter 3: misunderstanding about science; hypothesis, theory, law; McLean opinion; empirical science; interpretation of data; theological aspect.

Chapter 4: institutional and individual claims for evolution as scientific fact; mental prison.

Chapter 5: public trust; *Voices for Evolution*; distortions of creation science.

Chapter 6: scientific fraud; bias vs. creation; bigotry against creationists; indoctrination.

Chapter 7: scientific naturalism; reasons why evolution is accepted.

Chapter 8: Darwin's doubts; logical positivism; escaping from God.

Chapter 9: evidence for evolution; logical fallacies; legal reasoning; scientists who reject evolution; creation evidence; only two options; superiority of creation.

Chapter 10: everything from nothing; the Big Bang; superiority of creation.

Chapter 11: problems in origin of life experiments; the Miller experiment; chirality; problems worsen; biochemical bias; evolutionary origin impossible; evidence for creation; probability and large numbers; the odds against a molecule; googles and factorials; Texas silver dollar illustration; balls of electrons.

Chapter 12: Darwin's black box; blood clotting and cilium; scientific silence on biochemical evolution; JME; human consciousness; creation evidence.

Other Books by
John Ankerberg and John Weldon

BEHIND THE MASK OF MORMONISM

CULT WATCH

ENCYCLOPEDIA OF NEW AGE BELIEFS

THE "FACTS ON" SERIES
The Facts on Abortion
The Facts on Angels
The Facts on Astrology
The Facts on Creation vs. Evolution
The Facts on the Faith Movement
The Facts on False Teaching in the Church
The Facts on False Views of Jesus
The Facts on Halloween
The Facts on Holistic Health and the New Medicine
The Facts on Homosexuality
The Facts on Islam
The Facts on the Jehovah's Witnesses
The Facts on the King James Only Debate
The Facts on Life After Death
The Facts on the Masonic Lodge
The Facts on the Mormon Church
The Facts on Near-Death Experiences
The Facts on the New Age Movement
The Facts on the Occult
The Facts on Psychic Readings
The Facts on Rock Music
The Facts on Roman Catholicism
The Facts on Self-Esteem, Psychology, and the Recovery Movement
The Facts on Spirit Guides
The Facts on UFOs and Other Supernatural Phenomena

"KNOWING THE TRUTH ABOUT" SERIES
Knowing the Truth About the Trinity
Knowing the Truth About the Reliability of the Bible

PROTESTANTS AND CATHOLICS: DO THEY NOW AGREE?

READY WITH AN ANSWER

Decoding the Bible Code

by John Ankerberg with Clifford and Barbara Wilson.

Is there a secret code within the Bible that outlines future events like *The Bible Code* proclaims? Responding to those claims, *Decoding the Bible Code* is a well-researched examination of the "code" and the faulty methodology and reasoning behind it.